The
Discerning Traveler's
Guide to New England

The Discerning Traveler's Guide to New England

David and Linda Glickstein

St. Martin's Griffin
New York

Photographs by David Glickstein unless otherwise indicated

Maps by David Glickstein

Library of Congress Cataloging-in-Publication Data

Glickstein, David.
    The discerning traveler's guide to New England / David
and Linda Glickstein. — 2nd ed.
        p.   cm.
    Includes index.
    ISBN 0–312–15111–X
        1. New   England—Guidebooks.   I. Glickstein,   Linda.
II. Title.
F2.3.G55   1997
917.404'43—dc21   96–44500

First Griffin edition: May 1997

10 9 8 7 6 5 4 3 2 1

To Dorothy and Bernard Schiro

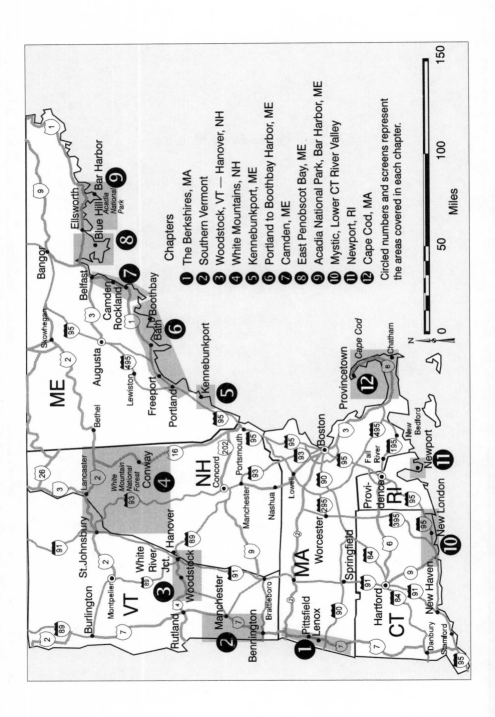

Chapters

1. The Berkshires, MA
2. Southern Vermont
3. Woodstock, VT — Hanover, NH
4. White Mountains, NH
5. Kennebunkport, ME
6. Portland to Boothbay Harbor, ME
7. Camden, ME
8. East Penobscot Bay, ME
9. Acadia National Park, Bar Harbor, ME
10. Mystic, Lower CT River Valley
11. Newport, RI
12. Cape Cod, MA

Circled numbers and screens represent the areas covered in each chapter.

Miles

0   50   100   150

Contents

viii CONTENTS

Introduction

Ten years ago we began publishing *The Discerning Traveler®*, a unique travel newsletter that covers destinations along the East Coast. The newsletter developed as a natural extension of our interest in traveling, which we have done at every opportunity over the past thirty years. When we stayed at small inns, hotels, and bed-and-breakfast homes, the owners often took time to recommend restaurants, craft studios, pleasant walks, and unusual shops to visit. Most of these places were not mentioned in the collection of guidebooks we brought along, so we started to build our own storehouse of knowledge. Soon our files bulged with clippings and notes, and our journals recorded our adventures. We developed a knack for designing trips and helped our friends plan theirs.

We started the *Discerning Traveler®* newsletter to give a larger audience of travelers a practical, easy-to-use guide that would help them develop the same appreciation of a place as the people who live there have. As we gather information for the newsletter, we talk with innkeepers, guests, and craftspeople, stay at different types of lodgings in the area, and eat a wide variety of meals. (We've often referred to our research methods as "poking with a purpose.") Our newsletter, and consequently this book, is far more personal than most other guides, since what is included is based almost exclusively on our own experiences.

For each issue of the newsletter we spend up to two weeks in a particular area. We stay at the inns, eat at the restaurants, and visit the attractions we write about. We drive the back roads and walk the side streets to find the best markets, roadside stands, crafts, shops, regional theater, museums, and historic sites. We look for, and usually find, that elusive something that can turn even a weekend getaway into a treasured experience. No one pays to be included in either the newsletter or this book.

The Discerning Traveler's Guide to New England is a guide to popular destinations in New England that have been featured in greater detail in issues of the *Discerning Traveler®* newsletter. The chapters are arranged so that, by following them in order, a traveler to New England can make a circle trip. We've featured areas that capture the diversity of New England, the preserved pockets of the past with historic homes, museums, national and state parks, and back roads leading to spectacular vistas.

Travelers using this guide will find virtually all the information necessary to experience the heart and soul of New England: the Maine coast, the pristine towns of Vermont, the rugged White Mountains of New Hampshire, the opulent mansions of Newport, the summer cultural scene in the Berkshires, Cape Cod National Seashore, and historic towns along the lower Connecticut River Valley.

Each chapter includes a short history of the region and firsthand reviews of accommodations, ranging from small, historic bed-and-breakfast inns to larger, full-service resorts. Restaurant reviews cover inexpensive regional and ethnic cuisine as well as gourmet restaurants of the highest caliber. The shops and craft studios we visit are, for the most part, small and family-owned. We describe museums and historic sites, walks and hikes, cruises, bicycle touring, downhill and cross-country skiing, horseback riding, and much more. To help you plan your trip, we supply a map of each area, a four- to five-day itinerary, our recommendations of what to see and do, and a detailed budget for two people.

We have made every attempt to verify prices, hours, and dates of operation at the time this book went to press. It always is wise to call ahead, however; many of the attractions, restaurants, and inns are small and subject to changes in management, prices, and policies.

Travelers who want more destinations to explore in New England can order copies of issues of the *Discerning Traveler*® newsletter. Each issue includes the same type of information as that contained in this book, but covers accommodations and restaurants in greater detail. Guides to the following destinations in New England are currently available: Litchfield County, Connecticut; Stowe and Southwest Vermont; Cape Ann, Boston, Nantucket, and Martha's Vineyard, Massachusetts; and Block Island, Rhode Island.

For travel to the Middle Atlantic area we suggest you consult *The Discerning Traveler's Guide to the Middle Atlantic States*. As is true with this book, many additional destinations are covered in issues of the *Discerning Traveler*® newsletter. The newsletter also covers destinations in the South and Canada. For subscription information to the *Discerning Traveler*® newsletter, see the back page of this book or send in the enclosed card for a sample issue.

We would appreciate any comments you might have, good or bad, about the inns, restaurants, and attractions reviewed in this book. Write to us at *The Discerning Traveler*®, 504 West Mermaid Lane, Philadelphia, Pennsylvania 19118. We wish you happy, healthy travels.

The
Discerning Traveler's
Guide to New England

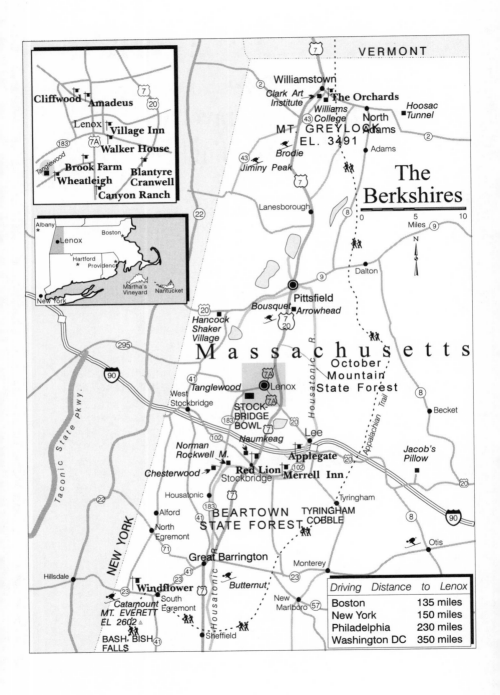

VERMONT

Cliffwood **Amadeus**

Lenox

Village Inn

Walker House

Brook Farm
Wheatleigh

Blantyre
Cranwell

Canyon Ranch

Williamstown

Clark Art Institute

The Orchards

Williams College

North Adams

Hoosac Tunnel

MT. GREYLOCK EL. 3491

Brodie

Jiminy Peak

Adams

The Berkshires

0   5   10
Miles

N

Lanesborough

Dalton

Pittsfield

Bousquet

Arrowhead

Hancock Shaker Village

M a s s a c h u s e t t s

October Mountain State Forest

Becket

Albany

Lenox

Boston

Hartford

Providence

Martha's Vineyard

Nantucket

New York

Tanglewood

⊙Lenox

STOCK-BRIDGE BOWL

Naumkeag

Lee

West Stockbridge

Norman Rockwell M.

Chesterwood

Red Lion Stockbridge

Applegate

Merrell Inn

Jacob's Pillow

Housatonic

Tyringham

Alford

North Egremont

BEARTOWN STATE FOREST

TYRINGHAM COBBLE

Hillsdale

Great Barrington

Monterey

Otis

Windflower

Catamount

MT. EVERETT EL 2602

South Egremont

Butternut

New Marlboro

Sheffield

BASH BISH FALLS

NEW YORK

Taconic State Pkwy.

Driving Distance to Lenox	
Boston	135 miles
New York	150 miles
Philadelphia	230 miles
Washington DC	350 miles

1

The Berkshires, Massachusetts

Champagne flutes reflect the wandering rays of the setting sun and candles flicker in silver candelabras. Baskets filled with croissants and dewy, freshly washed grapes sit on crisp white tablecloths next to platters of pâté and prosciutto and melon. Music lovers congregate comfortably on the great lawn for another splendid evening of picnicking and Prokofiev.

For more than fifty years, the Boston Symphony has made Tanglewood its summer home and has turned the Berkshire region into one of the great cultural destinations in the country. Today some fifty different organizations offer summer or year-round music, dance, theater, film, and art exhibits.

In the 1850s such writers as Hawthorne and Melville came to these venerable hills to write in peace and solitude. The popularity of the Berkshires as a vacation destination was tied to the nineteenth-century extension of the railroad from Boston, up the hills through the famous 4.75-mile Hoosac Tunnel (the longest bore in the world in 1875), through the Berkshires and on to Albany and points west.

The Gilded Age arrived in the Berkshires after a direct rail line was built from New York City to Pittsfield. Wealthy nineteenth-century industrialists built more than seventy sprawling "cottages" between Lenox and Stockbridge, making the area a landlocked Newport.

At the same time the world's first commercial electric system was built along the main street of Great Barrington. This enticed the General Electric Company to set up factories in Pittsfield; even today, GE is the major employer in the region. Paper mills pioneered the manufacture of wood pulp newsprint. Textile mills used the wool from sheep that grazed the hillsides.

All of this development had a price: before the turn of the century, railroad construction crews had chewed up trees by the thousands to make ties, and paper companies had deforested the hillsides for pulp wood. The forests were gone, the rivers were polluted.

Today, with the decline of heavy industry in the region, 75 percent of the land is again forested with more than 100,000 acres set aside as state forests and natural preserves. The Appalachian Trail winds for eighty-six miles through the Berkshires. Wild turkey, beaver, black bear, and the occasional moose are once again part of the animal population in the county.

More than a century after Hawthorne and Melville left the dirty, crowded, costly cities of the 1850s for the Berkshires, new urban settlers are coming to the region to escape the cities of the 1990s. Publishers, investment advisers, designers, commodities traders, and other professionals equipped with personal computers, fax machines, overnight mail, and access to the Internet conduct their business from these pristine hills.

For information on special events, contact **the Berkshire Visitors' Bureau** (Berkshire Common, Pittsfield, MA 01201; (413) 443-9186 or (800) 237-5747). Ask for an information booklet on the entire Berkshires and the excellent calendar of events listing all the arts organizations in the area.

For information on lodging in Lenox and Stockbridge, contact the **Lenox Chamber of Commerce** (Lenox Academy Building, 75 Main Street, Lenox, MA 01240; (413) 637-3646 or (800) 25-LENOX) or the **Stockbridge Chamber of Commerce** (6 Elm Street, P.O. Box 224, Stockbridge 01262; (413) 298-5200 or (413) 298-5327).

WHERE TO GO, WHAT TO DO

Cultural Events

In the Berkshires more than fifty different organizations offer music, dance, theater, film, and art exhibits during the summer months and increasingly throughout the year. Listed below are the most prominent. The Berkshire Visitors' Bureau (800) 237-5747) publishes an excellent calendar of cultural events.

Tanglewood. The Boston Symphony Orchestra at Tanglewood has made the Berkshires the summer cultural center of the country, if not the world. From July through late August, concerts are held at the music shed on Friday and Saturday nights and Sunday afternoon. The newly completed Seiji Ozawa Hall is used for chamber music, recitals, and student concerts on most other days. On Saturday mornings visitors can attend an open rehearsal for the Sunday program. Tanglewood also has jazz and contemporary music concerts. Series before and after the concert season.

Concert tickets are available for seats in the shed or Ozawa Hall, or for open seating on the lawn (bring a folding chair or blanket). Located on West Street, Route 183, Lenox, MA 01240. September through May (617) 266-1492, June through Labor Day (413) 637-1600.

Williamstown Theatre Festival. The finest actors and actresses in America appear here each summer. The Main Stage has five summer productions while the smaller Other Stage has six. Tuesday through Sunday, mid-June through August. 84 Spring Street, Box 517, Williamstown, MA 01267; (413) 597-3400.

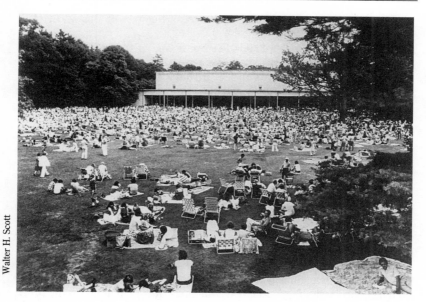

Walter H. Scott

Visitors picnic on the Great Lawn before the Boston Symphony performs at Tanglewood.

Berkshire Theatre Festival. The new Mainstage Theater has four summer productions. The Unicorn Theatre stages readings of new plays in development. At the Children's Theatre (noon, Wed.–Sat.), plays are performed by acting interns. Mainstage, Monday through Saturday, late June to Labor Day. Main Street, Stockbridge, MA 01262; (413) 298-5576.

Shakespeare & Company. There are four different stage settings on the grounds of Edith Wharton's former cottage, "The Mount." At the Mainstage open-air amphitheater, one Shakespearean comedy is performed throughout the summer, July and August. (Bring a jacket and bug repellent.) At the Wharton Theatre, in the drawing room of The Mount, stories by Wharton or her friend Henry James are adapted for the theater and performed in the afternoons, late May through October, with one December production. The Stables Theatre has a repertory of ten plays, about half Shakespearean, late May through Labor Day. Box office: Box 865, Plunkett Street, Lenox, MA 01240; (413) 637-3353.

Don't go to The Mount expecting to see signs of the lavish life depicted in Wharton's books and the movie *The Age of Innocence.* The Mount (built in 1901–02) is in need of extensive repairs and is undergoing restoration as funds become available. Guided tours of the house include stories of Wharton's life at The Mount. Late May to mid-October. Adults $6. Plunkett

Street, one mile south of Lenox at the south junction of 7 and 7A; (413) 637-1899.

Jacob's Pillow. Jacob's Pillow Festival is one of the leading centers of contemporary dance. Ninety minutes before each evening's programs, artists-in-residence give a free performance of works in progress on the outdoor stage. Tuesday through Saturday, late June through August. Located on Route 20, eight miles east of the Lee interchange off I-90. Box 287, Lee, MA 01238; (413) 243-0745.

South Mountain Concerts. Chamber music concerts, string quartets. September to early October. Temple of Music. On Route 7, north of Lenox; (413) 442-2106.

Aston Magna Festival. Concerts of sixteenth- and seventeenth-century music played on period instruments. Saturdays in July and early August. St. James Church, Great Barrington; (413) 528-3595.

Berkshire Opera Company. Two opera productions are given each summer on Saturday evenings, mid-July through August, at the chapel on the grounds of Cranwell. Route 20, Lenox; (413) 528-4420.

Berkshire Choral Festival Concert. Choral singers spend a week studying a piece with nationally known conductors culminating in a Saturday evening concert with the Springfield Symphony. July to mid-August. Route 41, Sheffield; (413) 229-3522.

Museums

Norman Rockwell Museum, Stockbridge. You can't help feeling the artist's humor and respect for the individual when you walk through this new museum dedicated to the works of Norman Rockwell (1894–1978), who illustrated his vision of middle America for over fifty years.

The museum is set on thirty-six acres overlooking the Housatonic River. Highlights include *The Four Freedoms,* a painting based on President Franklin D. Roosevelt's State of the Union message on January 6, 1941, that toured the United States during World War II and helped sell $130 million in war bonds; *Main Street Stockbridge at Christmastime;* and originals of some of Rockwell's 321 *Saturday Evening Post* covers. Open daily. Adults $8. Route 183, Stockbridge, MA 01262; (413) 298-4100.

Clark Art Institute, Williamstown. The neoclassical white marble main building and red granite addition on a quiet residential street house a truly outstanding collection of paintings from the seventeenth through nineteenth centuries. Here you can see paintings by Gainsborough, Rembrandt, Renoir, Degas, Monet, Toulouse-Lautrec, Cassatt, Remington, Homer, Sargent, and Fragonard, along with antique furniture, silver, prints, drawings, and illustrated books. Late nineteenth-century French Impressionists dominate the col-

Hancock Shaker Village, Pittsfield, MA

The 1826 Round Stone Barn is one of twenty buildings at Hancock Shaker Village, a living history museum.

lection. Open Tuesday through Sunday year-round; also open Monday in July and August. 225 South Street, Williamstown, MA 01267; (413) 458-9545.

Hancock Shaker Village, Pittsfield. This living history museum (twenty buildings set on 1,200 acres) has the largest collection of Shaker furniture and artifacts located on an original Shaker site. In the nineteenth century, 300 celibate men and women made their living and practiced their religion on this site. The famous round stone barn is a prime example of labor-saving Shaker design. The smaller buildings on the property house craftspeople who make the simple, elegant furniture, baskets, brooms, and oval Shaker boxes. Located at the junction of Routes 20 and 41. Open daily, Memorial Day through late October; weekends only, April, May, and November. Adults $10. Box 898, Pittsfield, MA 01202; (413) 443-0188.

Chesterwood. Daniel Chester French, one of America's greatest classical sculptors, lived and worked here six months of every year from 1898 until his death in 1931. His most famous work is the seated Abraham Lincoln in the Lincoln Memorial in Washington, D.C. Chesterwood displays the series of models of this work, some of them small enough to hold in your hand. The guided tour takes you into French's studio, which features a twenty-three-foot ceiling and a railroad track designed to move large works through the huge doors (so the artist could see his creations in the sunlight). The tour also includes the first floor of his Colonial Revival house. The grounds include nature trails, a restored barn with exhibits of Chester's work, and an outdoor changing exhibit of high-quality contemporary sculptures for sale. The property is owned and operated by the National Trust for Historic Preservation. Open daily. Adults $10. Route 183, P.O. Box 248, Stockbridge, MA 01262; (413) 298-3579.

Naumkeag. Deriving its name from a Native American word meaning "place of rest," this twenty-six-room Norman-style mansion was built in 1886 for Joseph Choate, the U.S. ambassador to Britain from 1899 to 1905, after a design by Stanford White. Outside you can stroll through the elaborate gardens; inside you'll see how a wealthy, cultured family lived at the turn of the century. Of particular note is the collection of Chinese export porcelain, Oriental rugs, and furniture that spans three centuries. May through October. Adults $6.50. Located one-half mile north of the intersection of Routes 7 and 102 on Prospect Street in Stockbridge; (413) 298-3239.

Arrowhead. It was here that Herman Melville, looking from his second-floor study north toward Mount Greylock, saw the specter of a giant whale and heard the wind filling "sails" as he and his good friend Nathaniel Hawthorne talked long into the night. Open late May to Labor Day, Friday through Monday; by appointment through October. Adults $5. Located off Route 7, 780 Holmes Road, Pittsfield, MA 01201; (413) 442-1793.

The Towns

Great Barrington

A mix of longtime residents (descendants of Colonial settlers), hippies from the sixties, New Age converts, and Manhattan escapees—make up this interesting town. The hub is Main Street around Castle and Railroad Streets. Interesting shops on Railroad Street include Bleu Lavande, which sells housewares imported from Provence; Tanglewool, for high-quality women's clothing; Liberty House, for lower-priced women's trendy clothing; and Church St. Trading Company, for antique furniture and chic home accessories. On Main Street look for T. P. Saddleblanket for upscale designer western clothing, or order custom work for your home at October Mountain Stained Glass.

The local hangout is 20 Railroad Street, featuring a long bar, good burgers, and large salads. For high-butterfat ice cream, good soups, and sandwiches, walk across the street to Bev's. The locals line up for their caffeine fix at Berkshire Coffee Roasting Company on Main Street. We like Baker's Wife, a bakery below street level with excellent almond macaroons and hazelnut-caramel bars. Castle Street Café is next to the Mahaiwe movie house on Castle Street, an ornate throwback to the past.

Heading south of town on Route 7, stop at Guido's. Everyone in the Berkshires with an interest in food finds his or her way to this popular purveyor of fine foods. Also along Route 7, visit the tiny Merrimac Smokehouse (955 South Main St., Great Barrington; 413-528-2004). The staff will vacuum-seal trout, salmon, and sturgeon for you to carry in a cooler. Heading north on Route 7, stop at the Marketplace for gourmet salads or sandwiches and at Catherine's for chocolates. DeWoolfson Down & Bed Feather Co. in the Jennifer House Commons shopping complex makes down pillows and comforters and sells fine imported cotton sheets and duvet covers. You can even try out different types of down pillows in the back room. Just beyond is Hickory Bill's and the Boiler Room Cafe.

Lee

An "upscale village-style" designer outlet mall is slated for construction at the Lee interchange of the Massachusetts Turnpike. This is sure to bring more traffic into this New England factory town, known for marble quarries and as a manufacturer of quality paper. Walk through the center of town and enjoy the Victorian houses and churches. Stop in at McClelland's drugstore (established in 1860) and have a twenty-five-cent cup of coffee at the old-fashioned soda fountain. Or head up the street to Joe's Diner, where you can listen to the local gossip and devour a substantial corned-beef sandwich.

Stockbridge

Sit on a rocker on the wide porch at the Red Lion Inn and soak up the ambience of this New England village made famous through Norman Rockwell's painting *Main Street Stockbridge at Christmastime*. Walk through the lobby of the Red Lion and through the dining rooms to the home of Country Curtains, where you can see many of the catalog curtains on display. The Stockbridge Chamber of Commerce, across the street, maintains a small information booth. Stand here and look at the real-life inspiration for Rockwell's painting.

Head west on Main Street across Route 7 to the 1739 Mission House, one of the original buildings in Stockbridge built by the first missionary to the Mahican Indians. The house, with its distinctive Connecticut River valley door, was moved to its present site and furnished with period pieces, and is today an excellent small museum of Colonial life in the Berkshires (late May to mid-October).

Worth a visit is Nijames Stockbridge Wine Cellar and Cheese Shop (413-298-3454) on Elm Street, which has excellent prices on French Bordeaux, Burgundies, and California Cabernets, and carries local products such as Monterey chèvre and Merrimac smoked salmon. If you are a glass collector, don't miss the Holsten Galleries (across the street next to the post office; (413) 298-3044), which specializes in work of renowned contemporary glass artists such as Harvey K. Littleton and Tom Patti.

West Stockbridge

This village has become a small center of craft studios and restaurants. New England Stained Glass Studios has exquisite Tiffany reproductions. Berkshire Center for Contemporary Glass lets you watch the glassblowers and take lessons. Charles H. Baldwin & Sons, a century-old business, manufactures extracts; the pure vanilla is excellent. Maple Hill Studio sells furniture, sculpture, and jewelry; Hotchkiss Mobiles, indoor and outdoor mobiles; and Waterside Gallery, quality sculpture and paintings. You can have lunch at Caffe Pomo d'oro (Friday and Saturday nights in the summer), dinner at La Bruschetta or Truc Orient Express, and ice cream well worth breaking your diet for anytime at Berkshire Ice Cream.

Lenox

In the summers of the 1880s this town was a hive of activity, with more than seventy huge estates or "cottages" built and operated for America's wealthy industrialists in the surrounding countryside. You can still experience a part of the Gilded Age by staying and dining in three of these "cottages" (see Where to Stay/Dine). On the site of two former cottages, Canyon Ranch Spa and Kripalu Center for Yoga and Health attract guests throughout the year for health and fitness. In Lenox, Tanglewood is the summer home of the Boston Symphony, which brings thousands of visitors to stay in the local inns, dine in the restaurants, and shop in many interesting galleries and boutiques. The Lenox Library at the corner of Main and Walker is an 1815 Greek Revival building. The main high-ceilinged reading room has a large collection of periodicals and comfortable seating. A gallery has continuing exhibits of local artists and craftspeople.

Eviva on Walker Street sells women's clothes by small American designers (many undiscovered) that you won't find at the outlets. Hoadley Gallery on Church Street has pottery and jewelry (a piece of Tom Hoadley's pottery was selected by the Clintons for the White House's collection). Ute Stebich Gallery has museum-quality folk art.

Williamstown

This pristine, well-planned old New England town is the home of Williams College, a highly regarded liberal arts institution, and the Clark Art Institute (see Museums). The Williams College Museum of Art has a permanent collection focusing on twentieth-century American, Asian, and other non-Western civilizations, as well as the finest collection of paintings by Maurice and Charles Prendergast. The 20,000 rare books at the Chapin Library include all four founding documents of the United States, and all the Shakespeare folios. Most of the stores, restaurants, and commercial buildings are on Spring Street, where there are several public parking lots.

Outdoor Recreation

Hiking

Seventy-five percent of Berkshire County is forested today with more than 100,000 acres in public protected parks. Eighty-six miles of the Appalachian Trail traverse the Berkshires. *Hikes and Walks in the Berkshire Hills* by Lauren Stevens (1990) and *A Guide to Natural Places in the Berkshire Hills* by Rene Laubach (1992), both published by Berkshire House in Stockbridge, are detailed sources. Here are a few of our favorite walks. *See* the Driving Tours section for directions.

Pleasant Valley Wildlife Sanctuary is an 1,100-acre Massachusetts Audubon Society property (admission $3) just north of Lenox off Route 7. Go west on West Dugway Road then bear left at West Mountain Road. Trail maps are available at the office.

Mount Greylock. You can get to Mount Greylock from Pittsfield or from North Adams. For serious hiking this is where you will want to go. For some of the best views take the one-mile hike to Stony Ledge.

Tyringham Cobble. South of Lee, this is about a one-hour walk to 400 feet above the beautiful Tyringham Valley, where you will get magnificent views of farms, the village and Hop Brook (*see* Driving Tours for directions and information.)

Bash Bish Falls. In the Southern Berkshires off Route 23 near Egremont, these are the most spectacular waterfalls in the region.

Berkshire Hiking Holidays. If you want to spend your time in the Berkshires hiking and leave the arrangements to others, Berkshire Hiking Holidays offers three- to five-day trips for small groups incorporating hiking, canoeing, cultural events, and staying in country inns. Box 2231, Lenox, MA 01240; (800) 877-9656.

Golf

Cranwell Resort's eighteen-hole 360-acre PGA championship course, built in the 1920s and in continuous play for sixty-seven years, circles the resort property. Many of the holes, especially the back nine, have a separate geographical identity. The eighth tee in front of the mansion has a sweeping sixty-mile vista of the Berkshire Hills to the south.

Horseback Riding

Undermountain Farm, located in a gorgeous valley close to Lenox, offers instruction ranging from beginner to advanced and private guided trail rides tailored to your ability (cantering is permitted). There is an indoor riding rink and instruction and trail rides are available year-round. 252 Undermountain Road, Lenox; (413) 637-3365.

Skiing

One of the Discerning Travelers learned how to ski at the Otis Ridge Junior Ski Camp in the 1950s. It was a good experience. Call (413) 499-7669 for the latest information on ski conditions at the downhill ski areas: Butternut, Catamount, Bousquet, Jiminy Peak, Brodie, and Otis Ridge. Cross-country skiing options include the state forests at Mount Washington and October Mountain. A couple of our favorites include Kennedy Park in downtown Lenox; Pleasant Valley Nature Center; Cranwell, which has groomed trails on the property; Brodie, for its fine ski touring center; and Stone Hill Loop (four miles), which begins at the Clark Art Institute parking lot.

Crafts

New England Stained Glass Studios. Hundreds of the highest quality Tiffany lampshade reproductions that rival the original are on display at this studio. Prices range from $50 to $15,000. 5 Center St., West Stockbridge; (413) 232-7181.

Berkshire Center for Contemporary Glass. Here you can watch masters work with glass, take lessons, or purchase a piece from the gallery. Located in West Stockbridge next to La Bruschetta restaurant; (413) 232-4666.

Joyous Spring Pottery. Michael Marcus, featured on a Charles Kuralt TV program, makes spectacular unglazed wood-fired pots that are sold in top galleries in the United States and Japan. His forty-three-foot-long Japanese wood-fired kiln, which he packs with over 1,200 pieces, is fired for twelve days once a year. His pots are one of a kind, inspired by traditional Japanese shapes, and have an earthy feel. Daily May to October, but best to call ahead. Art School Road, Monterey; (413) 528-4115.

Great Barrington Pottery. Since 1967, Richard Bennett, who learned his craft in Japan, has made Western-style table place settings using Japanese methods. His best works are pieces with a glaze that remind us of Chinese scroll painting. A Japanese woman performs tea ceremony at his teahouse in the summer. Daily, May to December, and weekends year-round. Route 41, Housatonic; (413) 274-6259.

Driving Tours

Stockbridge–Tyringham–Great Barrington–Housatonic

From **Stockbridge** head east on Route 102. Just before the Massachusetts Turnpike, turn right on Tyringham Road. You'll pass the **Gingerbread House Art Gallery** (admission), an architecturally fascinating thatched roof cottage. Just after the village of Tyringham, turn right on Jerusalem Road for one-quarter mile to **Tyringham Cobble**, a promontory that rises over 400 feet. The two-mile (one-hour) hike affords great views of the valley.

Turn right at Art School Road, the next road on your right, to **Joyous**

Spring Pottery. The restored **Bidwell House** farther up the road is a 1750 saltbox with a collection of eighteenth- and early nineteenth-century furniture pieces. (Daily, late May to mid-October, (413) 528-6888.) In Monterey turn right at Route 23 and continue to **Great Barrington**. Lunch options are **20 Railroad Street, Bev's, Hickory Bill's** just north of the center on Route 7, or takeout at the **Marketplace**. Head south on Route 7 through Great Barrington. **Merrimac Smoked Fish** (on the left two miles south of downtown) can provide the fixings for a truly gourmet lunch. With more than fifty antique shops along the road an avid antiquer could easily spend an entire day going from Great Barrington to Sheffield. At **Fellerman & Raabe Glassworks** south of Sheffield (413-229-8533) you can watch the glassmakers at work. Prices range from very reasonable on up. About a mile before the Connecticut state line turn left at Hewins Street, then right on Shunpike Road to get to **Butler Sculpture Park** (daily, May through October, (413) 229-8924). Robert Butler's contemporary curvilinear large sculptures are spread on the hillside, a beautiful spot with long spectacular views. Return to Great Barrington. Turn left on Route 183, which follows the Housatonic River. This is a scenic road, particularly in the fall, when the colors of the leaves reflect in the river. Five contemporary art galleries have opened in the town of **Housatonic (Housatonic Gallery, Front Street Gallery, Le Petit Musee, Spazi Contemporary**, and **River Contemporary Art**). For a detour, take Main Street to Route 41 north to **Great Barrington Pottery**, a production pottery making complete sets of dishes. Visit potter Richard Bennet's showrooms, Japanese gardens, and teahouse, where a tea ceremony is performed. Return to Route 183 and continue north. You will pass **Chesterwood** and the **Norman Rockwell Museum**. The **Botanical Garden** at Route 102 has fifteen acres of gardens and trails (May through October; (413) 298-3926), and is worth a stop. Turn right on Route 102 west to **Stockbridge**.

Lenox–West Stockbridge–Pittsfield–Mount Greylock–Williamstown

Start in **Lenox** on Route 7A heading north. Take an immediate left on Cliffwood Street, then left on Under Mountain Road past the **Under Mountain Stables**. This road ends at Route 183 (also known as West Street) at the entrance to Tanglewood. Take the next right off Route 183 (Richmond Hill Road) up a steep hill. Pull off at the overlook to see the view of the **Stockbridge Bowl vista**. Turn left on Lenox Branch Road to **West Stockbridge**. Stop for lunch at **Pomo d'oro** or get an ice-cream cone at **Berkshire Ice Cream**, delicious and very rich locally made ice cream. Go into **Baldwin & Sons** (413) 232-8519), a store with the feel of the past selling pure vanilla extract and other flavorings. At **New England Stained Glass Studio** see Tiffany lamp reproductions that are made here. Head north on Route 41 to Route 20 to tour **Hancock Shaker Village**. Take Route 20 to Pittsfield and turn left on Route 7. The **Berkshire Museum**, on your right, has a nice collection of Hudson

River painters. Continue north on Route 7 to Lanesborough. At Rockwell Road turn right and follow it to the Visitor Center for Mount Greylock. Here you can get information on guided walks and can get trail maps. It's another twenty-minute drive up to the summit of **Mount Greylock**, highest peak in Massachusetts. If the weather is clear you'll be treated to spectacular views. **Bascom Lodge**, a stone lodge at the summit, was built during the depression by the Civilian Conservation Corps and is now operated by the Appalachian Mountain Club. Lodging is in four private rooms and four dormitory-style bunk rooms that accommodate a total of twenty-eight. Breakfast and dinner (call by noon for dinner reservations) are served family style; lunch is available over the counter, mid-May to mid-October (413) 443-0011). If you are a hiker or a birder and are looking for inexpensive lodgings, this is a good option. Return to Route 7. At Route 43 stop at the **Store at Five Corners**, a gourmet food store, then continue on 43 to Williamstown. The **Clark Art Institute**, a wonderful museum with free admission, is reason enough to visit Williamstown at every opportunity. **Williams College** is also here. The **Williams Art Museum** is free and is worth a visit. **Spring Street** is the shopping street with a number of restaurants; Robins is good for lunch. For more elegant dining, we suggest the **Orchards**. Take Route 8 through Adams with a side trip to Dalton for a visit to **Crane Paper Museum** (open June through mid-October, weekdays 2 to 5 P.M.) and learn how the paper for all U.S. currency is made. Continue to Pittsfield on Route 9 and back to Lenox.

WHERE TO STAY

Minimum stays are generally three nights on weekends (Thursday through Sunday) during July and August and two nights (Friday and Saturday) at other times.

Blantyre, Lenox

A long drive winds through the woods of this eighty-five-acre property to an impressively maintained 1902 Tudor castle patterned after one in Scotland. Staying here gives you a rare chance to experience what life was like for the very well-to-do at the turn of the century. Now this castle is owned by the Fitzpatricks, owners of the Red Lion Inn and Country Curtains, and for many years has been most capably managed by Roderick Anderson.

The great hall has dark carved wood paneling, Oriental rugs, and a large wood-burning fireplace. The first floor includes a main dining room, a conservatory, and an outdoor terrace where lunch is served in the summer.

For the spirit of the Gilded Age stay in the main house, which has five large rooms and suites, each with a wood-burning fireplace, and three modest-sized rooms. The carriage house provides a more casual setting, with balconies or decks off each room and marble baths. Other facilities include a heated swim-

Lincoln Russell

Blantyre, built in 1902, was patterned after a Scottish Tudor castle.

ming pool, two tournament-sanctioned bent-grass croquet lawns, four Har-Tru tennis courts, a large indoor hot tub, a sauna, and a few fitness machines.

Open mid-May through October. Twenty-three rooms and suites, two cottages (for longer stays), all with private bath, $230–$650. Children over 12 welcome. 10% gratuity. Continental breakfast included. Tennis whites required on courts and croquet lawns. Blantyre Road (off Route 20), P.O. Box 995, Lenox, MA 01240. May through November, (413) 637-3556; November through April, (413) 298-1661.

Wheatleigh, Lenox

This elegant Florentine-inspired country palace, built in 1893 on twenty-two acres, is close to the back entrance of Tanglewood. The hotel, owned by Linfield and Susan Simon, has an airy, uncluttered, contemporary feel. The great hall has a baronial marble wood-burning fireplace and the Simons' collection of ceramics attractively offset by English antique and oriental furniture. The captivating views of the Berkshire hills from the glass doors leading to the terrace add to the magnificence of the setting.

Here we found spacious accommodations, lots of privacy, and a dining experience second to none. The top choices are the five very large rooms on the second floor that overlook the hills and a first-floor room that looks out on the gardens. Each of these rooms has a king-size bed and a fireplace; five also have balconies. The center room, the former sitting room between the count and the countess's rooms, is the most interesting architecturally, with a dome ceiling and curved walls, but the bath is small. All the rooms are air-conditioned and have televisions and VCRs (a selection of classic movies is available), as well as portable telephones. The owners recently added a state-of-the-art fitness room with a treadmill, life cycle, rowing machine, Stairmaster, and weight equipment, as well as a private massage room.

The grounds include an oval-shaped heated swimming pool set in a grove of towering pines and a newly resurfaced tennis court.

Seventeen rooms, all with private bath. Weekends July and August and fall, $195–$555; other times, $155–$395. Breakfast available but not included. Children over 12 welcome. No pets. Three-night minimum July and August. Hawthorne Road (off Route 183), Lenox, MA 01240; (413) 637-0610.

Cranwell Resort, Lenox

This brick Tudor mansion set high on a hill with a sixty-mile commanding view of the Southern Berkshires stands out as a landmark as you drive north on Route 20 from Lee. The 380-acre property includes the 1893 mansion as well as the Carriage House, Beecher's Cottage, Founders Hall, Cottage suites, a chapel, and an eighteen-hole championship golf course.

All of the rooms, among the largest in the area, have been redecorated with coordinating carpets, upholstery, and draperies. A unique feature is the marble baths in all the rooms throughout the resort except in Founders Hall. Beecher's Cottage is a little more deluxe than the Carriage House. Each of the Cottage suites has a private entrance, a living room, bedroom, and kitchen. Founders Hall was recently renovated to include rooms ranging from executive parlors to master suites with kitchenettes and a terrace.

The eighteen-hole PGA championship golf course encompasses the entire property. Other facilities include an outdoor swimming pool, two Har-Tru tennis courts, a 500-seat chapel used for weddings and for performances of the Berkshire Opera, indoor golf in the original gym, and multiple meeting rooms. Cranwell also has eleven kilometers of groomed and tracked cross-country ski trails and a snow-making machine. Restaurants in the mansion include Wyndhurst for fine dining and the seasonal English-style pub in the Golf Club.

Ninety-four rooms, all with private bath. May through October, $249–$459; other times, $99–$259. Continental breakfast included. Inquire about special golf and off-season packages. Children welcome. No pets. Route 20, Lenox, MA 01240; (413) 637-1364; (800) 272-6935.

Canyon Ranch, Lenox

Canyon Ranch in the Berkshires, situated on 120 acres belonging to Bellefontaine, one of the area's former grand cottages, is the ultimate in fitness and well-being. It is patterned after its highly successful namesake in Arizona. A staff of 450 allows for an extensive and highly individualized list of services.

Packages include three meals a day and all fitness classes. An average rate for a three-night stay in a deluxe room, June through October, Sunday through Tuesday, is $1,428 (single) or $1,218 (double occupancy); Wednesday through Saturday, $1,596 (single), $1,365 (double occupancy), plus 18% service charge and sales tax. Rates are lower in other seasons. Children must be at least 14 years old to stay or participate in activities. No pets. No smoking. 165 Kemble Street, Route 7A, Lenox, MA 01240; (413) 637-4100; (800) 742-9000.

The Orchards, Williamstown

This deluxe country hotel built in 1985 is the best place to stay in the Berkshires' North County. The hotel is built around stunningly landscaped central garden. The spacious rooms include either a king-size bed or two double beds, an armoire (where the television and VCR are hidden), dresser, and night tables—all top-quality English antiques.

During the winter the best rooms are the ones with wood-burning fireplaces. In summer, the rooms overlooking the interior garden and pond are our favorites. Other facilities include conference rooms, a restaurant, an outdoor pool, a small exercise room, a large indoor whirlpool, and bicycles.

Forty-seven rooms, all with private bath. Late May through mid-November, $160–$225; other times, $125–$175. Afternoon tea included. All meals available but not included. Children welcome. No pets. 222 Adams Road, Williamstown, MA 01267; (413) 458-9611; (800) 225-1517.

Red Lion Inn, Stockbridge

This venerable establishment in the center of Stockbridge is well known throughout the world from Norman Rockwell's famous painting *Main Street Stockbridge at Christmastime*. In continuous operation since the eighteenth century, the Red Lion has been owned by the Fitzpatrick family since 1968.

The first floor contains restaurants, the original Country Curtains store, a gift shop, and a grand front porch equipped with rocking chairs.

Rooms range from deluxe suites to small bed-and-breakfast rooms with shared baths. Favorites in the main building are the suites with views of the main street. Of the other buildings that make up this complex, our favorite is the Stafford House, located directly behind the main building, and the old Firehouse, which includes a second-floor master bedroom and a bath with a double whirlpool. The inn also has a swimming pool and a small exercise room.

One hundred eight rooms and suites. Late April through October, private-bath rooms and suites $94–$350, shared-bath rooms $62–$87. Other times, private-bath rooms and suites $87–$320, shared-bath rooms $62–$72. Children welcome. Breakfast included in shared-bath rooms only. No pets. Two-night minimum on summer weekends. Stockbridge, MA 01262; (413) 298-5545.

Cliffwood Inn, Lenox

Cliffwood, a one-and-a-half-acre property set back from the road on a quiet street of large, elegant homes, two blocks from the center of Lenox, was built in 1889 with many French-inspired details. Outfitting an inn with fine furnishings was no problem for owners Joy and Scottie Farrelly, as they had amassed a sizable collection of furniture, paintings, Oriental rugs, and accessories during twenty-five years of corporate moves among the capitals of Europe.

The first floor has inlaid hardwood floors, twelve-foot ceilings, gilded mirrors in the expansive living room, and a dining room graced by a Venetian chandelier and a 400-year-old sideboard. In summer, breakfast is served on the veranda, which overlooks the pool and landscaped grounds.

Top choices are the Helen Walker Room and the Jacob Gross Jr. Room, each with king-size four-poster canopy beds and a fireplace. The Nathaniel Foote Room, another good choice, has a queen-size canopy bed and fireplace.

A unique feature is the new indoor counter-current pool, a small pool with an adjustable current, and whirlpool large enough for three.

Seven rooms, all with private bath. July, August, and foliage season, weekends $120–$210; other times $85–$145. Continental breakfast included (except midweek low season); wine and hors d'oeuvres included. Three- or four-night weekend minimum in high season. Children over 13 welcome. No pets. No smoking. 25 Cliffwood Street, Lenox, MA 01240; (413) 637-3330; (800) 789-3331.

Historic Merrell Inn, South Lee

Arriving at this 200-year-old roadside inn one can easily feel transported back to the nineteenth century, when the building was a stagecoach stop. Faith and Charles Reynolds have conscientiously restored this property with wide board spruce floors, an original circular Colonial-era birdcage bar in the breakfast room, wood-burning fireplaces, and period antiques, including the 1800 grandfather clock that still chimes in the central hall. A gazebo on the back lawn overlooks the peaceful Housatonic River and the Berkshire Hills.

Our favorites are the three rooms with wood-burning fireplaces: Room 1, a first-floor room, and rooms 2 and 9 are all larger rooms with queen-canopy beds. Other popular choices are room 6 with a corona over the bed and room 7 with a fishnet canopy; both are on the third floor. All the rooms have phones and are air-conditioned.

The Tavern Room, where breakfast is served on Bennington pottery from 8:30 to 10 A.M., has a particularly pleasing feel with Windsor chairs, individual tables, and a wood-burning fireplace.

Nine rooms, all with private bath. Summer and fall weekends $115–$135, midweek and other times of the year $75–$95. Full breakfast and tea included. Children over 12 welcome. No smoking. No pets. Two- to three-night weekend minimum. 1565 Pleasant Street (Route 102), South Lee, MA 01260; (413) 243-1794; (800) 243-1794.

Applegate, Lee

This white-shingled Georgian Colonial, built in 1920 on six manicured acres, is owned by Nancy and Rick Cannata, a flight attendant and a pilot, who adjust their work schedules so one of them is always at the inn. The first floor has an open feel with a spacious entrance hall opening to an expansive living room with a piano, a wood-burning fireplace, and shelves of books. An adjoining winterized sunroom has a television/VCR.

Our favorite is room 1, with a four-poster king-size bed, a wood-burning fireplace, and a bath with a steam shower large enough for two. Of the other rooms four have queen-size beds, and one (room 3) also has a fireplace. Room 6, the smallest room, is a good value. Turndown service includes Godiva chocolates and brandy.

The breakfast room has another wood-burning fireplace. Ray and Bubba, the Cannatas' cockatiels, are favorites of all the guests. The property also includes a swimming pool in an attractive setting as well as a contemporary decorated carriage house apartment with two bedrooms, a bath with a double whirlpool tub, kitchen, living room, and deck.

Six rooms, all with private bath, and a two-bedroom apartment. June through October, weekends $120–$225; weekdays and other times of the year $85–$190. Continental breakfast, wine and cheese included. Apartment is $1,000 a week in the summer, $225 a night other times. Children over 12 welcome. No pets. Two- to three-night weekend minimum. No smoking. RR1, Box 576, 279 West Park Street, Lee, MA 01238; (413) 243-4451; (800) 691-9012.

Brook Farm Inn, Lenox

Sitting on the front porch on a summer morning we heard the soft strains of classical music wafting through the trees from the nearby Tanglewood Institute, a prestigious summer music school. Nothing could have been more appropriate, for the arts, both poetry and music, are an important part of this inn.

The light-filled, comfortable living room has a wood-burning fireplace and bookcases with about 1,500 books (half are poetry). Innkeepers Anne and Joe Miller have tape recorders and a collection of poetry tapes that you can borrow to listen to by the heated pool, as you lie in the hammock, sit on the wicker chairs on the front porch, or relax in your room. On Saturdays, Joe reads poetry while guests have tea and scones.

For a winter stay ask for one of the six rooms with fireplaces, five of which are wood-burning. The most popular are rooms 1, 2, and 4, each with a Shaker-style queen-size bed and a full bath. Room M on the first floor has a queen-size bed (twin beds during the summer) and a brick-front fireplace.

A buffet breakfast includes a hot dish such as cheese strata with salsa or French toast casserole topped with fruit. On summer Sunday mornings a student quintet from the Tanglewood Institute plays during breakfast.

Twelve rooms, each with private bath. Late June through October, weekends $110–$185. Weekdays and other times of the year $80–$130. Breakfast and tea included. Children over 15 welcome during the summer; younger children at other times; $20 additional. No pets. No smoking. Two- to three-night weekend minimum. 15 Hawthorne Street, Lenox, MA 02140; (413) 637-3013; (800) 285-POET.

Amadeus House, Lenox

We were first attracted to this 1820s cream-colored clapboard inn by the wide wraparound front porch, where a congenial group of guests were enjoying afternoon tea on a summer afternoon. As avid listeners of National Public Radio, we enjoyed talking with innkeepers John Felton, formerly its deputy foreign editor, and his wife, Marty Gottron. The informal small living room has a fireplace, an extensive classical music collection of over 500 CDs, and good reference books about the Berkshires.

Mozart, a first-floor room with a wood-burning stove and a private porch, is our favorite. Bach, with a queen-size and a twin bed, and Brahms, with a four-poster queen bed and wicker couch, are the other large rooms, each with a shower. Four smaller rooms are the bargain accommodations for this area. For longer stays there's a third-floor two-bedroom apartment.

A full breakfast, served at three tables from 8 to 9:30 A.M., includes a hot dish such as apple pancakes or orange waffles.

Seven rooms, five with private bath, and a two-bedroom apartment. July to Labor Day, weekends $85–$145 daily, apartment $900 per week; other times $60–$125; apartment $90–$175. Full breakfast and tea included (except in apartment). Children over 10 welcome. No smoking. No pets. Two- to three-night weekend minimum. 15 Cliffwood Street, Lenox, MA 01240; (413) 637-4770; (800) 205-4770.

The Village Inn, Lenox

Since 1775 guests have dined and lodged at this traditional inn located in the center of Lenox owned by Clifford Rudisill and Ray Wilson. The first floor has two dining rooms, a television room, and a formal parlor. The lower-level tavern serves light fare. All the rooms have window air conditioners and phones.

Six of the rooms have fireplaces, three have single whirlpool tubs, and all are furnished with country antiques. The standard and superior rooms have a queen-size bed or one king-size bed or two twin beds. The six small economy rooms have double beds and small baths; three have private hall baths. Favorites are 7, 20, and 8 (with whirlpool tubs and fireplaces) as well as large rooms 23 (fireplace) and 25, the largest, a corner room with a queen-size four-poster and large bathroom with a claw-foot tub. The third-floor suite has two bedrooms, a kitchenette, and a living room.

Thirty-two rooms including a two-bedroom suite, all with private bath. Summer, rooms $100–$210, suite $395. Other times of the year, rooms $60–$165, suite $220–$300. $10 additional on holiday weekends. Breakfast, tea, and dinner available but not included. Children over 6 welcome. No smoking. No pets. P.O. Box 1810, 16 Church Street, Lenox, MA 01240; (413) 637-0020; (800) 253-0917.

Walker House, Lenox

Innkeepers Richard and Peggy Houdek own this 1804 Federal on a three-acre lot in the center of Lenox. They have eight cats, and guests are welcome to bring pets. They have a large collection of recorded movies, operas, and plays that they show in the library equipped with a projection television, a seven-foot screen, and surround sound. The living room with a grand piano and the dining room have wood-burning fireplaces. Of the five rooms with fireplaces Mozart is the favorite. Puccini is a summer favorite as it has a porch.

Eight rooms, all with private bath. July through Labor Day, weekends $110–$190; midweek and other times of the year $80–$150. Continental breakfast and tea included. Children over 12 welcome. Pets welcome with prior approval. No smoking. Two- to three-night weekend minimum. 74 Walker Street, Lenox, MA 01240; (413) 637-1271; (800) 235-3098.

Windflower, Great Barrington

This 100-year-old Federal-style informal country inn is the kind of place where you can put up your feet and relax. Barbara and Gerald Liebert and their daughter Claudia and her husband, John Ryan, have operated the inn since 1980. There are two casual living rooms with wood-burning fireplaces, a screened porch, and a swimming pool.

All the rooms are air-conditioned and have small black-and-white televisions, and six have wood-burning fireplaces. Eleven of the rooms have queen-size beds and two have one king-size or two twin beds. A number of the rooms have four-poster canopy beds and old-fashioned claw-foot tubs. A nice selection of toiletries includes a loofah mitt scrub. Room 12, our favorite, has a massive stone wood-burning fireplace and a door opening to the side porch. Room 11 has a fireplace and a door to the same porch. Room 1, the master bedroom, has a queen and a twin bed, fireplace, and dressing room. Room 4, with a bay and a double window, and room 5, with two double windows, are large, sunny, corner front rooms with four-poster canopy beds.

Guests sit at their own table for breakfast, 8:30 to 9:30 A.M., which includes a hot dish such as French toast made with homemade challah or cottage cheese soufflé pancakes.

Thirteen rooms, all with private bath, $100–$180, breakfast and tea included. 15% meal gratuity. Children welcome, $35–$50 additional. No pets.

Two- to three-night weekend minimum. 684 South Egremont Road (Route 23), Great Barrington, MA 01230; (413) 528-2720; (800) 992-1993.

October Mountain Campground
For the budget-minded who like to camp, this well-run state park has fifty wooded sites with hot showers and flush toilets. Best of all, it is close to Lenox. Reservations are not accepted, so arrive by Thursday morning during the Tanglewood season. Woodland Road, Lee, MA 01238; (413) 243-1778.

WHERE TO DINE

Fine Dining

Wheatleigh, Lenox
The entrance to the formal dining room is through the great hall of this Florentine-inspired 1893 palace. A pair of antique Waterford chandeliers, two matching candelabras above the fireplace, and candlelit tables set the stage. The dining here is on the cutting edge of culinary innovation. Three five-course tasting menus are prepared each evening: a low-fat, a vegetarian, and a regular dinner menu. We chose courses from each of the three menus for a truly memorable dinner.

The low-fat dinner the night we dined included seviche of scallops, pumpkin soup with fresh fig quenelles, grilled steelhead salmon, breast of squab, a trio of sorbets, and a poached spiced seckel pear.

The vegetarian menu included three vegetable mousses, Monterey chèvre and roasted vegetable terrine, wild mushroom Napoleon, acorn squash filled with wild rice and pecans, fresh mission figs in red wine sauce with frozen anisette soufflé, and white and dark chocolate mousse with raspberries in a delicate pastry.

The dinner tasting menu included smoked salmon on buckwheat blini, foie gras terrine, halibut with a black trumpet mushroom sauce, roast veal with black truffle sauce, a selection of cheese, and a tarte tatin with sour cream quenelles. Each dish was beautifully coordinated with the china on which it was served. The portions are small and light, so we left the table satisfied but not uncomfortable. The wine list is extensive and expensive; all the great French growths are represented.

A second dining option during the summer is the Grill Room. In nice weather, dining on the portico takes advantage of the mountain views.

Dinner nightly, May through October; closed Tuesday November through April. Prix fixe dinners $55, $68; degustation dinner, $90. Grill Room: Sunday brunch and dinner, July and August, entrées $9.50–$24. Hawthorne Road (off Route 183), Lenox, MA 01240; (413) 637-0610.

Blantyre, Lenox

Dinner here is in the grand tradition of an English country house hotel, which is fitting, as Blantyre is a 1902 Tudor mansion built to replicate a grand Scottish manor house. Guests are greeted in the great Gothic hall, which features large furniture, leaded glass windows, fireplace, tapestries, and Oriental rugs. Have a drink and make your dinner selections before being seated in the dining room, which has dark carved walls and widely spaced tables beautifully set with Limoges floral-patterned green-and-gold china made for Blantyre.

The prix fixe dinner includes a selection of six appetizers, six entrées, and desserts. The extensive wine list represents over 250 vineyards.

Selections from a fall menu included appetizers of braised lamb cannelloni served over tender spinach with a light saffron sauce and grilled medallions of Maine lobster with a Thai curry and julienne of cucumber. Entrées included a breast of pheasant with pumpkin risotto with fried sage and chanterelles, roasted halibut with oysters, braised tiny onions and a cider sauce, and veal tenders with a fresh horseradish cream sauce. Following dessert, coffee and chocolates are served in the main hall. During the summer, guests who are going to Tanglewood can return for a postconcert dessert buffet.

Summer lunches at Blantyre are served in the conservatory or outside on the terrace. The menu includes caramelized onion pizetta with mozzarella, walnuts, and sage; Caesar salad; curried roast chicken salad; or grilled fish with stir-fried vegetables.

Dinner nightly, mid-May to early November. Prix fixe $70. Open for lunch (reservations needed) daily in July and August, entrées $13–$22. Route 20, Lenox, MA; (413) 637-3556.

Wyndhurst, Cranwell Resort, Lenox

The newly restored elegant formal dining room just off the great hall of this 100-year-old Tudor mansion has magnificent expansive vistas over the golf course and the Berkshire Hills. For starters we had a large salad of local organic baby greens and gravlax served with crème fraîche and salmon roe, and sautéed goat cheese from local Rawson Brook Farm with a pistachio crust served over julienne vegetables.

Entrée choices were grilled yellowfin tuna served over organic greens with a warm orange dressing and roasted rack of baby lamb rubbed with herbs, olive oil, and whole grain mustard served with roasted garlic and pinot noir wine sauce—a real treat. The dessert not to miss is the exceptional apple tart, a puff pastry round with thin slices of apples covered with a caramel sauce and topped with vanilla ice cream.

On Sundays an extensive and elaborate buffet brunch is served in the Music Room. For more casual dining we like the hunt decor of the restaurant in the clubhouse.

Dinner nightly, entrées $17–$26. Sunday brunch à la carte. Light fare lunch and dinner menu served in the tavern April through November. Route 20, Lenox, MA; (413) 637-1364.

John Andrew's, South Egremont

For creative new American cuisine at moderate prices this restaurant, owned by talented chef Danny Smith and his wife, Susan, wins many accolades. The restaurant is located in a wooded setting on Route 23, thirteen miles from Stockbridge.

One room has a wood-burning fireplace and the other has orange-rose sponge-painted walls and glass doors opening onto a deck. Lightly fried oysters coated with sourdough crumbs were served with mesclun greens and a pungent anchovy-mustard vinaigrette. Superb goat cheese flan served with slices of rare smoked duck and a few greens was a winner. Pasta dishes included cavatelli with anchovies, tomatoes, olive oil, and Swiss chard, and fettuccine with shiitake and porcini mushrooms and pine nuts. Entrées included braised lamb shank with roast garlic puree and white beans; ragout of rabbit; and roast monkfish with beet coulis. The moist pear-and-walnut cake served with cinnamon ice cream and white chocolate sauce was a delicious choice.

Dinner Thursday through Tuesday; daily in the summer. Entrées $13–$20. Route 23 South Egremont, MA (413) 528-3469.

Church Street Cafe, Lenox

This chef-owned American bistro located in the middle of Lenox is a longtime favorite of ours. The wonderfully flavorful Louisiana shrimp and andouille gumbo, a meal in itself, and spicy Maine crabcakes are always available. An autumn dinner included starters of barbecued duck in a corn pancake with tomatillo salsa and a salad of endive, pears, spiced hazelnuts, and roasted beets.

Entrées included roasted pork tenderloin with cider and sage sauce and sweet potato-apple gratin, pan-seared cod with crispy polenta, and garlic and cilantro fettuccine with smoked corn, chilies, pumpkin seeds, and shrimp.

The creative lunches include a sandwich of grilled eggplant, roasted red peppers, goat cheese, watercress, onion, and tomato on whole-grain bread and a green chili quesadilla.

Lunch and dinner, Tuesday through Saturday; daily in season. Lunch entrées $7–$10; dinner entrées $15–$22. 69 Church Street, Lenox, MA; (413) 637-2745.

Boiler Room Café, Great Barrington

As soon as we tasted chef-owner Michèle Miller's crusty, flavorful yeasty bread we knew we'd found a winner. The three small dining rooms of this Victorian home include one with red walls and abstract paintings, another with gold sprayed willow branches, and a third with a large twig wreath in the bay window.

We shared the Provençal appetizer plate of roasted garlic, braised artichoke with aioli, grilled lamb sausage, eggplant pâté, focaccio, aged chèvre, and olives. Other appetizers include Catalan vegetable soup with pieces of tuna and mussels, and duck confit with lentils and baby turnips. For entrées we had roast cod with rosemary and dried tomato oil and an excellent dish of wood-grilled tuna topped with tapenade served with a cake of thin-sliced potatoes. Grilled chorizo sausage with clams in a tomato sauce on pasta and baby back ribs with garlic mashed potatoes are other choices. For dessert we had a satisfying piece of rich, traditional chocolate cake.

Dinner Wednesday through Saturday, and Tuesday in season. Entrées $9–$21. 405 Stockbridge Road (Route 7) Great Barrington, MA; (413) 528-4280.

The Red Lion Inn, Stockbridge

Dining at the Red Lion is quintessential New England. Depending on your mood, choose the more formal traditional dining room (tie and jacket at dinner) or the intimate rough-hewn tavern room, both with the same menu; the outdoor patio for summer dining; or the cozy Lion's Den with a fireplace, pub menu, and live music each evening.

Hearty portions are the norm in the main dining room or the tavern: thick slabs of prime rib served with a popover, a traditional turkey dinner (the most popular entrée) with all the fixings, rack of lamb, shrimp scampi, sole meunière, and an entrée low in calories, fat, and sodium. They also have a children's menu and a few entrées that can be ordered in smaller portion sizes. Lunch choices include club sandwiches, burgers, fruit plate, chef salad, or hot entrées like salmon cakes, creamed chicken, or hot prime rib sandwich.

All meals daily. Lunch entrées $7–$14. Dinner entrées $16–$26. The Lions Den, lunch (except midweek winter), dinner, and late snacks $4–$13. Main Street, Stockbridge, MA; (413) 298-5545.

The Orchards, Williamstown

The plush dining room has the feel of a refined country club: double-story glass windows looking out at the landscaped central courtyard, upholstered Queen Anne chairs, and tables set with pink cloths and napkins.

Appetizers include apple walnut tortellini with sliced duck breast and calvados sauce and a tasty strudel made with sun-dried tomato, goat cheese, and shiitake mushrooms. The range of entrées includes a shellfish stew with a hearty broth, venison medallions with a cranberry and juniper berry sauce, and rack of lamb with a macadamia nut crust.

Lunch of Caesar salad topped with shrimp and scallops and tortellini with sun-dried tomatoes, feta cheese, and artichoke hearts was excellent.

Breakfast, lunch, and dinner daily. Lunch entrées $7–$12; dinner entrées $18–$28. 222 Adams Road, Williamstown, MA; (413) 458-9611.

La Bruschetta, West Stockbridge

We like the contemporary Italian cuisine and the excellent selection of reasonably priced Italian wines served at this no-frills restaurant, which has white walls, a tile floor, and bamboo chairs with upholstered seats. Antipasti starters include an excellent grilled radicchio wrapped in pancetta with local Monterey chèvre and sun-dried tomatoes; clams fra diavalo, Wellfleet littleneck clams in a spicy marinara sauce; or venison prosciutto with pear compote and provolone. We had an excellent, very garlicky orecchiette pasta with shrimps, escarole, and sun-dried tomatoes. Other entrées are roasted lamb shank with tomatoes, garlic, onions, and black olives served with gorgonzola polenta; and pork chops on a bed of grilled onions with a lemon, garlic, and jalapeno sauce. For dessert we had a dish of superbly rich dark chocolate gelato.

Dinner, Thursday through Tuesday; Friday through Sunday, November through April. Entrées $14–$18. 1 Harris Street, West Stockbridge, MA; (413) 232-7141.

Truc Orient Express, West Stockbridge

This Vietnamese restaurant opened in West Stockbridge more than ten years ago. Four of us ordered a selection of dishes to pass around the table. Appetizers included stuffed chicken wings, lemon skewered chicken, and vegetarian spring rolls. For the main course we enjoyed the shaking beef, filet mignon cubes in garlic on a bed of watercress; happy pancake, a rice crepe stuffed with shrimp and pork; seafood delight, shrimp and scallops in garlic and tomato sauce; and hot and sour shrimp soup with straw mushrooms and lemon grass.

Lunch and dinner, Tuesday through Sunday; daily in season. Lunch $6–$11. Dinner entrées $10–$17. Harris Street, West Stockbridge, MA; (413) 232-4204.

Jack's Grill and Restaurant, Housatonic

This fun new restaurant specializes in comfort foods like real mashed potatoes, pot roast, spaghetti with meat sauce, grilled pork chops with apple sauce, and hamburgers smothered with onions and mushrooms. Other menu items include spaghetti with aioli, Parmesan, and walnuts; chicken Caesar salad; peasant bean and sausage soup; grilled pizza with BBQ chicken; roasted chicken; and grilled fish. The building was once the general store for mill workers in this nineteenth-century factory town bordering the Housatonic River. The old shelves that once held the stock are filled with collections of lunch boxes, Fiestaware china, old tube radios, cookie jars, and much more. A model train makes its rounds on a track hung from the ceiling over the heads of the diners. The music is from the '40s and '50s.

This is the newest restaurant owned by the Fitzpatrick family, whose other properties include the Red Lion Inn, Blantyre, and Country Curtains.

Open spring through fall. Dinner, Tuesday though Sunday. Entrées $7–$14. Main Street, Housatonic, MA; (413) 274-1000.

Castle Street Cafe, Great Barrington

This casual high-ceilinged storefront dining room, a favorite with the locals, has brick walls with paintings and photographs of fruits and vegetables. We were impressed that chef-owner Michael Ballon lists on the back of the menu sixteen local farms and purveyors who provide items for the restaurant.

Start with fried shrimp dumplings, smoked brook trout, or a half portion of pasta. We had grilled veal chop with roasted garlic sauce served with mashed potatoes and grilled salmon with a mild curry sauce and rice, both tasty. Other choices are eggplant roulade stuffed with three cheeses, sautéed sea scallops with sun-dried tomatoes on top of fettuccine, calves' liver with orange marmalade and pearl onions, and roast duck with black currant sauce.

Dinner, Wednesday through Monday. Entrées $9–$22. 10 Castle Street, Great Barrington, MA; (413) 528-5244.

The Old Mill, South Egremont

This is a good place for traditional New England food and ambience. The restaurant, converted from an old mill, has two dining rooms with wood floors, white walls, and beamed ceilings. On busy Saturday nights an excellent magician keeps diners in the bar area entertained during the inevitable wait for a table.

For appetizers we had fish-and-vegetable soup topped with a large crouton, a grilled portabella mushroom with roasted red peppers, and a large Caesar salad. Entrées included roast codfish with mussels and clams, chicken pot pie with Parmesan mashed potatoes, sautéed pork chop, and calves' liver with fried onions. Our table of four split a serving of chocolate profiteroles, a large portion covered with chocolate sauce, as well as an excellent warm bread pudding with hazelnuts and Frangelico sauce.

Dinner, Tuesday through Sunday, daily in season. Reservations for groups of five or more only. Entrées $14–$23. Route 23, South Egremont, MA; (413) 528-1421.

Dakota, Pittsfield

This is a favorite of Berkshire residents and is a particularly good option if you're traveling with children. It has the rustic decor of a hunting lodge: fieldstone fireplace, wood floors, knotty pine walls, Indian artifacts, animal trophies, and birch bark canoes. There is an extensive salad bar, and entrée selections include teriyaki sirloin, prime rib, New York sirloin, Maine lobster, and mesquite-grilled chicken, shrimp, and sirloin. Finish the meal with mud pie.

Dinner nightly. Entrées $8–$18. 1035 South Street (Route 7), Pittsfield, MA; (413) 499-7900.

Informal Dining

Caffe Pomo d'oro, West Stockbridge

This cafe and gourmet takeout is located in the old train station in West Stockbridge. An excellent sandwich of toasted whole grain bread with grilled eggplant, tomato, and smoked mozzarella and a hearty bowl of homemade vegetable minestrone and bread convinced us that we'd like to make a return visit.

Breakfast and lunch, Thursday through Monday, $3–$7. Dinner Friday and Saturday, summer only, entrées $11–$16. 6 Depot Street, West Stockbridge, MA; (413) 232-4616.

20 Railroad Street, Great Barrington

Since 1977 this restaurant has had a wide local following. There's a long bar, tables are close together, smoking is permitted, and the menu has typical fare including big burgers, Reuben sandwiches, salads, and blackboard specials.

Lunch and dinner daily, $3–$12. 20 Railroad Street, Great Barrington, MA; (413) 528-9345.

Hickory Bill's Bar-B-Que, Great Barrington

The kitchen is built around a large steel box where the meat is smoked. Bill Ross dishes up pork, ribs, and chicken, which are available as platters and sandwiches. During warm weather, get takeout and sit at the picnic tables out back along the Housatonic River.

Lunch and dinner Tuesday through Saturday, $4–$10. 403 Stockbridge Road (Route 7) next to Boiler Room Cafe, Great Barrington, MA; (413) 528-1444.

Joe's Diner, South Lee

Joe's is usually crowded with hungry regulars. We prefer the counter to a booth: watching the activity on both sides of the counter is as much a highlight of Joe's as devouring one of his substantial corned beef sandwiches. Prices are low, portions large, and preparation simple. Open 24 hours Monday through Saturday; closed Sunday. 63 Center Street, South Lee, MA; (413) 243-9756.

Pappa Charlie's, Williamstown

The blackboard here announces sandwiches with such familiar names as Zonker Harris, Tomahawk, Moondog, Dick Cavett, and Jacques Cousteau. There's no telling what their namesakes think of these creations, but we like them a lot. Open daily. 18 Spring Street, Williamstown, MA; (413) 458-5969.

Crosby's, Lenox

This market is well known in the area for imaginative pricey preparations that can be ordered by the pound or individually packaged as part of a sumptuous picnic dinner. Soup, salads, cold meats, pâtés, cheeses, breads, tempting desserts—everything you need, from chowder to macadamias. Open daily. Call in advance for picnic boxes. 62 Church Street, Lenox, MA; (413) 637-3396.

Guido's, Pittsfield and Great Barrington

Everyone in the Berkshires with an interest in food finds his way to this popular purveyor of fine foods. We like the array of imaginative salads, ideal for picnics. There is a deli counter, a bakery, and produce as well as meats, fish, and grocery items. Open daily. Route 7, south of Pittsfield, and a second store on Route 7, south of Great Barrington, MA.

ITINERARY

If you are visiting during the summer you will want to take advantage of the many arts activities that abound in the Berkshires. We suggest you plan ahead and reserve tickets, especially for **Tanglewood** and **Williamstown Theatre.** See page 10 for recommended driving tours.

DAY ONE. In **Stockbridge** pick up a walking and driving guide to the town at the information booth across the street from the famous **Red Lion Inn.** Visit the **Norman Rockwell Museum;** then have a leisurely lunch at **Blantyre** (summer only) to experience one of the great Berkshire cottages. Continue on to **Lenox** to explore the town. Have dinner in Lenox at the **Church Street Cafe** or the **Village Inn.**

DAY TWO. Take the **driving tour** starting in Stockbridge through the Tyringham Valley with a stop for a hike to the top of the **Cobble.** Visit **Joyous Spring Pottery.** Lunch in **Great Barrington** at **Hickory Bill's** or **20 Railroad Street.** Explore the shops along Main and Railroad Street. Take Route 183 to **Housatonic** and browse through the art galleries. Take Main Street in Housatonic to Route 41 north to **Great Barrington Pottery.** Continue to **West Stockbridge** with a stop for a snack at **Berkshire Ice Cream.** Then take Route 102 back to Stockbridge. Have dinner at **John Andrew's** or **Boiler Room Cafe** or at the **Old Mill** or **Red Lion Inn** for a more traditional New England dinner.

DAY THREE. Start in **Lenox.** Take the **driving tour** to West Stockbridge, then go north on Route 41 to **Hancock Shaker Village.** Continue to **Williamstown** for lunch at **Pappa Charlie's,** a college favorite. Visit the **Clark Art Institute** and the **Williams College Art Museum,** and walk down Spring Street. Have an early dinner (or late lunch) at the **Orchards** or return to Lenox to dine elegantly at either **Wyndhurst** at Cranwell or at **Wheatleigh** or more casually in West Stockbridge at **La Bruschetta** or **Truc Orient Express.**

DAY FOUR. If the weather is nice drive north on Route 7, stopping at **Guido's** to purchase food for a picnic. Drive to the top of **Mount Greylock** and take one of the trails. An alternative is horseback riding at **Under Mountain Farm,** hiking at **Pleasant Valley Wildlife Sanctuary,** or golfing at **Cranwell.** Antiquing is excellent along Route 7 Great Barrington south to Sheffield. **Butler Sculpture Park** and **Fellerman and Raabe Glass Studio** are in the southern part of the county near Sheffield. For casual dining consider **Jack's** or **Castle Street Cafe.**

DAY FIVE. Museums and historic houses to consider visiting are **Chesterwood, Naumkeag, Arrowhead,** the **Berkshire Art Museum,** and the **Berkshire Botanical Gardens.** A good back road for bikers or scenic drives is the road through the Tyringham Valley (*see* Driving Tour), returning through Beartown State Forest (some dirt roads). We also liked the back roads starting at West Stockbridge heading south on a ridge looking at the farms around Alford and North Egremont. A county map is useful for back-roads touring.

BUDGETING YOUR TRIP

To help you get the most for the time and money you have to spend, here are some travel suggestions at three budget levels (cost per day with two people sharing a room), including lodging and meal tax, gratuity on meals, and service charge when it is added to your bill. Prices are approximate and are intended for planning purposes only. Lodgings are categorized by price, and depending on the room selected, may appear in more than one category. Lodging prices are based on peak summer rates. Meal prices at lunch include an average entrée and beverage. Dinner prices include an appetizer, entrée, dessert, and beverage. Wine or alcoholic beverages are not included.

Staying and dining at expensive lodgings and restaurants: From $410 to $1,170 per day for two.

Lodging: Blantyre, Wheatleigh, Cranwell Resort, Red Lion Inn (suites), The Orchards, Canyon Ranch (all meals and activities included).

Dining: Breakfast: included except at Wheatleigh, Cranwell, the Orchards, Red Lion. Lunch: Blantyre, Wheatleigh. Dinner: Blantyre and Wheatleigh.

Staying and dining at moderately priced lodgings and restaurants: From $210 to $360 per day for two.

Lodging: Cliffwood, Brook Farm Inn, Walker House, Village Inn, Amadeus House, Red Lion Inn, Historic Merrill Inn, Applegate, the Orchards, Windflower.

Dining: Breakfast: included except at Village Inn, Red Lion Inn, the Orchards. Lunch: the Orchards, Red Lion Inn, Church Street Cafe, Truc Orient Express. Dinner: Wyndhurst at Cranwell, Old Mill, Red Lion, The Orchards, John Andrew's, Church Street Cafe, Castle Street.

Staying and dining at less expensive lodgings and restaurants: From $140 to $190 per day for two.

Lodging: Amadeus House (shared bath), Red Lion Inn (shared bath).

Dining: Breakfast: included. Lunch: Pomo d'oro, Lion's Den (Red Lion Inn), Hickory Bill's, Joe's Diner, Pappa Charlie's. Dinner: La Bruschetta, Truc Orient Express, Boiler Room Cafe, Lion's Den at Red Lion Inn, Jack's Grill, Hickory Bill's, Joe's Diner.

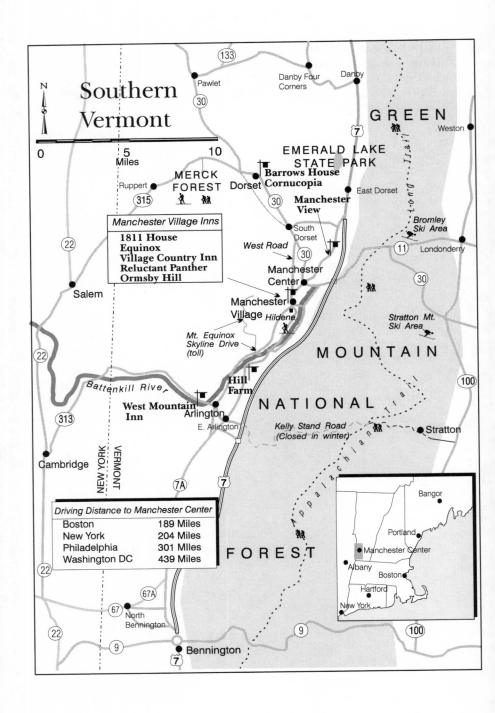

Southern Vermont

N

0   5   10
Miles

(133)

Pawlet

Danby Four Corners   Danby

GREEN

(30)

Weston

(7)

EMERALD LAKE STATE PARK

MERCK FOREST

Ruppert

Dorset   **Barrows House Cornucopia**

(315)

Manchester View

(22)

South Dorset

West Road

(30)

Long Trail

Bromley Ski Area

(11)   Londonderry

Manchester Village Inns

**1811 House
Equinox
Village Country Inn
Reluctant Panther
Ormsby Hill**

Manchester Center

(30)

Salem

Manchester Village   *Hildene*

Stratton Mt. Ski Area

Mt. Equinox Skyline Drive (toll)

MOUNTAIN

(100)

Battenkill River

Hill Farm

West Mountain Inn   Arlington

NATIONAL

E. Arlington

Kelly Stand Road (Closed in winter)   Stratton

(313)

Cambridge

NEW YORK   VERMONT

(22)

(7A)   (7)

Driving Distance to Manchester Center

Boston	189 Miles
New York	204 Miles
Philadelphia	301 Miles
Washington DC	439 Miles

FOREST

Appalachian Trail

(22)

Bangor

Portland

Manchester Center

Albany

Boston

Hartford

New York

(67A)

(67)   North Bennington

(22)

(9)   **Bennington**

(7)

(9)

(100)

2

Bennington, Manchester, and Dorset, Vermont

Today, southern Vermont has more "flatlanders" than native-born Vermonters. Just about every general store in the small towns carries the *New York
Times*, the *Wall Street Journal*, the *Boston Globe*, and, yes, even *Barron's*. Sophisticated and interesting restaurants, galleries, shops, and dozens of country
inns are thriving. Strict land-use laws hamper industrial growth but protect the
landscape for which Vermont is known.

Visitors can fish and canoe along the trout-laden Battenkill and Mettowee Rivers, and drive or bike through white villages with tall church
steeples and town greens, along the back roads through forests, along the
ridges with spectacular vistas, and past the rural landscape of working
farms. There is hiking on the Appalachian Trail and Long Trail in the
Green Mountain National Forest. This is the area where Norman Rockwell
worked in his early years, where he found the sincere, honest, homespun
folk he loved to paint. You can stay in enchanting country inns or in a
grand old turn-of-the-century resort hotel. Shop till you drop at the name-
brand discount, outlet, and factory stores of Ralph Lauren, Coach bags,
Anne Klein, Brooks Brothers, and dozens more. Enjoy quality theater and
golf at first-rate courses, and ski, ski, ski in winter.

Vermont wasn't always a haven for travelers and residents alike. The early
settlers in the eighteenth century eked out a living farming more rocks than
soil and braving the long, cold winters. Settlers continued to come until 1825,
when the Erie Canal from Albany to Buffalo opened the West to settlement.
As the land in Vermont filled up, the next generation of Vermonters, who were
tired of the long, cold winters and of tilling rocks on hillsides, migrated to farm
the more fertile lands in the Midwest or headed south to the large factories
in Massachusetts, Connecticut, and Rhode Island.

The decline in population continued for 140 years until the late 1960s and
early 1970s, when the back-to-nature movement brought thousands of new
residents to Vermont. They followed much the same route as the early settlers,
but this time in cars, pickup trucks, and Volkswagen vans. Today the rapid

growth of telecommunications has spawned a new group of Vermonters who work from their homes.

The images of Vermont are vibrant: dairy herds grazing on a hillside, steam and wood smoke rising from a sugar house in March, a fast-flowing stream, a country fair in late summer, and probably the most famous, the brilliant foliage in autumn, when it seems the whole world descends upon the state.

For further information on the area, contact the **Manchester and the Mountains Chamber of Commerce** (2 Main Street, RR 2, Box 3451, Manchester Center, VT 05255; (802) 362-2100).

WHERE TO GO, WHAT TO DO

The Towns

Manchester Center and Manchester Village

These two communities flow into each other. Manchester Center is one of the premier locations for upscale factory and company stores in New England. The traffic is heavy here, especially on crowded weekends. Most of the clothing stores are along Route 11/30 stretching from exit 4 of the Route 7 interchange into Manchester Center and along Route 7A to the Equinox in Manchester Village. Store locations change as leases expire, so check on arrival to find your favorites. Company stores include Anne Klein, Cole Haan, Polo/Ralph Lauren, Donna Karan, Ellen Tracy, Hickey Freeman, Coach leatherware, Joan and David, Polly Flinders (hand-smocked children's dresses), Liz Claiborne, London Fog, Orvis, Pendleton, Boston Trader, Jones New York, Brooks Brothers, Esprit, Nautica, and Williams-Sonoma (quality cookware). Other stores with good discounts include Herdsmen Leathers, which has an annual "penny sale." If you're not looking for big discounts, go to Pierre Deux for top fabrics, the Clift Collection for good women's clothing, and Christine's for trendy clothes. The best time to come for bargains is when the discount stores have sales. Check out the retail prices of the designers you like before you come to Manchester so that you'll know how much of a bargain you're really getting. If you love to shop, you can do plenty here.

Following are a few stores, galleries, and bookshops in the Manchester area that we like for specialized shopping (other than clothing):

Frog Hollow. A nonprofit visual arts organization featuring contemporary and traditional juried Vermont craft in all media. Across the street from the Equinox, Manchester Village; (802) 362-3321.

The Clift Collection. This is not a discount store, but it sells truly exceptional women's clothing you won't find everywhere. Across the street from the Equinox, Manchester Village; (802) 362-3377.

Northshire Books. Browsers are welcome at one of the finest independent bookstores in the United States. At the intersection of Routes 11/30 and 7A, Manchester Center; (802) 362-2200.

Orvis. The array of rods, flies, and fishing gadgets along with a complete selection of outdoor apparel is a sportsperson's delight. You can test the rods on the pond next to the store. Drastically discounted clothing is on the lower level. Route 7A, Manchester; (802) 362-3750.

The Enchanted Doll House. Twelve magical rooms feature play and collector dolls, dollhouses, and toys. Route 7, 2½ miles north of town, Manchester Center; (802) 362-1327.

Tilting at Windmills Gallery. This is one of the best galleries in New England, featuring works by contemporary, regional, national, and international artists. On Routes 11/30, 1 mile west of exit 4 of the Route 7 interchange, Manchester Center; (802) 362–3022.

Pierre's Gate. Sculptural tables of wood reproducing a stream bottom are most unusual. 554 Main Street, Manchester Center; (802) 362-1766.

Be sure to notice the old county courthouse located across from the Equinox and next to the 1811 House. The dome is leafed in gold. When the court is in session and the judge is not busy, she might give you a tour if your ask.

Hildene. This estate was built by Abraham Lincoln's son, Robert Todd Lincoln, who was chairman of the Pullman company (1897–1911) and summered here for many years between 1905 and his death in 1926. The house was occupied by members of his family until 1975, when it was given to the Church of Christ, Scientist who later decided to sell it. The local citizens raised the $200,000 necessary to purchase the home. Today the twenty-four room house and gardens have been meticulously restored. The gardens, designed to look like a stained glass window, are known particularly for their peonies. From the end of the garden there is an impressive view of the valley and of Mount Equinox.

The restored mechanical 1908 organ and one of the collection of 250 rolls is played for each tour. The mirror in the children's room was in Abraham Lincoln's dressing room at the White House. One of Lincoln's four remaining black silk top hats is also on display. Robert Todd was particularly proud of the grand front staircase. Notice the chandelier, which is purposely small so it does not distract from the grandeur of the sweeping staircase.

The Christmas candlelight tours are a highlight. Visitors are brought to the house by horse-drawn sleigh or wagons. The fireplaces are burning, candles are lit, Christmas carols are sung, and hot mulled cider and cookies are served. It is a magical time to visit this impressive home.

Open daily, mid-May through October; tours 9:30 A.M. to 4 P.M. Adults $7. Candlelight tours between Christmas and New Year's. On Route 7A two miles south of the junction of Routes 11/30, Box 377, Manchester, VT 05254; (802) 362-1788.

Equinox Skyline Drive. The twisting five-mile road takes you to the highest peak (3,816 feet) in the Taconic Range. Although increasing air pollution in the Northeast often obscures the views, on a clear crisp day in the spring or fall months you can see as far as Quebec, Massachusetts, New York, and New Hampshire. There are nature trails at the top. The views are magnificent and the drive is worthwhile if your car is in good condition, the road is nicknamed "burn-your-brakes road." If you decide to make the trip, come down the mountain in the lowest gear instead of riding your brakes.

Open daily, May through October, 8 A.M. to 10 P.M. $6 per car and driver; $2 additional adults. On Route 7A, five miles south of Manchester; (802) 362-1114.

American Museum of Fly Fishing. This historic collection pays tribute to American angling memorabilia and famous fishermen. Open daily early May through late October, 10 A.M. to 4 P.M. Seminary Avenue, Manchester Village, VT 05254; (802) 362-3300.

Southern Vermont Art Center. This twenty-eight room mansion situated at the end of a long winding drive on hundreds of acres is used for exhibitions of paintings and sculptures. The outdoor sculpture garden displays contemporary works. There are eleven galleries with rotating exhibits of works for sale, as well as traveling exhibitions. Solo and group exhibits often feature works of artists who live in the vicinity. The botany trail includes a waterfall, pool, trees, ferns, and wildflowers with identification markers. The setting for the café (*see* Where to Dine) in the glass solarium or outdoors on the terrace overlooking the sculpture garden couldn't be more ideal. Concerts and plays are held throughout the season in an adjacent building.

Open late May through late October, Tuesday through Saturday 10 A.M. to 5 P.M.; Sunday, noon to 5 P.M. Adults $3. West Road, Manchester, VT 05254; (802) 362-1405.

Dorset

Dorset fits our image of an idyllic Vermont village; the buildings are white with black or dark green shutters. The first settlers arrived here before the American Revolution. The first marble quarry on the North American continent was in Dorset; it was a fair-size industry from 1785 until 1920. The stone for the New York Public Library came from one of the local quarries. Today this quarry, which is on Route 30, is a popular swimming hole. The center of the village is Church Street, with its 175-year-old Peltier's General Store. Along with a sampling of the standard necessities, you'll find a large section of made-in-Vermont products, fine wines, home-baked muffins, and other gourmet goodies. After you leave the store, walk across the village green to the Dorset Inn, a good place for lunch or dinner. The Dorset church and the private country club are farther down the street. Turn left at Cheney Road to get to the marvelous old Dorset Playhouse, where the Dorset Theatre Festival performs during the summer, and take another left on Meadow Road to get back to Route 30.

A pretty drive is the loop of the Lower and Upper Hollow Roads. This road is the first road on your right after you pass the Barrows House as you approach the center of Dorset.

Stores to visit as you head back toward Manchester on Route 30:

Williams Department Store is an old-fashioned "no frills" store that's been owned by the same family for 100 years; it has a complete stock of practical items. It doesn't cater to tourists, so you'll need to look closely on the left side of the road for an old red building with a small sign.

J. K. Adams is a woodworking factory that makes items such as cutting boards, wine racks, and bowls. The store sells first- and second-quality items. There are good buys on seconds, especially the cutting boards on the second floor in the back. You can look down on the factory floor through a large window on the second floor; (802) 362-2303.

A word to the wise: Keep strictly to the speed limits as you drive on Route 30 or on West Road, particularly around Dorset. The police are particularly attentive in this area.

Pawlet and the Mettowee Valley

Route 30 out of Dorset heading toward Pawlet goes through the Mettowee Valley for seventeen miles. This is picture-perfect rural Vermont scenery, a valley of dairy and sheep farms, farm houses, silos, and tillable land. In 1986 the Mettowee Valley Conservation Project was formed by local citizens to help the remaining farmers resist the pressures of development, to protect farmland and open spaces, and to keep the land in productive use. The land trust pays working farmers for the development rights to their land, thus ensuring that the land will remain open for future generations.

If you like to bicycle, this is an attractive route that doesn't involve a lot of hill climbing. Keep on the lookout for wild turkeys pecking away in the cornfields. The Mettawee River is popular with fishermen. There are few overhanging trees, making it easy to cast without snagging your line.

Places to stop between Dorset and Pawlet:

Connaway Gallery. Jay Hall Connaway (1893–1970), one of the foremost marine and landscape artists who painted in the style of Winslow Homer, lived and worked on Monhegan Island in Maine year-round for seventeen years and in the Pawlet-Dorset area for about twenty years. The gallery is open by appointment only. On Route 30, five miles from Dorset; (802) 325-3107.

Susan Sargent Designs. Susan is an internationally known designer of innovative handwoven rugs and accent pillows. Route 30 Pawlet; (802) 325-3466.

Mach's General Store. At one time there was a working mill on this site, on top of the Flower River in the center of Pawlet. Wander to the back of the store and peer down the glass-covered square hole fifty feet to see the river rushing through a rock gorge. Next door is the *Brick-Oven Bakery*, where a wood-fired oven turns out bread, pastries, and pizza; (802) 325-6113.

The Pawlet Potter. Marion McChesney's pottery studio is across the street from the general store. We particularly admired the pastel free-form porcelain plates; (802) 325-3100.

Other studios in Pawlet to visit by appointment include *David Maness* for furniture, cabinets, frames (802-325-3603); *Jean Evans* for hooked rugs (802-325-3069); *Roy Egg* for original one-of-a-kind pottery, open weekends only in West Pawlet (no phone).

Danby

The Peel Gallery of Fine Art. Paintings, drawings, sculpture, and limited edition prints of fifty American artists are on display here. Prices range from $25 to $25,000. Closed on Tuesday except during the summer. Off Route 7, two miles north of Danby; (802) 293-5230.

The Gallery of Danby Green. Made up of two historic buildings along Route 7, this gallery is filled with dinnerware, gourmet cookware, and hand-crafted gift items made in Vermont. Route 7, Danby; (802) 293-5550.

Bennington

Bennington Museum. Most people who come to this museum have heard the name of Grandma (Anna Mary Robertson) Moses, but don't know that she was a local woman who started painting primitive nostalgic images of Vermont life when she was in her seventies. Between 1940, when she was discovered by a prominent New York gallery, and her death in 1961, she produced 1,500 paintings. Twenty-eight examples of her work are on display. Another gallery houses the Wasp, the only survivor of the twenty cars built by Karl Martin between 1920 and 1925 in Vermont. The front seat of this luxury operating roadster, with fenders that look like a wasp, is exposed to the elements and the backseat has a convertible parasol top. Other galleries of the museum house an extensive collection of pressed and molded glass, including a case of Tiffany Favrile. Other rooms display Bennington pottery and memorabilia from the Battle at Bennington, including a 1776 Stars and Stripes that's thought to be the oldest in existence.

Open daily, 9 A.M. to 5 P.M. Adults $5. West Main Street, Bennington VT, 05201; (802) 447-1571.

The Bennington Battle Monument. This 306-foot obelisk that was built in 1891 to commemorate the Battle of Bennington is the highest structure in Vermont. The 1777 battle was considered a turning point in the American Revolution. If the weather is clear, take the elevator to the top for great views.

Open daily, April through October, 9 A.M. to 5 P.M. Adults $1. Located ½ mile west of the junction of Route 9 and Route 7, then north to the end of Monument Avenue; (802) 447-0550.

Stores to visit in Bennington:

Bennington Potters. In production since 1948, this pottery is constantly designing new stoneware and terra-cotta styles. The white or black mugs with double finger holes are popular. There is a retail and a seconds store with discounts of 30 percent. A mail-order catalog is available. Monday through Saturday, 9:30 A.M. to 5 P.M. (till 8 P.M. in the summer); Sunday noon to 5:30 P.M. 324 County Street, Bennington, VT 05201; (802) 447-7531.

Hawkins House is a large craft store representing the work of 400 crafts-people. There's some of everything: lots of earrings, pottery, prints, and gift items, with special exhibits during the summer and fall. Prices are moderate. Monday through Saturday 10 A.M. to 5:30 P.M., Sunday noon to 5:30 P.M. 262 North Street, Route 7, Bennington; (802) 447-0488.

Sports

Fishing

Orvis Fly Fishing School. We signed up for the 2½-day Orvis school to learn more about this challenging, almost age-limitless sport. During the practice sessions of knot tying, casting, and catch-and-release on the Orvis pond and on the Battenkill River, the instructors, one for every four students, easily handled diverse levels of skill. Classes included a tour of the rod shop, a class in entomology, and an equipment demonstration.

If you are an avid fisherman, you can hire the instructors as guides for some after-hours fishing on the Battenkill or Mettowee Rivers. Cost is about $125 per person for four hours including all equipment.

Fly-fishing school held from mid-April through Labor Day weekend. Route 7A, Manchester, VT 05254; (800) 548-9548.

Falconry

The British School of Falconry at the Equinox. Take a hands-on lesson in the sport of flying hawks, and learn how to have a hawk land on your protected arm. If you become hooked on falconry you can take more advanced courses lasting up to four days. Located on River Road, Route 7A, Manchester Village, VT 05254; (802) 362-4780.

Hiking

The Green Mountain National Forest Ranger Station has maps and information about all the hiking trails in the Green Mountain National Forest. There are also trails at Emerald Lake State Park in North Dorset and Hapgood Pond Nature Trail in Peru. The ranger station is on Route 11/30 headed east toward Route 7 from Manchester. Drive past the entrance to Route 7. Manchester Ranger District, RR1, Box 1940, Manchester Center, VT 05255; (802) 362-2307. Open Monday through Friday, 8 A.M. to 4:30 P.M.

Another source for hiking trails and descriptions is *The Dayhiker's Guide to Vermont* published by the Green Mountain Club for $9.95. Available through the Green Mountain Club, Box 889, Montpelier, VT 05601-0889; (802) 223-3463.

Lye Brook Wilderness. This is the second largest wilderness area in the Green Mountain National Forest. The Lye Brook Trail provides access to the often photographed Lye Brook Falls. If you go to the ranger station, ask for the specific guide to this trail. To get to the start of the trail take Union Street (opposite the Equinox) to the "T-intersection." Turn left on Richville Road, then right on East Manchester Road, the second paved road. Follow the road under the Route 7 overpass. Take the first road (dirt) to the Falls area parking lot. Follow the blue blazes 2.8 miles to the Falls.

Kelly Stand Road. If you plan to take the drive from East Arlington to West Wardsboro, the back side of Stratton Mountain, get copies of the trail guides that start from various points along this road. The Appalachian and Long Trails cross the road. You can hike 3.3 miles to the top of Stratton Mountain (rated moderately difficult), the 3.9-mile Stratton Pond Trail (rated moderate), or the Grout Pond Trails, a series of loop trails that go around the pond, good for easy walking, cross-country skiing, and for snowmobiles (*see* Driving Tour for directions). Beware of the road note that the road is not plowed in the winter, and is badly rutted and muddy in the spring.

Merck Forest and Farmland Center. This 2,800-acre preserve is one of the best places to take a walk or a hike. Stop at the visitor center for a trail map and a schedule of activities.

If you are traveling with children, the center sponsors three- and four-day camping trips and day activities for younger children. The grounds house a garden, a nature center, and large work horses used for plowing and hay or sleigh rides. A short half-hour loop walk took us through a trail known as "the saddle," where we felt as though we were on top of the world with views in all directions. During the winter this is also a good area for cross-country skiing. The entrance to Merck Forest is not well marked. As you drive north on Route 30 from Dorset turn left onto Route 315. The entrance is 2.6 miles up the road on the left. Box 86, Rupert, VT 05768; (802) 394-7836.

Canoeing the Battenkill

This is the perfect type of canoeing, with ever-changing scenery and swift-moving water, including minirapids. Overhanging trees provide shade on hot days, and the shoreline has picnic spots. There is no one set route or time to arrive. If you are a novice you can paddle at a wider section of the Battenkill, where the water is calmer. Near the base camp there is a tricky bend where the Roaring Branch River meets the Battenkill River. We were transported a few miles down the road, given a map with landmarks and a choice of take-out points so we could have a shorter or longer paddle depending on how much we paddled, the water conditions, and our interest in stopping along the way.

Open mid-April through mid-October. Located on Route 7A north of Arlington. BattenKill Canoe, Arlington, VT 05250; (802) 362-2800; (800) 421-5268.

Downhill Skiing

Stratton. The largest ski area in the region, Stratton has a gondola that takes only eight minutes to reach the top of southern Vermont's highest mountain. The village square at the base of the mountain has shops, restaurants, and lodging. Located off Route 30. Snow conditions (taped message), (802) 297-2211. General information, (802) 297-2200; resort information, (800) 843-6867.

Bromley. One of the oldest ski areas in Vermont, Bromley opened in 1937 and has catered to families ever since. Located on Route 11 in Peru, VT. Ski conditions, (802) 824-5522. Call (802) 824-5458 if you want to stay on the mountain, (800) 677-7829 for area lodging service.

Summer Activities at the Ski Areas

During the summer Bromley operates an alpine slide that winds for almost a mile through woods and meadows. Open daily, Memorial Day through mid-October. On Route 11, Peru, VT; (802) 824-5522.

You can take the Stratton gondola to the top of southern Vermont's highest peak, bring a picnic lunch, and take a walk on the nature trail. Open daily, late June through mid-October; (802) 297-2200.

Cross-country Skiing

The key to cross-country skiing is altitude; the higher you get, the more likely you'll find snow.

Hildene. The former estate of Robert Todd Lincoln, Hildene today is a popular local place for cross-country skiing. Fifteen kilometers of trails wind through evergreens and forest land. The warming hut is the carriage barn, where there are ski rentals and light refreshments. Trail fees. Route 7A, Manchester; (802) 362-1788.

Wild Wings Ski Touring Center. At this popular family-oriented cross-country ski touring center, trails go through the Green Mountain National Forest. Located 2½ miles north of Peru, VT; (802) 824-6793.

Entertainment

The Dorset Theatre Festival. Casts from New York and Los Angeles present a season of five plays in the Dorset Playhouse, a theater constructed from pre-Revolutionary barns. Performances mid-June through August. Route 30, P.O. Box 307, Dorset, VT 05251; (802) 867-5777.

Weston Playhouse. This highly respected summer theater, which performs five comedies and musicals a year, celebrated its sixtieth anniversary in 1996. Professional actors from New York City play the leading roles. You can dine in the Playhouse restaurant before the show. Stay for the great after-theater Act IV Cabaret, featuring actors from the evening's production.

Located about 45 minutes from Manchester Center. Performances late June through early September. P.O. Box 216, Weston, VT 05161;(802) 824-5288.

Strattonfest. During this nine-week festival, folk, country and western, jazz, New Age, and classical musicians perform in the pavilion (sit on the lawn or under cover) at the Stratton base lodge at the Stratton ski resort complex; (802) 297-0100.

Driving Tours

Manchester—Dorset—Pawlet—Salem—Cambridge—Arlington

From Manchester, take Route 30 to Dorset. Continue on Route 30 through the Mettowee Valley to **Pawlet.** Have a light lunch at **the Station Restaurant** in Pawlet. Go back toward Dorset on Route 30 for a few miles. Turn right on Route 315; go 2.6 miles to **Merck Forest.** Continue on Route 153 to Salem, New York. Treat yourself to a cappuccino and chocolate truffles at **Steininger's.** Drive south on Route 22 toward Cambridge. You may want to stop at the **New Skete Monastery** in Cambridge to purchase a cheesecake that's made by the nuns, some smoked hams, bacon, or cheese made by the monks, or to see the gold-domed Russian-style church. To get there turn onto Route 313, then right on Ash Grove Road (look for a small sign); (518) 677-3928. Continue on Route 313 east to Arlington, then north on Route 7A to Manchester.

Manchester—Arlington—Kelly Stand Road—Stratton

Bring a picnic lunch (stop at **Al Ducci's Italian Pantry** in Manchester (Elm Street, Manchester Center; (802) 362-4449) for a gourmet spread). You can drive on Route 7A to Arlington or follow the River Road (it starts just after the Ekwanok Golf Club) and the Sunderland Hill Road all the way to East Arlington Road. Turn left on East Arlington Road; turn right at Old Mill Road, which brings you to Candle Mill Village in East Arlington. You can have your lunch along the Roaring Branch River or when you're hiking. Continue on Old Mill Road. After you cross the bridge over Route 7, take an immediate right onto the **Kelly Stand,** a hard-packed dirt road. (Do not attempt this drive if the weather is muddy or in late fall or early spring, since there is often snow here earlier and later than in other areas.) The drive is spectacular, following the Roaring Branch River about half the way. The Appalachian and Long Trails go through this wilderness, so you may want to take a hike (*see* Hiking) partway on one of the trails. When you get to the white town hall in Stratton, turn left and follow the signs to Stratton Resort Village. You can browse the shops at this famous ski resort, take in a performance at the summer festival, or take the gondola to the top of the mountain. After you come down the mountain, turn left on Route 30N to Manchester.

Manchester—Dorset—Pawlet—Danby—Manchester

From Manchester take Route 30 to **Dorset.** Drive through the Mettowee Valley to **Pawlet.** For a longer drive, continue on Route 30 to Wells, Lake St. Catherine State Park, and to Poultney, where you'll find several antique shops. Take Route 140 to Middletown Springs. Take the cutoff to travel the back roads to Danby Four Corners, which has a general store at the crossroads. **Danby** has gift shops with some locally made craft items. Go two miles north on Route 7 to the **Peel Gallery;** then return to Manchester.

WHERE TO STAY

Lodgings are arranged geographically from south to north.

West Mountain Inn, Arlington

This inn, owned by Wes and MaryAnn Carlson, sits on 150 acres of picture-perfect hillside overlooking the Battenkill River and the Red Mountain. Llamas and rabbits freely roam the property. Common rooms include the Great Room, a spacious room with a wood stove and a couple of seating areas, as well as a game room, a porch seating area, and a library nook.

The Rockwell Kent Suite is the most popular accommodation. The sleeping area has a cathedral ceiling and a king-size bed; the loft area is perfect if you're traveling with a child, as it has a twin-size bed; a spacious sitting area has a fireplace. The Grandma Moses Suite has a fireplace in the sitting room and a great view of the mountains and the Battenkill from the queen-size bed. The Governor Chittenden Room has a queen-size bed and a good view of the mountains.

The Mill House contains three town house units, each with two bedrooms, a kitchen, and a living room. Two units also have decks and wood stoves.

The inn is popular with families and bike groups, and is rented frequently for weddings and conferences. The 150-year-old barn on the property has been renovated and is used particularly for weddings and dances.

Dinner includes soup, salad, a choice of five or six entrées, and dessert. Sample entrées include shrimp and scallops in pesto cream sauce, rack of lamb with a Dijon honey glaze, roast duck, a vegetarian entrée, and fresh fish. Breakfast features a choice of entrées, such as Ooey Gooey (toast with fried eggs and cheddar cheese), and such desserts as apple pie à la mode or a Belgian waffle with ice cream and fruit. The inn can arrange for a baby-sitter so parents can have a quiet dinner.

Eighteen rooms and suites, each with private bath, $145–$239, breakfast and dinner for two included. Bed-and-breakfast rates $119–$189 available in some rooms. 15% service charge. Children welcome. Outside diners by reservation, $30. Two-night weekend minimum. Located ½ mile west of Arlington on Route 313. Box 481, Arlington, VT 05250; (802) 375-6516.

Hill Farm Inn, Arlington

This 1830 farmhouse and the 1790 guesthouse, operating as an inn for almost 100 years, overlook fields that border the Battenkill River. The innkeepers are George and Joanne Hardy.

Walk through the front door of the farmhouse and you'll find yourself in the dining room. Adjoining this room is a common room with a big fireplace, a piano, and lots of books and magazines.

Room 7, a suite, has a large sitting area, a high queen-size bed, a cathedral ceiling, and a porch with a good view. The Lilac Suite has a brass queen-size bed, a cozy living room with a wood stove and convertible couch, a kitchenette, and a porch entrance. Of the rooms with private baths, room 6 is our favorite because it is the largest, with a king-size bed and windows on both sides of the house. In the 1790 house, the best view is from room D, which has a king-size bed.

Four cabins, separate from the houses, are very small, traditional motels that date from the 1930s. Folks either love them or they hate them. Our favorite is the Willows, which is next to the pasture.

Dinner is served at individual tables at 7 P.M. and includes a choice of three entrées that guests select in advance. The night we stayed we had green bean soup, homemade bread, garden salad, glazed Cornish hen, orange rice, carrots and broccoli, and blueberry cheesecake.

Seventeen rooms, suites, and cottages, twelve with private bath, $105–$150, breakfast and dinner included. Bed-and-breakfast $65–$110. 15% service charge. Children welcome. Pets permitted in the cottages. Two-night weekend minimum. RR #2, Box 2015, Arlington, VT 05250; (802) 375-2269; (802) 882-2545.

The Inn at Ormsby Hill, Manchester

This large Federal manor house, located about a mile south of Manchester Village, has its origins in the 1760s. Innkeepers Ted and Chris Sprague, who formerly owned an inn on the Maine coast, have done major renovations to this property. With its panoramic view of the Green Mountains protected from development, spacious common areas, renovated and new rooms (nine with wood-burning or gas fireplaces and many with double whirlpool tubs), and a creative gourmet breakfast, this inn is now one of the best in this area. The interior has an open feel with three large common areas for guests. We like the more casual gathering room with the original oversize wood-burning fireplace and the long dining room, which has a sitting area at one end with windows on three sides facing the Green Mountains.

The Taft Room is the largest, and popular with honeymooners. It has a king-size canopy bed, vaulted ceiling, and wood-burning fireplace, plus a large bath with the largest double whirlpool in the inn and a separate two-person shower. The Pierrepont Room and Anne Eliza, newly built rooms, have king-size canopy beds and a gas fireplace. The Library, a first-floor handicap-accessible room, has the original hand-hewn beams, a king-size bed, wood-burning fireplace, and bath with double whirlpool and separate shower. All the rooms are air-conditioned.

A creative gourmet breakfast is served in the dining room from 8 to 10 A.M. or you can have a breakfast basket delivered to your room. We were served blueberry-peach crisp, strawberry frappé, and a memorable dish of creamy risotto with pancetta and grilled sliced portabella mushrooms. On Friday nights a soup, pasta, or stew with homemade bread is available so guests can dine whenever they arrive, and on Saturday Chris prepares a four-course gourmet dinner.

Ten rooms, all with private bath, $110–$200. Afternoon tea and breakfast included. Not appropriate for young children. No smoking. No pets. Route 7A, Manchester Center, VT 05255; (802) 362-1163; (800) 670-2841.

The Equinox, Manchester Village

The front entrance of this nineteenth-century resort, with its trademark high white fluted columns, stretches along Route 7A in the center of Manchester Village for some 600 yards. The 1,100-acre property includes an eighteen-hole golf course, tennis courts, pools, and a health spa, and the British School of Falconry. The new owners of The Equinox, a partnership led by the Guinness Company of England, have completed a multimillion-dollar renovation. The golf course has undergone a $4 million renovation and redesign by golf course architect Rees Jones. The hotel has the best-staffed concierge desk in New England outside Boston.

Most of the rooms in the main building are oversize, with twelve-foot ceilings. They have all been recently renovated and equipped with cable television and phones. Our favorite accommodations in the main inn are the nine suites, which are each furnished in a different style. The two-story Eisenhower Suite has the best views. On the first floor is a living room. Stairs lead to the cupola, where the queen-size bed is surrounded by windows, giving a bird's eye view of the town and the mountains. The most luxurious is the Green Mountain Suite, with mission oak furnishings made by a local cabinetmaker. Rooms 208 and 210, deluxe category rooms, are the only two in the main building that open onto a shared porch overlooking Route 7.

Thirty contemporary town house units are located behind the main building, next to the spa. Ten of these units are suites with wood-burning fireplaces, decks, living rooms with a full kitchen, and a bedroom with a queen-size bed. The standard town house rooms are smaller than the comparably priced rooms in the inn.

The building just to the north of the Equinox, once the country home of the fly-fishing entrepreneur, Charles F. Orvis, has been turned into the Charles

The front entrance of the Equinox, a grand resort built in the nineteenth century, stretches along Route 7A for some 600 yards.

Orvis Inn with nine deluxe one-and two-bedroom suites. The first floor has a sitting room staffed by a concierge. The lower level has a billiard room and a bar with complimentary drinks, champagne, and house wine. An expanded continental breakfast is included and is delivered to your room, or guests can go to the main building for a full buffet breakfast. Each suite has its own full kitchen, living room with a gas fireplace, and large marble-clad bath with a double whirlpool tub.

During the summer, the resort runs Equinox Camp for Kids at no extra charge. The property behind the hotel on Equinox Mountain is a nature preserve with miles of trails and a stocked fourteen-acre pond for catch and release fishing.

The Equinox has 183 guest rooms, suites, and town houses. Rooms $169–$299; suites $399–$559; one-, two-, and three-bedroom town houses $369–$659. Charles Orvis Inn has nine one- and two-bedroom suites $569–$899. Children welcome. No pets. Ask about special packages. Route 7A, Manchester Village, VT 05254; (802) 362-4700; (800)362-4747.

1811 House, Manchester Village

You'll know this inn is in a class by itself as soon as you walk through the door. The original structure was built in the 1770s and has operated as an inn since 1811. Today the house is a showcase for innkeepers Marnie and Bruce

The 1811 House in Manchester Village is a showcase of English and American antiques, prints, Oriental rugs, and magnificent perennial gardens.

Duff's extensive collection of English and American antiques, prints, and Oriental rugs. Bruce can usually be found working in his extensive magnificent perennial gardens during the summer months.

At the end of the day, head to the atmospheric English pub for one of Marnie's chocolate chip cookies or something stronger. The glasses are Waterford and the liquor selection includes forty-nine single-malt scotch whiskies.

One particularly appealing feature of the 1811 House is the variety of common rooms available to guests. A library and a living room each have a working fireplace. A basement game room with low overhead lamps has both table tennis and a regulation billiard table. The formal dining room has another fireplace and three separate tables.

The most romantic rooms are the six with wood-burning fireplaces and the one with a private balcony with a view of the landscaped grounds, pond, and Green Mountains. Three of the fireplace rooms are located in a reconstructed cottage next to the main inn. Our favorite takes up the entire second floor and has a peaked ceiling. In the main inn, the fireplace rooms include the suite on the first floor, with a king-size four-poster, and the two rooms on the second floor, each with queen-size canopy beds.

A full breakfast, served from 8 to 9:30 A.M., could be an English-style breakfast of fried eggs, scones, bacon, grilled tomatoes, apples, and mushrooms, or eggs Benedict.

Fourteen rooms each with private bath $110–$200. Afternoon tea and breakfast included. Children over 16 welcome. No pets. Two-night weekend minimum. Route 7A, Box 39, Manchester Village, VT 05254; (802) 362-1811; (800) 432-1811.

The Reluctant Panther, Manchester Village

The distinctive color of the main building, mauve with yellow shutters, makes this inn stand out next to the Equinox Hotel in the center of Manchester Village. Its owners are standouts as well: unlike many other innkeepers, Robert Bachofen was trained in hotel management in Switzerland, and had a top position at the Plaza Hotel in New York City before purchasing the inn. Maye, his wife, also had a career in hotel management.

The Bachofens have done major renovations, especially to the four suites, which are located in an adjacent building. The ultimate romantic indulgence is the Mark Skinner Suite, which has a bedroom with a king-size brass bed facing a wood-burning fireplace and an enormous bathroom with a double whirlpool in the center of the room, a separate shower, double pedestal sinks, and another wood-burning fireplace. The Seminary Suite is especially spacious. It has a king-size bed and fireplace and a large bath with a whirlpool tub. Other suites in this building are the Mary Porter Room with two fireplaces and the Village Suite with a wood stove.

In the main inn our favorites are room J, a deluxe room with a king-size bed, one of the larger rooms, and room B, a fireplace room with the best view of Mount Equinox. All rooms are air-conditioned and have telephones and televisions.

A full breakfast, served at individual marble-topped tables from 8:30 to 9:30 A.M., includes a hot dish such as French toast and bacon as well as large corn or blueberry muffins.

Sixteen rooms and suites, all with private bath, $158–$335, breakfast and dinner for two included. Service charge 15%. Bed-and-breakfast rates deduct $40. Not appropriate for young children. No smoking. No pets. West Road and Route 7A. Box 678, Manchester Village, VT 05254; (802) 362-2568; (800) 822-2331.

The Village Country Inn, Manchester Village

The Village Country Inn is ideally situated in historic Manchester Village. Shoppers can take advantage of the vast numbers of upscale outlets less than a mile down the road; for those who like to stroll, Manchester Village has marble sidewalks, historic homes, and galleries; and for those who want to relax at the inn, the chintz pillowed rockers on the front porch, the chaises around the large pool, or benches in the garden are most inviting.

Since purchasing this hundred-year-old building in 1985, innkeepers Anne and Jay Degen have done major renovations. They tore down walls to create large rooms and suites and added a flower garden with a half-moon bridge and fountains.

Room choices include two-room suites or large luxury rooms, garden rooms with private entrances, and smaller standard accommodations called sleeping rooms. All the rooms have phones and the larger accommodations have televisions. The largest rooms are Le Fleur and Rose Noir, which have king-size beds and overlook the garden. Janée's Suite, Francesca's Room, Renaissance, Lavender and Lace, and Love Letters are other top rooms with special features.

The four garden rooms open directly into the garden. The lower-priced sleeping rooms are smaller in size, perfectly adequate if you don't want to spend a lot of time in your room, and offer one of the best values in Manchester Village.

Thirty-three rooms and suites, all with private bath, $140–$275. Full breakfast and dinner for two included. 15% service charge. Not appropriate for children. No smoking. No pets. Located on Historic Route 7A. Box 408, Manchester Village, VT 05254; (802) 362-1792; (800) 370-0300.

Barrows House, Dorset

Innkeepers Jim and Linda McGinnis have a complex of eight buildings spread over twelve acres in the midst of this beautiful Vermont village six miles from Manchester Center. The main building houses the dining rooms on the first floor and guest accommodations on the second floor. Seven other buildings range from small single-suite cottages to a six-bedroom house. There are also two tennis courts, a swimming pool, a perennial garden, and a gazebo.

The most popular room is the suite in the Schubert House with a glass-enclosed porch and a spacious sitting area by the wood-burning fireplace. The two second-floor Stable suites each have a king-size bed, gas fireplace, a kitchenette, and a living room with a convertible couch and television. Dogs are permitted in Birds Nest, one of the private cottages. The Carriage House, a good option for a family, has a bedroom with a king-size bed, a living room with television and refrigerator, and a second-floor loft area with six single beds. Halstead, an apartment on the lower level of the innkeeper's home, has a living room with a wood-burning fireplace and is farther away than the other buildings.

If you are traveling with another couple or two, Truffles is an ideal accommodation. There are three bedrooms on the first floor, each with king-size beds. The living room is spacious, with a wood-burning fireplace and a full kitchen. The second floor has two bedrooms and a living room with a wood stove.

Twenty-eight rooms and suites, each with private bath, $180–$240, breakfast and dinner for two included. Bed-and-breakfast rates available. 15% service charge. Children welcome. Dogs permitted in three of the buildings. Two-night weekend minimum. Route 30, Dorset, VT 05251; (802) 867-4455, (800) 639-1620.

Cornucopia of Dorset

You will be pampered to perfection by innkeepers Bill and Linda Ley at this intimate nineteenth-century white clapboard dark green shuttered bed and breakfast located in the center of Dorset.

The entire first floor is common space for the guests. The dining room has a glass-walled sitting area with a pair of white couches and a television/VCR at one end. Other common areas include a small living room and a library, each with a fireplace. The terrace is set with Adirondack chairs and overlooks the manicured, cultivated narrow yard and the cottage.

In the main inn our favorite is Scallop, a corner room overlooking the main street, with floor-to-ceiling windows, a queen-size canopy bed, and a wood-burning fireplace. Dorset Hill, with a four-poster king-size bed and a stove fireplace, and Green Peak, a long, spacious room with a four-poster queen-size bed and wood-stove fireplace, both look out on the backyard. All rooms have phones, and rooms in the main house are air-conditioned.

For a romantic getaway stay in Owl's Head, a deluxe private cottage located behind the inn. The first-floor living room has a cathedral ceiling, a couch and easy chair facing a brick fireplace, a full kitchen, and an outdoor deck with chairs. The sleeping loft has a queen-size bed and two skylights.

The breakfast room has an exquisite Oriental rug and French doors that open onto the terrace and garden. Breakfast, served from 8 to 9 A.M. at two large tables, includes fresh-squeezed juice, a fruit course, and an entrée such as a baked puff pancake served with fresh fruit and maple syrup or croissants a l'orange.

Four rooms, each with private bath, $105–$140, and a cottage, $185–$205. 10% service charge. Afternoon tea, early morning coffee, and full breakfast included. Not appropriate for children. No pets. No smoking. Two-night weekend minimum. Route 30, Dorset, VT 05251; (802) 867-5751.

Manchester View Motel, Manchester Center

This is the best of the motels in the area, with rooms ranging from standard basic units to deluxe one- and two-bedroom luxury units with wood-burning or gas jet fireplaces and single or double whirlpool tubs. Most units have outdoor decks or patios with excellent views of the Green Mountains. Other amenities include an exercise room, an outdoor swimming pool, and access to the golf and tennis facilities at the Manchester Country Club. During the summer and on weekends in the winter a continental breakfast is available in "the Barn," another building on the property.

Thirty-five rooms, one- and two-bedroom suites, each with private bath, $74–$165. In season fireplace rooms and suites are $25–$35 additional. Children welcome. No pets. Breakfast available. Located on Route 7A, one and three-quarters miles north of Manchester Center, Box 1268, Manchester Center, VT 05255; (802) 362-2739.

WHERE TO DINE

Fine Dining

Mistral's

This intimate restaurant, owned by Chery and Dana Markey, is located off Route 11/30 on the way to the ski areas four miles from the main intersection in Manchester Center. It was once a toll stop on the old Boston-to-Albany route. Of the two rooms with large windows that overlook a small gorge with a rushing stream, our preference is the more intimate smaller room with a bar at one end. The trees are lit with little white lights, so be sure to request a window table.

Starters might include risotto with wild mushrooms and coquilles and langoustines St. Jacques. The duck, a specialty, is prepared with different sauces. An excellent Chateaubriand for two is prepared tableside. A recent menu also included rack of lamb for two; Norwegian salmon cannelloni stuffed with lobster and vegetables; trout stuffed with scallop mousse; and medallions of veal with prosciutto, mushrooms, and artichoke hearts. For dessert try the coup mistral, coffee ice cream with Frangelico rolled in hazelnuts and topped with a chocolate sauce.

Dinner, Thursday through Tuesday. Entrées $18–$26. Toll Gate Road, just outside of Manchester. (802) 362-1779.

Chantecleer, East Dorset

As you walk in the door you will see a ceramic rooster for which this restaurant is named. Your eyes are then drawn to the massive fieldstone fireplace that soars to the peak of the high roof of this converted dairy barn. The prime spot is the table in front of the fireplace in the smaller, more intimate room. We were seated in the larger, lower-ceilinged dining room with fifteen well-spaced tables, barnboard-and-plaster walls, and Windsor chairs. Contemporary Wolfard oil lamps on the tables provide pleasant lighting. The restaurant is sophisticated and elegant.

Appetizers might include risotto with mushrooms and sausage, potato pancakes served with a thick crabmeat and lime butter sauce, and Caesar salad, prepared tableside. The cheese fondue that we saw at a nearby table looked like fun.

The rack of lamb, four thick rib chops coated with herbs and broiled rare, was excellent. Other entrées included filet mignon with a macadamia nut sauce, roast duckling with onion jelly and duck sauce, and Wiener schnitzel. An assortment of vegetables and a choice of roasted potatoes, spaetzle, curried rice, or linguini with capers and ginger comes with the entrée.

Desserts included an alpine torte, with thin layers of flourless chocolate cake and buttercream frosting, and trifle, rum-soaked sponge cake with fresh fruit topped with Bavarian cream sauce.

Closed late October to Thanksgiving and mid-April to mid-May. Dinner nightly except Tuesday in the summer and Monday and Tuesday in the winter. Entrées $18–$25. Route 7A 3.5 miles north of Manchester Center, East Dorset, VT; (802) 362-1616.

Main Street Café, North Bennington

If you crave excellent Northern Italian cooking with good, strong flavors, make the effort to visit this out-of-the-way storefront restaurant in the quiet village of North Bennington. There is nothing extraordinary about the exterior or the decor, but the personality of the chef and the food preparation put this restaurant in a class by itself. Enthusiastic chef-owner Jeff Ben David tries to greet each table personally and introduce the specials he's cooking. We find the best approach is to ignore the menu, indicate your likes or dislikes, and give Jeff a free hand to do his thing.

Jeff's motto is, "If the only problem is that there's too much food then there is no problem." Dishes were served family-style. The little plates of appetizers filled our table: eggplant topped with sun-dried tomato sauce, grilled chicken wrapped in eggplant with melted mozzarella, cannelloni and grilled scallops on slices of smoked salmon. Following a salad we were served a large platter of angel-hair pasta topped with swordfish and grilled shrimp, a platter of grilled vegetables, and another dish of angel-hair pasta with chicken and portabella mushrooms. The meal was bountiful and delicious, and the friendly atmosphere of the room was contagious. There is a fine selection of reasonably priced quality Italian wines.

Dinner, Tuesday through Sunday. Entrées $12–$20. Route 7A south from Arlington to Route 67A (2 miles). 1 Prospect Street, North Bennington, VT; (802) 442-3210.

Barrows House, Dorset

The main dining room is on two levels. Walls are covered with a cabbage rose paper that coordinates with the flowered plates and rose checked tablecloths. The sunny greenhouse room, used for breakfast and dinner, has a wall and ceiling of glass that give it an airy feel we found as appealing on sunny days as in the midst of a heavy downpour, when the cascading rivulets of water made an artistic pattern overhead.

Appetizers to try are the smoked salmon bruschetta with grilled eggplant, tomato, and basil; or the house specialty, Maine crab cakes prepared with the traditional Old Bay seasoning.

The grilled tournedos of beef came with Maine crabmeat and black bean salad topped with cheddar cheese. Grilled swordfish was on a bed of chipotle pepper and roasted corn puree. Wild mushroom ravioli was topped with sun-dried tomatoes, roasted eggplant, broccoli, basil, and goat cheese. A menu of lighter fare included such dishes as steamed mussels with tomatoes and fusilli, grilled duck breast with a spicy peanut sauce, and sautéed calves' liver with bacon and onions.

The tavern, where the locals often congregate, has the same menu but a more informal feel. Before you leave, take a look at the stuffed velour moose on the wall, front and back.

Dinner nightly. Entrées $10–$24. Route 30, Dorset, VT; (802) 867-4455.

The Dorset Inn, Dorset

This classic New England inn has three dining rooms. Lunch is served in the greenhouse room, with such selections as chicken salad, avocado club sandwich, or the Dorset Inn country salad of greens topped with teriyaki chicken, corn, green beans, mushrooms, and croutons. Our favorite is the more casual tavern dining room, which has a fireplace and a long bar. There is also a formal, more subdued dining room.

At dinner the menu in the tavern and the dining room is the same, a combination of lower-priced tavern fare selections and more expensive entrées. For starters, choose from yam fritters with maple syrup, steamed mussels in red pepper butter sauce with grilled French bread, or mozzarella garlic toast. Continue with spicy beef or turkey chili; spinach salad topped with pieces of duck, bacon bits, and feta cheese; or hearty baked eggplant crepes stuffed with spinach and ricotta covered with tomato sauce and mozzarella. The entrées range from New England classics of fresh calves' liver with bacon and onions or loin lamb chops with shallots and garlic confit to such specials as chicken breast stuffed with Brie and coriander or veal tenderloin stuffed with spinach and mushrooms and wrapped in prosciutto.

Lunch daily, $5–$10. Dinner nightly, entrées $9–$20. Route 30, Dorset, VT; (802) 867-5500.

The Village Country Inn, Manchester Village

Since the Degens have added a garden and fountains to the property, the outdoor patio next to the pool is an even more inviting summer dining option, a secluded alfresco dining spot not visible from the front of the inn. For dining throughout the year, the inn has a large French country dining room with springlike green-and-white flowered wallpaper.

Dinner includes choice of appetizer, salad, entrée, and a selection from the dessert tray. For starters we suggest escargot Bourguignonne, scallops Alfredo, and the fish wrapped in puff pastry. Ten entrée selections are offered nightly, including a vegetarian dish and a light option such as tofu with shrimp, pasta, and hazelnuts. A favorite is venison with a Burgundy wine sauce. Pork tenderloin with a green peppercorn sauce or roast pheasant with apple raisin sauce satisfy a range of tastes.

Dinner, Thursday through Monday. Entrées $16–$19. Route 7A, Manchester Village, VT; (802) 362-1792.

The Reluctant Panther, Manchester Village

Before dinner, have a drink in the bar or on the outside terrace before moving to the intimate dining room with a greenhouse window. The menu is relatively small but changes nightly. We started with appetizers of sliced seafood sausage served with a basil mayonnaise and a curried tomato bisque attractively presented in an ostrich-egg-shaped double cup made at nearby Bennington Pottery. Caesar salad served with grilled shrimp had a pungent dressing rich with garlic and anchovy flavors.

For entrées, locally raised tender pheasant was served on a bed of cooked apples with thin asparagus spears, slivered carrots, and roasted little potatoes. Osso buco was a large, tender portion of veal covered with a rich tomato sauce served on a bed of saffron risotto in a black dish. Other entrées included scallopini of veal with mushrooms, shallots, and roasted garlic; tenderloin of beef with choron sauce; and pan-grilled swordfish on a bed of warm pepper sauce. Our dessert choices were a white and dark chocolate terrine with hazelnut sauce and a red wine poached pear with crème anglaise and toasted hazelnuts. Nice complements to the meal were the hors d'oeuvre of smoked salmon on a toast round and the chocolate truffle that came with our coffee.

Dinner, Thursday through Monday except April and November, daily in foliage season. Entrées $20–$26. West Road and Route 7A. Box 678, Manchester Village, VT; (802) 362-2568; (800) 822-2331.

The Equinox, Manchester Village

This resort hotel has a variety of dining options. We prefer Marsh Tavern, to the right of the large lobby, where you can sit next to one of the original fireplaces inscribed "L. C. Orvis 1832" on the marble face. For lunch we enjoyed the sautéed crab cakes and the crispy pieces of chicken served over local field greens. Creative sandwiches included thin-sliced lamb in a pita pocket with tomato, lettuce, and a yogurt dressing; Vermont goat cheese, roasted peppers, arugula and onions on rye; and roast turkey with bacon, lettuce, and tomato. Moderately priced dinner options include lamb stew, grilled free-range chicken, filet mignon or sirloin, or a burger.

Marsh Tavern: lunch daily, $8–$13; dinner nightly, entrées $9–$19. Colonnade: summer, dinner Wednesday through Sunday; winter, Friday and Saturday. Entrées $21–$25. Route 7A, Manchester Village, VT; (802) 362-4700.

Ye Olde Tavern, Manchester Center

Built in 1790, this tavern was frequented by Vermont's founding fathers. The well-worn wooden floors, exposed hand-hewn beams, and old wooden high-backed booths are reminiscent of the Colonial era. For appetizers try the house-smoked trout and the pan-blackened chicken fingers. Entrées included crisp roast duck with raspberry sauce, veal sautéed with mustard and caper sauce, and broiled scallops served with a lobster cream sauce. Light entrées such as broiled rainbow trout, steak and scallops, or broiled Delmonico steak are a lower-cost alternative, served without the fancy sauces and the soup and salad courses.

Lunch features salads, sandwiches, a variety of burgers, and a selection of broiled chicken, steak, scallops, and trout.

Lunch daily, $6–$9. Dinner nightly, $9–$19. Main Street, Manchester Center, VT; (802) 362-3770.

Informal Dining

Alldays and Onions, Bennington

This is a combination deli, wine shop, and gourmet restaurant. You can build a sandwich from assorted cheeses, meats, and condiments such as hummus, sprouts, and honeycup mustard. The salad sampler is priced by weight; we had curried chicken salad, smoked chicken with pasta, and a julienned vegetable salad. There are tables inside and on the flagstone terrace.

The dinner menu changes weekly. Roasted eggplant terrine with herbed mayonnaise, tagliatelle with smoked shrimp and wild mushrooms, or grilled boned quail are possible appetizers. The entrées might include swordfish with roasted pepper and olive butter or grilled chicken with lingonberries.

Lunch, Monday through Saturday, $4–$6. Dinner, Tuesday through Saturday (summer), Thursday through Saturday (winter). Entrées $11–$19. 519 Main Street, Bennington, VT; (802) 447-0043.

The Little Rooster, Manchester

The owners of Chantecleer (*see* page 49) also own this little café on Route 7A close to the outlets. This is a great place for lunch. Choices include a grilled fresh tuna Niçoise salad or a Caesar salad and sandwiches such as a steak sandwich on toasted garlic bread; a roast beef sandwich with pickled red cabbage, watercress, and horseradish dill dressing; crabmeat cakes on a baguette; or a grilled Reuben sandwich.

Breakfast and lunch, Thursday through Tuesday. Closed one week in April and November. $6–$9. Route 7A, Manchester, VT; (802) 362-3496.

Southern Vermont Art Center, Manchester

The Equinox Hotel operates the café in this twenty-eight-room mansion situated at the end of a long drive on hundreds of acres. After viewing the exhibits of paintings and sculptures, visitors can dine in the glass solarium or outdoors on the terrace overlooking the sculpture garden. The lunch menu includes sandwiches such as roast beef with horseradish, herbed mushroom with bacon, pâté de campagne, and salads such as chef's vegetable.

Open mid-May through October. Lunch, Tuesday through Sunday, $4–$7. Dinner, served only on evenings of a performance, entrées $10–$15. West Road, Manchester, VT; (802) 362-4220.

Up for Breakfast, Manchester Center

If breakfast is your favorite meal, don't miss this little second-floor hideaway across the street from the Quality Restaurant. The good, strong coffee is made from freshly ground beans. Fresh-squeezed juices include orange, pink grapefruit, and carrot. We had the strawberry lemon soufflé pancakes, which had a distinctive lemon flavor. Other selections listed on the blackboard were a sour cream omelette made with lamb sausage, red onions, and mushrooms; wild turkey hash with andouille sausage; apple cheddar omelette; Cajun frittata; and huevos rancheros. There was also a large selection of muffins including morning glory, one of our favorites, as well as Irish scones. Breakfast daily, weekdays to noon, weekends to 1 P.M., $4–$8. Main Street, Manchester Center, VT; (802) 362-4204.

The Station Restaurant, Pawlet

The walls of this former railroad station, which was moved to this site, are covered with old railroad pictures, timetables, tickets, posters, and railroad lanterns. The cooking is basic and the customers are local. (Notice their mugs on the wall.) We had good pea and vegetable beef soup, a traditional fried egg sandwich with ketchup served on homemade bread, and a slice of homemade blueberry maple cream pie accompanied by Wilcox rum raisin ice cream.

Breakfast and lunch daily. School Street, Pawlet, VT; (802) 325-3041.

Steininger's, Salem, NY

The exterior of this bright green building looks like an Irish bar, but inside, the Steininger family produces chocolates in the finest European tradition. Try the Grand Marnier truffle, the hazelnut gianduia, or the winter's leaf, made with white chocolate and minced roasted almonds. The chocolates are exquisitely packaged in padded fabric boxes or less expensively in plain boxes.

There are five glass-topped tables and a changing list of lunch or tea items. On our visit it included roast beef or ham-and-cheese melt on a croissant, homemade soup, cherry pie, chocolate tea muffins, and chocolate chip cookies. Our cappuccino was served with cinnamon sticks, shaved chocolate, and schlag, thick whipped cream. Check the back counter for bargain prices on "distressed chocolate."

Open Monday through Saturday for lunch and tea. At the intersection of Route 22 and Route 153. Main Street, Salem, NY; (518) 854-3830.

Mother Myrick's, Manchester Center

This high-profile ice-cream and candy shop and café has won rave reviews. The buttercrunch is exceptional and is also available by mail order. When you're tired of shopping, treat yourself to something fattening: an ice-cream sundae, ice-cream float, Vermont harvest cheesecake, dark chocolate cake, or a few pieces of candy.

Open daily. Route 7A, Manchester Center, VT; (802) 362-1560.

ITINERARY

DAY ONE. One of the major attractions of this area is the quantity of shopping opportunities in Manchester. Take a few hours to orient yourself and to decide where you want to shop. Drive north on Route 30 through the Mettowee Valley to Pawlet for lunch at the **Station Restaurant**. Visit stores in **Pawlet**. On your way back take a detour to **Merck Forest** for a short walk. Chocoholics will want to continue to Salem to visit **Steininger's**. Have dinner at **Barrows House** or at **Mistral's**.

DAY TWO. Get a picnic lunch at **Al Ducci's** in Manchester. Drive south to East Arlington, briefly visit the stores, then take the **Kelly Stand Road**, stopping for a hike on the Appalachian Trail. Drive to Stratton to see the base camp village. Have an elegant dinner at **Chantecleer**.

DAY THREE. Take a tour of **Hildene**. Continue to Bennington to visit the Bennington Pottery. Have lunch at **Alldays and Onions** followed by a visit to the **Bennington Museum**. You may also want to visit the **Battle Monument**. Return to Manchester on Route 7A if you want to shop or on Route 7 if you want to get to the stores in Manchester. Have an excellent dinner at the **Main Street Café** in North Bennington.

DAY FOUR. **Canoeing** on the Battenkill is a lot of fun. Decide how many hours you want to spend on the river and the staff will arrange your pickup spot accordingly. Bring a picnic lunch. In the late afternoon stop in at the **1811 House** for a drink, then dine at the **Reluctant Panther** or the **Village Country Inn**.

DAY FIVE. Hire a guide for **fly-fishing**; go to **Bromley** to ride on the alpine slide; take one of the **driving tours**; visit the **Southern Vermont Art Center** and have lunch at the café; or go **shopping** in Manchester.

BUDGETING YOUR TRIP

To help you get the most for the time and money you have to spend, here are some travel suggestions at three budget levels (cost per day with two people sharing a room) including lodging and meal tax, gratuity on meals, and service charge when it is added to your bill. Prices are approximate and are intended for planning purposes only. Lodgings are categorized by price, and depending on the room selected may appear in more than one category. Meal prices at lunch include an average entrée, and beverage. Dinner prices include an appetizer, entrée, dessert, and beverage. Wine or alcoholic beverages are not included.

Staying and dining at expensive lodgings and restaurants: From $330 to $740 per day for two.

Lodging: Barrows House (includes dinner), the Village Country Inn (includes dinner), the Reluctant Panther (includes dinner), Cornucopia of Dorset, 1811 House, the Inn at Ormsby Hill, the Equinox, the Charles Orvis Inn, Manchester View Motel.

Dining: Breakfast: included except at Manchester View Motel and the Equinox. Lunch: Dorset Inn, the Equinox (Marsh Tavern). Dinner: Chantecleer, Mistral's, the Equinox, the Reluctant Panther.

Staying and dining at moderately priced lodgings and restaurants: From $250 to $300 per day for two.

Lodging: Barrows House (includes dinner), the Village Country Inn (includes dinner), the Reluctant Panther (includes dinner), West Mountain Inn (includes dinner), Cornucopia of Dorset, 1811 House, the Inn at Ormsby Hill, Manchester View Motel.

Dining: Breakfast: included except at the Manchester View Motel. Lunch: Ye Olde Tavern, the Little Rooster, Southern Vermont Art Center, Alldays and Onions, Steininger's. Dinner: Dorset Inn, Barrows House, the Village Country Inn, Main Street Café.

Staying and dining at less expensive lodgings and restaurants: From $150 to $220 per day for two.

Lodging: Hill Farm Inn, Manchester View Motel.

Dining: Breakfast: included except at Manchester View Motel. Lunch: Up for Breakfast, the Station Restaurant, takeout at Alldays and Onions. Dinner: Ye Olde Tavern, Alldays and Onions, Dorset Inn (tavern).

3

Woodstock, Vermont, and Hanover, New Hampshire

One of the most beautiful towns in America, cradled between lush green hills, Woodstock was first settled over 200 years ago. By the mid-1800s Woodstock was an attractive self-contained town of sturdy brick and granite buildings with a population of about 1,200. Its green was surrounded by classic examples of Georgian and Federal architecture, and the Ottauquechee River and Kedron Brook flowed through town, supplying water power for a full complement of outlying mills—grist, carding, woolen, linseed oil, and lumber. The tradesmen, in turn, made carriages, clocks, musical instruments, combs, and other goods.

Prominent statesmen, entrepreneurs, and artists called Woodstock home. George Perkins Marsh, who created the concept of modern ecology with his book *Man and Nature* (1864), lived here. Frederick Billings built and operated a model dairy farm. Hiram Powers sculpted the *Greek Slave,* a popular but controversial work of art now on display in the Corcoran Gallery in Washington, D.C.

The Civil War years saw many of Vermont's young people leave and never return. Many young men gave their lives for the Union cause.

In the latter part of the nineteenth century, newly affluent Americans flocked to Europe to take the waters. Sanderson, an enterprising Woodstocker, claimed his "waters" were the equal of those in Europe. Eventually, "flatlanders" (people not born in Vermont) started to come for the waters and pure mountain air.

In 1934 two unrelated events changed the town of Woodstock forever. Yankee ingenuity, a Model-T engine, and a cable were put to work on Gilbert's farm, located along Route 12 on the southern flank of Mount Tom. The result was the first rope tow in the country. From these humble beginnings the Vermont ski industry grew to become one of the mainstays of the state's economy.

The second event was the marriage of Laurance S. Rockefeller to Mary Billings French, a union of two families of great means and interest in

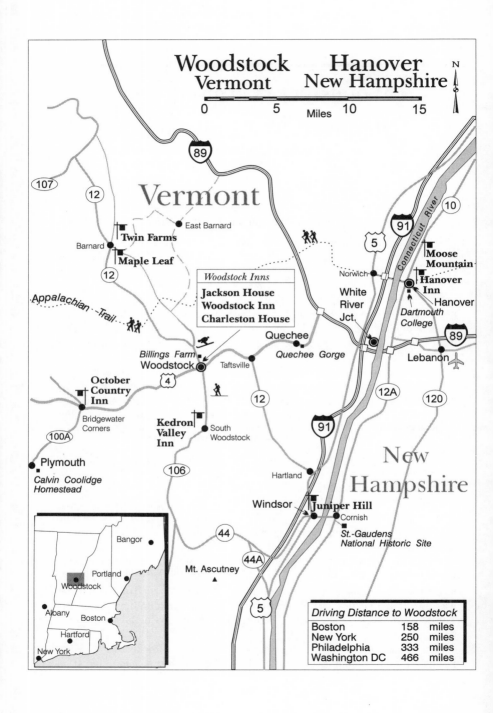

conserving the area. In the decades since, the Rockefellers and town leaders have worked to preserve the historic character of Woodstock. Strict laws regulate new development. Utility lines are buried underground. Much of the surrounding hillside is protected and will never be developed. The Billings Farm, now a museum, provides a comprehensive look at the day-to-day life of the Vermont hill farmer.

Four of the town's churches still ring bells cast by Paul Revere, and magnificent nineteenth-century homes still line the oval green and the side streets. There have been inevitable changes as well: parking meters have replaced hitching posts. The sheep on the town green are gone, replaced by bicycle tour groups at rest. Gillingham's, a traditional general store in the center of Woodstock, survives, but most of the craftspeople and small industries have been replaced by restaurants, upscale gift shops, art galleries, and a number of real-estate offices.

Surrounding the community is the Vermont countryside—lush and green in summer; blazing red, orange, and yellow in autumn (when it seems the whole world descends upon the state); pure white in winter; brown in mud season; and ever so delicate in spring.

For information on special events, contact the **Woodstock Area Chamber of Commerce** (18 Central Street, Woodstock, VT 05091; (802)457-3555) or the **Hanover Area Chamber of Commerce** (216 Nugget Building, Box 5105, Hanover, NH 03755; (603)643-3115).

WHERE TO GO, WHAT TO DO

Billings Farm and Museum, Woodstock. We were impressed with the low-key, noncommercial attitude here—as well as with the variety of activities. The day of our visit we tasted hand-churned butter made by a group of enthusiastic ten-year-olds, watched a hand-milking contest, saw a master craftsman cane chairs, and had a personal tour of a prizewinning herd of Jersey cows.

This working dairy farm and museum was opened to the public in 1983 as a memorial to Mrs. Rockefeller's grandfather, Frederick Billings. Mr. Billings started his enterprise with cows from the Isle of Jersey in 1871 and eventually developed his own blue-ribbon herd. (The Jersey cow produces milk with the highest butterfat content.)

Down on the farm, you can see a room filled with dairy trophies and ribbons, tour a separate room for calves, and visit the main dairy (preferably during the midafternoon milking). A hay wagon pulled by huge Belgian workhorses is also a good way to tour the farm.

In the museum, four interconnected barns offer exhibits and demonstrations tracing the daily life of a Vermont family hill farm in 1890. The lives and times of these hearty New England farmers come alive as you look in on a fully stocked general store; see stone walls and wood fences under constuction; imagine old-time maple sugaring with wooden buckets, taps, and boiling-down supplies; and examine plows, carriages, a school, a workshop, and more. In addition, the original Billings farmhouse was recently restored and is now open for visitors.

Special events are held throughout the year. In September, border collies herd the sheep, which are then sheared to provide the wool for the farm's spinning and weaving demonstrations. October is harvest time, and brings a husking bee and barn dance.

Open May to late October, daily, 10 A.M. to 5 P.M.; November and December, weekends 10 A.M. to 4 P.M. Adults $6. Route 12, Woodstock, VT; (802) 457-2355.

Marsh-Billings National Historical Park. Mary Billings, granddaughter of Frederick Billings, and her husband, Laurance Rockefeller, recently donated a mansion and about 600 acres of woodlands to form a new National Historical Park. The mansion was home to conservationist George Perkins Marsh in the early 1800s. It was purchased by Frederick Billings in 1869, who used scientific farming methods at the Billings Farm (see above) based on Marsh's environment-saving principles. While it was not yet open to the public as we went to press, we suggest you make inquiries with the local chamber of commerce.

The Vermont Raptor Center, Woodstock. Bald eagles, great horned owls, and peregrine falcons are just three of the twenty-six species of raptors (birds of prey) that, because of permanent injuries which prevent their release to the wild, now live in spacious outdoor habitats on the grounds of the Vermont Institute of Natural Science. A plaque explaining the cause of each bird's injury is attached to each of the large cages. Hundreds of other birds of prey are also treated here every year, many of which are eventually returned to the wild. In addition, self-guided nature trails wind through the seventy-seven-acre property.

Open year-round. May through October, daily 10 A.M. to 4 P.M. November through April, closed Sunday. Adults $5. Church Hill Road, Woodstock, VT; (802) 457-2779.

The Dana House, Woodstock. On display here at the headquarters of the Woodstock Historical Society is a collection of furnishings dating from 1800 to 1860, nineteenth-century clothing and toys, and etchings of John Taylor Arms, an artist who lived in nearby Pomfret. Also on the property is a barn with a collection of nineteenth-century tools, sleds, and a splendid sleigh.

Open May through October, Monday through Saturday, 10 A.M. to 5 P.M.; Sunday, 2 to 5 P.M. and weekends in December. Admission free. 26 Elm Street, Woodstock, VT; (802) 457-1822.

Stores and galleries in and around Woodstock. The village police strictly enforce parking laws, so watch the meters and the no-parking zones carefully to avoid a ticket. A seasonal (June to October) information booth on the Woodstock town green has maps of the town and other brochures. For daily and weekly events check the "town crier" blackboard located at the corner of Elm and Central Streets. The days and times of walking tours of the town are also posted here. The commercial district is small enough to peruse in a couple of hours. The following are among our favorites:

Gallery on the Green. The work of forty New England artists represented includes the glass and bronze works of local artist Peter Bramhall. Corner of Elm Street; (802) 457-4956.

Woodstock Folk Art Prints and Antiquities. Sabra Field and Woody Jackson's original watercolors and silkscreens are among the work of forty New England artists represented. 6 Elm Street; (802) 457–2012.

F. H. Gillingham and Sons. This must-see Vermont institution, owned by the same family since 1886, offers Vermont specialty food items, housewares, and hardware. A mail-order catalog is also available. Elm Street; (802) 457-2100 or (800) 344-6668.

Morgan-Ballou. Quality women's clothing and accessories include Dia sweaters, which are handmade in Vermont. Elm Street; (802) 457-1321.

The House of Walsh across the street has men's and women's clothing; (802) 457-3900.

The Yankee Bookshop. This store has an impressive selection of books about Vermont and New England. 12 Central Street; (802) 457-2411.

Who Is Sylvia? One of the finest secondhand clothing stores we've seen, this shop is in an old firehouse straddling Kedron Brook. The building alone is worth a visit. 26 Central Street;(802) 457-1110.

Grayson Gallery. The majority of the artists represented here are from Vermont. 43 Central Street; (802) 457-1171.

Stephen Huneck Gallery. Animal lovers will enjoy the bold, whimsical paintings, wood carvings, and folk sculptures of animals by this internationally known painter and sculptor. 49 Central Street; (802) 457-3206.

Red Cupboard Gift Shop. Even the locals come here to send gift packages of Vermont products to their friends. Just west of Woodstock on Route 4; (802) 457-3722.

These two local craftspeople have pieces in galleries in Woodstock. To visit their studios, call for an appointment.

Sabra Field. Her wood-block prints have appeared on a UNICEF card, on the cover of *Vermont Life* magazine, on a hot-air balloon, and on the 1991 Vermont bicentennial United States postage stamp. The simplicity of her prints captures the essence of the Vermont countryside. Best of all, her prices are affordable, with prints starting under $50. We enjoyed visiting the gallery, talking with Sabra, and watching the wood-block engraving and printing process. Folk Art Prints and Antiquities in Woodstock carries her work. Tontine Press, Box 114, RFD 2 (East Barnard), South Royalton, VT 05068; (802) 763-7092.

Peter Bramhall. His richly interpenetrating glass globular forms are highly unusual. Drawing on the colors he sees in nature, Peter classifies his pieces based on the colors of the glass. He has an ocean series and a winter sunset series, among others, and the glass interiors range from six to twenty-two inches in diameter and sell from $300 to $1,500. Peter also does bronze sculptures that sell from $7,500 to $100,000. His glass and bronze are for sale at Gallery on the Green in Woodstock. His home and workshop, located on 400 wooded acres, includes three studios and a gallery (open by arrangement). Christine Merriman, whose Merry Woman Studio is also on the the premises, makes handmade raku tiles that can be fashioned into nameplates, fireplace screens, and placemat tiles and murals. Box 18, Bridgewater Center Road, Bridgewater, VT 05034; (802) 672-5141.

The Towns

Plymouth

Calvin Coolidge Homestead, Plymouth. The thirtieth president of the United States, nicknamed "Silent Cal," was sworn into office by his father in this tiny hamlet after President Warren Harding died in 1923. Coolidge was elected to a full term by a huge majority in 1924 and served until 1928, when he declined to run again.

Plymouth Notch was his birthplace and the village where he grew up, as well as the place he vacationed throughout his life and where he is buried. The countryside is bucolic, and development has yet to scar the surrounding hillsides. The contrast between the simple "summer White House" of the 1920s and the pageantry that accompanies the president's every move today is striking.

The village has an information center, a general store, a wooden barn full of carriages and period farm implements, a dining room, a cheese factory, the small house where Coolidge was born, and the house where he vacationed while president. The focus of the displays and guided tours is on the town more than on Coolidge and his political career.

Open daily, late May to mid-October, 9:30 A.M. to 5:30 P.M. Adults $4.50. Six miles south of U.S. 4 on Vermont 100A; (802) 672-3773.

Plymouth Cheese Company. The cheese most typical of this area is Vermont granular curd cheese, and the company that makes it is still owned by Calvin Coolidge's son, John Coolidge. Mild, medium, sharp, extra sharp, sage, pimento, and caraway are available by the piece at the factory or in three-pound wheels by mail order. Open year-round. Mid-May to mid-October, daily, 8 A.M. to 5:30 P.M.; mid-October to mid-May, 8 A.M. to 4:30 P.M. Closed Saturday and Sunday after Thanksgiving. In the village. Box 1, Plymouth, VT 05056; (802) 672-3650.

Quechee

Simon Pearce Glass, Quechee. Simon Pearce, a glassblower from Ireland, came to Vermont in 1981 and discovered an old mill and dam that were idle. One of the local success stories of the 1980s is how Pearce successfully installed a modern water-driven turbine (to power the furnaces and pottery kilns) and turned this once run-down property on the Ottauquechee River into a tourist center. Walk downstairs to see the glassblowers and potters at work. Each piece of glass is handblown, each pot hand-thrown.

Functional, attractively displayed hand-blown glassware such as pitchers, carafes, goblets, mugs, and bowls, as well as handmade country furniture and Irish woolen clothing, all of the highest quality, can be purchased on the premises. Firsts and seconds of pottery are also for sale. Be aware that on rainy days during the tourist season the mill is packed with people. (Pearce has opened a larger facility for glassblowing in Windsor.) After taking it all in you will probably be hungry, so meander across the room to Pearce's restaurant, where the tables are set with his glassware and pottery. Try to get a window table overlooking the dam.

Open daily 9 A.M. to 9 A.M. Glassblowing 9 A.M. to 5 P.M. The Mill, just off Route 4, Quechee, VT 05059; (802) 295-2711.

Quechee Gorge. The one-mile path to the bottom of the gorge follows along the waterfalls and rapids carved by the Ottauquechee River. The bridge spanning the gorge at Route 4 is 165 feet from the bottom and offers great views of the downstream side.

Windsor

Simon Pearce Glass, Windsor. This manufacturing facility and retail shop is the newest of Simon Pearce's ventures. The retail shop has first and seconds of glassware and pottery. The high point of the visit is watching the glassblowers at work from the catwalk that circles the factory floor. We've heard that a restaurant is planned for this site. Open daily, 9 A.M. to 6 P.M. Situated in an industrial park north of Windsor on Route 5; (802) 674-6280.

The Old Constitution House. It was here in Elijah West's Tavern that Vermont was declared an independent republic in 1777, and it remained so until 1791, when it was admitted to the Union as the fourteenth state. Open Memorial Day through Columbus Day, Wednesday through Sunday. Route 5, Windsor; (802) 828-3051.

Vermont State Craft Gallery. Crafts by more than 200 Vermont artisans fill two floors of this nineteenth-century Windsor House. Open daily except in the winter. 54 Main Street; (802) 674-6729.

The American Precision Museum. The system and machinery for making interchangeable machine parts that could be mass-assembled was developed in Windsor. You'll see machine tools, many displayed with the products they were used to make—rifles, sewing machines, typewriters, steam engines, coffee percolators, even a Model T. Many of these tools are artistic works in themselves, beautifully carved and painted with shells, flowers, and birds. Open daily, late May through October. Adults $3. Route 5, South Main Street; (802) 674-5781.

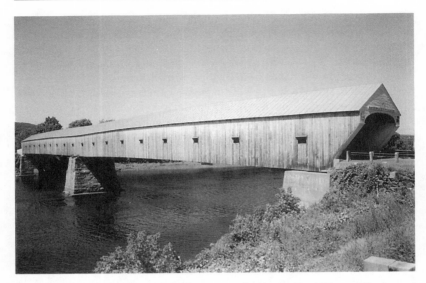

The 460-foot Windsor-Cornish bridge across the Connecticut River is the longest covered bridge in the United States.

Windsor-Cornish Covered Bridge. This 460-foot bridge, spanning the Connecticut River from Windsor to Cornish, NH, is the longest in the United States.

Cornish

Saint-Gaudens National Historic Site. Drive over the covered bridge and up the hill to see how Augustus Saint-Gaudens, the first major American sculptor, tossed away classical robes and dressed his subjects in current fashions. President Theodore Roosevelt, a friend and admirer, commissioned him to design the relief sculptures used on the penny, ten- and twenty-dollar gold pieces. Visitors can tour his house; the gardens; the Little Studio and the New Gallery, which contain the sculptor's works; the Picture Gallery, which has contemporary art exhibits; and the stable, with a collection of horse-drawn vehicles. Concerts are held on Sundays, early July to mid-August. Open daily, Memorial Day through October. Adults $2. Off Route 12A, Cornish, NH; (603) 675-2175.

Hanover, New Hampshire

Hanover, the home of Dartmouth College, spreads itself around the expansive elm-tree-lined green. Inhabited by just over 10,000 mostly Dartmouth-affiliated students, professors, educators, and graduates who don't want to leave, the town has picture-book New England architecture. Stroll the streets, stop in the galleries, coffee shops, museums, and soak up the atmosphere of "Big Green" Dartmouth.

Hood Museum of Art. Here's a trivia question for you: Who painted the familiar "sap gathering" picture found on the metal Vermont maple syrup cans? The answer is Paul Sample, one of the highly regarded painters associated with the American Regionalist style during the 1930s and 1940s. Sample was a 1920 graduate of Dartmouth College, and the Hood Museum has a permanent collection of his paintings on display. The museum's collection also includes Assyrian reliefs and twentieth-century paintings by Rothko, Picasso, and Stella.

Open Tuesday through Saturday, 10 A.M. to 5 P.M., also Wednesday 5 to 9 P.M., and Sunday noon to 5 P.M. Admission free. Located on the green next to the Hanover Inn, Hanover, NH; (603) 646-2900.

Baker Memorial Library. For something completely different, walk across the green to the basement of the library for a look at *An Epic of American Civilization,* the outstanding and dramatic series of frescoes painted by the Mexican muralist Jose Clemente Orozco from 1932 to 1934 while he was artist-in-residence. Open daily 8 A.M. to 5 P.M. during campus holidays, other times 8 A.M. to midnight; (802) 646-2560.

Hopkins Center for the Arts. A full and varied slate of plays, concerts, recitals, and foreign films is available at different venues on the Dartmouth campus throughout the year. The complex of three theaters and a recital hall designed by Wallace Harrison was the prototype for his design of Lincoln Center in New York City.

Tickets can be purchased by phone with a credit card. The box office is open Tuesday through Saturday, 10 A.M. to 6 P.M. Dartmouth College, Hanover, NH 03755; (603) 646-2422.

Dartmouth Bookstore. This is one of the great bookstores in northern New England, with more than 100,000 titles. 33 South Main Street, Hanover, NH; (800) 624-8800.

Hanover League of New Hampshire Craftsmen. If you like local and regional handicrafts but aren't quite ready to spend a few hundred dollars for a vase, this shop has a fine assortment of crafts and home furnishings jury-selected for quality. Items include furniture, jewelry, pottery, ironwork, wood carving, glassware, pewter, prints, lamps, and shades. There are also workshops and craft classes offered in many mediums.

Open Monday through Saturday, 9:30 A.M. to 5 P.M. Behind Hopkins Center. 13 Lebanon Street, Hanover, NH; (603) 643-5050.

Anichini Outlet Store. Here you will find the highest-quality linens, including the unbleached cottons used at Twin Farms, at 50 percent off retail prices. No mail order, but the store will ship your purchases. Open Monday through Saturday 10 A.M. to 9 P.M., Sunday noon to 5 P.M. Powerhouse Shopping Mall, Route 10, West Lebanon, NH; (603) 298-8656.

Sports

Downhill Skiing

Suicide Six. This ski area near Woodstock is good for families, as its size and terrain are more manageable than the larger Vermont ski slopes. The lift lines are also shorter and the food at the cafeteria has a good reputation. Eighteen trails. Woodstock, VT; (802) 457-1666; snow conditions, (802) 457-1622.

Cross-country Skiing

Woodstock Ski Touring Center. Skiing is available on two sets of groomed trails; the Mount Peg trails (thirty-one kilometers) are laid out over the golf course and surrounding hills; the Mount Tom trails (twenty-five kilometers) are located near the Suicide Six ski area off Route 12, north of the village. Headquarters at Woodstock Country Club, Route 106, Woodstock; (802) 457-2114.

Golf

The Woodstock Country Club. This is a famous old eighteen-hole Robert Trent Jones–designed course that is part of the Woodstock Inn complex. There is water at over a dozen holes. Route 106, Woodstock, VT; (802) 457-1100.

Swimming

Silver Lake State Park. In addition to being a good place to go swimming, the park offers canoe and boat rentals, and picnic and camping facilities for a fee. From Barnard, go a quarter-mile north on Town Road; (802) 234-9451.

Driving Tour

Woodstock–Windsor–Cornish–Quechee

From Woodstock, head south on Route 106 past the Woodstock Country Club and Kedron Valley Inn. Continue on Route 106 past the Green Mountain Horse Association and Eastern Magnesium Talc Company, a major producer of talcum powder. This is a beautiful drive through wooded countryside. Turn left on Route 44. About three miles beyond Brownsville the road forks to become Route 44A.

If you want to drive to within 500 feet of the summit of Mount Ascutney, take the right fork (Route 44A) to the forest ranger's cottage and continue up Mount Ascutney. There's a scenic overlook and trail leading to the top (elevation 3,144 feet). Continue on Route 44A to Route 5. Take Route 5 north to Windsor.

If you don't want to go to Mount Ascutney, continue on Route 44 to Windsor. Stop at the **Craft Center** and the **American Precision Museum**. Cross the 460-foot-long **Windsor-Cornish covered bridge**. After you cross the bridge, bear left on Route 12A up the hill to **Saint-Gaudens National Historic Site**. Return to Route 5 with a stop north of the town at **Simon Pearce's** glass factory and store. At Hartland turn left at Route 12; continue to Taftsville. Stop at the Taftsville Country Store. Cross Route 4 and drive over the red covered bridge. Turn left onto River Road, a dirt road that follows the Ottauquechee River back to the middle of Woodstock, or take Route 4 directly back to Woodstock.

WHERE TO STAY

Lodgings are arranged geographically from west to east.

October Country Inn, Bridgewater Corners, VT

This is one of the most relaxed and welcoming inns we have stayed at during our travels. During the spring-to-fall season bike groups regularly stay here. Guests congregate in the public areas after a day spent touring. There is a spacious wooden deck with a hot tub and a swimming pool on the hillside. The common room, furnished with couches and easy chairs, a hundred-year-old wood stove and a fireplace, has shelves of recently published books purchased on forays to the Dartmouth bookstore, lots of games and puzzles, and a cookie jar for afternoon nibbling. Innkeepers Patrick Runkel and Richard Sims have an eclectic collection of contemporary art with many pieces made by local artists. Be sure to look at the guest logs, which are filled with excellent drawings and snippets of poetry, and browse through the photographs of guests taken over many years.

Many guests return here year after year, and soon feel as though they're part of the extended family. Over the years we've watched Patrick and Richard make many improvements such as the installation of the deck and hot tub, skylights in some rooms, and the enlargement of bedrooms and baths.

An excellent hearty dinner is served family-style. Patrick is in charge of the kitchen. On one of our visits dinner included garlic baked chicken, eggplant parmigiana, a fennel salad, and chocolate cake with raspberry cassis sauce. Other nights the theme is French country, Greek, African, Mexican, Hungarian, or Chinese.

A hearty breakfast buffet includes breads for toasting, muffins, granola, fruit, juice, plus a hot dish such as omelettes, pancakes, or French toast.

Ten rooms, eight with private bath. $124–$158, breakfast and dinner for two included. 10% service charge. Children welcome. No smoking. No pets. Located at the junction of Routes 4 and 100A. Bridgewater Corners, VT 05035; (802) 672-3412; (800) 648-8421.

October Country Inn is one of the most relaxed and welcoming inns in New England.

Jackson House, Woodstock, VT

The inn, purchased by Juan and Gloria Florin in the fall of 1996, is set on a landscaped three-acre parcel one and a half miles west of Woodstock. It has been painstakingly restored and appointed with museum-quality furnishings. The gardens are spectacular and include an English garden with an important sculpture by Judith Brown.

The house was built in 1890 for a lumber merchant who demanded the finest woods and craftsmanship available at the time. The floors are maintained in such superb condition that in winter, guests are asked to wear slippers. The bedrooms and suites are furnished with exquisite period antiques, such as an 1860 cannonball bed and a French sleigh bed from the Empire period. All rooms are air-conditioned.

Our top choice is Regency, a huge apartment with a full kitchen and living room, a wood-burning stove, an entertainment center, and a Brazilian mahogany four-poster bed. Nicholas and Francesca are third-floor one-room suites with decks that overlook the grounds. A well-equipped exercise room with large-screen television and film library, steam room, universal gym, exercise machines, and juice bar is in the basement.

A highlight is the 6 to 7 P.M. innkeeper's reception. The night we were there, we sipped champagne and sampled caviar, pâté, Swedish meatballs, carpaccio, hot cheese puffs, and imported cheese.

Twelve rooms and suites, all with private bath, $135–$250. Hors d'oeuvres and a full breakfast included. Children over 14 welcome. No smoking. No pets. Route 4 West, Woodstock, VT 05091; (802) 457-2065.

Woodstock Inn & Resort, Woodstock, VT

More than just a full-service inn, this is a deluxe year-round resort complex located in the center of Woodstock. The classic lobby has a mammoth ten-foot-wide stone fireplace. Owner Laurance Rockefeller's wonderful collection of regional art is found in the classic New England–style lobby and throughout the common areas. Rooms in the main inn are furnished with locally made ash furniture, colorful handmade quilts made in Vermont, and prints by local artist Sabra Field. Rooms in the Tavern Wing are newer, with cherry wood furniture and fabrics in darker, richer tones. The thirty rooms in the Tavern Wing are all premium rooms; sixteen have wood-burning fireplaces. Each of the four Tavern Suites has a king-size cherry wood bed, large bath with a double sink, shower and separate tub, and a sitting room with a fireplace, wet bar, and half bath. We also like the three porch rooms, which have two double beds and folding doors to a sitting porch.

The Woodstock Country Club, just south of the inn, has an eighteen-hole Robert Trent Jones course which in the winter is a ski-touring center with thirty-one kilometers of groomed trails. The Sports Center, located one and a half miles from the inn, has two indoor and ten outdoor tennis courts, two squash courts, two racquetball courts, a thirty-by-sixty-foot lap pool, whirlpool, Nautilus machines, steam bath, saunas, and massage room. In addition, the Suicide Six ski area is just four miles northwest of town.

One hundred forty-four rooms and suites, all with private bath, rooms $149–$285, suites $399–$499 (meals not included). Children welcome. No pets. Use of the indoor health and fitness center is included. Package plans available. Fourteen the Green, Woodstock, VT 05091; (802) 457-1100 or (800) 448-7900.

The Charleston House, Woodstock, VT

This 1835 Greek Revival house on Woodstock's main street is within strolling distance of all the shops and restaurants in town. The building is furnished with period antiques, fine reproductions, and an eclectic selection of art and Oriental rugs. The twin chintz-covered couches and welcoming fireplace in the living room make this a particularly inviting gathering spot.

Owners Barbara and Bill Hough have completed a major addition of two deluxe suites added to the back of the inn, Mount Peg and Summer Kitchen. Both rooms have gas fireplaces, televisions, and double whirlpool tubs, and they have king- and queen-canopy beds, respectively. Pomfret Hills room, where we stayed, is another good choice. It is a good-sized room with a queen-size bed, cable television, and full bath. Families prefer Mount Tom, the third-floor suite which has a king-size bed, a double bed, a sitting room with a futon couch, and an oversize shower.

Barbara and Bill serve breakfast to all guests at one large table. When the inn is full there are two breakfast sittings. A fruit dish is followed by a hot dish such as feathered eggs and croissant or buttermilk pancakes and bacon. Barbara has compiled her recipes into a breakfast cookbook, which is available for purchase.

Seven rooms, all with private bath, $110–$175. Afternoon tea and breakfast included. Children over 6 welcome. No pets. 21 Pleasant Street, Woodstock, VT 05091; (802) 457-3843.

The Maple Leaf Inn, Barnard, VT

This newly built inn owned by Gary and Janet Robison has a quiet wooded setting twelve miles north of Woodstock. Gary, a former construction engineer for Exxon, and Janet, a former teacher, moved here from Texas and opened the inn in 1994. They designed the inn so that all the first- and second-floor rooms would have wood-burning fireplaces and four would have double-whirlpool tubs. All the rooms have king-size beds, phones, and televisions that can be swiveled to view from the bed or from the sitting area. Rooms have overhead fans but are not air-conditioned. The Country Garden Room on the first floor is wheelchair accessible. The four rooms on the second floor are named for the seasons. The Winter Room is the largest. The two rooms on the third floor are smaller and do not have fireplaces or whirlpool tubs.

The breakfast room, decorated with Janet's "Love stamp" needlepoint pictures, has a fireplace. Breakfast is served at individual tables from 8:30 to 10 A.M. The day we stayed we had sautéed bananas, stuffed French toast, and scones.

Seven rooms, all with private bath, $100–$160. Not appropriate for children. Afternoon tea and breakfast included. No smoking. No pets. Box 273, Barnard, VT 05031; (802) 234-5342; (800) 51-MAPLE.

Twin Farms, Barnard, VT

This 240-acre grand estate is one of the finest hideaways we have ever seen. The farmhouse was the country home of Dorothy and Sinclair Lewis in the 1930s and '40s. Owners Laila and Thurston Twigg-Smith spent millions of dollars renovating, constructing additions and numerous new buildings, and doing an incredible job of decorating. Stunning pieces of art and antiques from their personal collection were combined to create a quietly elegant, unpretentious atmosphere.

The price is unquestionably high, but is worth it if you are looking for this kind of exclusive place. The main house has a two-story central living room and a second living room/game room and an open bar. The ultramodern pub building has a Wurlitzer jukebox, a forty-six-inch television, pool table, stocked bar, and lounge sitting area. A fitness center that rivals any that we have used in deluxe hotels is underneath this adult playground. After exercising, cross the road to the building with a Japanese furo, a soaking tub. There is also a private ski slope and tow, a swimming and stocked fishing pond with canoes and rowboats, tennis courts, and miles of hiking trails.

Each accommodation has a wood-burning fireplace, a large seating area, and a large bath with a separate oversize shower and a tub. The eight cottages set in the woods are the most luxurious and expensive. The ultimate is the Studio, a two-story stone building with white plush carpeting and couches, a Frank Stella painting over one of the two fireplaces, an enclosed deck with a whirlpool, and a view of the woods. The bedroom on the second floor has a king-size bed, a second fireplace, and a bath with a copper-lined 300-gallon tub.

The dining room has two large fieldstone Rumford fireplaces at either end of the high arched room. Guests are served a set gourmet lunch and dinner with wines at their own table; individual requests or diets can be accommodated.

Fourteen suites and cottages. $700–$1,500. 15% service additional. Breakfast, lunch, dinner, alcoholic beverages, and all activities and equipment for two are included. Closed in April. Not appropriate for children under 18. No pets. Barnard, Vermont 05031; (802) 234-9999; (800) TWIN-FARMS.

Kedron Valley Inn, South Woodstock, VT

This is one of those rare country inns that has an outstanding gourmet kitchen and welcomes families too, including well-behaved pets. The fifteen-acre complex is located in the village of South Woodstock, and includes the 1822 brick inn, an equally old roadside tavern that has been converted into spacious accommodations, a log lodge, and a one-and-a-half-acre swimming pond with sand beach.

Quilts from the innkeepers Max and Merrily Comins' extensive collection hang in the common areas and decorate the wall or the bed in each of the rooms.

Fourteen of the rooms have wood-burning fireplaces. Our favorite is room 17, a deluxe suite in the main house with a bedroom and sitting room separated by a bifold door. The bedroom has a queen-size canopy bed; the sitting room has a fireplace. The bath has two sinks, a double whirlpool tub, and a separate shower. In the Tavern Building we like room 24, a duplex with a bath, daybed, and TV on the first floor and a second-floor loft with a queen-size canopy bed, fireplace, and a small rooftop deck. Room 22, also in the Tavern Building, is a large room with a queen-size canopy bed and glass-enclosed fireplace. You can also enjoy the fine view of the surrounding hills from the chaise lounges on the room's private porch. Midrange rooms all have queen-size beds; many also have wood stoves. Most of the rooms in the log lodge have one queen-size and one twin bed and exposed log walls decorated with quilts. All rooms have televisions and seven have air-conditioning.

A full breakfast includes a choice of hot dish such as Cajun hash or cheddar-Swiss omelettes.

Twenty-eight rooms, all with private bath, $166–$261, breakfast and dinner for two included. Peak times $20 additional. Bed-and-breakfast rates $120–$215. 15% service charge. Children and pets welcome. Located five miles south of Woodstock on Route 106. South Woodstock, VT 05071; (802) 457-1473.

As you make the last turn up the country road to Juniper Hill, this imposing mansion takes you by surprise.

Juniper Hill Inn, Windsor, VT

As you make the last turn up the country road, the sight of this imposing mansion on the hillside takes you by surprise. You enter through the Great Hall, a central sitting room thirty by forty feet with English golden oak paneling. Off this room are two dining rooms, another sitting room with a fireplace, and a gentleman's library study. There is a terrace, rolling lawn with well-tended perennial borders, and a swimming pool. The innkeepers are Susanne and Rob Pearl, who purchased the inn in July 1992.

Room 1, the largest and the one most popular with honeymooners, is a corner room with a great view of the mounains. Both the queen-size canopy bed and the sofa face the wood-burning fireplace. Room 4, at the opposite corner of the second floor, has a Charleston Rice four-poster queen bed and a sofa that faces the fireplace. Room 7, another newly redone room with a queen-size bed facing the fireplace plus a twin bed, is also a favorite. Room 20, with a wood stove and a private porch, and room 21, also with a wood stove, are in a separate wing of the house over the library. All nine rooms on the second floor have fireplaces, and third-floor rooms all have high ceilings.

Guests can have dinner at the inn; the menu of three entrées changes nightly. The night we stayed we were served mushroom leek soup, salad, and a choice of poached salmon with a dill-and-caper sauce, grilled chicken breast topped with pesto, or charbroiled filet mignon with béarnaise sauce. The dessert was peach bread pudding with warm caramel sauce. After a day of touring we enjoyed a nice wine and the relaxing candlelit atmosphere of the dining room.

Breakfast includes a choice of a hot dish such as eggs or blueberry pancakes or their special French toast stuffed with cream cheese, honeynuts, and fresh peaches.

Sixteen rooms, each with private bath, nine with fireplaces, $90–140. Full breakfast included. Children over 12 welcome. No pets. No smoking. Dinner available nightly by reservation, $25–$29. Dinner for outside diners by reservation Wednesday through Sunday at 7 P.M. One-quarter mile north of Windsor (Route 5). RR1 Box 79, Juniper Hill Road, Windsor, VT 05089; (802) 674-5273; (800) 359-2541.

The Hanover Inn at Dartmouth College, Hanover, NH

This four-story brick neo-Georgian hotel owned and operated by Dartmouth College overlooks the campus green. It is the only place to stay in Hanover, and is booked far in advance for all college occasions such as football games and graduation. The interior recently received a much-needed refurbishing. The price of a room depends on whether it has a view of the campus or the city. All the rooms are newly carpeted, and baths have green marble countertops. The best rooms are 321 and 327, the ones usually reserved for visiting dignitaries when they are in town to lecture. The fourth-floor rooms have more limited views and slightly less space, as they have dormer windows. Dining options at the hotel include the Ivy Grill for casual meals or the formal Daniel Webster Room. Lunch also is served on the front terrace during the summer.

Ninety-two rooms, all with private bath, $207–$277. All meals available. Children welcome. No pets. Box 151, On the Green, Hanover, NH 03755; (603) 643-4300; (800) 443-7024.

Moose Mountain Lodge, Etna, NH

"On the mountain nothing needs to be perfect," reads the sign over the door of this rustic log-and-stone lodge. That relaxed attitude is exactly what makes Moose Mountain an ideal getaway. In fact, Kay and Peter Shumway had one request when we asked how to describe the 350-acre mountaintop home: "Please understate us." So we'll try to recommend Moose Mountain in an understated manner.

First, the lodge has panoramic views of the Green Mountains sixty-five miles to the west. In winter, it has thirty-five kilometers of cross-country ski trails and ice-skating on a nearby pond. In summer, Tulla, the family's weimaraner, happily will lead you on a hike through the woods, where you can pick wild berries and return for a refreshing swim in the pond. (You might even see a moose; we spotted tracks by the beaver pond.) And yes, we have seen acres of rainbow-colored wildflowers before—but only in mail-order seed catalogs.

The accommodations are appropriately simple. Most of the small rooms are furnished with log beds made by Kay, while others have double beds, twin beds, or bunk beds. All rooms are strictly functional, and fine for guests who plan to spend most of their time outdoors or in the large living room. During the summer the lodge is frequently used by bicycle touring groups. The greatest attraction here is the honest, healthy living. The food isn't nouvelle, just well prepared, plentiful, and served family style.

Open mid-June to late October and December 26 through early March. Twelve rooms, all with shared bath. $170 for two, breakfast and dinner included. $130 bed-and-breakfast. Lunch available in the winter. Children over 5 welcome. No smoking. No pets. Two-night weekend minimum. Box 272, Etna, NH 03750; (603) 643-3529.

WHERE TO DINE

Fine Dining

Hemingway's, Killington

Ted and Linda Fondulas, the husband-and-wife team that owns and operates this four-star restaurant, are perfectionists. If you enjoy fine dining, this is the one restaurant in the area you should not miss.

The most formal dining room is the Paris Room, with its crystal chandeliers. The plant-filled Garden Room overlooks the patio and herb garden, and has a wood-burning fireplace. Downstairs, four tables are nestled in a stone-walled wine cellar.

Subtle details make this restaurant unique. Linda creates individually designed flower arrangements for each table, and paintings, bronzes, and stone and glass sculptures by local artists are tastefully placed throughout the rooms. Ted oversees the kitchen and is the maître d' and sommelier. A four-course prix fixe menu includes choices of about five starters, three first courses, four main courses, and five desserts or cheese. Diners can also have a vegetarian menu or a set wine dinner with four wines chosen to complement each course.

The first courses included a grilled Provençal vegetable pie and a napoleon of wild mushrooms with tarragon phyllo pastry. Second courses included seared diver scallops with truffled potatoes and caramelized onion and risotto with grilled asparagus and plum tomato. The entrées were a succulent locally raised pan-roasted free-range poussin (baby chicken) with basmati rice, and pepper-crusted yellowfin tuna with mesclun greens in a crispy potato basket.

For dessert you can choose a cheese course. We also had a fresh fruit charlotte with a vanilla and raspberry web. With coffee we received a plate of truffles and miniature cookies.

Dinner, Wednesday through Sunday. Closed early November and mid-April to mid-May. Prix fixe menus $40–$46. Wine-tasting menu $65. Five miles east of Killington. Route 4, Killington, VT; (802) 422-3886.

Woodstock Inn

The main dining room is one of the most beautiful in Vermont and overlooks lush gardens, a putting green, and the Vermont Hills. The paintings are part of the inn's extensive collection of work by New England artists and worth a look even if you don't dine here. The kitchen has vastly improved in the last two years. Appetizers include duckling ravioli with prosciutto, mushroom broth, and sweet potato confetti; pistachio-coated Vermont Brie with fruits and flat bread; and Burgundy snails in flaky pastry with spinach, mushrooms, and red wine sauce. Entrées include Vermont-raised rack of lamb with truffle-whipped potatoes, eggplant, and garlic chips; and portabella mushroom and eggplant lasagna or pan-seared jumbo sea scallops in a madras curry with wilted spinach, pappadams, and grilled bananas. The menu suggests wines available by the glass for each entrée.

Sunday brunch is a major event at the hotel and rivals the best we have sampled in luxury city hotels, complete with omelette and carving stations, cold and hot plates, and an array of beautiful desserts.

Dinner nightly. Entrées $18–27. Jackets required. Fourteen the Green, Woodstock, VT; (802) 457-1100.

Kedron Valley Inn, South Woodstock

This inn serves exceptionally good food in a casual, relaxed environment where children are welcome. Among the entrées on our visit was a marvelously tender boneless breast of chicken rolled in pistachio nuts; a filet of salmon stuffed with herbed seafood mousse, wrapped in puff pastry; and shrimp, scallops, and lobster sautéed with wild mushrooms and shallots in white wine. Filet mignon, lamb tenderloin, a vegetarian plate, and shrimp and penne pasta are other choices.

A lighter tavern menu is available nightly and can be served in the dining room or in the living-room bar. Shrimp and Caesar salad, grilled chicken curry, or country-style pizza, a sourdough crust filled with tomatoes, three different cheeses, and pepperoni, are some of the selections. There's also a children's menu.

Dinner, Thursday through Monday. Entrées $16–$22. Tavern menu $7–$15. Route 106, South Woodstock, VT; (802) 457-1473.

The Prince and the Pauper, Woodstock

Along with checking the "town crier" blackboard for special events in and around Woodstock, be sure to wander down Elm Street to peek at the weekly dinner selections offered by the Prince and the Pauper. You'll find them posted in a glass-enclosed case in front of the entrance to the restaurant. Inside, we found dark wood, a beamed ceiling, paintings by local artists, and a bar made from old ship-hatch covers.

The restaurant offers a prix fixe menu that includes appetizer, salad, entrée, and coffee as well as an à la carte bistro menu served at tables in the bar section and a couple of booths in the dining room. Grilled Indonesian chicken marinated and grilled with a spicy peanut sauce, a daily pasta, and excellent hearth-baked pizza with such toppings as Vermont goat cheese, Niçoise olives, sun-dried tomatoes, and fresh herbs. Entrées from the regular menu include the house specialty of boneless lamb, duxelles, and spinach encased in a puff-pastry shell; roasted duckling with raspberries and cassis; and tournedos. A fine wine list features many unusual California selections and a good choice of wines by the glass.

Dinner nightly. Prix fixe $30. Bistro menu $10–$16. 24 Elm Street, Woodstock, VT; (802) 457-1818.

Barnard Inn, Barnard

This 1796 brick building is just south of the village of Barnard. New owners Marie France and Philip Filipovic formerly owned one of the top restaurants in Montreal. The restaurant's four dining rooms are lit by wall sconces and flickering candles in hurricane lamps. Their collection of Quebec art and crafts decorate the spotlessly clean plaster walls. Exposed wood beams, white country curtains, and wide, well-worn floors all help create a homey atmosphere. The house-smoked salmon with potato laces and a large portabella mushroom garnished with fresh mozzarella and roasted sweet pepper over spinach were excellent appetizers. The tender salad greens come from the chef's garden. Bouillabaisse is served in a copper pot. A half portion is served and the remainder is kept warm over a candle. The crispy roast duck, a favorite for many years, served partially deboned in three pieces, is still on the menu. The venison tenderloin is grilled and served with a raspberry vinegar and bitter chocolate sauce. The cheese course was a sampling of French Brie, Vermont cheddar, Danish blue, and French Roblechon very attractively served with an apple carved to look like a swan. One of the fancier desserts is the chocolate success meringue cake with chocolate filling, and homemade vanilla ice cream. The decaf coffee was served in individual pots. The bill was presented in a lacquered case along with a homemade chocolate truffle.

Dinner, Tuesday through Sunday. Closed Sunday in winter. Entrées $10–$30. Prix fixe $33. Located ten miles north of Woodstock. Route 12, Barnard, VT; (802) 234-9961.

Wild Grass, Woodstock

This new restaurant, touted by local innkeepers, serves creative American dishes in an airy dining room with large windows on the east side of Woodstock. The signature item here is the unusual crispy sage leaves served with assorted dipping sauces. Selections include spicy cioppino with clams, mussels, shrimp, crab, and fish in a rich tomato sauce; angel-hair pasta tossed with grilled wild mushrooms, yellow squash, snap peas, artichoke hearts, roasted garlic, with a red pepper coulis; adobo rubbed lamb with black bean cakes and plaintain fritters; and Jamaican jerk chicken with sweet potato puree and wilted greens.

Dinner nightly. Entrées $10–$15. On Route 4 just east of the center of Woodstock, VT; (802) 457-1917.

Simon Pearce Restaurant, Quechee

The restoration of this old woolen mill is a dynamic example of the right way to preserve the history of a region. When the weather cooperates, we like to sit overlooking the waterfall that powers the generator for the glass factory on site. The four tables along the large windows inside offer the best views of the river and the water flowing over the dam. Be sure to ask for one when making a reservation.

The hickory-smoked coho salmon (smoked here at the mill) and marinated grilled chicken with spicy peanut sauce are two of our favorite appetizers. On visits over the past years we have also enjoyed grilled pork tenderloin with corn and black bean salsa, penne pasta with broccoli rabe, sun-dried tomatoes and pine nuts in a parsley pesto sauce, and the roasted duck with mango chutney sauce. The first-rate Guinness stew adds just the right Irish flavor to the menu. For dessert, try the frozen white chocolate mousse cake. The large wine list has many expensive selections.

After dining from pottery thrown at the mill and sipping wine from glasses created on the factory floor below, you surely will be tempted to purchase something to take home. The restaurant is crowded at lunch during the tourist season and on rainy days.

Lunch and dinner daily. Lunch $8–$11; dinner entrées $15–$21. The Mill, Quechee, VT 05059; (802) 295-1470.

Informal Dining

Wasp Diner, Woodstock

This tiny thirteen-stool white shack with green shutters is tucked along Main Street in Woodstock beyond the Grand Union, and is a favorite with locals for breakfast and lunch. Tourists usually can't find it, as there is no sign.

The White Cottage

This fast-food restaurant on Route 4 west of town specializes in fried clams and burgers served at picnic tables along the river in the summer.

Mountain Creamery, Woodstock

A turkey for sandwiches and soups is roasted daily at this small luncheonette in the center of Woodstock. We feasted our eyes on the macadamia–chocolate chip–coconut cookies, maple walnut bars, and coconut–chocolate chip macaroons—but somehow managed to resist them. We also watched as waffle cones were made on the griddle and packed with scoops of Mountain Creamery's own ice cream (mud pie, mint Oreo, and Reese's peanut butter, among other flavors).

We reasoned that the large sandwich piled with freshly sliced meat that we split was much better for us than two big ice-cream cones. To resist further temptation, however, we took our sandwich to a picnic table in the tiny park located next to the restaurant along the banks of Kedron Brook.

Open daily for breakfast, lunch, and takeout. 33 Central Street (Route 4), Woodstock, VT 05091; (802) 457-1715.

Village Diner Restaurant, Bridgewater

If you arrive in the Woodstock area late at night, you'll be glad you know about this twenty-four-hour diner. The stools and booths are upholstered in blue vinyl; the jukebox is always playing; and the day we visited, there was an unmistakable haze of cigarette smoke in the air. We're not talking gourmet dining here, but you'll like the prices. The bowl of fish chowder, while heavy on the potatoes, was a good value. The fried clam roll, on the other hand, was made with clam strips (we've been spoiled by the real thing). The pies and portions are also more than adequate; we had no complaints with the coconut cream.

Open daily, 24 hours. Route 4, Bridgewater, VT 05034; (802) 672-5363.

Barnard Bakeshop, Barnard

Located in the post office building across the street from the general store, this gourmet shop is run by Michael and Jacky Recchiuti. Michael is the pastry chef at Twin Farms. In addition to the fresh baked pastries, breads, preserves, vinegars, chutneys, and sauces made at Twin Farms, you'll find many of the items used at the inn such as the Anichini unbleached 310-count Egyptian cotton sheets, robes, and towels. This is a great spot to stop for a coffee or cappuccino and pastry while on a drive through the countryside.

Open Thursday through Monday, 9 A.M. to 5 P.M. Off Route 12 at Silver Lake, Barnard, VT; (802) 234-6432.

Old Pete's, Hanover

Formerly called Peter Christian's, known by students and locals as "P. C.'s" the name change took place in 1996. This is the type of eatery that seems to exist on the perimeter of every Ivy League campus. You walk down a few steps, pass through a heavy old carved door, and enter a dimly lit grotto. The "decor" consists of old wooden booths illuminated by electric lanterns, exposed brick walls, and tables tucked into nooks and crannies. Order a few mugs of ale or beer to quaff with a sandwich, salad, or soup. Tea and scones are served in the afternoon, and the dinner menu includes such dishes as shepherd's pie, deep-dish turkey pie, lasagna, and beef stew. But don't try eating here during the football season unless you're fond of noisy crowds and Dartmouth pep songs.

Open daily, lunch, dinner, and late-night snacks $3–$10. 39 South Main Street, Hanover, NH; (603) 643-2345.

ITINERARY

If you plan to visit the Woodstock area in winter, it is probably to go downhill skiing at **Suicide Six** or cross-country skiing at the **Woodstock Ski Touring Center**. If your visit is in the spring, summer, or fall, you may want to spend a few days **hiking, biking,** or **horseback riding** from inn to inn. If **golf** is your sport, your itinerary naturally will revolve around your tee times. Any of the inns reviewed above can be used as a home base for all of these activities. We have included dinner in the following itinerary, but you should note that many inns include dinner in their room rates.

DAY ONE. Drive to **Woodstock** to check the "town crier" blackboard at the corner of Central and Elm for special events that may be of interest. Spend an hour or so at the **Billings Farm and Museum;** then, having reserved a window table at **Simon Pearce's Restaurant,** take River Road to Quechee. Head downstairs to watch the glassblowers and potters before visiting the shop. After lunch, drive to the bridge on Route 4 for a look at the **Quechee Gorge.** Drive to **Hanover and Dartmouth** to visit the lovely campus, shops, and **Hood Museum of Art.** Dine at the **Barnard Inn.**

DAY TWO. Visit **Calvin Coolidge's birthplace** in Plymouth. If you're hungry, you can get lunch or a snack here at **Wilder House**. Visit the **Raptor Center** at the Vermont Institute of Natural Science in Woodstock. Explore the galleries and shops in Woodstock. Dine at **Hemingway's.**

DAY THREE. Follow the driving tour to South Woodstock and Windsor. Visit **Saint-Gaudens Historic Site**. Dine at the **Kedron Valley Inn** or at **Wild Grass.**

DAY FOUR. This is the day to get out into the country. Hike to the bottom of **Quechee George** to the top of Mount Tom in Woodstock or to Mount Ascutney in Weathersfield. Rent bikes and tour the countryside. Go horseback riding at the Kedron Valley Stables. If you're a golfer, reserve a tee time at the Woodstock Country Club. Dine at the **Prince and the Pauper** or at **Simon Pearce.**

BUDGETING YOUR TRIP

To help you get the most for the time and money you have to spend, here are some travel suggestions at three budget levels (cost per day with two people sharing a room) including lodging and meal tax, gratuity on meals, and service charge when it is added to your bill. Prices are approximate and are intended for planning purposes only. Lodgings are categorized by price and depending on the room selected may appear in more than one category. Meal prices at lunch include an average entrée and beverage. Dinner prices include an appetizer, entrée, dessert, and beverage. Wine or alcoholic beverages are not included.

Staying and dining at expensive lodgings and restaurants: From $350 to $1,850 per day for two.

Lodging: Twin Farms, Woodstock Inn (Tavern Wing and suites), Hanover Inn, Jackson House (apartment).

Dining: Breakfast: included except the Woodstock Inn, Hanover Inn. Lunch: Woodstock Inn, Simon Pearce Restaurant. Dinner: Hemingway's, Barnard Inn, Woodstock Inn.

Staying and dining at moderately priced lodgings and restaurants: From $250 to $350 per day for two.

Lodging: Kedron Valley Inn, Woodstock Inn, Maple Leaf Inn, Charleston House, Juniper Hill Inn.

Dining: Breakfast: included except at the Woodstock Inn. Lunch: Mountain Creamery, Old Pete's. Dinner: Prince and the Pauper, Simon Pearce Restaurant, Kedron Valley Inn, Juniper Hill Inn.

Staying and dining at less expensive lodgings and restaurants: From $160 to $230 per day for two.

Lodging: October Country Inn, Moose Mountain Lodge, Juniper Hill Inn, Maple Leaf Inn, Kedron Valley Inn.

Dining: Breakfast: included. Lunch: Mountain Creamery, Wasp Diner, White Cottage, Village Diner, Barnard Bakeshop, Old Pete's. Dinner: Prince and Pauper (bistro), Wild Grass, Village Diner, Old Pete's.

4

The White Mountains of New Hampshire

I t was one of those rare September days on top of Mount Washington, when you can see the Atlantic Ocean off the coast of Maine some 130 miles in the distance. This is the highest point in the northeastern United States (6,288 feet). The temperature was in the sixties, the wind was blowing about twenty miles per hour, and it looked as though the entire world was spread out before us. The little Cog Railway engine was hissing steam. The engineer, covered in soot from his coal-fired engine, was in the cab tooting his whistle. The conductor called "Allaboard" and the train, the oldest steam tourist railroad in the world, started down the mountain.

The winter weather on this mountain duplicates the worst conditions in Antarctica, which could include winds in excess of 100 miles per hour and huge snowdrifts. The first recorded ascent of Mount Washington was in June 1642 by Darby Field and two Native Americans. Today about 50,000 hikers a year make the strenuous climb up the mountain. A few express frustration when they arrive at the top and see the visitors (about 200,000 annually) that made the climb the easy way, by the Cog Railway and in their own automobiles. The mountain has been easily accessible since 1861, when stagecoaches first took tourists to the top, the Mount Washington Cog Railway opened in 1869.

As early as 1605, European explorers, saw the mountains from the ocean. The railroads came to the area after the Civil War, bringing thousands of summer visitors who stayed at the grand hotels and resorts that were built in the valleys. Lumbermen also came in the nineteenth century, clear-cutting whole mountains, clogging streams with the logs, and causing erosion and fires on a vast scale. The Appalachian Mountain Club was organized in 1876 to preserve the mountains and forests. By 1911 the club had put enough pressure on Congress to establish the White Mountain National Forest. Thus began the long road back to the wonderful landscape we enjoy today.

In the 1930s Americans discovered skiing, and the invention of the ski lift gave the White Mountains a winter tourist season. Cross-country skiing had been a quiet sport for many years, but in the seventies waxless skis and trail-

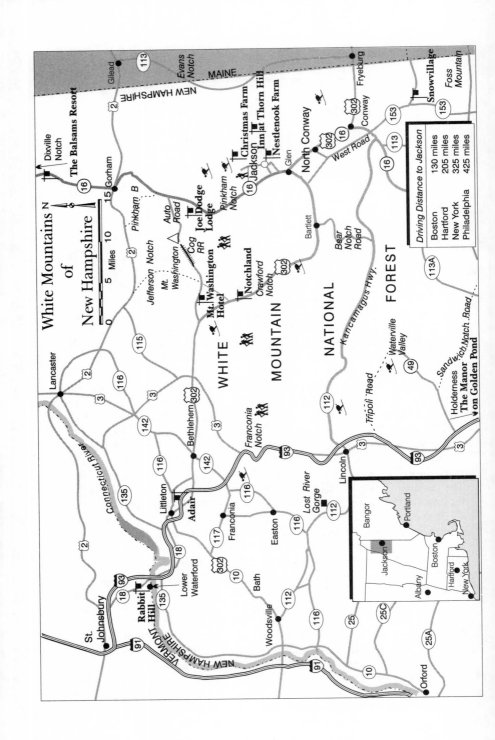

White Mountains
of
New Hampshire

N

0 5 Miles 10 15

Driving Distance to Jackson
Boston   130 miles
Hartford   205 miles
New York   325 miles
Philadelphia 425 miles

MAINE

NEW HAMPSHIRE

Evans Notch

Gilead
113

Snowvillage
Foss Mountain

Fryeburg
153

Conway
302
153

Dixville Notch
The Balsams Resort

Gorham
16
2

North Conway
302
16

West Road
113
16

Pinkham B
2

Auto Road

Joe Dodge Lodge
Pinkham Notch

Christmas Farm
Inn at Thorn Hill
Nestlenook Farm
Jackson
16
Glen

Jefferson Notch

Mt. Washington
Cog RR

Notchland
Mt. Washington Hotel
Crawford Notch
302

Bartlett

Bear Notch Road

WHITE

MOUNTAIN

NATIONAL

FOREST

115

Kancamagus Hwy.

113A

Lancaster
2

116
3

142
3

116

Bethlehem
302
3

Franconia Notch

142

93

Waterville Valley
49

Tripoli Road

Holderness
The Manor on Golden Pond

Sandwich Notch Road

Connecticut River

135

116

Littleton

Adair
116

117
Franconia

Easton
116

Lincoln
3

112

Lost River Gorge
112

Bath

302
10

Woodsville

112

116

St. Johnsbury
2

18
93

Rabbit Hill
18
135

Lower Waterford

VERMONT
NEW HAMPSHIRE

91

25

25C

Orford
25A

10

91

Bangor
Portland

Jackson

Albany
Boston

Hartford
New York

grooming machines caused a surge of interest in this sport, another reason to visit the White Mountains in winter. All these visitors needed someplace to stay. The condominium boom of the 1980s, not unlike the resort boom of the 1880s, brought many more people to the mountains. The latest craze is outlet shopping. The road between Conway and North Conway is often a slow-moving line of shoppers doing the "Conway crawl." Whether you come in the summer to hike the trails or drive through the notches, or in the winter to ski, you're sure to be impressed with the rugged beauty and grandeur of the White Mountains.

For information on special events, contact the **White Mountains Visitor's Center** (Exit 32 off I-93, Route 112, Kancamagus Highway, Box 10, North Woodstock, NH 03262; (603) 745-8720, or (800) FIND MTS outside NH), open daily 8:30 A.M. to 5 P.M., or the **Mount Washington Valley Chamber of Commerce** (Main Street, Box 2300, North Conway, NH 03860; (603) 356-3171, or (800) 367-3364, open daily 9 A.M. to 5 P.M.

WHERE TO GO, WHAT TO DO

Seeing the White Mountains by Car

An introductory driving tour

The White Mountain National Forest in northern New Hampshire and part of western Maine covers more than 750,000 acres, about the size of Rhode Island. There are eighty-six mountains, forty of which are more than 4,000 feet high, including Mount Washington at 6,288 feet, the highest point with the most severe weather in the northeastern United States.

If you have never been to the White Mountains, take a drive through the major notches, as the passes are called, with a good map. If you are coming from the north on I-93 you will drive through Franconia Notch, home of the world-famous Old Man in the Mountain, an unusual rock formation. Get off at exit 32 in Lincoln and stop at the White Mountains Visitor's Center.

Continue on through the Kancamagus Highway (pronounced kan-kuh-MAW-gus), named after an Indian chief who lived here in the seventeenth century. The thirty-four-mile "Kanc," as locals called it, was started in the 1930s by the Civilian Conservation Corps and wasn't completely finished until 1959. There are miles of trails, four overlooks, four picnic areas, and six campgrounds. We have seen moose in the marshy areas along this road. Take note of the location of the intersection of the Bear Notch Road (closed in the winter) since this is the connector road that bypasses the crowded North Conway shopping area. Just before you get to Conway on the left side is the Saco Ranger Station (603) 447-5448, open seven days a week and staffed by knowledgeable rangers with excellent information on the trails in the area.

Take a left on Route 16 passing from Conway to North Conway for an introduction to the tremendous growth of outlet shopping. To avoid the traffic and shopping in North Conway take the West Road, which starts at the light where Route 153 intersects Route 16. Assuming you elect to take the shopping route, the road splits at Glen. Route 16 goes to the right and the east of Mount Washington and Route 302 goes to the left and the west of Mount Washington.

Take the right-hand road. Route 16 skirts Jackson Village and passes through Pinkham Notch, where you can get information on the trails, reservations at the huts, and meals at the Appalachian Mountain Club. Continue on past the start of the Mount Washington Auto Road entrance. Turn left onto Route 2 in Gorham. Turn left on Route 115 to Route 3 and left on Route 302. On your left you will pass the entrance road to the base station of the Cog Railway. Almost immediately you will see the picturesque grand old Mount Washington Hotel and, if the day is clear, the top of Mount Washington. Moose are often seen along the sides of the road here at dusk, so take care. This road cuts through Crawford Notch and continues to the junction of Route 16 and Route 302 in Glen.

Jackson–Mount Washington–the Balsams–Stark–Crawford Notch or Jefferson Notch

Starting at Jackson, drive north on Route 16. Stop at the Glen Ellis Falls for an easy quarter-mile hike down the stairs. Along the way you will see the falls drop sixty-four feet. Continue to the Pinkham Notch Camp of the Appalachian Mountain Club, a good stop for information, maps, trail guides, lunch, or a snack. Take the auto road or go in a touring van to the top of Mount Washington. Turn left on Route 2 at Gorham, then follow Route 16 through the industrial town of Berlin. The smell is from the paper mills. The Androscoggin River runs parallel to the road. This is a great fishing and whitewater canoeing area. The prettiest section is the Thirteen-mile Scenic Area, south of Errol. Turn left on Route 26 to Dixville Notch where the Balsams, one of the grand hotels, is majestically framed by the mountains and a lake. The buffet lunch here is well worth the stop (*see* Where to Stay/Dine). Return to Milan, then turn right on Route 110B/110 to the village of Stark with a picture-perfect white church and covered bridge. At Groveton head south on Route 3 to Lancaster. Take Route 2 to the Jefferson Notch Road (*see* Back roads), then Route 302 past the Mount Washington Hotel through the Crawford Notch to Glen and north on Route 16 to Jackson. If the weather is not appropriate for the Jefferson Notch Road or if you are looking for an activity for children, take Route 3 to Route 2 with possible stops at Santa's Village one mile northwest of Jefferson; ((603) 586-4445) and Six Gun City (¼ mile west of the junction of Route 115; (603) 586-4592). Continue on Route 2 to Gorham and soute on Route 16 back to Jackson.

Littleton–Franconia Notch–North Woodstock–Sugar Hill

Stop at the Village Bookstore in Littleton for guides to the area. Head south on I-93 through Franconia Notch, stopping to walk to the Flume and view the Old Man in the Mountain rock formation. Other options are to take the nine-mile off-road bike path from Echo Lake to the Flume or to ride the tram to the top of Cannon Mountain. At North Woodstock head west on Route 112, stopping at Lost River to explore the chasms and the caves. Head north on Route 302 past the covered bridge and the country store in Bath, said to be this country's oldest. Turn onto Route 117 to Polly's Pancake Parlor (*see* Where to Dine). Take Route 117 back to I-93.

Jackson–Gorham–Evans Notch–Conway–Kancamagus–Lincoln

From Jackson take Route 16 to Gorham, then turn right on Route 2 to Gilead. Head south on Route 113 through Evans Notch. *Note*: The views of the notch are better when viewed heading south through the notch. The road is not maintained in winter. Of all the notches that you can drive through in the White Mountains, this is the least well known. Continue on Route 113 to Frye-burg, where a major fair is held in late September. Turn right on Route 302 to Conway. Stop at the ranger station for a map of the Kancamagus (Route 112). Highlights on the Kancamagus are the Lower Falls (6.7 miles), a good place to swim; Rocky Gorge Scenic Area (8.4 miles), where you walk across the rocks onto a wooden footbridge to view the gorge; Bear Notch Road (11.8 miles), the connector road to Bartlett; Passaconaway Historic Site (12.3 miles), an early settler's home, where costumed guides are on hand; Sabbaday Falls (14.9 miles), a series of cascading falls; Lily Pond (18.1 miles), where moose are often seen on the north side of the road; and Wilderness Trail Parking Lot (28.8 miles), where there is a long suspension bridge over the river. In Lincoln there is a visitors center just before the entrance to I-93 and many places to have lunch. You can head north on Route 3, where you'll find Clark's Trading Post, Whale's Tale Water Park, and the gondola rides at Loon Mountain. Continue on I-93; turn right on Route 3; turn right on Route 302 through the Crawford Notch to Glen; turn left on Route 16 to Jackson. An alternative and far shorter route is to take the Kancamagus in the opposite direction and take Bear Notch Road to Route 302 and north to Jackson on Route 16.

Back roads. For these back-road driving tours we recommend detailed county maps, signs often are down or nonexistent, and it's easy to get lost.

If your idea of back-roading is finding the narrow dirt or gravel roads that are barely wide enough for two cars and passable only in the summer and early fall, here are four roads you'll enjoy. A four-wheel-drive vehicle is not required unless you have a low car or travel in spring mud season.

Tripoli Road is an eleven-mile road that starts at exit 31 off I-93, south of North Woodstock, and goes through woodland forests to Waterville Valley. During the summer, particularly on weekends, this is an extremely popular camping area since there are no fees and no restrictions on the number of campers per site.

Sandwich Notch Road is a left turn off Route 49 about six miles south of Waterville Valley. The narrow dirt road winds for ten miles through the forests and through clearings to Center Sandwich. We found this road a bit more rutted than the Tripoli Road; if you have difficulty on the Tripoli Road, skip this route and take Route 49 back to I-93. Sandwich Notch Road starting from the Waterville Valley end is more clearly marked.

Jefferson Notch Road. From Route 302 follow the Cog Railway Base Station Road to Jefferson Notch Road. The southern part of this nine-mile gravel twisty road is in better condition than the northern part. The road reaches the highest point of any public road in New Hampshire. Coming from the south, the notch is at mileage 3.4 at an elevation of 3,008 feet. The road ends at Valley Road, where you turn right to get to Route 2.

Pinkham B Road. This is a short wilderness road connecting Route 16 north of the Mount Washington auto road with Route 2. The popular Dolly Copp Campground is off this road. Trailheads to some of the higher peaks in the Presidential Range start off this road.

Seeing the White Mountains on Foot

Whether your aim is to spend an hour, a day, or several days on the trail, the White Mountains offer opportunities for all types of hikers on more than 1,000 miles of trails. The majority of people we passed while walking on anything but roadside trails came prepared with hiking boots. The terrain in the White Mountains is rocky. Break in a pair of hiking boots before you come; their thick soles and ankle support reduce the chance of injury. Plan to hike with a pack large enough to hold sweaters, rain gear, snacks, and water. The temperature drops ten to twenty degrees when you climb above the tree line and the effect of wind in the exposed areas will make you glad that you carried extra clothing. Don't drink water on the trail unless you properly treat it no matter how pristine it looks; it could contain *Giardia lamblia*, an organism that causes an extremely unpleasant intestinal disorder called giardiasis. Carry insect repellent, especially during June and early July when the black flies are most active. Timely weather information can be obtained from the National Weather Service at (603) 225-5191.

The Appalachian Mountain Club. The AMC maintains one self-service and seven full-service "huts" in the White Mountains, spaced about a day's hike apart. Hikers walk from hut to hut carrying only their personal belongings, a sheet or sleeping bag, and food for lunch. The full-service huts are staffed by four or more employees who prepare meals and pack in food a couple of times a week. Accommodations at the huts are in coed bunk rooms. At some of the huts there are two bunk rooms on either side of a central dining room, each holding eighteen to twenty-five people in bunk beds stacked three or four high. Other huts have a couple of buildings with smaller sleeping quarters holding four to fifteen people with standard two-person bunk beds. Accommodations include flush or chemical toilets. When we arrived at Zealand Hut we were greeted by the cook, who was preparing a turkey dinner for the thirty-six hikers who would be spending the night. Other nights chicken, ham, roast beef, or a vegetarian entrée is served with freshly baked bread, salad, vegetable, and dessert. Fresh eggs or pancakes are the usual breakfast.

Summer weekends tend to be booked far in advance. (Reservations are taken for the following year starting on November 1.) Since some of the full-service huts remain open through the mid-October fall foliage season, the weeks after Labor Day are an ideal, less crowded time to stay at the huts. The accommodations at the different huts and the surrounding terrain vary considerably; some huts are best for a family, while others are geared toward more serious hikers. During the summer, the AMC operates a shuttle bus to take hikers from their car to the trailhead. Some of the huts are open throughout the year on a self-service basis. They make a good base for wilderness cross-country skiing, snowshoeing, or hiking.

To learn more about the specific huts, the self-service hostel at Crawford Notch, or the Joe Dodge Lodge at Pinkham Notch Camp (*see* Where to Stay) and how to make reservations, write or call the Appalachian Mountain Club for a guide to the huts (603-466-2721 ext. 116). To make reservations at one of the eight huts or at the Joe Dodge Lodge at Pinkham Notch call (603) 466-2727 or write to Reservations, Pinkham Notch Camp, Gorham, NH 03581.

Pinkham Notch Camp. Route 16, north of Jackson. This is the Appalachian Mountain Club's North Country base. If you haven't planned ahead, you can stop by or call to see if there is room at one of the huts. The best chance for a last-minute reservation is midweek in June or after Labor Day. You can get information here about any of the trails, and purchase supplies, maps, and trail guides. If you are hiking to the huts, you will want either the *AMC White Mountain Guide* or the *AMC Guide to Mt. Washington and the Presidential Range*. If short one- or two-hour hikes are more your style, *Short Hikes & Ski Trips around Pinkham Notch* or *Waterfalls of the White Mountains* will provide you with a good variety of hikes for this area of the White Mountains.

Limmer hiking boots. Since 1951 the Limmer family has made hiking boots to order in Intervale, New Hampshire. Limmer boots are worn by serious hikers throughout the world. The tops are made from a single piece of thick leather sewn with a single seam on the instep strengthened with six rows of stitches; the Vibram soles can be replaced; and each pair is customized to your foot. If you order a pair, you must wait twelve to thirteen months to receive it. The price is finalized at the time the boots are made, but the hiking boots cost about $270 and golf or walking shoes cost about $125. If you have a standard-sized foot, Limmer boots machine-made in Germany are far less expensive and are in stock at the Limmer workshop.

Open Monday through Saturday, 8 A.M. to 5 P.M. If you are coming from the south, the building is on the left before you get to Mountain Vale Inn. Route 16A, P.O. Box 88, Intervale, NH 03845; (603) 356-5378.

Mount Washington

There are three ways to get to the 6,288-foot summit: walk; take the Cog Railway that climbs up from Crawford Notch on the west side, or drive your own car or take the touring van up the auto road that starts from the eastern side of the mountain at Pinkham Notch.

The Tuckerman's Ravine Trail. The most popular hiking trail to the summit leaves from Pinkham Notch camp. Allow about 4.5 hours of strenuous hiking with an elevation gain of 4,200 feet. The slope starting at the base of Tuckerman's Ravine to the top is especially steep.

Cog Railway. Completed in 1869, this is the oldest operating railroad in the world whose sole purpose is to haul tourists. The little coal-fired engines with slanted smokestacks (built this way because of the steep incline) push one car up the track. The center rail of the track is notched for the cogwheels. The cog provides the traction (and braking) so that the train, going up an average grade of 25 percent and traveling at four miles per hour, can make it up the 3.25-mile track to the top of the mountain. Open early May to early November, weather permitting; weekends only at the beginning and end of the season. Adults $35. Three hours round-trip. Route 302, Bretton Woods, NH 03589; (603) 846-5404; (800) 922-8825, ext 2.

Auto Road. If there is good visibility at the top of Mount Washington, change your plans for the day and drive to the top, since about half of the time the top of the mountain has a cloud cover. The day we went up in early September there was 100-mile visibility and the next day it was only fifty feet! The company that owns and maintains the road has eleven vans with driver-guides that make continuous trips throughout the day. A disadvantage is that the van ride allows thirty minutes on top of the mountain, barely time to dash through the museum and visit the Tip Top House, a museum in the original lodge.

Mid-May to mid-October, daily (weather permitting). Private car (includes audio tour on cassette tape) toll: car and driver $14, adult passenger $5. Guided fare: adults $18. Route 16, Pinkham Notch, NH (mailing address Box 278, Gorham, NH 03518); (603) 466-3988.

Seeing the White Mountains on Skis

Cross-country Skiing. Many travelers consider Jackson the top cross-country ski center in New England. The Jackson Ski Touring Foundation main-

The Cog Railway train carries passengers to the top of Mount Washington.

tains 156 kilometers of trails in and around Jackson; about half of them are groomed and tracked and the other half are mapped and marked by level of difficulty. The trails cross town-owned lands, National Forest lands, and through townspeople's lands, so the terrain varies widely. We like this area for cross-country skiing because you can take a loop trail from your inn and have a choice of restaurants in Jackson for lunch. The most popular trail is the seven-mile Ellis River trail that goes at a gentle upgrade to Dana Place Inn, where you can stop for lunch (check in advance to make sure the restaurant is open). If you don't want to ski back you can take a shuttle bus, which operates on the weekends and at peak times (check on that day to make sure the shuttle is operating). The Jack Frost Ski Shop, located in the center of Jackson, has sports clothing and rental equipment.

There are also cross-country touring centers at the Balsams, Bretton Woods, Franconia, Loon, and Waterville Valley.

Downhill Skiing. There are nine ski areas within the White Mountains: Attitash, the Balsams/Wilderness, Black Mountain, Bretton Woods, Cannon, Cranmore, Loon, Waterville Valley, and Wildcat. You can write or call to get the current year's free *Ski the White Mountains of New Hampshire* guide, which lists phone numbers for each of the ski areas along with rates, information on ski lessons, children's programs, and discount packages. White Mountains Visitor's Center, Box 10, North Woodstock, NH 03262; (603) 745-8720; (800) FIND-MTS (outside NH).

Other Activities

Cannon Aerial Tram. This is our pick of the trams or gondola rides. The tram car holds eighty people and rises steeply to the 4,200-foot summit that's above the timberline. If the weather is clear you can see into Maine, Vermont, and Canada. Plan on taking the panoramic Rim Trail and going to the observation fire tower. There are cafeterias at the base and the summit. To learn about the history of skiing, visit the New England Ski Museum located next to the base station.

Open mid-May through October. Adults $9. Exit 2 off I-93, Franconia Notch, NH; (603) 823-5563.

The Flume. On a hot day, this is one of our favorite places to visit. It's even a good choice for a misty or cloudy day for the views from the boardwalks down into the chasm. The Flume, a minicanyon about 700 feet long, is a narrow gorge with sheer walls. The boardwalk and system of staircases takes you through the gorge.

Open mid-May through late October. Adults $6. Exit 1 off I-93, Route 3, Franconia Notch, NH; (603) 745-8391.

Lost River. You can look down into this 300-foot-deep gorge or you can walk into it on a ¾-mile handcrafted wooden walkway. The self-guided tour winds down the steps and along the boardwalk past giant boulders and the rushing stream that tumbles through the gorge. You can bypass the caves or squeeze past boulders, climb up and down the ladders and walkways that go through the small caves such as the Lemon Squeezer, the Dungeon, and the Judgment Hall, and crawl and slither your way through openings that only one of us was small enough to navigate. Pay attention to the rules on the guide sheet, especially the one that says "put your wallet in your front pocket or give it to someone who is not going through the caves." The path is lit by small candles in the caves and daylight from the entrance or exit.

Open mid-May through late October. Adults $7. On Route 112, six miles west of North Woodstock. Lost River Reservation, North Woodstock, NH; (603) 745-8031.

Heritage New Hampshire. The state comes alive in this EPCOT Center–like walk through 200 years of New Hampshire history. You start with a cup of Switchel (water, sugar, ginger, molasses, and vinegar) and a rosewater cookie in England. Then you board a ship for New Hampshire that creaks and groans and rolls while a costumed interpreter tells you about the conditions of your voyage. You walk along a path and sense the isolation of a settler's cabin as you feel the cold ice and hear the wind. A life-size figure of George Washington speaks to you in the town square and fireworks light up the sky. A mill with images of children reminds you of the poor working conditions during the Industrial Revolution. The highlight is a simulated train trip through Crawford Notch.

Open mid-May through mid-October. Adults $7.50. Route 16 (next to Story Land), Glen, NH; (603) 383-9776.

Story Land. This educational landscaped amusement park brings to life the storybook characters of childhood. The park has fifteen theme rides and lots of places for young children to play. Highlights include a roller coaster, a spaceship to the moon, a raft ride where you're guaranteed to get wet, a teacup ride, and antique autos to drive. Live animals include the Billy Goats Gruff, Three Little Pigs, Mary's Little Lamb, and Baa Baa Black Sheep. The park is done in excellent taste and is well maintained.

Open daily mid-June to Labor Day, weekends only to Columbus Day. Admission $15 per person. Route 16, Glen, NH; (603) 383-4293.

Other family attractions. The White Mountains abound with summer activities, many geared to children. In the North Lincoln area the Whale's Tale Water Park has water slides, including a flume and a speed slide. Clark's Trading Post has trained bears, a train ride, and other activities. At Attitash in Bartlett there's an alpine slide and a water slide. In North Conway there's the Conway Scenic Railroad, and in Lincoln there's the Hobo Railroad. On Route 2 near Jefferson there's Six Gun City with a Wild West theme and Santa's Village. You can take a gondola ride to the top of the mountain at Loon or Wildcat ski areas.

Canoeing. Saco Bound Canoe Center rents canoes and kayaks. You can take a full- or half-day trip on the Saco River with transportation provided back to the start, or you can paddle to a campsite on the river. If you don't want your camping gear to get wet, you can set up camp at the "Landing," a wilderness campsite eleven miles down the river, and then return to start your paddle.

The Saco Bound Canoe Center is located on Route 113 east of Center Conway. Box 119, Center Conway, NH 03813; (603) 447-2177 or-3801.

Shopping in North Conway. Some love this area and others do what they can to avoid it. If the weather is rainy, expect a crowd of shoppers and a traffic jam (the Conway Crawl). The stores span about five miles of Route 16, from Conway to North Conway. The largest concentration is at the Settlers' Green Mall, with more than fifty stores that include Patagonia, J. Crew, Eddie Bauer, Brookstone, and the Globe Travel bookstore, as well as a large Sheraton Motor Inn. Other stores along the strip are Benetton, Polo/Ralph Lauren, Calvin Klein, Chuck Roast (outdoor clothing and soft luggage made locally), Timberland, Cole Haan, Leslie Fay, Dansk, Carroll Reed, and an L. L. Bean factory store. There are many more! There is no sales tax in New Hampshire.

League of New Hampshire Craftsmen. This organization runs stores throughout the state that sell craft items made by New Hampshire artists. We spent a considerable amount of time in the North Conway store, where the merchandise included Shaker boxes, inlaid tables, paintings, jewelry, pottery, and more. The store is open daily and is on Route 16, North Conway; (603) 356-2441. (Heading south on Route 16, it is on the right side of the road two doors before Peach's, a good spot for lunch.) There is another store at 99 Main Street in Lincoln, (603) 745-2166.

WHERE TO STAY

Lodgings are arranged geographically from north to south. All are in New Hampshire unless otherwise noted.

The Balsams Grand Resort, Dixville Notch
This 15,000-acre complex with its own golf course and ski slope is one of the grand destination resort hotels built in the nineteenth century.

The main building has a clay roof, turrets, towers, and a grand veranda. Rooms typically have wall-to-wall carpeting, two double beds or a king-size bed, wicker chairs with coordinated cushions, painted bureaus, and a dressing table. About fifteen rooms are renovated during each of the two off-seasons when the hotel is closed. The best rooms are 168, 268, 368, and 468, a curved corner room with six windows and views of the mountains, the flower garden, pool, lake, and Dixville Notch. Business conferences are scheduled during May, June, September, and October only. Men must wear a tie and jacket at dinner.

Open late May to mid-October and mid-December to early April. Two hundred eleven rooms and suites, all with private bath, $198–$390 for two including two meals (winter) and $306–$390 for two including three meals (summer) and use of all the facilities. Tower suite $580. 15% service charge except in summer. Extras: golf carts, ski lessons, rentals. Children welcome. No pets. Dixville Notch, NH 03576; (800) 255-0600 (outside NH); (800) 255-0800 (in NH).

Rabbit Hill Inn, Lower Waterford, VT
Tucked in the Vermont hillside overlooking the Connecticut River valley and the White Mountains of New Hampshire is Lower Waterford, a picturesque New England village. The steepled church, post office, library, and eighteenth-century homes are all painted traditional white with dark green shutters. In this storybook setting you'll find the utterly romantic Rabbit Hill Inn.

Hospitality starts when you arrive at teatime, served from 2:30 P.M. by new owners Leslie and Brian Mulcahy. The inn offers numerous large, romantic rooms with double whirlpool tubs and gas fireplaces. The newest of these "fantasy chambers" include the Loft, with its own secret staircase; the Nest, with a canopy that can be drawn completely around the bed; and the Turnabout, which is also wheelchair-accessible. Tavern Secret has a bookcase wall that opens into a huge bath with an oversize double whirlpool tub with a view of the fireplace. The third-floor Cummings Suite has a living room with a fireplace and a large private screened porch with an expansive view of the White Mountains.

Before and after dinner, guests congregate in the common rooms or the tavern for a drink in front of the fireplace. When you retire to your room, you will find that your bed has been turned down, a candle lit, and a handmade present left for you to take home. Breakfast, served at individual tables, includes a choice of two entrées.

Twenty-one rooms and suites, each with private bath, $179–$269. Full breakfast, afternoon tea, and dinner included. 15% service charge. Children over 12 welcome. No pets. No smoking. Route 18, Lower Waterford, VT 05848; (802) 748-5168; (800) 76-BUNNY.

Adair, Bethlehem

This large white three-story imposing mansion sits on 200 acres at the northern edge of the White Mountains. In 1992 Hardy and Patricia Banfield and their daughter Nancy converted it from a private home to a comfortable inn.

The front center entry hall opens into a large living room with a wood-burning fireplace and groupings of sofas and easy chairs. To the left of the main hall is the dining room. The basement Tap Room is another huge room with an honor bar, a stocked refrigerator with complimentary sodas and juices, television with VCR and a collection of movies, a piano, games, and a 1927 pool table. There is also a huge granite fireplace in this room. The wooded property includes a water garden with goldfish and a tennis court.

The second floor has four good-sized rooms, three of which have gas fireplaces. Lafayette, a suite, has French doors opening to a sitting room with a fireplace stove. Another recently completed suite has a king-size sleigh bed and gas fireplace, deck, and bath with an oversize double whirlpool tub and a separate shower.

Patricia has a collection of teapots and china cups which guests use to brew their choice of tea, served along with sweet breads or cookies. A cheese platter and beverages are set out in the game room before dinner.

Breakfast features steaming hot popovers, plus an entrée such as egg blossoms, a mixture of cheese and eggs in a flaky phyllo crust; eggs Benedict; or cinnamon raisin French toast made with Bailey's Irish Cream.

Nine rooms, all with private bath, $205–$290, breakfast, tea, and dinner included. Bed-and-breakfast rates $135–$220. Children welcome. No smoking. No pets. I-93 exit 40 right at end of the ramp, then immediate left. Old Littleton Road, Bethlehem, NH 03574; (603) 444-2600; (800) 441-2606.

The Mount Washington Hotel, Bretton Woods

This massive white structure is a New England icon of a bygone era. In addition to the hotel, which is not winterized, the property includes the Bretton Arms, a restored Victorian inn; the Lodge at Bretton Woods, which is more like a motel with an indoor pool, sauna, and Jacuzzi; and Bretton Woods Town-houses, which range in size from one to five bedrooms.

The hotel is open late May through mid-October. One hundred seventy-five rooms, all with private bath, $185–$225. Full breakfast and dinner included. The Bretton Arms Inn, $99–$129; Lodge, $89–$129; and condominiums, $115–$335 are open year-round. Lower rates midweek. Children welcome. 16% service charge on the meal portion of the rates. Route 302, Bretton Woods, NH 03575; (603) 278-1000; (800) 258-0330.

The Notchland Inn, an 1862 granite mansion, sits on a 400-acre property in the midst of the White Mountains.

The Notchland Inn, Harts Location

This secluded 1862 granite mansion sits on a spectacular 400-acre property in the midst of the White Mountains. The front parlor was designed by Gustav Stickley, a founder of the nineteenth-century Arts and Crafts movement. Combine the location with good dining and warm welcoming innkeepers Ed Butler, a former health professional, and Les Schoof, formerly the managing director of the American Ballet Theatre in New York City, and you have a winner. Coco, the owners' Bernese mountain dog, welcomes guests; other animals on the property include a Belgian draft horse, two llamas, and two miniature horses.

After a day of hiking or skiing, guests can soak in the wood-fired hot tub that sits in the gazebo next to the pond (and from which there's a great view). The Davis Path to Mount Crawford starts across the road, and hiking trails to

Arethusa Falls and Frankenstein Cliffs are close by. The inn has 8,000-foot frontage on the Saco River, one of the best swimming holes in the area, and five miles of groomed cross-country ski trails.

All rooms and suites have queen-or king-size beds and wood-burning fireplaces. The Kinsman Suite has a king-size bed and a large living room with an exquisite Japanese wedding kimono mounted on the wall. Our favorite is the Crawford Room, the front corner room with a king-size bed. Two additional suites located over the dining room with whirlpool tubs and fireplaces are under construction. We also like Dixville, the second-floor suite in the School-house, a building next to the inn, for its large, arched living-room window with a view of the valley.

Eleven rooms and suites, all with private bath, $150–$190. Foliage and holiday periods $180–$230. Breakfast and dinner for two included. 15% gratuity. Bed-and-breakfast rates $40 less. Children welcome. Baby-sitting available. No smoking. No pets. Hart's Location, NH 03812; (603) 374-6131; (800) 866-6131.

Joe Dodge Lodge, AMC, Pinkham Notch

This is a good place to stay and eat if you have come to the White Mountains to hike or if you don't want to spend much money. Rooms are on two floors and share toilets. Most of the accommodations are two- or four-bunk bed-rooms; two rooms have double beds. The small rooms are clean and furnished simply with a wooden bench and a simple wooden bureau. When you arrive you are given a towel; bring your own washcloth and soap. We stayed for two nights and enjoyed the accessibility to the trails, the views of the mountains, and the wood-burning fireplace in the library and the living room. During our stay, other guests included families, hikers, and people attending outdoor courses at Pinkham Notch.

The Lodge is next to the Appalachian Mountain Club's Pinkham Notch headquarters, which has information on hiking, serves meals, and sells maps, books, and hiking equipment. Courses are given throughout the year for all ages in backpacking, photography, ecology, geology, and other subjects.

Thirty-two rooms; nine rooms with double beds accommodating two to four people. Bathrooms on the first and second floors. Standard rates on weekends, February, late June through early September, and holidays, adults $29 (bunk room). Larger private rooms start at $65. Members of the AMC get a $7 discount per night. Breakfast $6, dinner $12. Tax included. Located on Route 16 at Pinkham Notch. Appalachian Mountain Club, Box 298, Gorham, NH 03581; (603) 466-2727 for reservations; (603) 466-2721, ext. 116 for information.

Christmas Farm Inn, Jackson Village

This is an inn equally appropriate for families with children and honeymooners seeking privacy. Bill and Sydna Zeliff have owned the inn for many years. Guest accommodations include the Main Inn, the Salt Box, the Barn, and seven cottages extending up a hill in Jackson Village. There is a heated pool, a cabana and snack bar, shuffleboard, a putting green, a volleyball area, a play area with children's toys, and a hot tub. The first floor of the Barn is a multipurpose room used for group functions or as a recreation center with bumper pool, large-screen television, video games, Ping-Pong, and board games. In the winter it is a cross-country ski center, and on winter weekends a skiers' lunch is served here.

The rooms in the Main Inn and the Salt Box building are decorated with Laura Ashley fabrics. Five of the rooms in these two buildings have double Jacuzzis set into alcoves in the bedroom. All rooms have telephones.

Of the cottages, the North Pole, at the top of the hill, has the best view. Its interior is similar to the other two-bedroom cottages: a casual country living room with a fireplace, cable television, couches, and easy chairs. We like the rustic Log Cabin with log walls and a high-ceilinged living room with a fireplace.

Thirty rooms, suites, and cottages, all with private bath, $136–$190, breakfast and dinner for two included. Children welcome. 15% service charge. No pets. Box CC, Jackson Village, NH 03846; (603) 383-4313; (800) HI-ELVES.

The Inn at Thorn Hill, Jackson Village

This 1895 home designed by Stanford White is up the street from the center of Jackson Village. Innkeepers Jim and Ibby Cooper purchased the property in 1992 and since then have made it one of the top inns in the area with one of the best restaurants in the state.

The first floor includes two common rooms, a restaurant, bar, and lounge area with a television, and a wicker-filled front porch with views of the mountains. Within the main inn our favorites are room 1, with a Victorian queen-size bed, and room 2, which has a queen-size bed with a carved high headboard and front view of the mountains. Both rooms have original wood floors with Oriental rugs. Other rooms and suites are equally large with views of the mountains.

The three cottages, certainly the most deluxe accommodations and perfect for guests seeking seclusion, were recently renovated and expanded. Each has a huge new bath with a double whirlpool tub and separate shower as well as a gas fireplace.

The carriage house has country-style rooms with knotty pine walls, a queen-size bed and a daybed, and a first-floor great room with a wood-burning fireplace, which makes it a particularly popular building in winter. There's a hot tub on the deck and a large swimming pool adjacent to this building.

A full breakfast, served from 8 to 9:30 A.M., includes a cold buffet of juices, fruit, cereals, and sweet breads. Entrées the day we stayed included delicious crispy French toast rolled in corn flakes topped with blueberry plum sauce, and cheddar-and-tomato omelettes.

Seventeen rooms and suites, and three cottages, $150–$250, breakfast and dinner for two included. 15% service charge. Bed-and-breakfast rate $15 less per person. Children over 12 welcome. No pets. No smoking. Thorn Hill Road, Box A, Jackson Village, NH 03846; (603) 383-4242; (800) 289-8990.

Nestlenook Farm, Jackson Village

This deluxe Victorian bed-and-breakfast is situated on sixty-five acres over-looking formal gardens, a heated swimming pool, a Victorian chapel, and a three-acre stocked trout pond.

Guests can enjoy a vast amount of private space whether they come in the summer or winter. In winter, activities include horse-drawn sleigh rides, ice-skating on the pond, and hot chocolate and cookies in front of the massive fireplace in the gazebo. In summer, guests can go horseback riding or swim in the pool. The basement recreation room has a billiard table, a dartboard, and a state-of-the-art surround-sound video system for evenings and rainy days.

All rooms have phones and whirlpool tubs (five are double whirlpools); one room has a wood-burning fireplace. The Murdoch and McConnell Suites have air-conditioning; the others have fans. Our top choice is the third-floor Mur-doch Suite with a bath as big as a bedroom; you can view the grounds from the double whirlpool tub. The king-size bed in the William Paskell Room faces the wood-burning fireplace.

Wine and cheese are served in the afternoon, and in the evening you can munch fresh popcorn while you view movies on laser disc. Breakfast includes fresh orange juice, fruit, cereals, and an entrée such as Belgian waffles with whipped cream and fruit, cinnamon French toast, or oven-baked omelettes.

Seven rooms and suites, all with private bath, $125–$215. Foliage season and winter, $175–$270. Breakfast and hors d'oeuvres included. Sleigh rides, mountain bikes, Nordic skiing, ice-skating, rowboats, and fishing included. 15% service charge. Children over 12 welcome. No pets. No smoking. Dinsmore Road, Jackson Village, NH 03846; (603) 383-9443; (800) 659-9443.

Snowvillage Inn, Snowville

It's the out-of-the-way location at the base of Foss Mountain, the views of the Presidential Range, and personable innkeepers Barbara and Kevin Flynn that give this inn a special charm. A spectacular perennial border lining both sides of the long entrance drive leads to the red clapboard inn framed by the moun-tains.

The inn includes the main building; the carriage house, which has been converted into eight pine-paneled, simply furnished rooms; and a newer building with four rooms, each with a wood-burning fireplace, a queen-size bed, and easy chairs. These rooms surround a central high-ceilinged lounge with another wood-burning fireplace and a picture window. Staying in the main inn gives guests easy access to the long screened porch, which has fabulous views of the mountains. The Robert Frost Room in the main inn is directly above this porch and has a full front view of the mountains from the queen-size bed.

A hearty traditional breakfast includes a full menu with a choices of eggs, pancakes, French toast, or a fitness breakfast of yogurt, fresh fruit, and cereal.

At some point during your stay be sure to drive up the dirt road behind the inn and walk up Foss Mountain to experience one of the best panoramic views of the White Mountains that's easily accessible without a lot of climbing. The inn also has cross-country ski equipment and ten kilometers of trails.

Eighteen rooms, all with private bath, $139–$189, full breakfast and dinner for two included. Foliage and winter holidays $159–$209. Limited outside dining by reservation. Children over 6 welcome. 15% service charge. No smoking. No pets. From Conway go 7 miles south on Route 153 to Snowville sign. Snowville, NH 03849; (603) 447-2818; (800) 447-4345.

The Manor on Golden Pond, Holderness

This deluxe 1907 inn on thirteen acres on a hill overlooking and fronting Squam Lake is just south of the White Mountains. Since purchasing the inn in 1992, innkeepers David and Bambi Arnold have upscaled the inn and have totally redone every room with an individual decor, quality furnishings, and fine designer fabrics. Common areas include two sitting rooms, the Three Cocks Pub, and terraces set with lawn furniture.

Within the inn, ten rooms have wood-burning fireplaces; many also have private decks with lake views. All rooms have televisions and phones. The three best rooms are Norfolk, Avon, and Wellington, each a large room with an extra-large double whirlpool tub in an alcove, a king-size bed, a wood-burning fireplace, a private deck, and a separate bath with a shower. Stratford is designed to look like a trapper's lodge with a king-size canopy bed, barnboard walls with mounted antlers, snowshoes, animal skins, and a bearskin rug. Windsor, a fireplace room, has the best panoramic view of the lake.

The carriage house rooms are far more simply furnished. Among the cottages, Dover has a fireplace and is the only one next to the lake. Two additional cottages also have fireplaces. Inn facilities also include a tennis court, a large swimming pool, and canoes. The lake has a small beach area and a swimming raft. During the summer you can take a sight-seeing boat around the lake.

Breakfast includes a cold buffet of juice, fruit salad, yogurt, and granola as well as a hot entrée such as pancakes with sausage patties.

The inn has seventeen rooms and suites, all with private bath, $190–$325, dinner and breakfast for two included. 15% service charge. Children over 12 welcome in the inn. No smoking. No pets. The carriage house, four rooms with private bath and two suites with kitchen (rented by the night) and four two-bedroom cottages with kitchens do not include meals (rented by the week, $950–$1500). Children welcome. No pets. Box T, Route 3, Holderness, NH 03245; (603) 968-3348; (800) 545-2141.

WHERE TO DINE

Fine Dining

The Inn at Thorn Hill, Jackson

This small restaurant in a well-regarded Victorian inn operated by innkeepers Jim and Ibby Cooper is one of the finest in New Hampshire. Ask to sit in the larger of the two dining rooms.

Appetizers on the July evening we dined included smoked swordfish samosa, a pan-fried pastry filled with grilled smoked swordfish, fresh artichokes, and oven-dried tomatoes; and chicken and Gorgonzola involtini, marinated herbed chicken and Gorgonzola cheese roasted in grape leaves and served with a sauce of wild mushrooms and roasted fresh tomatoes.

Entrées included a large portion of fresh linguine with calamari, mussels, and seared greens in a tomato curry sauce with pickled garlic and toasted cashews; grilled sirloin steak with a pepper pumpkin seed crust and a zinfandel and fresh tarragon sauce; and mahimahi served on mushroom polenta with a sun-dried tomato and bacon cream sauce. The award-winning wine list is extensive and includes a special selection of wines chosen to complement the current menu. For dessert, chocolate lovers will go for the flourless chocolate cake; we had cappuccino bread pudding and ripe native strawberries with crème anglaise.

Closed midweek in April. Dinner nightly, 6 to 9 P.M. Entrées $17–$20. A limited number of reservations are accepted for guests not staying at the inn. No smoking. Thorn Hill Road, Jackson Village, NH; (603) 383-4242.

Rabbit Hill Inn, Lower Waterford, VT

Dining at the Rabbit Hill Inn is a creative and well-orchestrated culinary experience. The background music is provided by an accomplished guitarist, who built a seven-string instrument specifically to play at the inn. "Rabbity" details include the butter pats, napkin rings, and porcelain table decorations.

The prix fixe dinner includes choices at each course and changes seasonally. Appetizers from recent spring and summer menus included chicken and foie gras timbale with chervil and roasted corn, smoked Vermont tenderloin of lamb with grilled sweet potato polenta, and tuna ceviche. A choice of salads included grilled cucumber and melon with roasted red peppers and spiced cashews, a salad of baby greens, or a classic Caesar salad. A taste of pineapple cranberry sorbet in champagne followed.

Entrées included a grilled duck breast with Chinese spices served with pineapple bread pudding; eggplant, potato, and oyster mushroom gratin with fresh mozzarella cheese; and smoked tenderloin of beef and grilled grits with goat cheese and fried green peas.

For dessert we had thin Hungarian hazelnut pancakes covered with peaches and strawberries and a caramel sauce, and frozen chocolate mousse cake with layers of mocha, white chocolate, and dark chocolate topped with hot fudge and whipped cream.

Dinner nightly. Seatings at 6 and 8:15 P.M. Prix fixe $34. A limited number of reservations are accepted for guests not staying at the inn. Route 18, Lower Waterford, VT; (802) 748-5168; (800) 76-BUNNY.

Christmas Farm Inn, Jackson

It's always Christmas at the Christmas Farm Inn; the decor features a red-and-green carpet, red-and-green wallpaper, green-and-white tablecloths, and a showcase of Christmas plates illuminated with tiny white lights.

The menu has a large selection of heart-healthy items. Sample entrées include vegetable stuffed chicken; mixed grill of lamb, pork, and portabella mushrooms; grilled smoked sirloin with grilled onion salsa; and Thai shrimp with spicy curry. The menu also includes a choice of pastas and sauces. Saturday night specials are fish chowder and prime rib.

Dinner nightly. A limited number of reservations are accepted for guests not staying at the inn. Entrées $14–$19. Route 16B, Jackson Village, NH; (603) 383-4313.

Snowvillage Inn, Snowville

Hors d'oeuvres are served in the living room by a large wood-burning fireplace or on the screened porch with wicker furniture and great mountain views. Dinner is served from 6:30 to 8 P.M. in the wood-paneled Swiss country dining room with a view of the mountains. A four-course dinner always includes Mediterranean fish soup with Swiss cheese and rouille as one of the appetizer choices. Melon and prosciutto and two kinds of pâté were on the summer menu. A salad is followed by a selection of about seven entrées: roast duck with port sauce, grilled shrimp with red pepper puree, poached salmon or baked halibut with beurre blanc, and rack of lamb were some of the choices on a recent menu. A rich chocolate cake topped off our meal.

Dinner nightly 6 to 8:30 P.M., entrées $16–$22. A limited number of reservations are accepted for guests not staying at the inn. From Conway go 7 miles south on Route 153 to Snowville sign. Snowville, NH 03849; (603) 447-2818; (800) 447-4345.

The Notchland Inn, Harts Location

Dinner at this secluded 1862 granite mansion is served at 7 P.M. at individual tables. One side of the dining room overlooks the pond and the gazebo, while the other side has a view of the perennial gardens and the mountains. The good home-style cooking includes a choice of two soups, two appetizers, three entrées, salad, and three desserts. The soups, appetizers, and desserts are brought around to the table on a tray so you can decide on the spot which choice catches your fancy. The night we stayed we tried the white bean and dill as well as the creamed broccoli and watercress soups. For the second course we tried small pieces of puff pastry topped with mozzarella and sliced tomato, and mussels broiled with garlic butter. Entrée choices were tender boneless rolled chicken with Brie and herbs, grilled shrimp, and a small steak served with mashed yams and spinach. From the rolling dessert cart we had the summer fruit pie and the white and dark chocolate truffle cake. It's a tradition at this inn to have seconds on dessert.

Dinner nightly for inn guests. A limited number of reservations are accepted for guests not staying at the inn, Wednesday through Sunday, 7 P.M. Prix fixe $30. Route 302, Hart's Location, NH; (603) 374–6131; (800) 866-6131.

Tim-Bir Alley at Adair, Bethlehem

This restaurant is operated by a husband-and-wife team at Adair (*see* Where to Stay), and the food is some of the best in the region. The menu includes three appetizers and a soup, six entrées, and four desserts.

For starters try the thin grilled eggplant slices topped with feta cheese, chopped tomato, and a light basil sauce or sautéed shrimp on Brie and onion pancakes with dill cream. The entrées are served on large glass plates with a creative selection of vegetables. Sliced roasted pork with slivered almonds and poached pears was surrounded by a tiny potato pancake topped with a dollop of sour cream, polenta with basil pesto, broccoli, roasted potato with sour cream and dill, a zucchini-and-ricotta pancake, and baby carrots. Catfish was served with a corn tomato salsa and the same vegetable display. Desserts range from a peach-blueberry strudel with strawberry puree and caramel sauce to a chocolate hazelnut pâté with Kahlúa cream.

Dinner served Wednesday through Saturday, Sunday during the summer and foliage season. Entrées $14–$17. No credit cards. Old Littleton Road, Bethlehem, NH; (603) 444-2600.

Manor on Golden Pond, Holderness

This deluxe 1907 inn is on thirteen acres and overlooks Squam Lake. Before dinner have a drink in the Cocks Pub, an intimate piano bar with small copper-topped tables and numerous decorative roosters.

Two dining rooms include the dark wood-paneled former billiard room with beamed ceiling and leaded windows and a second room adjacent to the pub that overlooks a terrace. The presentation of the plates is particularly attractive. The leisurely five-course meal includes a choice of three appetizers and three desserts. The menu changes every night. Dinner might start with chilled carrot soup followed by crispy skate with Thai sauce, rabbit and duck cassoulet, or layered phyllo with wild mushrooms. The salad also changes nightly. We had entrées of steamed mussels in flavorful broth with garlic bread, and medium rare sliced Magret duck breast. The third choice was a veal chop. The evening's dessert might be wine-poached pears with chocolate crème fraîche or strawberry sorbet with white chocolate mousse.

Dinner nightly, prix fixe $50. A limited number of reservations are accepted for guests not staying at the inn. Route 3, Holderness, NH; (603) 968-3348; (800) 545-2141.

Informal Dining

Polly's Pancake House, Sugar Hill

This family-run restaurant has a view of Kinsman Ridge and the Easton Valley below. Each waitress cooks her customers' orders on a griddle to one side of the dining room. A regular order is six three-inch pancakes; choose from plain, cornmeal, buckwheat, whole wheat, or oatmeal-buttermilk pancakes or waffles with blueberry, walnut, or coconut fillings. The maple syrup, maple sugar, and maple spread served with the pancakes are made right here.

The lunch menu includes cob-smoked bacon, lettuce, and tomato on toasted homemade oatmeal bread, grilled Reubens, or Croque Monsieur.

Open late April through mid-October, Monday through Thursday, breakfast and lunch; Friday through Sunday, 7 A.M. to 7 P.M. $3–$13. Route 117, Sugar Hill, NH; (603) 823-5575.

Wildcat Inn and Tavern, Jackson

This rambling old building houses five intimate dining rooms and an atmospheric pub with two wood-burning fireplaces. For lunch try the lobster Benedict or a large sandwich of turkey, avocado, bacon, and melted cheddar or another of avocado slices, sprouts, tomato, and mushrooms served open-face on dark rye with melted cheese.

At dinner we were seated in one of the candlelit smaller porch dining rooms. The blackened swordfish was a thick steak with béarnaise sauce. The Extravaganza is a large plate of shrimp, lobster, and scallops sautéed with garlic, green peppers, onions, mushrooms, and tomatoes. Lower-priced tavern suppers include Korean-grilled chicken breast served with a salad, and baked lasagna.

More than sixteen desserts are listed on small chalkboards. We shared the wilderness ice-cream pie built with a chocolate cookie crust, a layer of ice cream blended with crème de cacao, another layer of ice cream blended with crème de menthe, topped with hot fudge and whipped cream.

Breakfast, lunch, and dinner daily. Lunch $6–$9. Dinner entrées $15–$21. Jackson Village, NH; (603) 383-4245.

The Thompson House Eatery, Jackson

For summer dining we particularly like the outdoor awning-covered patio at this casual old red farmhouse restaurant. Bring your appetite, as the chef-owner believes in large portions. The bread basket had slices of raisin and chocolate chip bread. A bowl of greens came with a crock of cranberry salad dressing and a muffin tin filled with assorted crunchy toppings. Chicken San Remo, a mound of sautéed chicken, sweet peppers, onions, eggplant, and sun-dried tomatoes, was more than we could finish. Large gulf shrimp and bay scallops were broiled with sweet red peppers in roasted garlic olive oil and white wine, served over roasted leeks and fennel.

Open daily, mid-December through March, May through early October. Lunch, $4–$10. Dinner, $7–$18. Route 16 and 16A, Jackson Village, NH; (603) 383-9341.

The Red Parka Pub, Glen

There is always a crowd at the Red Parka Pub, a popular hangout approaching its twenty-fifth anniversary. A great staff, big drinks, and large portions of sirloin steaks, barbecued ribs, and prime rib packs them in. They also have a great kids' menu (the restaurant is located just down the road from Story Land).

Dinner nightly. Entrées $7–$18. Route 302, Glen, NH; (603) 383-4344.

The Balsams, Dixville Notch

If you've ever had the opportunity to make a North Atlantic passage on the great ocean liners of the past, you will feel at home in this large dining room. Each place is set with nine pieces of silverware at lunch, ten or more at dinner. The lunch buffet features three tables laden with food. The cold table includes sliced meats, cheeses, fresh fruits, and salads. A selection of hot dishes might be linguine with creamed seafood sauce, grilled Italian sausages with tomato sauce, baked stuffed Atlantic salmon with hollandaise sauce, and steamship round of beef au jus. It is hard not to overindulge at the dessert table, even if you only try a sampling of the chocolate bourbon pecan pie, blackberry mousse, éclair, cream puffs, cannoli, and assorted cakes.

Lunch daily. Prix fixe $16. Reservations recommended. Route 26, Dixville Notch, NH; (800) 255-0800 in NH; (800) 255-0600 in U.S.

Appalachian Mountain Club, Pinkham Notch

If you happen to be taking short hikes in the area or just driving through Pinkham Notch, this is a great spot for a quick cafeteria-style lunch of soup, sandwich, or salad as well as for information, maps, and books on the area. You can also come for a family-style all-you-can-eat dinner and join the hungry hikers at the long picnic tables.

Cafeteria open 9 A.M. to 4 P.M., dinner at 6 P.M. $12. Reservations advised for dinner. Route 16, Pinkham Notch, NH; (603) 466-2727.

ITINERARY

This itinerary is based on a visit to the White Mountains in the late spring to fall season, when most of the commercial attractions are open. To truly experience the White Mountains, make arrangements for an overnight stay at one of the AMC huts. During the winter months, activities center around downhill or cross-country skiing.

DAY ONE. Take the **introductory driving tour**. Have lunch at the Appalachian Mountain Club and get hiking information. If it is a clear day, drive on the **auto road** to the top of Mount Washington or an excursion on the **Cog Railway.**

DAY TWO. This is a day for exploring Franconia Notch. The driving tour starts from Littleton. If you are staying in the Jackson/Conway area, however, take the **Kancamagus Highway** to Lincoln. Take a walk through the **Flume** and take the tramway up **Cannon Mountain;** there are cafeterias at the base and the summit, or take a detour to **Polly's Pancake Parlor** in Sugar Hill for lunch followed by a walk through **Lost River Gorge.**

DAY THREE. Pack a picnic lunch and take a hike. We liked the hike to Zealand Hut (three hours round-trip) because it is easy, you can eat lunch by the falls, and can see what a typical Appalachian Mountain Club hut looks like. For a 360-degree view, hike to the top of Kearsarge Mountain (five hours round-trip) or to Foss Mountain (thirty minutes). Another option is the **driving tour to Dixville Notch** with lunch at the **Balsams**.

DAY FOUR. If you are traveling with younger children you will want to visit **Story Land**. Next door is **Heritage New Hampshire**. The area abounds with other attractions of interest to children. Some will be tempted by the over **200 shops in North Conway.**

BUDGETING YOUR TRIP

To help you get the most for the time and money you have to spend, here are some travel suggestions at three budget levels (cost per day with two people sharing a room) including lodging and meal tax, gratuity on meals, and service charge when it is added to your bill. Prices are approximate and are intended for planning purposes only. *Note:* lodgings are categorized by price and depending on the room selected may appear in more than one category. Meal prices at lunch include an average entrée and beverage. Dinner prices include an appetizer, entrée, dessert, and beverage. Wine or alcoholic beverages are not included.

Staying and dining at expensive lodgings and restaurants: From $240 to $720 per day for two.

Lodging: Rabbit Hill Inn (fireplace rooms and suites), Adair (fireplace rooms and suites), the Inn at Thorn Hill, Mount Washington Hotel, the Balsams (all meals and activities included), Nestlenook Farm, Manor on Golden Pond.

Dining: Breakfast: included. Lunch: the Balsams. Dinner: Rabbit Hill Inn, the Inn at Thorn Hill, Snowvillage Inn, Notchland Inn, Manor on Golden Pond.

Staying and dining at moderately priced lodgings and restaurants: From $180 to $235 per day for two.

Lodging: Rabbit Hill Inn, Snowvillage Inn, the Inn at Thorn Hill, Christmas Farm Inn, the Notchland Inn, Adair.

Dining: Breakfast: included. Lunch: Polly's Pancake House, Thompson House Eatery, Wildcat Tavern. Dinner: Tim-Bir Alley, Wildcat Inn, Christmas Farm Inn, Rabbit Hill Inn, the Inn at Thorn Hill, Snowvillage Inn.

Staying and dining at less expensive lodgings and restaurants: From $110 to $130 per day for two.

Lodging: Joe Dodge Lodge.

Dining: Breakfast: included except at Joe Dodge Lodge. Lunch: Appalachian Mountain Club. Dinner: Thompson House Eatery, Red Parka Pub; Appalachian Mountain Club.

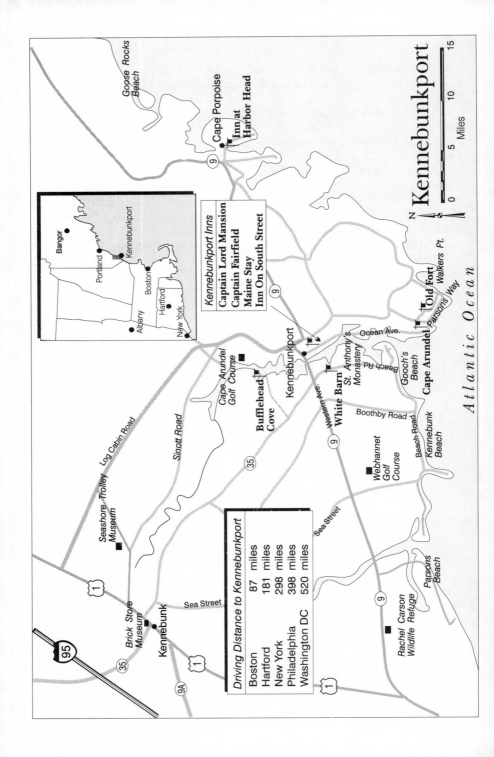

Kennebunkport

Atlantic Ocean

Goose Rocks Beach

Cape Porpoise

Inn/at Harbor Head

Bangor
Portland
Kennebunkport
Boston
Albany
Hartford
New York

Kennebunkport Inns
Captain Lord Mansion
Captain Fairfield
Maine Stay
Inn On South Street

Cape Arundel Golf Course

Bufflehead Cove

Kennebunkport

White Barn

St. Anthony's Monastery

Ocean Ave.

Old Fort

Cape Arundel

Walkers Pt.

Parsons Way

Gooch's Beach

Beach Rd.

Western Ave.

Boothby Road

Beach Road

Kennebunk Beach

Webhannet Golf Course

Sinott Road

Log Cabin Road

Seashore Trolley Museum

Sea Street

Brick Store Museum

Kennebunk

Sea Street

Rachel Carson Wildlife Refuge

Parsons Beach

Driving Distance to Kennebunkport

Boston	87	miles
Hartford	181	miles
New York	298	miles
Philadelphia	398	miles
Washington DC	520	miles

N

0   5   10   15 Miles

5

Kennebunkport, Maine

The pace of life slows as you get close enough to smell the salt air of this southern Maine seacoast town. In a compact area small enough that you can leave your car and walk or bicycle almost anywhere, an abundance of galleries and shops awaits browsers. You can dine in restaurants ranging from elegant gourmet eateries to characteristically dilapidated casual lobster shacks, sun yourself on quiet, sandy beaches, and stay in a range of quality inns and small bed-and-breakfasts.

The historic homes and tree-lined streets indicate that past generations put down roots in this area. There are no neon signs, fast-food franchises, arcades, or shopping malls.

As you walk around Dock Square in the center of Kennebunkport, which is packed with tourists on busy summer weekends, try to imagine ships unloading their cargo into the building that today houses the Book Port bookstore. The existing spiral staircase led to the loft and up to the lookout tower where residents watched for incoming ships.

As tensions with England grew, especially the rift over the tea tax, American sailing ships expanded their trading territory and began to make the long journey to China to trade for tea. Larger, sturdier, and faster boats were needed for the voyage. The coast of Maine became a hub of activity as shipyards liberally sprung up along the protected coves. At one time, more than thirty stood in the Kennebunkport area.

The enterprising families who owned and captained the ships and conducted trading in the years after the American Revolution made a great deal of money. It was during this period of prosperity that many of the Federal homes were built, such as the thirty-six-room Captain Lord Mansion Inn that stands majestically at the top of the town green.

Shipbuilding started a slow decline after the Civil War. The supply of available lumber along the coast depleted just as the new technology of steam-powered ships overtook the wind-powered clipper ships.

By 1873, the Boston and Kennebunkport Sea Shore Company had amassed 600 or 700 acres of property along the ocean, including five miles of ocean frontage. By the turn of the century, thirty grand hotels, numerous rambling single-family shingle cottages, and the extension of the railroad and trolley lines had contributed to Kennebunkport's resurgence in popularity and prosperity. In the intervening years the automobile, changing lifestyles, and shorter vacations caused the demise of most of these hotels and created the demand for a new type of lodging, the bed-and-breakfast inn.

In 1903 George Herbert Walker, son of a wealthy St. Louis dry goods merchant, purchased an eleven-acre parcel of land bordered on three sides by water, constructed two large homes, and renamed the parcel Walker Point. Little did he know that in the latter part of the century his grandson George Herbert Walker Bush would be the forty-first president of the United States and use the property as the summer White House.

For information on special events, contact the **Kennebunk-Kennebunkport Chamber of Commerce and Information Center** (Route 35, Lower Village near the intersection with Route 9; Box 740, Kennebunk, ME 04043; (207) 967-0857), open daily June through September; weekdays the rest of the year.

WHERE TO GO, WHAT TO DO

Walks and Drives

A walk, jog, bike ride, or drive through Kennebunkport. This tour is about four miles long. Start at Dock Square in front of the 200-year-old rum warehouse, now the Book Port bookstore. In the past, this section of town housed sailing lofts, warehouses, and ship chandlers. Today it is filled with shops, and it's a fun place to browse.

Continue up Spring Street. Cross to the far side of Maine Street to get a good look at the attractive Federal-era houses built from profits made in the trading and shipbuilding industry in the first half of the nineteenth century.

Continue past the Victorian Maine Stay Inn. Turn right at South Street past the Inn at South Street.

At the end of South Street, turn right. The Captain Fairfield Inn as well as the Captain Lord Mansion, a prominent Federal-era mansion and one of the outstanding inns in the country, will be right in front of you. The town green is in front of the mansion. This is where George Bush spoke to the local populace after his presidential election victory. Walk along the green to Ocean Avenue.

Turn left on Ocean Avenue. The harbor is on your right, and soon it will come into full view. In about a mile, you will cross a bridge with a tidal cove on your left. Port Lobster Company, a wholesale and retail lobster and fish market, makes an excellent low-cost lobster roll. Mabel's next door is a good sit-down lunch stop. The government wharf where lobstermen unload their catch is behind the buildings across from Mabel's. The Colony, one of the last of the grand summer Victorian hotels, looms into view on the left as you continue down Ocean Avenue.

After you pass the Colony you will come to Parsons Way, a stretch of land with benches and paths overlooking the Atlantic Ocean given to the town of Kennebunkport by Henry Parsons. When the tide and the wind are up, the endless drama of the sea unfolds before you.

Continue past the dark, mysterious-looking house that sits alone on the rocks facing the ocean. Farther along, you'll see cars pulled off the road. Curious visitors with binoculars and cameras are taking pictures of Walker's Point, the summer home of former president George Bush. It is an impressive point of land. Blowing Cave, another landmark in this cove, produces a large "whump" sound when waves rush in and displace the air in the cave. On a good day, the spray will shoot as high as thirty feet.

Walk back along Ocean Avenue. Turn right at Spouting Rock Avenue, next to Cape Arundel Inn, to get a close look at the large Victorian-era seaside shingle cottages. Continue past the Old Fort Inn to the Colony. From here, you can continue along Boston Avenue and South Maine Street. Turn left at Maine Street and continue back beyond the Maine Stay Inn for a look at more summer cottages. A left turn down Union Street brings you back to Dock Square.

Cleaves Cove. This is an isolated small cove that is not signed, but is open to the public. From the guard station at Walker's Point, drive or walk $8/10$ mile along Ocean Avenue. Park just beyond the white stucco wall with paving stones on top. Follow the short unmarked tarred path. Bear right as the path turns to gravel. This is a beautiful isolated spot to sit on the rocks and to view Bumpkin Island, home to cormorants, seagulls, and seals. Bring your binoculars.

Cape Porpoise. When you've been to Cape Porpoise, you know you've been to Maine. This is a bona-fide commercial fishing harbor. Walk the docks, watch the lobstermen, visit Bradbury's Market and Nunan's. Take care as you drive here from Kennebunkport; the speed limits are strictly enforced.

Rachel Carson National Wildlife Refuge. The one-mile groomed trail marked with explanatory signs that explain such terms as *estuary, salt hay, salt pannes,* and *tidal creeks* is an excellent way to learn about the salt marsh ecosystem. It's a pleasant walk on level ground. Open daily. Free admission. A mile off U.S. 1 on Route 9 east in Wells, ME; (207) 646-9226.

St. Anthony's Franciscan Monastery. Visitors are welcome to Sunday morning church services at this monastery, home to about twenty Lithuanian monks. If you visit during the first week of December, attend the moving candlelight community carol sing held outdoors. During the summer the monastery operates a no-frills guesthouse. Any time of the year, you can follow the path from the end of the parking lot near the outdoor shrine to the boathouse, which has an excellent view of the Kennebunk River. The trolley bus stops during the summer, or you can walk from Kennebunkport. Beach Street, Kennebunk, ME 04046; (207)967-2011.

Beaches

The following beaches are some of the finest in Maine. They are clean and not crowded, probably because the absence of changing rooms, snack bars, and rest rooms discourages day-trippers. However, this is Maine; the water is cold. There is no charge to use the beaches but you will need a parking permit during the summer. Most of the inns provide these for their guests; however, as the parking is along the edge of the roadway, the limited space fills quickly. If you have to drive, get to the beach early or wait until late in the day. Otherwise, park where you can find a legal spot and walk a few blocks.

Kennebunk Beach. This is the closest beach to town. You can take the trolley here from Kennebunkport. Gooch's Beach and Middle Beach are the parts closest to town that have good surf. The far end is called Mother's Beach; the water is shallow.

Goose Rocks Beach. This is a favorite sandy beach that's rarely crowded. The houses are on the other side of the road and are fairly well hidden by the dune grasses. It's a good swimming beach, and the water is not as cold as it is in other parts of the area. From Kennebunkport take Route 9 north to the Clock Farm Corner. Turn right on Dyke Road.

Parson's Beach. Sugar maples form a canopy over the alley that leads to this privately owned beach. This is a favorite spot for painters. The area available for free parking holds only six cars. You can't park along the road, so the best way to get here in season is by bicycle. From Kennebunkport take Route 9, going toward Route 1. After you cross the Mousam River and pass a horse farm, turn left to get to the beach.

Shops and Galleries

More than sixty artists, either with their own studios or represented by galleries, belong to the Art Guild of the Kennebunks. The map they publish for the early August art show marks the location of all the galleries and studios in the area. Look in the galleries for a copy of this map or write to Art Guild of the Kennebunks, Box 2658, Kennebunkport, ME 04046.

You can see most of the studios and galleries on a walking tour. Start in Dock Square in Kennebunkport. Walk down Ocean Avenue a few blocks before taking Pearl Street over to Maine Street. Cross Route 9 and continue to the Congregational Church, then turn left and make your way back to Dock

Square. Cross the bridge into Lower Village, where you'll find galleries on Route 9, north on Route 35, and on Chase Hill Road and Beach Street.

There are also a few galleries on Route 9 in Cape Porpoise. Following are a few galleries and shops of note.

Kennebunk Book Port. Ships unloaded their cargo in this building, the oldest in the square. The elegant spiral staircase climbs to the loft and up to the lookout tower where nineteenth-century residents watched for incoming ships.

Choose a book or two from the extensive collection and spend some time reading on the couch. Open daily year-round. 10 Dock Square, Kennebunkport; (207) 967-3815.

Meserves Market. This neighborhood grocer is open daily and carries a bit of everything, including free tide tables. Western Avenue, Route 9, Kennebunkport; (207) 967-5762.

Mast Cove Galleries. The largest group gallery in the area has selections in graphics, painting, and sculpture. Mast Cove Lane and Maine Street, Kennebunkport; (207) 967-3453.

Goose Rocks Pottery. Bob and Lou Lipkin make stoneware and porcelain pottery. The tiles at the Inn at Harbor Head were done by Lou. Wharf Lane, Kennebunkport; (207) 967-2105.

Joan Moshimer. Joan sells handmade hooked rugs, yarns, and dyes out of her home studio. North Street, Kennebunkport; (207) 967-3711.

The Ellenberger Gallery. Roger W. Ellenberger paints classic New England coastal harbor scenes in acrylic and watercolor. Look for his paintings at the Captain Lord Mansion. Route 35, Lower Village, Kennebunkport; (207) 967-3824.

Nancy St. Lawrence. Watercolors of the Kennebunks are her specialty. Ocean Avenue, Kennebunkport; (207) 967-3170.

Museums

Brick Store Museum. Anyone interested in the maritime history of the Kennebunks will enjoy the changing exhibits on the first floor and the collection of Federal furniture, ship models, and portraits on the second floor.

Mid-June to mid-October, walking tours of the historic district of Kennebunk and a tour of the Taylor-Barry House are given Wednesday at 10 A.M. and Friday at 1 P.M., $3. Museum open Tuesday through Saturday, 10 A.M. to 4:30 P.M.. Adults $3. 117 Main Street, Kennebunk, ME, (207) 985-4802.

Seashore Trolley Museum. As the trolley pulled out on the main line the conductor picked up the paddle indicating we had the right-of-way on the rails. After the four-mile run, we crossed the tracks and tried out a different vintage trolley. During the summer they may have 4 or 5 of the more than 100 trolleys running on any given day. You're welcome to ride all day on the same ticket. Following the ride, we visited the trolley barn, where the conductor told us stories of the history of each car. Trolley buffs will want to visit the repair shops or volunteer to work on these relics.

Open daily, May through October. Hours vary. Adults $6. Located about three miles from Kennebunkport. Follow North Street, also called Log Cabin Road, to the museum. Kennebunkport, ME; (207) 967-2800.

Other Activities

Biking

Cape-Able Bike. One of the best ways to explore the area and to beat the town and beach traffic is to go by bicycle. If you're exploring more than one area of Maine, stop here first and rent your bikes and equipment for a week or two. Owner and dedicated cyclist Peter Sargent will gladly suggest the best rides along the way.

Open throughout the year, daily Memorial Day through Labor Day; shorter hours in spring and fall. Townhouse Corners, off Log Cabin Road, Kennebunkport, ME 04046; (207) 967-4382.

Golf

Cape Arundel Golf Club. This is the golf course George Bush plays; we've been told he does the course in two and a half hours. Eighteen holes. Kennebunkport; (207) 967-3494.

Webhannet Golf Club. These fairways are tighter and slightly more challenging. Eighteen holes. Kennebunk Beach; (207) 967-2061.

Whale Watching

This is high on our list of suggested activities, providing the seas aren't rough. Species found along the coast of Maine include humpbacks, finbacks, minkes, right whales, and white-sided dolphins. On our trip, we saw nineteen humpbacks, including a couple of mother-and-baby pairs. Remember, the whales move with the fish supply, so the kind of whales and the exact destination of the boats will vary from day to day. Both of these boats go to the Jeffries Ledge, an upheaval about twenty miles off the coast.

Nautilus. This sixty-five-foot boat holds up to 100 passengers and is faster than the *Indian* (see below). The captain provides the commentary. Memorial Day to mid-October from the Arundel Shipyard, located behind the Mobil station next to the bridge on Route 9. $25–30. Kennebunkport; (207) 967-5595.

Indian. This seventy-five-foot boat holds up to seventy-two passengers. This is a slower boat than the *Nautilus,* so you will spend longer getting to the whales. A marine mammalogist is on board. Trips leave late June through September from the Arundel Wharf on Ocean Avenue. Kennebunkport; (207) 967-5912.

Ogunquit

If you are looking for additional shops and galleries, you'll find a large concentration of both in Ogunquit and in Perkins Cove.

Marginal Way. A walk on the Marginal Way, a mile-long footpath along the cliffs connecting Ogunquit with Perkins Cove, should not be missed. When the weather turns stormy, put on your rain gear and watch the show of waves crashing against the rocks; your memory of Maine will be far more lasting than the temporary discomfort of the chill, damp air. Make a reservation at one of the front window tables at Hurricanes in Perkins Cove before taking your walk so you can warm up and continue to watch the fury of the sea.

Lobstering trips. On the docks and next to fishermen's homes, you'll see piles of lobster traps. If you want to learn how the lobstermen bait, set, and haul in their traps, take the fifty-minute Finestkind cruise. July through Labor Day. Trips leave from Barnacle Billy's Dock in Perkins Cove; (207) 646-5227.

Ogunquit Playhouse. This well-known summer theater opened in 1932. The ten-week season includes six comedies or musicals. If a show is sold out, cancellations sometimes are available at the box office about an hour before the performance. Late June through Labor Day. Monday through Saturday and matinees on Wednesday and Thursday. On Route 1, Ogunquit; (207) 646-5511.

WHERE TO STAY

White Barn Inn

This deluxe country house hotel, situated a quarter of a mile from the ocean on a quiet street in Kennebunkport, combines spectacular formal dining with rooms that range from spacious and well appointed to smaller and more traditional. The owners are Laurie Bongiorno, who runs the restaurant, and his wife, Laurie Cameron, the innkeeper.

The top accommodations are in May's Annex, a carriage house with six deluxe rooms. Each room has a sitting area with a wood-burning fireplace, couches or large easy chairs, and a king-size four-poster bed. The large bathrooms have marble floors, single whirlpool baths, and a separate glass-enclosed, marble-lined shower.

May's Cottage has been renovated to include a king-size bed, double-sided wood-burning fireplace, and patio overlooking the swimming pool. The bath has a double whirlpool and separate shower. The Gate House Cottage rooms in a third outbuilding are not as luxurious as those in May's Annex or the Cottage, but each has a fireplace and a bath with a single whirlpool tub. All rooms in the outbuildings have phones and televisions. Rooms in the main inn, the original farmhouse, are on the small side but are attractively furnished in traditional New England decor with print wallpaper, hand-painted furniture, and double, queen, or twin beds.

Breakfast includes freshly squeezed orange juice, a basket of pastries, a fruit plate, and an assortment of cereals. A full breakfast is available for an additional fee.

Twenty-four rooms, all with private bath. June through October, $150–$375. Continental breakfast, tea, and use of bicycles included. Children over 12 welcome; rooms are double occupancy only. No smoking. No pets. Two-night weekend minimum. 37 Beach Street, Box 560C, Kennebunkport, ME 04046; (207) 967-2321.

The Captain Lord Mansion

Rick Litchfield and Bev Davis own this distinguished mansion, built in 1812 by a sea captain and situated in Kennebunkport on a hill at the edge of the town green. The quietly elegant common room has high ceilings, antique furniture, and Oriental carpets. The bedrooms have nineteenth-century antique furniture, and most have gas fireplaces.

First- and second-floor rooms have nine-and-a-half-foot ceilings. One of our favorite fireplace rooms is the expansive first-floor Brig Merchant, with a king-size bed and a large bath with a double whirlpool, oversize shower, double sink, and exercise equpment. Ship Callender also has a double whirlpool, and Schooner Champion has an antique soaking tub and steam shower. The Lincoln Room on the second floor has an 1820 English four-poster queen-size bed. Ship Harvest, on the third floor, has a country look with a king-size four-poster bed and a mural scene of Kennebunkport in the 1800s.

Breakfast, served family style at two long tables in the country kitchen with seatings at 8:30 and 9:30 A.M., includes muffins, breads, and fruit followed by a hot entrée such as vegetable quiche, Belgian waffles, or malted blueberry pancakes.

Phoebe's Fantasy is a separate building with four rooms, two with king-size and two with queen-size beds. The common gathering room has a large-screen television, a fireplace, and an attractive plush chintz sofa. Guests who stay at Phoebe's Fantasy are served breakfast in this building.

Nineteen rooms, all with private bath. May through December, $159–$349. Lower rates at other times. Afternoon tea and full breakfast included. Children over 6 welcome. No pets. Two-night weekend minimum. Box 800, Kennebunkport, ME 04046; (207) 967-3141.

The Captain Lord Mansion overlooks the town green.

The Inn at Harbor Head, Cape Porpoise

This waterfront cottage owned by innkeepers Joan and Dave Sutter overlooks the harbor of Cape Porpoise, two and a half miles from the center of Kennebunkport. Guests like to lie in the hammock or sit by the water to sketch or read. In cooler weather they can sit in the antique-filled living room or the library, which has a wood-burning fireplace and a view of the harbor.

The Summer Suite has a striking water view. The large bathroom has a double Jacuzzi, a peaked ceiling, a skylight, and a bidet, the bedroom has a king-size bed and a gas fireplace. The Harbor Suite has a queen-size pencil-post bed, a love seat facing French doors opening to a deck with a view of the harbor, and a tiny corner bath. You'll notice a Japanese influence in the small Garden Room, which opens onto a private deck, set with a table and chairs, that offers a beautiful view of the water.

For breakfast, guests dine together at one large table. A typical breakfast includes fresh orange juice, homemade muffins, a fruit course such as peaches and blueberries in spiced white wine, and a hot dish such as ricotta-stuffed French toast with a fruit sauce or sourdough rounds sautéed with chicken, shallots, and a cream sauce.

Five rooms, all with private bath. Open late April through October, $135–$250. Full breakfast and afternoon hors d'oeuvres included. Children over 12 welcome. No pets. No smoking. Two-night weekend minimum. 41 Pier Road, Kennebunkport, ME 04046; (207) 967-5564.

Bufflehead Cove Inn

Named for the diving sea ducks that winter here, Bufflehead Cove Inn is located on six private acres at the end of a dirt road that winds past several small ponds, less than a mile from the center of Kennebunkport. The location is so peaceful that we could happily spend hours on the porch or the viewing deck, reading and looking at the myriad waterfowl. Innkeepers Harriet and Jim Gott are natives of the area. Jim is also a commercial fisherman for shrimp and lobster.

For total privacy we suggest the Hideaway, a new, large, airy room with a private porch and floor-length windows that overlook the cove. A double-sided gas fireplace separates the king-size bed from the sitting area. The huge bath has a skylight over the double whirlpool tub, and there's a separate shower. Within the main part of the inn we particularly like the Balcony Room, which has a brass queen-size bed, a gas fireplace, and a porch that overlooks the cove. The Cove Suite has two rooms with a gas fireplace in the living room and a balcony overlooking the cove. The Garden Studio has its own entrance, a large sitting area, and a patio in a small courtyard; this is the only room where pets are permitted.

Breakfast is served 8:30 to 9:30 A.M. outdoors in the summer at five tables or inside at two tables. The day we stayed we had fresh orange juice, blueberries, sweet bread, and French toast stuffed with cream cheese and apples with bacon.

Four rooms and two suites, all with private bath, $95–$220. Full breakfast and afternoon wine and cheese included. Children over 12. Pets with permission. No smoking. Two-night weekend minimum. Located ½ mile off Route 35. Box 499, Kennebunkport, ME 04046; (207) 967-3879.

The Maine Stay Inn

This inn, owned and run by Carol and Lindsay Copeland, suits guests who like to talk with the innkeepers, as well as families, honeymooners, or people wanting more privacy. The main inn is an 1860 Victorian Italianate structure; the property also includes eleven self-sufficient cottages and a grassy area with barbecue grills, lounge chairs, and a croquet set.

The first-floor suite has a spacious sitting room with a fireplace. Room 14 is a small first-floor room with windows on three sides, a gas fireplace, private deck, and a private entrance.

Lindsay and Carol have painted all eleven cottage interiors white or papered them in summery colors and added bright, crisp flowered linens and pillows. Ten of the cottages have kitchens. Four have wood-burning fireplaces and one has a gas fireplace. Cottage 6, with two bedrooms and a living room, is a good choice for families. All rooms and cottages have televisions and air-conditioning.

Breakfast includes juices, fresh fruits, granola, breads for toasting, muffins, and such entrées as baked French toast, ham-and-cheese omelettes, or a blintz soufflé. Guests staying in the cottages can arrange to have a breakfast basket delivered to their door.

Seventeen rooms, suites, and cottages, all with private bath. Late June to mid-October, $125–$220. Lower rates at other times of the year. Breakfast and afternoon tea included. Children welcome; baby-sitting by prior arrangement. No smoking. No pets. Two-night weekend minimum. 34 Maine Street, Box 500A, Kennebunkport, ME 04046; (207) 967-2117, (800) 950-2117.

Old Fort Inn

Innkeepers Sheila and David Aldrich have combined the best elements of a mini-resort and a bed-and-breakfast country inn. Of all the inns we've reviewed in this area, this is the only one with a large freshwater swimming pool, a tennis court, shuffleboard, horseshoes, and laundry facilities for guests' use.

Fourteen of the rooms are located in the converted carriage house. All the rooms have air-conditioning, wet bars with a sink and a refrigerator, televisions, and phones. One of the suites is over the antique shop and overlooks the swimming pool; suitable for three people as it has a sitting room, a family room with a convertible sofa, plus a bedroom with a king-size bed and a large bath.

A buffet breakfast is set out in the lodge, an 1880s converted barn with a massive brick fireplace, an exposed beam ceiling, and comfortable sofas and chairs. On nice days guests like to take their trays and sit by the pool. Breakfast includes juices, fresh fruit, homemade granola, yogurt, croissants, muffins, sticky buns, or fruit breads, and quiche.

Open mid-April through early December. Sixteen rooms and suites, $130–$290. Breakfast included. Not comfortable for children under 12. No pets. No smoking. Two-night weekend minimum. Old Fort Avenue, Box M, Kennebunkport, ME 04046; (207) 967-5353.

Captain Fairfield Inn

This 1813 Federal mansion, owned by innkeepers Bonnie and Dennis Tallagnon, is a former sea captain's home next to the Captain Lord Mansion overlooking the town green. All rooms have queen-size beds; three have wood-burning fireplaces. Of these, room 1, the former library, has a canopy bed, a private porch, and a deep double-sized soaking tub. Room 4 has an old porcelain tub and a separate shower. Room 6 is the third room with a fireplace. Rooms 6 through 9 are newer rooms decorated in the style of an English garden. Our favorite is room 9, a corner room with an iron queen-size canopy bed and the best view of the perennial gardens.

Dennis, a former Swiss chef, prepares a particularly attractive breakfast.

We were served an excellent fresh fruit cup topped with mango slices, blueberry muffins, and homemade blueberry jam. The choice of main dishes the day we stayed was strawberry crepes or eggs Benedict with a spicy hollandaise sauce.

Nine rooms, all with private bath. Full breakfast and afternoon tea included. Mid-June through December, $95–$195; other times $85–$175. Children over 6 welcome. No smoking. No pets. Two-night weekend minimum. Corner of Pleasant and Green Streets, P.O. Box 1308, Kennebunkport, ME 04046; (207) 967-4454; (800) 322-1928.

Inn on South Street

This early nineteenth-century Greek Revival home owned by Eva and Jacques Downs has a second-floor common room with items that reflect the innkeepers' interest in China: Chinese coffee and end tables, bowls, wall hangings, and rugs, as well as export china reminiscent of what a nineteenth-century captain of a China clipper would have brought back. Jacques, an historian who is a walking encyclopedia on the China trade, is a professor at the nearby University of New England.

We particularly like the luxury apartment suite, which has its own private entrance from the garden. It has a living room, a bedroom with a gas fireplace and queen four-poster, a bath with a double whirlpool tub, and a kitchen. Eva delivers a full gourmet breakfast to this suite as well as early morning coffee and afternoon refreshments.

There are three other rooms in the house, all with queen-size beds. The first floor Perkins Room has a fireplace and four-poster queen-size canopy bed and daybed.

Eva serves breakfast at one large table in the large country kitchen at 8:30 A.M. A sample menu includes juice, homemade breads and jam, and an entrée such as an orange soufflé with warm strawberries, German apple pancakes, or blueberry blintzes.

Three rooms and one suite, all with private bath. Open April through October and December. July through October, $135–$190. Other times $85–$175. Breakfast and afternoon refreshment included. Children over 12 welcome. No pets. No smoking. Two-night weekend minimum. South Street, Box 478A, Kennebunkport, ME 04046; (207) 967-5151.

Cape Arundel Inn

If you want to stay at an inn where you can see the waves dash against the rocky shoreline and get a glimpse of Walker's Point, President Bush's summer White House, this is the place to be. With a highly regarded restaurant on the first floor and a regular clientele that returns each year, it's easy to understand that the rooms with a prime view are some of the most sought-after summer accommodations in Kennebunkport.

Most of the rooms in the main building are large and simply furnished, with carpeted floors and white bedspreads. Room 2 has twin four-poster pineapple beds, a large picture window, and a private deck overlooking the water. Room 3, another spacious room, has four curved windows overlooking the water, and two double beds. Room 4 is a smaller corner room with great views of the ocean and two twin beds that can be made into a king.

Next door are six basic motel units, each with a private balcony that faces the ocean. One unit has a kitchen.

Open late May through October. Fourteen rooms, all with private bath, $90–$145. Children welcome in the motel units. A full breakfast is available but is not included in the rate. No pets. Ocean Avenue, Box 530A, Kennebunkport, ME 04046; (207) 967-2125.

WHERE TO DINE

Fine Dining

The White Barn Inn

The candlelit main dining room is a classic New England barn with seasoned wood interior walls, oil paintings, exposed rafters, and a second floor filled with an assortment of items one might have found stashed in an old barn: a hay rake, old steamer trunks, baskets, pulleys, a pair of ice tongs, a rocking chair, scales, and old signs advertising elixirs, old harnesses, and house paints. A large picture window in each of the two barn dining rooms looks onto a viewing porch seasonally decorated with bales of hay or cornstalks, old rocking chairs, a wooden sleigh, farm tools, and pots of flowers. At the front of the main dining room, our preference of the two barn dining rooms, there are cocktail tables and a piano bar.

The menu changes weekly and includes a choice of about eight appetizers, eight entrées, and six desserts. The formal, elegant dinner includes a selection of hors d'oeuvres, an appetizer, sorbet or soup as a palate cleanser, entrée, and dessert. For starters we were particularly impressed with the lobster spring roll and the cappuccino mushroom soup of shiitake and oyster mushrooms with foie gras. Steamed tender lobster over homemade fettucine was a memorable entrée. Other choices included a combination dish of roasted rack of lamb encrusted with pecans and roasted leg of venison, breast of farm-raised chicken with portabella mushrooms wrapped in pastry, and grilled Maine salmon over vegetables. For dessert we suggest the caramelized apples with calvados ice cream, caramel sauce, and a phyllo flower, and the trio of chocolate desserts including a terrine, mousse, and sorbet.

Dinner nightly April through December; Wednesday through Sunday in February and March. Jacket requested. Prix fixe $56. 37 Beach Street, Kennebunkport, ME; (207) 967-2321.

The main dining room at the White Barn Inn is a classic New England barn.

Grissini, Kennebunk

This popular new Tuscan-style restaurant is owned by Laurie Bongiorno of the White Barn Inn. The chefs and waiters are from Italy. The atmosphere is sophisticated yet comfortable: parchment paper covers the tables, the ceiling has exposed pipes, and there's a stone patio for outdoor dining. Slices of different kinds of homemade bread are placed directly on the table; tear off pieces and dip them into the olive oil. Lighter fare includes Tuscan white bean soup with duck sausage or pizza with assorted toppings and a salad. Homemade pasta combinations include pappardelle with shiitake, oyster and portabella mushrooms; linguine with seafood; fettuccine with grilled chicken, pesto, and brandied apples; and tagliolini with pesto and pine nuts. Other menu items might include wood-grilled chicken with Tuscan mashed potatoes, osso buco, and Maine trout steamed in foil. Tiramisu and strawberries with balsamic vinegar and mascarpone cheese are among the dessert selections.

Lunch and dinner daily except mid-February to mid-March. $4–$14. 27 Western Avenue, Kennebunk, ME; (207) 967-2211.

Seascapes, Cape Porpoise

The large picture windows in the dining room overlook a working lobster harbor. At high tide, the water comes up to the building. Italian fluted glasses, brightly colored country-style pottery service plates, wooden fish napkin rings, and flowers give the dining room a fresh feel. Before dinner, have a glass of wine in the lounge, which has a wood-burning fireplace. There's a second wood-burning fireplace in the dining room.

The style of cooking borrows heavily from countries of the Pacific Rim, and the presentations are outstanding. Maine lobster and crab egg roll includes seaweed and pickled ginger salad; steamed mussels are served in a broth flavored with spicy salsa and andouille sausage; and the Caesar salad is mixed with prosciutto and Parmesan and wrapped in a large grilled flour tortilla. Grilled rack of lamb comes with a maple-encrusted goat cheese topping, and pheasant and lobster are served with ginger wild rice.

Lunch (summer only), and dinner daily, late April through October. Lunch, $5–$16; dinner entrées $19–$28. Cape Porpoise Harbor, Kennebunkport, ME; (207) 967-8500.

Arrows, Ogunquit

For fine dining along the Maine coast, this outstanding restaurant is well worth the twenty-five-minute drive from Kennebunkport. Chef-owners Clark Frasier and Mark Gaier perform their culinary magic in a Colonial farmhouse with large windows overlooking lit gardens filled with many of the vegetables, herbs, and flowers used in the restaurant.

Clark and Mark rotate weeks as chef and host. For an appetizer try the bento box, a Japanese lunch box with three divided trays, which comes with a changing variety of about six small items such as paper-wrapped chicken, crispy catfish, and papaya salad. The Boston lettuce salad with spicy maple pecans and Roquefort cheese was excellent.

The menu changes weekly but always includes three fish, two beef, and one pheasant or duck entrée. Selections from a recent menu included plank-roasted salmon with pearl onions, haricots verts, yellow beans, couscous and mango chutney and grilled rib veal chop with chanterelles, artichoke hearts, radicchio, and risotto.

Late April through Thanksgiving. Dinner, Tuesday through Sunday during July and August. Wednesday through Sunday, June and September to mid-October, Friday through Sunday at other times. Entrées $28–$33. Located on Berwick Road, Ogunquit, ME; (207) 361-1100.

Cape Arundel Inn

This turn-of-the-century seaside shingle cottage, now a successful inn and restaurant, features good food and panoramic views of the Maine seacoast. All diners enjoy a view of the rocky shore from the sixty seats arranged on two levels. (The corner table with the best view of the water is number 6.) Couples are in luck here, because all the tables for two are placed along the windows. Delightful photographs of Kennebunkport during its Victorian summer resort era decorate the walls and set the stage for gracious, old-fashioned service.

For starters, try the sauté of lobster and artichoke hearts with truffles and puff pastry, scallops seviche with avocado, or spicy shrimp and pancetta with melon salsa.

Entrées include duck breast with jasmine honey glaze and pear chutney, lime-marinated scallops with pea pods, champagne and avocado crème fraîche, broiled swordfish with papaya and macadamia nut butter, and, of course, steamed Maine lobster.

Open late May through October. Breakfast daily. Dinner Monday through Saturday, entrées $17–$23. Ocean Avenue, Kennebunkport, ME; (207) 967-2125.

Hurricane's, Ogunquit, Perkins Cove

On a stormy day at high tide when the waves are crashing on the rocks, head to Perkins Cove for fine dining and a spectacular show of nature's force. This is one of the ultimate Maine dining spots, highlighted by the big picture windows that allow diners a full view of the Atlantic.

Appetizers include lobster ravioli, poached oysters with corn pancakes, and raw oysters and clams. An unusually tasty salad that comes with dinner includes greens with roasted shallots, pistachio nuts, and a peppercorn dressing.

We couldn't resist the daily special entrée, a platter of steamers and a boiled lobster. Other entrées include crab-stuffed filet of sole; breast of chicken stuffed with feta cheese, spinach, and pine nuts; and herb-roasted rack of lamb. On Sunday, there's a jazz brunch.

Open daily for lunch, $6–$12, and dinner, entrées $11–$20. Closed on Tuesday in the off-season. Oarweed Lane, Perkins Cove, Ogunquit, ME; (207) 646-6348.

Windows on the Water, Kennebunk

Although the water view has evaporated with the construction of a new group of stores on the docks just below this crisp, contemporary dining spot, the open kitchen continues to turn out a varied selection of fresh grilled and sautéed seafood. Patrons can sit on Windsor chairs at well-spaced tables in the dining rooms or, in pleasant weather, on the brick deck set with white plastic furniture.

The lobster-stuffed potato, which put this restaurant on the map, was served at President Bush's inauguration. Pan-blackened Cajun scallops served with a cooling cucumber dill salad was a nice contrast of flavors.

Tuna, salmon, swordfish, halibut, perch, and shrimp are served charbroiled and accompanied by a variety of sauces such as orange pineapple salsa, warm fruit compote, printemps sauce, lemon Chambord butter, toasted pecan butter, or saffron cream. The chunky lemon Parmesan salad dressing was a refreshing change. The wine list includes a selection of fifteen half bottles. Desserts included a chocolate pecan pie and a blueberry cream pie made with cream cheese.

Lunch and dinner daily. Closed on Monday, November through April. Lunch $5–$11. Dinner entrées $16–$21. Chase Hill Road, Kennebunkport, ME; (207) 967-3313.

Informal Dining

Mabel's Lobster Claw

"I can't take any credit for the lobsters. All I do is bless them and throw them in," explained Mabel Hanson, who operates this small restaurant that serves excellent food on bare wood tables. When we stopped by to make reservations, Mabel teasingly asked if we wanted to help her make pies in exchange for our dinner. After a good laugh, we reserved the left front corner table where George Bush always sits.

Lobster Savannah is a split lobster filled with scallops, shrimp, and fresh mushrooms in a creamy Newburg sauce, one of Mabel's specialties. Lobster stew, fried clams, and her famous lobster roll—lobster meat tossed in a light Russian dressing, served with a lettuce leaf in a butter-grilled hot dog roll—are all excellent.

The old-fashioned desserts include traditional Maine blueberry pie served à la mode.

Late April to mid-October, lunch and dinner daily. Entrees $7–$27. Ocean Avenue, Kennebunkport, ME; (207) 967-2562.

Allison's

This is Kennebunkport's local hangout. The high noise level combines the sounds of two televisions over the long bar, records, and the animated laughter of relaxed people having a good time. A collection of trophies near the dartboard attests to the prowess of the patrons.

The menu includes twelve burger concoctions ranging from the Buffalo, with blue cheese and hot spicy red sauce, to a melt with lots of American cheese and sautéed onions on grilled rye. You can add guacamole and jalapeño peppers to any burger for an extra charge. More substantial dinners include broiled haddock, scallops, swordfish, and, of course, lobster. For pub noshing, there are cheese and meat nachos, fried potato skins, and Buffalo-style chicken wings.

Daily, breakfast (daily in summer and weekends other times), lunch,

dinner, and pub dining; children's menu. Lunch $2–$7. Dinner entrées $10–
$15. 5 Dock Square, Kennebunkport, ME; (207) 967-4841.

Lobster Pounds

No trip to this area of the coast of Maine is complete without a lobster dinner.
Following is a selection of our favorite lobster pounds, where you can roll up
your sleeves and attack your lobster with gusto.

Nunan's Lobster Hut, Cape Porpoise. This is a run-down, much-beloved
institution that works. Loyal diners wait in line to rub elbows in this wonderfully cramped black-and-red building. Diners sit at picnic tables and feed on
lobsters, steamers, and blueberry pie. (Kids who aren't lobster lovers can order peanut-butter-and-jelly sandwiches.) After dinner, diners wash their hands
in the corner at the porcelain sink.

Late April to mid-October. Dinner. No credit cards. Route 9, Cape Porpoise,
ME; (207) 967-4435.

The Lobster Pot, Cape Porpoise. If you don't want to stand in line at
Nunan's, continue north on Route 9 for about a mile to this family restaurant,
a large airy room with a lobster tank, long tables, and place mats that kids can
color on (crayons are supplied). The menu has a full spectrum of traditional
shore food, ranging from lobster to fried seafood. Steak is available for the
beef fan.

Weekends late March and April, daily May to early December. Breakfast,
lunch, $2–$7, and dinner, entrées $9–$21. Route 9, Cape Porpoise, ME; (207)
967-4607.

Clam Shack, Kennebunkport. You can order fried clams or a lobster roll
at Shackford and Gooch's take-out stand on the bridge that separates Kennebunk from Kennebunkport, but watch out for the seagulls who are adept at
swooping down and picking off a fried clam.

May through October. On the bridge in Kennebunkport; (207) 967-3321.

Cape Porpoise Lobster Company, Cape Porpoise. This is a good stop
for a take-out lobster roll or a cooked lobster for a picnic. 15 Pier Road, Cape
Porpoise, ME; (207) 967-4268.

Preble and Sons, Cape Porpoise. This is a wholesale and retail operation. The staff will steam your lobster if you want to put together a picnic.

Open all year, 7 A.M. to 5:30 P.M. (last lobster order in for steaming by 5
P.M.). Route 9, Cape Porpoise, Kennebunkport, ME; (207) 967-4620.

ITINERARY

DAY ONE. Take the four-mile **walking tour,** which starts in Dock Square and
goes through the historic district and along Ocean Drive. Have lunch at **Ma-**

bel's; then complete the walk. Drive or bike to **Goose Rocks Beach.** Dine at the **White Barn Inn** or overlooking the water at **Cape Arundel Inn.**

DAY TWO. Take a walk or the trolley bus to **Kennebunk Beach,** stopping at the **Franciscan Monastery** on the way. Have lunch on the outdoor deck at **Windows on the Water** or at **Allison's.** Spend the afternoon visiting shops and galleries or antiquing along Route 1, followed by a walk in Ogunquit on the Marginal Way. Have dinner at **Hurricane's** or at **Arrows.**

DAY THREE. If you want to play golf, make arrangements for an early game, as both courses are closed to the public in the middle of the day. Go **whale watching** or **rent bicycles** and explore Ocean Drive, stopping at **Cleaves Cove** and **Cape Porpoise.** Get a lobster roll at **Cape Porpoise Lobster Company.** Visit the **Trolley Museum,** or go to **Parson's Beach,** the **Rachel Carson National Wildlife Refuge.** An alternative is to spend the day on a whale-watching trip. Have an informal dinner at **Grissini** or **Mabel's** or overlooking the water at **Seascapes.**

BUDGETING YOUR TRIP

To help you get the most for the time and money you have to spend, here are some travel suggestions at three budget levels (cost per day with two people sharing a room), including lodging and meal tax, gratuity on meals, and service charge when it is added to your bill. Prices are approximate and are intended for planning purposes only. *Note:* lodgings are categorized by price and depending on the room selected may appear in more than one category. Meal prices at lunch include an average entrée and beverage. Dinner prices include an appetizer, entrée, dessert, and beverage. Wine or alcoholic beverages are not included.

Staying and dining at expensive lodgings and restaurants: From $400 to $580 per day for two.

Lodging: Captain Lord Mansion, White Barn Inn, Inn at Harbor Head, Bufflehead Cove, Old Fort Inn, Maine Stay Inn.

Dining: Breakfast: included. Lunch: Seascapes, Hurricane's, Windows on the Water. Dinner: White Barn Inn, Arrows.

Staying and dining at moderately priced lodgings and restaurants: From $240–$340 per day for two.

Lodging: Captain Lord Mansion, White Barn Inn, Inn at Harbor Head, Inn on South Street, Captain Fairfield Inn, Old Fort Inn, Maine Stay Inn, Cape Arundel Inn, Bufflehead Cove.

Dining: Breakfast: included except at Cape Arundel Inn. Lunch: Lobster Pot, Mabel's, Allison's. Dinner: Mabel's, Hurricane's, Windows on the Water, Cape Arundel Inn, Seascapes.

Staying and dining at less expensive inns and restaurants: From $150 to $170 per day for two.

Lodging: Captain Fairfield Inn, Cape Arundel Inn.

Dining: Breakfast: included. Lunch: Allison's, the Lobster Pot, Clam Shack, Cape Porpoise Lobster Company. Dinner: Allison's, the Lobster Pot, Nunan's, Grissini, Mabel's, Hurricane's.

6

Portland to Boothbay Harbor, Maine

Portland, with a population of 66,000, is likened to San Francisco by the many young professionals and artists who have moved here in the past decade. Like San Francisco it is bordered by water on three sides. Portland is a wonderful city to explore on foot and by ferry (a number of the islands in Casco Bay are part of the city). There is an active commercial waterfront, an abundance of good restaurants, a symphony orchestra, a string quartet, and a highly regarded theater company.

The Old Port Exchange area with its paving-block streets, brick sidewalks, and gaslights is a major tourist attraction in the city. The four-and five-story granite and brick buildings, many of which were built in the Victorian style after a great fire in 1866, provide a pleasing-looking streetscape that extends along 100-foot-wide Commercial Street, from the Casco Bay Lines ferry terminal (public rest rooms are available here) to the visitors center and the streets leading away from the water.

Most of the stores in the Old Port Exchange are locally owned and sell out-of-the-ordinary merchandise. Visit galleries, crafts shops, antiquarian bookshops (there are nine throughout the city), coffee shops, stores with trendy clothing, pubs, and even a store that specializes in old bottles. A few of our favorites in the Old Port include *Nancy Margolis Gallery,* 367 Fore Street, (207) 775-3822, which has fine pottery and jewelry; *Abacus,* 44 Exchange Street, (207) 772-4880), which has contemporary crafts and jewelry from throughout the country; and *Joseph's,* 410 Fore Street, (207) 773-1274, which has top-quality designer-name women's and men's clothing.

For information on special events, contact the following:

Portland Visitors Bureau. 305 Commercial Street, Portland, ME 04101-4641; (207) 772-5800. Summer: Monday through Saturday, 8:30 A.M. to 6:30 P.M.; Sunday 9 A.M. to 2 P.M. Winter: Monday through Friday, 9 A.M. to 5 P.M.; Saturday and Sunday, 10 A.M. to 3 P.M.

Freeport Merchants Association. 10 Morse Street, Box 452, Freeport, ME 04032; (800) 865-1994.

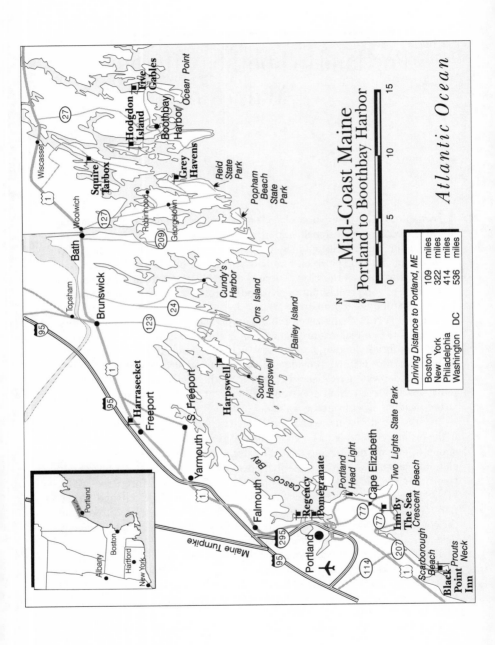

Mid-Coast Maine
Portland to Boothbay Harbor

Atlantic Ocean

N

Driving Distance to Portland, ME		
Boston	109	miles
New York	322	miles
Philadelphia	414	miles
Washington DC	536	miles

0   5   10   15

Wiscasset

Woolwich

Bath

Topsham

Brunswick

Harraseeket
Freeport

S. Freeport

Yarmouth

Harpswell

South
Harpswell

Cundy's
Harbor

Orrs Island

Bailey Island

Falmouth

Casco Bay

Portland

Maine Turnpike

Regency
Pomegranate

Portland
Head Light

Two Lights State Park

Cape Elizabeth

Crescent Beach

Inn By
The Sea

Scarborough
Beach

Black
Point
Inn

Prouts
Neck

Squire
Tarbox

Robinhood

Georgetown

Grey
Havens

Reid State
Park

Popham
Beach
State
Park

Hodgdon
Island

Five
Gables

Boothbay
Harbor

Ocean Point

Albany

Hartford

New York

Boston

Portland

Boothbay Harbor Chamber of Commerce. Located on Route 27 just before the town. P.O. Box 356, Boothbay Harbor, ME 04538; (207) 633-2353.

Chamber of Commerce of the Bath/Brunswick Region. 59 Pleasant Street, Brunswick, ME 04011; (207) 725-8797.

WHERE TO GO, WHAT TO DO

Portland Museum of Art. From the exterior we thought the museum's I. M. Pei–designed 1983 addition of gray concrete looked a bit out of place in this town of nineteenth-century architecture. Inside, however, the dramatic use of space and the light from the curved glass stairwells and the half-moon-shaped window added to our enjoyment. The museum has a large collection of Winslow Homer's paintings, drawings, and prints, some of which are always on permanent exhibition. Homer settled on Prout's Neck, a promontory located thirteen miles south of Portland where many of his finest seascapes of the Maine coast were painted.

The Payson collection of Impressionist paintings includes works by Renoir, Picasso, Degas, and Van Gogh.

Open Tuesday through Saturday, 10 A.M. to 5 P.M.; Thursday 10 A.M. to 9 P.M.; Sunday noon to 5 P.M. Adults $6. Free admission first Saturday morning of the month and Thursday evening. Corner of High and Congress Streets, Portland, ME 04101; (207) 773-ARTS.

The Western Promenade. This district of Portland, on the National Register of Historic Places, is one of America's best-preserved Victorian residential neighborhoods, with dozens of large homes built in the latter part of the nineteenth century.

The Victoria Mansion. This brownstone gem with a distinctive square Italianate tower is on the National Register of Historic Places. The house is filled with opulent furnishings, carved woodwork, stained and etched glass, and colorful frescoes. Open Memorial Day through October and December. Adults $4. 109 Danforth Street, Portland; (207) 772-4841.

Henry Wadsworth Longfellow House. The home where Longfellow spent his childhood is now a national historic landmark. It is open to visitors June through October. Adults $4. 485 Congress Street, Portland; (207) 879-0427.

Portland City Hall. This Congress Street building includes a large concert hall where the Portland Symphony performs. Check for performances on the Kotzschmar Organ, one of the largest municipal organs in the country. 389 Congress St, Portland; (207) 874-8300.

Back Bay Cove. If you want to jog, bike, or walk, try the three-and-a-half-mile waterfront trail that circles Back Cove. Part of the path runs parallel to I-295.

Casco Bay Islands. Approximately 135 islands, some privately owned and others that are a part of the city of Portland, are scattered throughout Casco Bay, which stretches twenty miles from Cape Elizabeth to Bailey Island. Casco

The Portland Head Light is the most photographed lighthouse in Maine.

Bay Lines coastal ferry service was founded by residents of these islands in 1845.

The mail and freight boat, a two-and-three-quarter-hour run, goes daily to six islands. The sunset run goes to the same islands. If your time is short and you want to experience one of the islands, take the seventeen-minute ride to Peaks Island, the most populated island (1,500 year-round and 6,000 summer residents), and walk or bike around this suburb of Portland.

Bailey Island Cruise. This guided boat tour leaves from Portland and cruises through the islands in Casco Bay to Bailey Island, docking at Cook's Landing, next to Cook's Lobster House, at noon. Have a meal at Cook's Lobster House or take the Bailey Island Nature Watch cruise. Bailey Island Cruise and Bailey Island Nature Watch, third week of June through Labor Day. Stop at the ferry terminal for a current ferry schedule. Commercial and Franklin Streets, Portland; (207) 774-7871.

A driving tour from Cape Elizabeth to Prouts Neck, including the Portland Head Light, Two Lights State Park, Crescent Beach, Scarborough Beach, and Prouts Neck. The Portland Head Light, commissioned by George Washington in 1791, is the most photographed of all the lighthouses in Maine. From Portland take Route 77 (State Street) across the bridge to South Portland. Turn left on Cottage Road/Shore Road and follow it to Fort Williams State Park for dramatic views of the crashing water on the rocks and the white lighthouse. A maritime museum is under construction in the lighthouse. Kite flying is popular here on breezy days. When you leave Fort Williams, continue on the

Shore Road back to Route 77. Turn left at Two Lights Road and follow it to Two Lights Lobster Shack. Take your lobster or fried clams to the picnic tables perched at the edge of the bluff. A little farther along Route 77 is the Inn at the Sea. Swimming and beach-walking possibilities include Crescent Beach State Park on Route 77 and Scarborough Beach State Park on Route 207 just before you reach Prouts Neck, an exclusive community at the tip of the peninsula. (Note that parking is not permitted along the side of the road unless you are staying at the local inn.) Winslow Homer's studio is still here, owned by his family and open to visitors in the summer. There is also a bird sanctuary tucked into the middle of this tip of land. If you've brought bicycles, park at Scarborough Beach and make the loop, plan to have lunch at Black Point Inn and take a walk afterward. Return to Portland on Route 77 or take Route 207 to Route 1.

Freeport

The main attraction here is the L. L. Bean store. Open twenty-four hours a day, it has experts on hunting, fishing, camping, biking, canoeing, and kayaking on site, as well as a large book section and "how to" videotapes set up in the sporting goods section.

The *Visitors Guide to Freeport* lists more than 100 other stores, restaurants, and lodgings. The main visitors center is on Depot Street between Mill and Bow Streets, one block below Main Street (Route 1), (800) 865-1994. Other than L. L. Bean, our favorite store is Fila. There are excellent discounts for the discontinued or overstocked styles of Dooney and Bourke or Coach bags. Everyone has her favorites, and it's often a question of what is in stock at any given time. For shoes, visit Cole Haan, Reebok/Rockport, Nike, Bass, and Timberland; for casual sportswear, Polo/Ralph Lauren, J. Crew, Patagonia, Nautica, and Boston Traders. For higher fashion, try Laura Ashley, Harve Bernard, Hickey Freeman, Anne Klein, or Calvin Klein.

Desert of Maine. This thirty-five-acre oddity was once part of a farm. A combination of overplanting, lack of crop rotation, and massive land clearing started the soil erosion that spread and exposed the sand and mineral deposits which came from a glacier about 8,000 years ago. Open May through mid-October. Adults $6. Exit 19 from I-95, 3 miles from Freeport; (207) 865-6962.

South Freeport. When you tire of shopping, drive two miles to the dock in South Freeport to Harraseeket Lunch and Lobster Company for lobster and fried clams to eat at the picnic tables overlooking the working harbor. If you are driving north from Portland and wish to bypass the Freeport Route 1 traffic, take the more scenic route through South Freeport. With our detailed DeLorme Maine Atlas, which we strongly suggest should be in your car for backroading, we were able to avoid both Freeport and Brunswick as we made our way to the Harpswells. Turn off Route 1 south of Freeport and follow signs to South Freeport, continue on Pleasant Hill Road till it ends, turn right on Main

Street, then left on Middle Bay Road to Route 123, the main road that goes down Harpswell Neck.

Brunswick and the Harpswells

Bowdoin College and the Brunswick Naval Air Station are in Brunswick. Park along the edge of the campus and walk on the tree-shaded walkways to the college museum. The Peary-Macmillan Arctic Museum in Hubbard Hall has displays about these two explorers' expeditions.

Bowdoin College Museum. Plan to stop at this free museum housed in the Walker Art Building. A rotunda leads to several galleries with a wide-ranging collection of American paintings from the Colonial period through the twentieth century. The Gilbert Stuart portraits of Jefferson and Madison are noteworthy, and the Winslow Homer gallery on the lower level has changing exhibits of Homer's prints, drawings, and paintings. On our visit we saw a photograph of Homer working in his studio at Prout's Neck on *The Gulf Stream,* the magnificent painting of a man adrift at sea that hangs in the Metropolitan Museum of Art in New York City. Open Tuesday through Saturday, 10 A.M. to 5 P.M. and Sunday, 2 to 5 P.M.; (207) 725-3275.

Maine State Music Theatre. Five professional musicals are performed on the Bowdoin College campus, June through August. P.O. Box 656, Brunswick, ME 04011; (207) 725-8769.

Eagle Island. Admiral Peary, the first person to set foot on the North Pole, had a summer home on Eagle Island, a seventeen-acre island off the Harpswells. He left the island to the state, and his house is now a small museum open during the summer. The Atlantic Seal Cruises (207-865-6112) leaves from South Freeport for three-hour excursions to see the museum and explore the island. Atlantic Seal Cruises also has foliage trips and lobstering demonstrations.

Drive to South Harpswell and Bailey Island. From Brunswick take Route 123 south, which goes through the Bowdoin College campus. Note the location of Mountain Road, about six and a half miles south of the campus, since you will want to take it to cross over to Bailey Island on your way back up the peninsula. Widgeon Cove studio, which sells jewelry and handmade decorative papers, is just off Route 123 south of Mountain Road; (207) 833-6081. Harpswell Inn is a half mile down Lookout Point Road. In Harpswell Center the church and meetinghouse both date from the mid-1700s. Ash Cove pottery is farther down Route 123 on the right; (207) 833-6004. Take a right turn off Route 123 to Basin Point and follow this back road two and a half miles to the end to the Dolphin Marina and Restaurant, one of the great finds of this trip. Continue down Route 123 past Estes Lobster House, which has a picturesque location but is open only seasonally. At the end of the road look for the sign that says "Potts Point Road Association—Private." Follow this extremely bumpy road $\frac{4}{10}$ mile to the end, where there is parking for three cars and a tiny, rocky beach with great views. Return north to Mountain Road and take a right to reach Orrs and Bailey Islands.

Mountain Road and the lower section of Route 24 out to Bailey Island have the best views in the Harpswells. On Orrs Island, look for the sign for Crib-stone Artisans, an artists' cooperative. The one-of-a-kind cribstone bridge con-necting Orrs Island and Bailey Island is made out of granite blocks with space between to allow the changing tides to pass through the bridge. Jack Baker's Oceanview Restaurant is at the bridge, and farther on is Cook's Lobster House.

The Giants Stairs. Don't leave Bailey Island without taking a short walk to view a series of giant boulders that create steps down to the rugged coastline. A plaque at the spot says that land was presented to the town in 1910 by a captain and his wife. Starting at the Log Cabin Restaurant go nine-tenths of a mile and turn left at Washington Avenue (yellow house on the corner). Park next to a small brown shingled building, a rustic Episcopal church with four columns on the porch, but no steeple. Follow the footpath that leads straight toward the water and then turns to the right, about a ten-minute walk to the Giants Stairs.

If you want to continue exploring, take the road to Cundy's Harbor located four and a half miles off Route 24. Holbrook's Lobster Wharf is open season-ally.

Bath

You will know you are near Bath when you see the giant red-and-white crane of the Bath Iron Works looming overhead. This company, one of the largest employers in Maine, has been building large ships for more than 100 years. When you cross the Kennebec River you will see one or more of the navy's Aegis Destroyer–class ships, which are built and repaired here. To avoid the inevitable bottleneck of traffic over the bridge, particularly during the summer, plan your trip to avoid the 4 P.M. shift change. In Bath we enjoyed walking along Washington Street to look at the mansions built from the profits of the sixteen shipyards that prospered in the second half of the eighteenth century. Several of the mansions are now comfortable bed-and-breakfasts.

Maine Maritime Museum. This ten-acre museum is at the south end of town along the Kennebec River just below the Bath Iron Works. Here you can see and experience 400 years of Maine's maritime history. In the Maritime History Building, paintings, models, videos, and artifacts tell the story of Maine and the sea. The history of the Bath Iron Works is shown in photographs and models.

The best time to come is May through mid-November, when you can also tour five buildings in the former Percy & Small Shipyard. On weekdays you can watch the apprentices restore and build wooden boats. Children enjoy going aboard the Grand Banks schooner *Sherman Zwicker* to learn about cod fishing. We particularly liked the exhibit building devoted to lobstering and the Maine coast.

During the summer months the *Hardy II* cruises the Kennebec River, making six daily fifty-minute trips up to the Bath Iron Works and down to Doubling Point. Since visitors are not allowed in the factory, this view of the activity is as close as you can get. When a ship is launched, special cruises allow visitors to watch the activity from the water. Signs at the museum list launching times, but it's best to call the museum in advance for dates and times.

The main building is open year-round 9:30 A.M. to 5 P.M. The shipyard is open May through Thanksgiving weekend. Adults $7. 243 Washington Street, Bath, ME; (207) 443-1316.

Driving tour to Reid State Park. After you cross the bridge from Bath you are in Woolwich. Head south on Route 127. The Osprey (*see* Where to Dine), located at the far end of a marina in Robinhood, off Route 127 before Georgetown, has top-notch views and food. If you've eaten at the Osprey you will have seen the examples of Georgetown Pottery, which are available at the pottery farther down the peninsula on Route 127.

Reid State Park is an idyllic spot. Some of the picnic tables are set on the rocks and others are at the edge of a grove of trees. We took a trail along the rocks and felt the impact of the waves as they crashed below us.

The park has two beaches, rest rooms with flush toilets, and a snack bar. The state park is open year-round with a charge during the season, mid-April to mid-October. At other times of the year, park on the road and walk in. Located on Route 127, fourteen miles south of Bath; (207) 371-2303.

On your return just after you pass Grey Havens (*see* Where to Stay) you will come to the intersection with Route 127, where an American flag is painted on a rock. Turn right and go to Five Islands, a working fishing harbor with a small seasonal lobster restaurant (*see* Where to Dine) on the docks. Locals believe some of the best lobsters in the world are caught in this harbor. Just before the bridge leaving Georgetown Island, turn left at Indian Point Road. The road takes you through the backside of Reid State Park, with good views of the water and historic homes, then loops back. Birders will enjoy a visit to the Audubon Society Josephine Sanctuary, located near Georgetown Center.

Wiscasset

This village is one of the prettiest in Maine. The road curves around the courthouse and leads down the hill to the bridge over the Sheepscot River. You can see a few of the sea captains' homes, antique stores, and an enticing array of stores on both sides of the road by the bridge. As you cross the bridge and see your first glimpses of the water, you may spot the hulks of two wooden schooners, built in 1917 and 1918, lying on their sides in the Sheepscot River. Le Garage (*see* Where to Dine) on Water Street overlooks them.

In Wiscasset, drive down the side roads near the water to get a better look at the sea captains' homes. The area around the Musical Wonder House (see below) is particularly elegant.

Antique Dealers. Wiscasset has a concentration of antique shops, most of which are found on Main Street. The antique dealers put out a yearly map showing the location of seventeen shops in the village; the map is free at the shops in town. Here are a few: Marston House, Main Street at Middle Street, (207) 882-6010, American country furniture and accessories. Nonesuch House, 1 Middle Street, (207) 882-6768, a number of dealers with a jumble of items spread over a few floors. Newton Marine Antiques, on U.S. 1 just before Wiscasset, (207) 882-7208, quality antiques, scrimshaw, paintings.

Musical Wonder House. "What should I play today?" Danilo Konvalinka, founder-owner of this unique museum, asked as he sat down to his Steinway baby-grand pianola. "A little Mozart," we replied, and from his boxes of classical music rolls he picked excerpts from *Don Giovani,* placed them into this interpretative player piano, pumped the foot pedals, and entertained us for ten minutes. The one-hour tour includes three downstairs rooms that are filled with dozens of working music boxes and mechanical music machines in mint operating condition. Danilo explains the history of the music box and demonstrates examples of Swiss, French, Austrian, German, and American pieces from different periods in his large 1852 sea captain's mansion.

For visitors with a serious interest in these machines, Danilo offers a three-hour tour that includes many more examples in the upstairs rooms. The house has a gift shop with music boxes and an extensive collection of recordings of music boxes and the Steinway grand pianola in the house.

Open daily Memorial Day through Mid-October, 10 A.M. to 5 P.M. One-hour guided tour $12.50. 18 High Street, Wiscasset, ME 04578; (800) 339-7163 (in Maine); (800) 336-3725 (out of Maine).

Boothbay Harbor Peninsula

Edgecomb Potters Gallery. Located three and a half miles south of Route 1 ((207) 882-6802), this gallery is one of our favorites. Edgecomb is the largest pottery in Maine, with a large gallery that displays functional pieces in distinctive vibrant reds, purples, and deep blues.

Boothbay Harbor. During the summer Boothbay Harbor is a popular vacation destination. The town has attractions galore, including shops, restaurants, and activities for children and adults. Many motels ring the picturesque harbor.

If you want to get out on the water, pick up a Boothbay Harbor visitors guide at the information booth on the way into town. These are three excursions we particularly like:

Trip to Monhegan Island. The *Balmy Days* leaves from Boothbay Harbor (pier 8) in the morning and returns in the late afternoon. You will have about four hours on Monhegan Island to walk the trails, have a lobster bake, or visit artists' studios; (207) 633-2284.

Sailing Trip. The *Appledore,* a sixty-foot windjammer, has four trips in the bay around Boothbay Harbor daily, leaving from pier 6; (207) 633-6598.

Clambake at Cabbage Island. If you've never had a real clambake with lobster, corn, clams, potatoes, and eggs steamed in seaweed over the coals, we suggest the trip to Cabbage Island (*see* Where to Dine) for lunch or dinner; (207) 633-7200.

Driving tour around Boothbay, Southport Island, and to Ocean Point. At the intersection of Route 27 in Boothbay, bear right and follow signs to Hodgdon House (*see* Where to Stay). The road crosses a number of bridges before you get to the inn. Turn left at the road just before the inn and follow signs to Sawyers Island. The road will dead-end at a private ferry landing. On your return, follow Samoset Drive to Lakeside Drive.

Once back on Route 27, follow the signs to Southport Island. Take Route 27 to the tip at Newagen, where there is a good view of the Cuckolds Lighthouse. Go back on Route 238. Take the turn to Capitol Island. When the road turns to a two-track dirt road, park your car and walk. The dirt road makes a pretty one-mile loop through the woods, with private drives leading to summer homes along the shore. For a lobster dinner, stop at Robinson's Wharf (*see* Where to Dine).

After visiting Boothbay Harbor and driving to Spruce Point, take Route 96 to East Boothbay. Five Gables Inn (*see* Where to Stay) is located on Murray Hill Road and has a view of the water. Lobsterman's Wharf (*see* Where to Dine) in East Boothbay is another good choice. Continue on Route 96, taking the right-hand side road that hugs the shore. The last stretch of this road, which ends at Ocean Point, is one of the great panoramas of the Maine coastline.

WHERE TO STAY

Prouts Neck to Portland

Black Point Inn Resort, Prouts Neck

The setting for this 115-year-old inn is within a private enclave on a spectacular point of land along the rocky coast of Maine. In past years guests stayed for a month or two during July and August, known as "the social season." Now the stays are generally a week or less, but enduring traditions include jackets required for dinner, finger bowls, dancing on the weekends, and a pianist for afternoon tea.

The resort has ten all-weather and four clay tennis courts, an indoor pool, a whirlpool, exercise machines, and a large swimming pool that overlooks the ocean. There are fifteen bicycles and two sailboats, a bird sanctuary with a half-mile trail, and a cliff trail along the ocean. Winslow Homer's studio is just down the road from the inn and is open to visitors in the summer. Guests have privileges at three golf courses in the area.

Accommodations are in the main building and in four lovely cottages ranging in size from five to nine bedrooms. Each cottage has at least one common room with a wood-burning fireplace. Rooms throughout the resort are spacious and have traditional cherry reproduction furnishings, including both a queen-size and a twin bed. All have air-conditioning, a telephone, and a radio. Many rooms have water views. The five-course dinner menu changes daily, but one of the seven entrées is always lobster.

Open May through late November. Eighty rooms and suites, all with private bath. Summer: $280–$400 for two including breakfast and dinner. Spring and fall: $240–$320. 15% service charge. November $90–$200 (bed-and-breakfast). Three-night minimum stay during the summer, two nights at other times. Children under 8 welcome during early July and late August. No pets. Prouts Neck, Scarborough, ME 04074; (207) 883-4126; (800) 258-0003.

Inn by the Sea, Cape Elizabeth

This gray shingled complex of a main building and four cottage buildings borders Crescent Beach State Park. Unlike other accommodations in the area, all of the rooms are suites with full kitchens. Original Audubon prints of seacoast birds hang in the marble-tiled lobby and dining room.

The best suites in the main building are the two-level Loft Suites; the lower level has a kitchen, a spacious living room with a two-story cathedral ceiling, and a small deck area, while the upper level has two double beds, a bath with a soaking tub, and a separate shower.

The cottages have wide wraparound porches or decks and expansive views of the marsh grasses and the ocean in the distance. All of the cottage units have two bedrooms; some have wood stoves. Some cottage units are on two levels with skylights and peaked ceilings. All of the suites have televisions, VCRs, and telephones, but are not air-conditioned.

Facilities include an outdoor swimming pool, a tennis court, and bicycles. A boardwalk leads from the inn to Crescent Beach State Park, a grand sand beach overlooking the Atlantic Ocean. Guests can cook their own breakfast or splurge on the inn's variation of eggs Benedict made with fresh lobster meat.

Forty-three one- and two-bedroom suites, all with full kitchens. July and August, $180–$410. Other times, $125–280. Packages available midweek and off-season. Breakfast and dinner served nightly but not included in the rates. Children welcome. No pets. Route 77, Cape Elizabeth, ME 04107; (207) 799-3134; (800) 888-IBTS.

Pomegranate Inn, Portland

This 1884 Colonial Revival sits on a corner lot in the Western Promenade district of Portland, one of America's best-preserved Victorian residential neighborhoods. This district is about a twenty-minute walk from the Old Port.

The inn is decorated with a profusion of paintings and antiques collected by owner Isabel Smiles, an interior decorator. The dining room features marbleized columns, mantel, and floors, bedrooms have large, bold abstract patterns painted on the walls.

The two largest rooms are room 2 on the third floor, with a king-size bed, and room 4 on the second floor, with twin beds. Next door, the second-floor suite includes a living room with a gas fireplace and a small bedroom with a queen-size bed. The Garden Room is a wheelchair-accessible ground floor room with a marble bath and an outdoor sitting area. All rooms have small televisions, telephones, and air-conditioning. On our visit, the main dish at breakfast was grilled mushrooms and tomatoes on polenta.

Seven rooms and an apartment, all with private bath. May through October, $125–$165. Other times, $95–$125. Two-night weekend minimum in season. Children over 16 welcome. No pets. 49 Neal Street, Portland, ME 04102; (207) 772-1006; (800) 356-0408.

Regency Hotel, Portland

This historic brick four-story full-service hotel is situated in the middle of the Old Port. The ten water-view rooms are our favorites; the best views are on the second and third floors. (No smoking is permitted on the second floor.) You can request one of these rooms, but they are assigned on your day of arrival. Rooms have a king-size or two double beds, two telephones, a television, and marble-topped sinks. The two Regency suites, which do not have water views, have a large sitting area, a minibar, and a king-size bed.

The hotel has an excellent health club. Aerobic classes, a twenty-four-station Nautilus, Stairmasters, rowing machines, treadmills, and a twenty-person whirlpool are free to hotel guests; for an extra fee you can get a massage or use the tanning booths.

Ninety-five rooms and suites, all with private bath. Mid-July through mid-October, $159–$229. Lower rates at other times. Weekend packages, November through May. Children welcome. No pets. 20 Milk Street, Portland, ME 04101; (207) 774-4200; (800) 727-3436.

Freeport to the Harpswells

Harraseeket Inn, Freeport

This full-service inn, comprising two nineteenth-century homes and a large modern building designed to blend into the architecture of the town, is located on the Main Street of Freeport, just two blocks from L. L. Bean and the myriad outlet shops. The inn has a fine restaurant (*see* Where to Dine), a tavern decorated in the style of a Maine woods camp, and a range of accommodations. Morning coffee is served from 6 A.M., and a complimentary afternoon tea that includes sweets, sandwiches, fruit, and cheese is served from 4 to 5 P.M. in a large drawing room with mahogany paneling and a fireplace.

The rooms are spacious. Standard rooms have a king-size bed and deluxe rooms have a wood-burning fireplace that faces the bed and a bath with a whirlpool Jacuzzi. A few of the rooms have a slightly larger than single-size whirlpool in the bedroom, as well as a separate bath with a shower. The suites include a wet bar and sitting area, and can be equipped with a microwave by request. All rooms have phones and televisions.

The buffet breakfast includes hot cereal and granola, fresh fruit, muffins, and about six silver-domed chafing dishes with selections of bacon, sausage, French toast, frittata, and fried potatoes.

Fifty-four rooms and suites, all with private bath. Mid-May through October, $150–$225. Other times of the year, rooms $95–$205. Full breakfast and afternoon tea included. Children welcome. No pets. No minimum-stay requirement. 162 Main Street, Freeport, ME 04032; (207) 865-9377; (800) 342-6423.

Harpswell Inn, South Harpswell

The inn, a large white house with dark shutters located at the end of a side road in Harpswell Neck, sits atop a knoll at Lookout Point overlooking the islands in Middle Bay and is owned by innkeepers Susan and Bill Menz. Built in 1761, it served as the cookhouse for a thriving shipyard that produced schooners and brigs during the mid nineteenth century.

The great room is large and comfortable, with a baby grand piano, a wood-burning stone fireplace, and Oriental rugs. The innkeepers are most enthusiastic. Top choices are the two new luxury suites in a separate building. The Captains Quarters, with the better view, has a wall of windows overlooking the water, a deck, a full kitchen, a cathedral ceiling in the bedroom and bath, and a gas fireplace. Eagle's Nest is a two-story suite with a cathedral ceiling, kitchenette, half bath, and living room with gas fireplace on the first floor and a bedroom, bath, and deck on the second floor.

In the inn we like Sunset, a two-floor suite good for a family; the first-floor Rackliffe Room, with a four-poster queen-size bed, and the Sunrise Room on the third floor, with a queen-size canopy bed.

Breakfast includes a hot dish such as blueberry-and-cream French toast, blueberry pancakes, or an egg, cheese, and sausage casserole.

Fourteen rooms, eight with private bath; six rooms share two baths. Mid-June through October, $64–$150. Other times, $54–$150. Full breakfast included. Children over 10 welcome. No pets. No smoking. Two-night weekend minimum in season. 141 Lookout Point Road, RR1 Box 141, South Harpswell, ME 04079; (207) 833-5509.

Georgetown, Boothbay, and Newcastle

The Grey Havens Inn, Georgetown Island

You can hear the waves crashing on the rocks and smell the salt air at this gloriously preserved relic located right on the water. Built in 1904, it is the last shingle-style hotel of its type still in existence on the Maine coast. This is *the* place to stay if you really want to feel the ocean.

The massive fireplace, built of large cobblestones gathered from nearby beaches, is the centerpiece of the great room. A twelve-foot long picture window overlooks the porch and the ocean. Owners Bill and Haley Eberhart told us some guests hope there will be a storm during their stay because the views of the water from the inn are so dramatic.

The Ocean Front Suite, our top choice, is an extra-long room with a king-size bed, a private balcony, and a full front view of the water. The four corner turret rooms also have water views but do not have balconies. Most of the ten remaining rooms also face the ocean and are furnished with period pieces such as iron, brass, or antique wood beds; the walls and ceilings throughout the building are yellow pine. The inn has a rowboat guests can use to explore a secluded island.

A continental buffet breakfast includes blueberry muffins, fresh fruit, cereal, and breads.

Open April through mid-December. Fourteen rooms, twelve with private bath either in the room or across the hall, $100–$195. Breakfast included. Children over 7 welcome. No pets. Two night weekend minimum in season. From Bath, south on Route 127 for 11 miles following the signs to Reid State Park. P.O. Box 308, Seguinland Road, Georgetown, ME 04548; (207) 371-2616.

Squire Tarbox Inn, Wiscasset

This inn has a quiet wooded setting south of Wiscasset on Westport Island. Innkeepers Karen and Bill Mitman raise Nubian goats and also have a horse, two donkeys, and several chickens. The inn is a collection of connecting Maine buildings from different centuries. The original cape house dates from 1763. Samuel Tarbox added a Federal-style home which has four large guest rooms and a comfortable living room, each with a wood-burning fireplace. The other seven rooms are the barn rooms, four of which open off the casual double-story barn sitting room, which has a wood stove; the other three rooms have private entrances.

There's much to see on the property. The 1820 post-and-beam barn has two rope swings. Beyond are the goats' sheds, which are kept extremely clean. A 1,000-foot path leads through a wooded area to a saltwater inlet with a floating dock, a rowboat for guests' use, and a small screened building with two chairs. Stay a few days and you'll soon adjust to the easy rhythm of this idyllic spot.

Dining at this inn is a memorable experience, far more than just a delicious dinner by a wood-burning fireplace. It begins with an informal cocktail hour that features a sampling of goat cheeses made at the inn. Dinner is served at 7 P.M., and at 9 P.M. most guests wander out to the barn to watch Karen milk the goats.

Squire Tarbox Inn is a collection of connecting Maine buildings from the eighteenth and nineteenth centuries.

The breakfast buffet includes fruit, home-baked breads, goat cheese, and granola.

Open mid-May through October. Eleven rooms, all with private bath, $135–$240, breakfast and dinner for two included; bed-and-breakfast, $65–$175. 12% service charge. Children over 12 welcome. No pets. Dinner, 7 P.M. Prix fixe, $29. Two-night weekend minimum. RR 2, Box 620, Wiscasset, ME 04578; (207) 882-7693.

Hodgdon Island Inn, Boothbay

This bed-and-breakfast on the water is definitely off the tourist path, but it's only a few miles west of busy Boothbay Harbor. All the rooms have views of a protected cove and a manually operated swing bridge. Innkeepers Joe and Sydney Klenk purchased the house in 1990 and renovated the interior to create six rooms, each with a new bath. They also have added a swimming pool.

All rooms have water views. Room 6 is the largest, with a king-size bed, a bath with tub/shower (most of the others only have showers), and access to a private porch that it shares with room 5. Room 4, with a king-size bed, and room 3, with a queen-size bed, each has a bay window.

Six rooms, all with private bath. May through October, $85–$105. Other times, $65–$75. Children over 12 welcome. Full breakfast included. No smoking. No pets. Located 3½ miles from Boothbay Harbor. Box 492, Trevett, ME 04571; (207) 633-7474.

Five Gables Inn, East Boothbay

If you want to be in a quiet village three miles from Boothbay Harbor and a short walk from the Lobsterman's Wharf Restaurant, this is a good place to stay. New innkeepers Mike and De Kennedy purchased this restored Maine nineteenth-century summer hotel overlooking Linekin Bay in 1995.

In nice weather guests have breakfast on the wide front porch, which looks out over the rooftops to the water. In cooler weather, breakfast is served in the common room at tables looking out onto the porch or in a seating area with a fireplace and easy chairs.

The largest room is room 14 on the third floor, with a king-size bed, a good view, and a fireplace. We also like rooms 8 and 10, corner rooms with views. Three second-floor rooms have queen-size beds and a fireplace, and one on the first floor has a double bed and fireplace. The gabled rooms on the third floor are cozy and comfortable with good views, but tall guests might find the ceilings too low.

Mike serves a multicourse breakfast buffet from 8 to 9:30 A.M. that includes a hot dish such as a tomato-and-basil frittata, quiche, French toast, or zucchini walnut pancakes with bacon or sausages. During the summer, guests eat at tables on the front porch.

Open mid-May to mid-November. Sixteen rooms, all with private bath, $90–$155. Full breakfast and afternoon snacks included. Children over 8 welcome. No smoking. No pets. Murray Hill Road, East Boothbay, ME 04544; (207) 633-4551; (800) 451-5048.

WHERE TO DINE

Portland

Street and Co.

This small, popular restaurant located on a narrow cobblestone street in the Old Port area serves large portions of exceptionally well prepared, simply cooked seafood. You can watch the chefs at work in the open kitchen in full view of the diners inside and those seated outside at tables spread along the narrow brick sidewalk. Individual sauté pans are whisked from the stove and placed directly on the attractive copper-clad tables.

Starters included excellent steamed clams with white wine and garlic broth, crab cakes, and sautéed crab served over a crouton. We had a generous thick portion of Cajun swordfish and a halibut filet served with mango butter. Calamari marinara, mussels or clams in a red or white sauce, and shrimp with tomatoes and capers are served over linguine and arrive at your table in individual pans. Other entrées include scallops in Pernod cream sauce, lobster diavalo for two, and sole Française.

Dinner nightly. Entrées $12–$18. 33 Wharf Street, Portland, ME; (207) 775-0887.

Fore Street

Sam Haywood, formerly the chef at Haraseeket Inn in Freeport, is the owner of this new downtown restaurant that overlooks the ferry terminal. It is a large room with an open kitchen, featuring a wood-fired brick oven as well as a rotisserie, and windows on three sides with views of the water. The metal-topped booths along one wall are popular. Other tables are copper-topped. The food preparation is straightforward, popular items include grilled pheasant, rabbit, and hanger steak and seafood, pizzettes, and salads.

Dinner nightly. Entrées $12–$18. 288 Fore Street, Portland, ME; (207) 775-2717.

Back Bay Grill

This is one of the top upscale gourmet restaurants in Portland, attracting the city's movers and shakers. The two high-ceilinged white-walled airy rooms are decorated with large abstract oil paintings and a wall mural of Portland's Back Bay. There is an open kitchen at the rear of the front dining room.

A single ravioli stuffed with Gorgonzola and surrounded with grilled leeks and a pungent brown sauce was a distinctive appetizer. The sweet-potato-and-lime bisque was accented with rhubarb chutney, a good contrast of taste and texture. Farm-raised salmon comes from nearby Rockland. The swordfish was served over couscous with grilled goat cheese wrapped in a radicchio leaf, and a thick grilled veal chop with peppercorn sauce came with braised endive.

Desserts are creative preparations: grilled strawberries tossed with cassis and pineapple-mint sorbet, grilled shortcake drizzled with Frangelico served with nougat ice cream, and plum-port sorbet in a chocolate tulip wafer.

Dinner, Monday through Saturday. Entrées $15–$20. 65 Portland Street, Portland, ME; (207) 772-8833.

Informal Dining in Portland

DeMillo's Floating Restaurant

This is the only place in Portland where you can dine outside next to the water. This boat restaurant is extraordinarily popular with locals as well as tourists. The traditional menu includes well-prepared lobster, steaks, and Italian fare. Long Wharf, Commercial Street, Portland; (207) 772-2216.

Raffles Cafe Bookstore

Located in the center of the business district, this bookstore-café is a good place to talk over coffee and muffins in the morning or a vegetarian lunch. 555 Congress Street, Portland; (207) 761-3930.

Portland Coffee Roasting

The smell of roasting coffee beans tempted us to stop for rich strong coffee and a pastry at this European-style café, a convenient place to rest and reconnoiter during your tour of the Old Port. 111 Comercial Street, Portland; (207) 761-9525.

Becky's on Hobson's Wharf

Portland still has a large fishing industry, and this diner is in the middle of the action on Hobson's Wharf. The early shift opens this diner at 4 A.M. 390 Commercial Street, Portland; (207) 773-7070.

Cape Elizabeth to Boothbay Harbor

Inn by the Sea, Cape Elizabeth

The restaurant, an attractive, airy dining room located about twenty minutes south of Portland, has a view of the water. For summer dining we like the porch room, particularly the tables with a water view.

There are always a couple of lobster preparations on the menu. Starters might include duck breast on a salad of spinach and arugula, spinach greens and caramelized walnuts with grilled portabella mushrooms and warm bacon dressing, lobster bisque, or lobster ravioli. Mixed seafood grill, crab cakes, grilled marinated chicken, grilled Thai sea scallops, shrimp Szechuan, rack of lamb, grilled tournedos, and a combination of lobster, shrimp, and scallops served over angel-hair pasta with peppers and asparagus are a selection of entrées.

Lunch and dinner daily. Lunch $7–$11. Dinner entrées $10–$25. Route 77, Cape Elizabeth, ME; (207) 799-3134; (800) 888-IBTS.

Harraseeket Inn, Freeport

We have a lot of respect for this kitchen. Salads feature locally grown organic greens, and a sea salad combines different seaweeds and smoked Maine shellfish. Other appetizers include farm-raised Pemaquid oysters; raviolini filled with winter squash and fresh savory; quail marinated with maple syrup; and two chilled soups, lobster and vichyssoise, served in one bowl.

A speciality in the Maine Dining Room is tableside preparation of Caesar salads, selected entrées, and flaming desserts. Rack of lamb cut tableside had an excellent white garlic cream sauce. Duck was carved tableside and prepared with port, peaches, and fried ginger. The chateaubriand covered with wild mushrooms was a spectacular presentation. The two-inch-high tenderloin steak, a popular entrée, is covered with shallots, mustard, and parsley. For dessert we had strawberry-rhubarb pie and a trio of sorbets.

The casual Broad Arrow Tavern is decorated to feel like a Maine backwoods hunting and fishing camp. The menu includes a bucket of steamed clams, Pemaquid oysters, baked beans with brown bread pancakes, lobster roll, grilled vegetable sandwich, or such entrées as fried clams, scallops, steamed lobster, grilled sirloin steak, or macaroni and Maine cheddar cheese.

Buffet breakfast. Lunch and dinner in the Broad Arrow Tavern, $3–$16. Buffet lunch during the summer, $12, and dinner nightly in the Maine Dining Room, entrées $15–$24. 162 Main Street, Freeport, ME; (207) 865-9377; (800) 342-6423.

The Osprey, Robinhood

"The osprey come back every year in the beginning of April to rebuild their nests on the number three day marker," we were told by our knowledgeable waitress, who brought a pair of binoculars to our window table. (Each marker has a number that corresponds to a navigational chart of the water.) The restaurant is on the second floor of an inconspicuous building in the back of a boatyard.

Try sushi-style tuna rolls, roasted oysters, shrimp and crab cakes, homemade sausage, or smoked trout for appetizers. Most of the pasta is homemade, with combinations such as mussels and fettuccine, ravioli with Asian duck, and black sesame pasta with pickled ginger. Entrées include fire-roasted leg of lamb with chipotle peppers, shelled and grilled lobster with zinfandel butter served over fettuccine, and grilled swordfish.

Lunch selections include a grilled steak sandwich with roasted garlic potatoes and smoked turkey with Granny Smith apples and Gorgonzola.

May through mid-October, lunch and dinner daily. Lunch $6–9. Dinner entrées $18–$24. South on Route 127 from Woolwich for six miles; left on Robinhood Road to the marina. Robinhood Road, Robinhood, ME; (207) 371-2530.

The Robinhood Free Meetinghouse, Robinhood

Chef-owner Michael Gagné, formerly the owner of the Osprey (see above), serves dinner in this 1855 historic church. The church still has its original pews (used for weddings), and the choir loft is used as a dining room, albeit a cavernous one with sixteen-foot ceilings. The menu is a tour of world cuisines, from saltimbocca to scallops Niçoise in puff pastry with sun-dried tomatoes to Wiener schnitzel with German potato pancakes, lingonberries, and sour cream. Jumbo shrimp and scallops are sautéed with bok choy, mushrooms, oyster sauce, preserved black beans, and chili paste. For beef traditionalists there are tournedos, grilled sirloin with crabmeat, and a Szechuan sirloin. All told, the menu has thirty-eight entrées and almost an equal number of soups, salads, pastas, and appetizers.

For lunch we had a superb artichoke strudel with a chunky sauce of tomatoes, mushrooms, and herbs topped with cheese. We also recommend the appetizer of shiitake, crimini, button, and oyster mushrooms on pasta. Other good choices are rice-paper-wrapped salad of avocado, crab, and oriental vegetables, and the homemade sausage sampler.

For dessert, try profiteroles or the individual apple raisin strudel with crème anglaise. If you plan to visit midweek in the spring or fall, ask about scheduled wine-tasting and cooking-school dinners.

Dinner daily and Sunday brunch, May through October. Call for days at other times. Entrées $16–$22. South on Route 127 from Woolwich, six miles; left on Robinhood Road for one mile (one-eighth mile beyond the marina). Robinhood Road, Robinhood, ME; (207) 371-2188.

Squire Tarbox Inn, Wesport Island

Dinner at this inn includes a visit to the barn, where a small herd of Nubian goats is milked each evening at 9 P.M. An informal cocktail hour at 6 P.M. features a sampling of goat cheeses made at the inn's small licensed cheese plant. We tried a creamy chèvre with chives and garlic, a Tellicherry crottin rolled in cracked pepper, and an aged hard Caerphilly that had a smooth texture and mellow flavor. Some of the guests gathered around an old-fashioned player piano; some relaxed by the fireplace or the wood stoves in rooms filled with interesting books about Maine; and others strolled down to the water.

The walls in the dining room are old barnboards, and a brick fireplace creates the ambience. We were seated with two other couples who were staying at the inn. A single entrée four-course dinner is served each evening, although substitutions can be arranged. We started with mushrooms stuffed with spinach and walnuts followed by a salad of mixed greens with balsamic dressing. Slightly sweet buns made from goat whey are always served. The entrée, boneless breast of chicken stuffed with herbed chèvre in a puff pastry shell, was served with fresh asparagus, honey-glazed baby carrots, and pan-roasted potatoes. Dessert was an orange almond tart with whipped cream. Other nights, the main entrée might be grilled swordfish, roast pork, broiled scallops, or poached salmon.

After dessert, diners are invited to the shed to observe the milking process explained by innkeeper and chief goat-milker and cheese maker Karen Mitman.

Dinner nightly, mid-May through October. By advance reservation only. Cocktails 6 P.M., dinner 7 P.M. Prix fixe $31. Located on Route 144 on Westport Island, 8½ miles from Route 1. RR 2, Box 620, Wiscasset, ME; (207) 882-7693.

Kristina's, Bath

This contemporary two-story restaurant and bakery, a favorite with area residents, has a wide-ranging menu. Entrées include haddock baked with crabmeat, spinach fettuccine with grilled chicken, spicy seafood stew, and tenderloin with grilled wild mushrooms. Lunch includes a variety of salads, burgers, and creative sandwiches.

At Sunday brunch, wild berry crisp topped with whipped cream starts the meal. Entrée selections include Kristina's French toast, cinnamon swirl bread filled with cream cheese, apples, and raisins; grilled sourdough bread with scrambled eggs, couscous, and chutney; and huevos rancheros, a tortilla topped with refried beans, poached eggs, salsa, sour cream, cheese, and avocado.

Breakfast, lunch, and dinner daily, Memorial Day though Labor Day. Other times, all meals Wednesday through Saturday, breakfast and lunch Sunday. Entrées $12–$18. 160 Center Street, Bath, ME; (207) 442-8577.

Jack Baker's Oceanview, Bailey Island

This small restaurant located at the south end of the Bailey bridge is perched on the edge of land looking out to sea. The window tables are right on the water. Owner Jack Baker greets you in the entrance lounge, which has a wood-burning fireplace. The menu offers well-prepared basic fare at low prices. We had baked scrod dusted with bread crumbs and Maine shrimp alfredo on fettuccine, served with a basket of corn fritters. Landlubber choices include chicken pot pie and steak. At lunch, try the crabmeat melt on an English muffin or the Maine shrimp roll.

Open daily year-round. Lunch $4–$9. Dinner entrées $9–$16. Bailey Island, ME; (207) 833-5366.

The Dolphin, South Harpswell

Only a local or someone with an inside tip will know to turn off the main road to find this place. During the summer, however, there can be a long wait at lunchtime. The hearty lobster stew or the less expensive fish chowder are the dishes to order here. We had a bowl of stew with a large blueberry muffin, and couldn't resist a piece of the rhubarb pie with ice cream for dessert.

Open daily year-round, 8 A.M. to 8 P.M. Route 123 through West Harpswell; right at Basin Point Road for 2½ miles to the end. South Harpswell; (207) 833-6000.

Le Garage, Wiscasset

This large restaurant on the bank of the Sheepscot overlooking the two decaying wooden schooner hulks serves consistently good food. The menu includes chicken pie, steaks, lamb, pork chops, and prime rib (Saturday only)

as well as haddock, Maine shrimp, scallops, lobster pie, and lobster casserole.
Open year-round except January for lunch and dinner. Entrées $8–$16.
Water Street, Wiscasset; (207) 882-5409.

No Anchovies, Boothbay Harbor

This casual pizza parlor and Italian restaurant has a couple of tables with great
harbor views and serves excellent thin-crust pizza. Open seasonally. Just off
Townsend Avenue, Boothbay Harbor, ME; (207) 633-2130.

Lobster Pounds

No trip to the coast of Maine is complete without a lobster dinner. Here's a
selection of our favorite lobster pounds, from Cape Elizabeth just south of
Portland to East Boothbay, where you can roll up your sleeves and attack your
lobster with gusto.

Two Lights Lobster Shack. Portland area residents have enjoyed the lobster here for more than fifty years. Have your boiled lobster at picnic tables
not more than twenty feet from the waves crashing on the rocks. Open April
through mid-October. Off Route 77, at the end of Two Lights Road, Cape
Elizabeth; (207) 799-1677.

Harraseeket Lunch and Lobster Company. When you tire of the crowds
and shopping in Freeport, drive two miles south to this quiet little fishing
harbor and boatyard for lobsters and fried seafood. Open seasonally. South
Freeport; (207) 865-4888.

Estes Lobster House. This large lobster house, located on a thin strip of
land just before the tip of South Harpswell, has great views in all directions.
Open seasonally for lunch and dinner. Route 123, South Harpswell; (207) 833-
6340.

Cook's Lobster House. Fishing boats unload here. This is a large family
restaurant with a full menu and great views. Avoid the noon hour during the
summer when the Casco Bay cruise boat docks. Open year-round for lunch
and dinner. Route 24, Bailey Island; (207) 833-2818.

Five Islands Lobster. This out-of-the-way lobster shack is on the dock of
a working harbor. Open seasonally. Route 127 to Georgetown, left on Five
Islands Road; (207) 371-2950.

Clambake at Cabbage Island. Take a three-and-a-half hour (round-trip)
excursion to an island just off Boothbay Harbor and enjoy a real clambake
steamed dinner with all the fixings. You'll have plenty of time to explore the
island. Mid-June through Labor Day. Boothbay Harbor; (207) 633-7200.

Robinson's Wharf. This is the place to go for lobster in the rough if you
are staying in Boothbay Harbor and want to escape the crowds. Open seasonally. Route 27, Southport Island; (207) 633-3830.

Lobsterman's Wharf. This is a little fishing community with a local lobster restaurant on the docks of the Damariscotta River. Open seasonally. Route 96, East Boothbay; (207) 633-3443.

ITINERARY

DAY ONE. Start in **Portland** at the visitors center. We suggest getting a city map and a state atlas or a map of the coast of Maine. Drive down the street to the **Casco Bay Lines** ferry terminal for a current schedule. Visit the **Art Museum**. Follow the **driving tour to Cape Elizabeth and Prouts Neck**. For lunch, stop at **Two Lights Lobster Shack** and sit at the picnic tables overlooking the water. Stop at the **Portland Head Light,** the most photographed lighthouse along the coast. Return to Portland to walk through the **Old Port Exchange,** followed by dinner at **Back Bay Grill, Street and Co.,** or **Fore Street.**

DAY TWO. Take one of the Casco Bay ferries. Bring a picnic if you want to explore one of the islands (returning on the later mail boat) or take the Bailey Island Cruise with the option of lunch at **Cook's Lobster House.** Shoppers may want to spend a day at the outlet stores in **Freeport.** Drive to South Freeport for lunch on the docks at the **Harraseeket Lunch and Lobster Co.** Have dinner at the **Harraseeket Inn** in Freeport or back in Portland.

DAY THREE. Take the **driving tour to South Harpswell and Bailey Island.** Have lunch at the out-of-the-way **Dolphin Restaurant** or, if there is a long wait, go to **Estes** in South Harpswell, **Cook's** on Bailey Island, or **Holbrook's Lobster Wharf** in Cundy Harbor. Be sure to take the walk to the **Giant Stairs** when you are on Bailey Island. Continue to **Bath** to the **Maritime Museum** and take the boat trip to see the **Bath Iron Works**. Take the **driving tour to Reid State Park** and stop for dinner on your return at **the Osprey** or **the Robinhood Meetinghouse** in Robinhood, at **Kristina's** in Bath, or at the **Squire Tarbox Inn** on Westport Island.

DAY FOUR. Start in **Wiscasset** at **Musical Wonder House** to hear the antique music boxes; then visit the antique stores along Main Street. Have lunch at **Le Garage,** which overlooks the Sheepscot River. Drive south on Route 27 toward **Boothbay Harbor,** stopping at **Edgecomb Potters.** Follow the **drives around Boothbay, Southport Island and from East Boothbay to Ocean Point.** Be prepared for traffic and a lot of tourists in season in Boothbay Harbor. Have a clambake on **Cabbage Island,** or lobster at **Lobsterman's Wharf** in East Boothbay or at **Robinson's Wharf** in Southport.

BUDGETING YOUR TRIP

To help you get the most for the time and money you have to spend, here are some travel suggestions at three budget levels (cost per day with two people sharing a room), including lodging and meal tax, gratuity on meals, and service charge when it is added to your bill. Prices are approximate and are intended for planning purposes only. Lodgings are categorized by price and depending on the room selected may appear in more than one category. Meal prices at lunch include an average entrée and beverage. Dinner prices include an appetizer, entrée, dessert, and beverage. Wine or alcoholic beverages are not included.

Staying and dining at expensive lodgings and restaurants: From $300 to $530 per day for two.

Lodging: Black Point Inn, Harraseeket Inn, Inn by the Sea, Regency Hotel.

Dining: Breakfast: included except at Inn by the Sea. Lunch: Inn by the Sea, Harraseeket Inn, the Osprey. Dinner: Inn by the Sea, Back Bay Grill, Harraseeket Inn, the Osprey, Robinhood Meetinghouse, Squire Tarbox.

Staying and dining at moderately priced lodgings and restaurants: From $185 to $280 per day for two.

Lodging: Squire Tarbox, Grey Havens, Regency Hotel, Harraseeket, Pomegranate Inn, Five Gables Inn, Harpswell Inn.

Dining: Breakfast: included except at the Regency Hotel. Lunch: Kristina's, Le Garage, Dolphin, Cook's, Harraseeket Lunch and Lobster. Dinner: Street and Co; Fore Street, Broad Arrow Tavern at Harraseeket, Kristina's, Le Garage; lobster dinner at Cabbage Island, DeMillo's, Cook's.

Staying and dining at less expensive lodgings and restaurant: From $130 to $175 per day for two.

Lodging: Harpswell Inn, Hodgdon House, Five Gables Inn.

Dining: Breakfast: included. Lunch: Two Lights, Harraseeket Lunch and Lobster, Estes, Cook's, Five Islands, No Anchovies, Becky's, Raffles. Dinner: Baker's Oceanview, the Dolphin, No Anchovies, lobster dinner at Two Lights, Harraseeket Lunch, Estes, Five Islands, Robinson's Wharf, Lobsterman's Wharf.

7

Camden, Maine

C amden, where the mountains meet the sea, has one of the most beautiful harbors on the East Coast and is the most popular stop along the Maine coast between Kennebunkport and Bar Harbor. While its narrow streets are packed with tourists during the summer, the town of just over 4,000 year-round residents is not overly dependent on tourism. The largest employer in town is the credit card company MBNA, which recently converted a run-down nineteenth-century mill into a regional telemarketing center. The 6,500-acre Camden Hills State Park looms right behind the town. Walk down Bay View Street. Be sure to take the walking and driving tours outlined later in this chapter to see the Camden that few tourists see.

For information on special events, contact the following:

Rockport-Camden-Lincolnville Chamber of Commerce. Located on the Public Landing in Camden. Open Monday through Saturday throughout the year, daily 9 A.M. to 4 P.M. weekdays 10 A.M. to 5 P.M. Saturday May through mid-October noon to 4 P.M. Box 919, Camden, ME 04843; (207) 236-4404.

Damariscotta Region Chamber of Commerce. Box 13, Damariscotta, ME 04543; (207) 563-8340.

Rockland-Thomaston Chamber of Commerce. Harbor Park, Box 508, Rockland, ME 04841; (207) 596-0376.

WHERE TO GO, WHAT TO DO

Rockport. This quiet seaside village lacks the commercialism of Camden. Stop first at the Marine Park, where there are picnic and cookout facilities, benches along the harbor, remnants of lime kilns that once operated here, and a statue of Andre, a pet seal who lived in Rockport for twenty-seven years until his death in 1986. *Maine Coast Artists* on Russell Avenue (207-236-2875), is an art gallery with changing exhibits featuring Maine artists. *Anne Kilham Designs,* 142 Russell Avenue (207-236-8127), is owned by a local artist who sells her prints, note cards, calendars, and watercolors. *Rockport Apprenticeship* on Sea Street (207-236-6071) is a school of wooden boatbuilding; visitors are welcome to watch from the second-floor gallery, June through October.

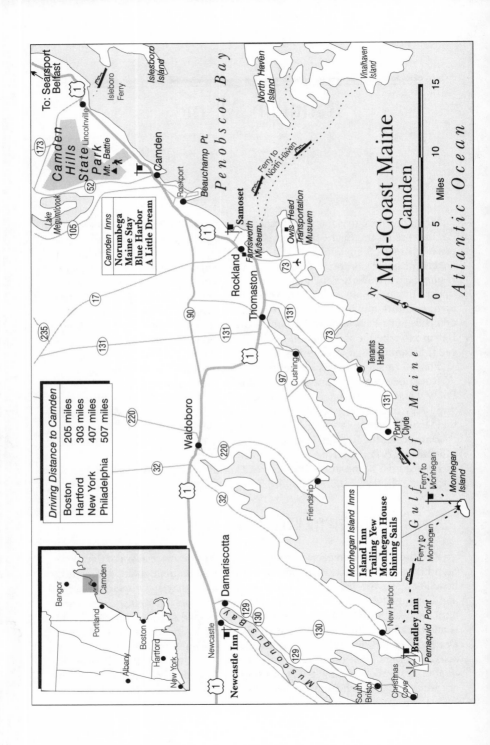

Mid-Coast Maine
Camden

Atlantic Ocean

Penobscot Bay

Gulf of Maine

To: Searsport
Belfast

Camden Hills State Park

Lincolnville

Mt. Battie

Camden

Rockport

Beauchamp Pt.

Lake Megunticook

Islesboro Ferry

Isleboro Island

North Haven Island

Vinalhaven Island

Ferry to North Haven

Owl's Head Transportation Musuem

Samoset

Rockland
Thomaston
Farnsworth Museum

Cushing

Tenants Harbor

Port Clyde

Monhegan Island

Ferry to Monhegan

Waldoboro

Friendship

Newcastle

Damariscotta

South Bristol

Christmas Cove

New Harbor

Bradley Inn

Pemaquid Point

Newcastle Inn

Muscongus Bay

Camden Inns
Norumbega
Maine Stay
Blue Harbor
A Little Dream

Driving Distance to Camden

Boston	205 miles
Hartford	303 miles
New York	407 miles
Philadelphia	507 miles

Monhegan Island Inns
Island Inn
Trailing Yew
Monhegan House
Shining Sails

Bangor
Portland
Camden
Albany
Boston
Hartford
New York

N

Miles
0   5   10   15

Bay Chamber Concerts ((207) 236-2823) sponsors year-round chamber music concerts in the Rockport Opera House. Concerts are held on Thursday and Friday evenings from mid-July through August and once a month September through June.

Rockland. This is the commercial hub of midcoast Maine. Most of the windjammers leave from here, as do ferries to North Haven ((207) 867-4441) and Vinalhaven ((207) 863-4421). Of major interest to all visitors is the Farnsworth Museum in town and Owls Head Transportation Museum a few miles outside of town.

Damariscotta. Newcastle and Damariscotta are on opposite sides of the Damariscotta River. At *Victorian Stable Gallery,* Water Street, Damariscotta ((207) 563-1991, open June through October), we were impressed with the collection of high-quality weaving, pewter, baskets, wall hangings, pottery, and other crafts. All of the work is made by Maine artists, and this collection is one of the finest we've seen in Maine. *Damariscotta Potter,* Northey Square, Damariscotta ((207) 563-8843) sells colorful ceramics hand-painted with pink flowers and blue leaves. *Round Top Center for the Arts,* Business Route 1, Damariscotta ((207) 563-1507) has changing exhibits and workshops on a beautiful farm. The center sponsors an open-air concert with the Portland Symphony in late July. *Round Top Ice Cream,* Business Route 1, Damariscotta (207-563-5307) is an ice-cream stand open May through mid-October that has been in business since 1924 and is located on the same farm as the Round Top Center for the Arts.

Fort William Henry at Pemaquid Harbor, built by the English to lay claim to this part of the country, was destroyed by the French in 1692. Artifacts are on display in the reproduction of the fort, was built on the original foundation. Archaeological excavations are under way. Displays at a nearby museum tell the history of the fort and early settlement in this region. Daily, Memorial Day to Labor Day, 9 A.M. to 5:30 P.M.; weekends, 9 A.M. to 5 P.M. through October. Adults $2. Pemaquid Point, ME; (207) 677-2423.

Monhegan Island. Is your idea of a vacation hiking through woodlands and sitting perched on rocks overlooking the Atlantic as the sun sets? Are you adventurous enough to don your foul-weather gear and hike to the cliffs, the highest on the New England coast, to watch the waves crash on the rocks in the middle of a storm? How about getting up at dawn to watch the sun rise from Pulpit Rock? If these experiences speak to you, then staying on Monhegan Island could be the experience of a lifetime. While winters are difficult and only about seventy people live year-round on the island, summers bring an influx of artists and visitors who spend their days reading, walking on trails, and visiting artists' studios.

Monhegan is ten miles from the nearest mainland. The entire island is less than a mile square, so walking is the only mode of transportation. (If you are staying overnight, a truck will bring your bags to your lodging.) There's limited electricity on the island; many of the houses use gas or kerosene lamps. The inns and cottages have a far simpler, more rustic feel than you will find on the mainland.

The booklet *A Visitor's Guide to Monhegan Island* describes the facilities and activities on the island. You can obtain a free copy by sending a stamped self-addressed envelope to any of the inns on the island, or on boats that go to the island. Ask for a trail map showing the seventeen miles of trails. A special feature of this island is the natural beauty of the trails and the views of the water. The Cathedral Woods path contains little woodland fairy houses made of pebbles by the children who live on the island. Pick up a free map of the artists' studio locations and times that they welcome visitors. For longer stays you can take advantage of the excellent well-stocked library.

Getting to the island: *From Port Clyde.* The least expensive way to get to Monhegan Island year-round is to take the mail boat *Laura B.* Monhegan Boat Line, Capt. James Barstow, P.O. Box 238, Port Clyde, ME 04855; (207) 372-8848.

From New Harbor. Hardy III leaves from Shaw's Wharf from Memorial Day to mid-October; 9 A.M. departure, 4 P.M. return. Hardy Boat Shaw's Wharf, New Harbor, ME; (207) 677-2026; (800) 278-3346.

From Boothbay Harbor. Balmy Days II leaves from pier 8, Memorial Day to mid-October; 9:30 A.M. departure, 4:15 P.M. return. Capt. Bob Campbell, Box 102M, 62 Commercial Street, Boothbay Harbor, ME 04538; (207) 633-2284; (800) 278-3346.

Museums

The Farnsworth Art Museum, Rockland

The collection at this museum emphasizes New England artists, and includes Wyeth paintings of local Maine scenes. A notation for the reproduction of Wyeth's *Christina's World* (the original is in the Museum of Modern Art in New York City) explains that it was painted on the Olsen Farm in Cushing, near Friendship. The museum now owns this farm and conducts tours. Also on display are works from the Hudson River School, American impressionists from the Old Lyme School, major works of Andrew, N. C., and Jamie Wyeth, a large collection of Louise Nevelson's sculpture, as well as paintings by Fitz Hugh Lane, Winslow Homer, and Edward Hopper. The Farnsworth homestead, a Greek Revival home with high Victorian decor and furnishings, is also part of the museum complex.

Open daily, June through September. Monday through Saturday, 10 A.M. to 5 P.M.; Sunday, 1 to 5 P.M. Closed Mondays, October through May. The homestead is open June through September. Adults, $5. 19 Elm Street, Rockland, ME; (207) 596-6457.

Owls Head Transportation Museum, Owls Head

Classic car, airplane, and motorcycle enthusiasts will definitely want to visit this museum. During the week the vehicles are on static display, but on selected weekends from mid-May through October, the equipment comes to life. Watch the Red Baron's Fokker Triplane, WWII fighters, antique and classic autos, trucks, motorcycles, and carriages in action. Visit the restoration workshop. Special weekend events include a Fabulous Fifties auto meet and air show, a military aviation and acrobatics show, a convertible meet and air show, an auction of antique autos, an antique truck meet and air show, a Chevrolet meet, a Sensational Sixties meet, and an annual transportation rally.

Open daily, April through October, 10 A.M. to 5 P.M. Other times, Monday through Friday, 10 A.M. to 4 P.M. and Sunday, 10 A.M. to 3 P.M. Adults $5. Located two miles south of Rockland on Route 73. Owls Head, ME; (207) 594-4418.

Penobscot Marine Museum, Searsport

We gained a deep appreciation for life at sea after viewing the harrowing movie taken by a young sailor with an early movie camera aboard a cargo carrier rounding Cape Horn in the early 1900s. This museum is a tribute to the men and women who built and sailed these wooden ships throughout the world. A complex of eight buildings tells the story of the great age of sail through lectures, models, exhibits, photographs, and paintings. The exceptional collection of marine paintings includes nineteenth-century European and Chinese ship portraits and works by Thomas and James Buttersworth.

Open Memorial Day through mid-October. Monday through Saturday, 10 A.M. to 5 P.M.; Sunday, noon to 5 P.M. Adults, $5. Church Street, Searsport, ME; (207) 548-2529.

Knox Mill Museum, Camden

This little museum illustrates the history of this former woolen mill with photographs, a film, and machinery. Movie buffs will recognize this as the "Harrington Mill" from the 1957 film *Peyton Place*. Open weekdays 8 A.M. to 7 P.M. MBNA, 32 Washington Street, Camden, ME; (207) 236-1400.

Getting Out on the Water

The windjammer fleet, a collection of fifteen operating historic sailing ships, recreates for its passengers an era when nations were settled and world trading patterns were established. The sailing ships, which have no inboard power, cruise the world-famous waters of the central Maine coast on three- and six-day trips from late May through early October. August and September usually have the best sailing weather, with crisp, clear days and winds from the north and west.

Windjammers compete in the annual Great Schooner Race in Penobscot Bay.

Folks that take these trips either love the experience and return every year or so, or hate it. The sleeping quarters are tight; some of the cabins barely have room to stand. The bunks are generally six feet long, with no extra room at either end. There are only a couple of toilets, called "heads," on board, and on most of the windjammers passengers shower on deck with a handheld showerhead. Hearty family-style meals are prepared on a wood stove; one night of the trip features a lobster feast on shore. Days are spent cruising the waters to destinations determined by the wind. In the late afternoon the ship anchors, allowing guests to go ashore or swim.

For the right kind of person, a windjammer cruise is the ideal summer vacation. The wind whips through your hair; the wooden ship creaks; the freedom of the open seas captures the imagination and creates a spirit of adventure. Passengers help with the sails, read those books they never got to all year, and talk with their fellow shipmates.

The schooners sail out of Camden, Rockland, or Rockport. This list and description is not complete; it is meant to give a picture of the options available. Please note that we have the *Pauline* in this list even though she is not a windjammer.

Schooner Stephen Taber, launched in 1871, is the oldest documented sailing vessel in continuous use in the United States. At 115 feet, it is the smallest of the windjammers and takes only twenty-two passengers. You'll be sailing with the owners, Ken and Ellen Barnes, who bought the vessel in 1979. The schooner sails from Rockland. 70 Elm Street, Camden, ME 04843; (207) 236-3520; (800) 999-7352.

Victory Chimes is the largest of the windjammers. It is 170 feet long and can take up to forty-four passengers. Creature comforts include slightly larger cabins than the other windjammers, below-deck showers and toilets, and a sink in each cabin with hot and cold running water. Kip Files, one of the owners, is the captain. The schooner sails out of Rockland. P.O. Box 1401, Rockland, ME 04841; (207) 594-0755; (800) 745-5651.

Schooner Mary Day is the newest of the windjammers; it was built in 1962 specifically to take passengers. A forward lounge area has a wood stove, a favorite gathering spot on rainy days; there is an organ in the dining saloon. The captain is Steve Cobb, who sails with his wife, Chris. On this schooner, as on the *Stephen Taber,* the toilets and the shower are on the deck. The *Mary Day* runs trips with special themes such as a trip with a naturalist, island weeks anchoring in small coves away from the mainland, and a folk music cruise. The windjammer sails out of Camden. Box 798, Camden, ME 04843; (207) 236-2750; (800) 992-2218.

The Isaac Evans is one of three windjammers operated by the North End Shipyard Schooners. Most windjammer vacations are not appropriate for children under 14, but this schooner has special three-day trips for families with children from age 8 up. The schooners sail from Rockland. P.O. Box 482, Rockland, ME 04841, (800) 648-4544.

Pauline is an eighty-three-foot former sardine boat that was refitted in 1988–89 as a luxury cruising vessel with a capacity of twelve passengers. *Pauline* has a powerful yet quiet engine so passengers can explore more of midcoast Maine: Penobscot Bay, Blue Hill through the Eggemoggin Reach, Monhegan Island, or Bar Harbor. Cabins have longer berths, plenty of headroom, and hot and cold running water. Toilets and showers are below deck. A plush wood-paneled saloon has a wood stove, sofa and easy chairs, and a library of nautical titles. Topside is an open deck. Dinners are individually served on china plates. Of interest to naturalists are the puffin and wildlife cruises in the second half of July. The *Pauline* sails out of Rockland. Windjammer Wharf, P.O. Box 1050, Rockland, ME 04841; (207) 236-3520; (800) 999-7352.

If spending three or six nights on the water doesn't fit your plans, you can get out on the water for trips lasting one to three hours. Walk along the wharf in Camden and you'll find tables with information about the available options, including these:

Schooner Surprise. The trip on this fifty-five-foot schooner, built in 1918 and owned by Barbara and Jack Moore, is highly recommended. Two- and three-hour trips leave from Camden Public Landing, Memorial Day through mid-October; (207) 236-4687 (evenings).

The Lively Lady. If you want to learn more about lobstering you can take a one-and-a-half-hour cruise in the bay with Captain Alan Philbrick. As the crew haul the traps they explain the skills and tools of this trade. Trips leave two to four times daily, June through September. Sharp's Wharf, Camden; (207) 236-6672.

Sports

Adventure trips and equipment rentals. A few miles south of Camden you'll notice Maine Sports, a new, modern building next to a pond that's used to try out the kayaks and canoes. The store has a full supply of sports equipment and sports clothing; the staff runs sea kayaking tours, fishing trips, canoe trips, bike trips, and whitewater rafting trips. You can also rent mountain bikes, sea kayaks, canoes, paddling accessories, camping gear, and fishing rods if you want to plan your own trip. Write or call for a catalog of trips and rental prices. P.O. Box 956, Route 1, Rockport, ME 04856; (800) 722-0826; (800) 244-8799 (in Maine).

Hiking. In Camden, the mountains and the sea are so close together that you can go sailing in the morning and take a strenuous hike to the top of Maiden Cliffs, a rock outcropping that rises 800 feet from the shores of Lake Megunticook, in the afternoon. At sunset you can drive to the top of Mount Battie ($1.50 per person), where there is a tower and much-photographed views of the town, the harbor, and Penobscot Bay.

The campground is popular; expect to find it full by 3 P.M. in July and August. There are 112 campsites open from May 15 to October 15.

Twenty-five miles of hiking trails in Camden Hills State Park include paths along the 1,700 feet of rocky coastline on fairly level terrain or at elevations going up to 1,380 feet in the state park. In addition to the Maiden Cliff Trail we are particularly fond of the hike to Bald Rock; the panoramic views of Penobscot Bay are particularly breathtaking. A map of the trail system with a description of each trail is available at the park headquarters.

Skiing. We don't know of any other ski slope on the East Coast where you can look out at the ocean from the top of the mountain. The Camden Snow Bowl is owned by the town and has nine trails, a 400-foot toboggan chute, and ice-skating. You can bring your own toboggan and pay per run or rent one on site. The proximity of the ski slopes to the water makes the weather milder here than farther inland. The ski area has snowmaking machines for the major slopes as well as a ski school and rental shop. We suggest making advance calls before planning a winter skiing trip to Camden, as the weather is often milder than inland and snow conditions may not be good. (207) 236-3438. Snow conditions: (207) 236-4418.

Driving Tours

Camden–Lincolnville–Belfast–Searsport

From the center of Camden, drive north on Route 1 for 10 miles. After you pass the Northport Diner look for the "blind walker" caution sign. Go straight on this road for four-tenths of a mile to Saturday Cove. Once past the cove take the right fork. Continue for about three and a half miles. This is the Bluff Shore Road, which hugs the coast and affords good views. Look for the miniature Victorian homes in Bayside, once the site of a Methodist Revivalist summer tent community. Turn right when this road rejoins Route 1.

Stop in Belfast to walk through the historic district and admire some of the finest examples of Greek Revival, Federal, and Victorian architecture in Maine. Not too many years ago Belfast was a center of the poultry industry. Today artists are buying the historic homes. Take a ride on the scenic Belfast and Moosehead Lake Railroad. After you leave Belfast and cross the bridge, look for the sign for Young's Lobster Pound.

Searsport is known for its many antique shops. If antiquing is your passion, come early in the day. The Penobscot Marine Museum in Searsport has a particularly outstanding movie about life on board the early ships. From Searsport it is about a forty-five-minute drive back to Camden.

Camden–Rockport–Rockland–Owl's Head–Port Clyde

Walk along Camden's waterfront to see sailboats and through side streets to explore gift shops, galleries, and restaurants. While the waterfront can become congested in the summer, the residential area just a few blocks away is always tranquil. Walk north along Route 1, past the library. Turn right on Eaton Street and look over the low fence at the manicured gardens. To get the full impact of the panorama of Camden, drive to the top of Mount Battie (entrance is in Camden Hills State Park) and look down onto the harbor.

Back in the car, take the back roads from Camden to Rockport. From Bayview Street in the center of Camden, turn left onto Russell Avenue, past a field where the unusual Belted Galloway cattle graze contentedly. Turn left on Calderwood Lane, stopping at the peaceful *Children's Chapel* on Vesper Hill. Here, the paved road changes to dirt—Beauchamp Road—and continues along Beauchamp Point. Stop along this narrow road that hugs the coast and walk out on the rocks for views of Rockport Harbor.

Route 1 heads to Rockland, where the *Farnsworth Museum* houses an outstanding collection of Wyeth family paintings. The Wyeth family spends its summers in this area of Maine.

Your next destination is *Owls Head* (Route 1 south, right on Route 73, left at a sign pointing to the airport, left at Owls Head flagpole). Just before the road ends, take the last left (Lighthouse Road). A walkway leads to the lighthouse. Be sure to walk around the lighthouse to the far side, where a path takes you to the edge of a cliff, one of Maine's great panoramic vistas.

Camden Harbor is one of the most picturesque on the East Coast.

The *Owls Head Transportation Museum* is best visited on selected week-ends May through October, when equipment like the Red Baron's Fokker triplane, and antique and classic autos, trucks, and motorcycles take you back to an earlier period.

Our absolute favorite lobster-in-the-rough spot is on Route 73 between South Thomaston and St. George. Look for the *"Miller's Lobster"* sign pointing left down a dirt road. This is the real thing! The menu is short and sweet: lobster, steamed grit-free soft clams, lobster rolls, crabmeat rolls, fresh home-made pies (try the rhubarb), and for nonseafood eaters, hot dogs and potato chips. Sit at picnic tables along the rocks and watch the ospreys.

New Harbor–Pemaquid Point–Damariscotta

Moody's Diner in Waldoboro is a Maine institution, known for traditional fare at reasonable prices. After a stack of pancakes, head south on Route 32. At the Chamberlain post office (south of Round Pond), turn left for a short loop around Long Cove Point for a look at classic Maine summer cottages and excellent water views. Stop at the *Rachel Carson Salt Pond Preserve*, where the great conservationist researched her book *The Edge of the Sea*. The view from the deck at Shaw's Lobster Pound in New Harbor overlooks one of the most photographed and painted fishing harbors in Maine. Shaw's has changed hands in the last couple of years and has gone upscale, but the lobster and fishing boats still unload their catch here. The Hardy boat leaves from Shaw's

Lobster Pond for trips to Monhegan Island and to see the puffins at Easter Egg Rock.

The view of Back Cove, an idyllic fishing harbor, is worth the effort to find. From New Harbor, head south on Route 130, then left at the Samoset Fire Company to the end of the road. Walk to the middle of the wooden bridge and look back at the idyllic fishing harbor scene.

Pemaquid Point and the lighthouse, one of the icons of the Maine coast, is at the end of Route 130. Visit the lighthouse and museum, explore the rocks and tidal pools, and soak up the sights and smells. Pemaquid Beach (left off Route 130 at the first crossroad) is a protected sand beach but still very cold, so all we felt like doing was wading! Stop at Captain's Catch on the way to the beach for the best fried, freshly shucked, and locally dug whole clams (not strips) in this part of Maine. This is the kind of place we always look for— away from the major tourist areas, frequented by the locals and the regular summer people, and supplied with seafood caught by local fishermen. *Fort William Henry* is off this road.

Take Route 130 to Route 129 toward South Bristol. Continue to Christmas Cove for a drink at the *Dory Bar*, a picturesque harborside watering hole at the Coveside Inn. Take Route 129 back to Damariscotta. If you need an ice cream fix, stop at *Round Top* on Business Route 1 in Damariscotta.

WHERE TO STAY

Norumbega, Camden

This 1886 turreted stone castle is a much-photographed curiosity. The spacious common rooms have hardwood inlaid floors, two wood-burning fireplaces, and English Victorian furniture. There is a formal dining room, a glass-walled dining room with views of the water, and a veranda where breakfast is served on warm days. The garden level lounge has a restored antique billiard table.

Accommodations are on the second and third floors, in the fourth-floor penthouse suite, and on the lower garden level, where the rooms open directly onto the rolling lawn. Five of the rooms have wood-burning fireplaces. If you want to have the feeling of staying in a grand castle we suggest staying on the upper floors. The rooms at the back of the house are our preference because they are quiet and offer distant views of the water. Traffic sounds from Route 1 are audible from the front rooms.

The deluxe penthouse suite (the only room that is air-conditioned) has a private spiral staircase, a king-size bed, a living room with a three-sided glass fireplace, a private deck, a refrigerator stocked with champagne and sodas, and a bath with a two-person bathtub, a double sink, and a separate shower.

The Warwick Room has a full front view of Penobscot Bay, a fireplace, and a private deck. The Windsor Room (Route 1 side) is a turret room with five curved windows. Arundel, a room on the garden level, has a double Jacuzzi in a large bathroom and a private deck. East Lake Suite, on the garden level, has two bathrooms, a sitting room and large bedroom, and a deck but is not a good choice for light sleepers as it is under the kitchen.

Twelve rooms and one penthouse suite, all with private bath. July through mid-October, rooms $195–$450. Other times of the year, rooms $135–$375. Snacks and full breakfast included. Children over 7 welcome. No pets. 61 High Street (Route 1), Camden, ME 04843; (207) 236-4646.

Samoset Resort, Rockport

Look no further if you prefer a full-service destination resort on the Maine coast. This complex, situated on 230 acres overlooking Penobscot Bay, has something for everyone. There's golf, an indoor pool and two hot tubs, two racquetball courts, one indoor and four outdoor tennis courts, a full fitness center, and a room filled with a full array of video games. Some visitors describe the setting of the eighteen-hole oceanside golf course as the "Pebble Beach of the East."

Most rooms have two double beds; some have queens; all have wall-to-wall carpeting. The suites are all on the fourth floor with the best water views, and all have been redecorated. Each suite has a living room with a wet bar, a bath with a double sink vanity, and a larger wooden deck with two chairs and a chaise. All rooms have decks of varying sizes and individually controlled air-conditioning.

Seventy-two time-share units with a full kitchen and washer/dryer can be rented by the night. Daily maid service or room service is not available in these units. The resort runs a children's camp during the summer and programs during school holiday periods.

One hundred fifty rooms and suites, 72 time-share units, all with private bath. Mid-June through Labor Day, rooms and suites, $215–$305, one- and two-bedroom time-share units $260–$390. At other times of the year, rooms and suites $115–$215, time-share units $170–$280. Package plans available. Children welcome, no additional charge. No pets. Rockport, ME 04856; (207) 594-2511; (800) 341-1650 (outside Maine).

A Little Dream, Camden

We sat on the blue Victorian sofa in the pink-tiled sunroom sipping a glass of strawberry iced tea and nibbling smoked trout pâté. Everywhere we looked was another vignette of artfully arranged Victoriana: teddy bears, antique dolls, quilts, an old-fashioned wheelbarrow filled with plants, piles of hatboxes, a violin propped on the mantel. The oversize stuffed animals, folk art toys, and Italian marionette belong to Joanne Ball and her husband Billy Fontana's collection, which is attractively displayed throughout the inn and in the Toy Room, a small second-floor room arranged as a display area.

The Master Bedroom has a king-size canopy bed, television, and private deck. The Blue Turret Room, a first-floor room that faces Route 1, has a gas jet fireplace. Travels, the third room in the inn, has a small deck. The carriage house is set back farther from the street and has two units, each with queen-size beds and wet bars. The front unit is bright and airy with a large deck that has water views in winter. The back unit has a steep spiral staircase leading to a loft sitting area.

Breakfast (8 to 9:30 A.M.) includes gourmet coffees or teas and a choice of entrée such as smoked salmon, Brie-and-apple, or cheddar-cheese-and-ham omelettes, fruit crepes; heart-shaped banana-pecan waffles; or smoked trout with a vichyssoise sauce and dilled eggs. The candlelit table is set with lacy cloths, stemmed glassware, and sweet bread under a glass dome.

Five rooms, all with private bath. Memorial Day through October, $129–$149. Other times of the year $95–$115. Afternoon tea and full breakfast included. Not appropriate for children. No pets. No smoking. 66 High Street (Route 1), Camden, ME 04843; (207) 236-8742.

Maine Stay Inn, Camden

"Big house, little house, back house, barn" goes the nineteenth-century children's verse that describes these connected white farm buildings and others like them throughout New England. The Maine Stay, owned by retired navy captain Peter Smith, his wife, Donny, and her twin sister, Diana Robson, is filled with furniture and art from the family's worldwide travels. Common space includes two front parlors with fireplaces and a television room. Should you want to go hiking, bicycling, antiquing, or exploring the back roads, Peter has detailed instructions for any of thirty different trips or activities stored in his computer.

The secluded ground floor Carriage House Room is a favorite for its wood stove and French doors opening onto a private patio that overlooks a two-acre wooded area next to the inn. The Clark Suite was made from two rooms and now has a separate sitting room with a gas fireplace. The Robson Room is at the back of the inn and overlooks the rock garden and the woods. A family on a budget can take the Stitchery Room, a third-floor shared-bath room and a connecting room with a twin bed.

At 8:30 A.M. Peter announces breakfast in true navy tradition with his boatswain's pipe. The three tables are set with sterling silver, Waterford crystal or Simon Pearce's handblown glass, and Spode or Ansle English bone china. Our breakfast included French toast served with maple and blueberry syrup and sausages.

Eight rooms, six with private bath. June through October, $75–$125. Other times of the year, 20% less. Afternoon tea and full breakfast included. Children over 8 welcome. No pets. 22 High Street (Route 1), Camden, ME 04843; (207) 236-9636.

Blue Harbor House, Camden

The focus of activity in this classic New England Cape, owned and operated by transplanted Californians Jody Schmoll and Dennis Hayden, is the large glass-walled living and dining room. At one end there are bookcases, couches, and a television. The breakfast tables can be used to play cards or board games, and dishes filled with candy, fruit, and cookies are available for afternoon munching.

Our choice of accommodations is the quiet back suites, each with a private entrance, where we heard none of the Route 1 traffic sounds. Room C is a large room with a high four-poster king-size bed, a convertible couch, a television, a full kitchen, and a spacious bath with a whirlpool tub. Room B is approximately the same size, has a separate living room with a television, a full kitchen, a bedroom with a king-size four-poster bed, and a bath with a whirlpool tub.

The innkeepers have added individually-controlled room air conditioners to all of the front rooms, which help muffle the Route 1 traffic sounds. We liked room 7, a first-floor front room with a four-poster queen-size bed and pine furniture, as well as room C1, a quiet room in the back of the inn with a queen-size bed.

Breakfast, served from 8 to 9:30 A.M. might be an individual cheese soufflé with fresh asparagus and bacon or blueberry pancakes served with blueberry butter and maple syrup.

Ten rooms, all with private bath. Mid-May through mid-October, $95–$135. Lower rates at other times. Afternoon tea and full breakfast included. Children welcome. No pets. Dinner available by prior reservation, $30 per person. Bicycles available. Two-night minimum stay during July and August. 67 Elm Street (Route 1), Camden, ME 04843; (207) 236-3196; (800) 248-3196.

The Newcastle Inn, Newcastle

This white clapboard, black shuttered Federal Colonial inn close to the Damariscotta River is owned by Rebecca and Howard Levitan. After a day spent touring, guests can return to a quiet setting knowing that a fine gourmet dinner awaits them.

The first floor has two sitting rooms, one with a wood-burning fireplace, and a glass-walled porch room with a white wicker sofa and chairs and a cast-iron wood stove.

We prefer the rooms with views of the Damariscotta River. In cool weather, we also enjoy the rooms with gas fireplaces. The top choice is room 17, a particularly large room with a king-size bed, five windows with good river views, and a bath with a double whirlpool tub. Room 6 has a queen-size canopy bed, a river view, and a bath with a double whirlpool tub and a separate shower. Room 5, also with a queen-size bed, is larger than room 6 and has a fireplace and a river view. Room 11, a first-floor room, has a view of the water from the queen-size bed and is the only room with a private deck. On the third floor our favorite is room 8, with a queen-size canopy bed and a bath almost as large as the bedroom.

Breakfast is served from 8 to 9 A.M. During the summer it is delightful to sit out on the new deck at the back of the inn, which has river views.

Fourteen rooms, all with private bath. Mid-June through October, $95–$200. Lower rates at other times of the year. 15 % service charge. Breakfast included. Three- or five-course dinner available $27.50, $35. Not appropriate for young children. No pets. No smoking. River Road, Newcastle, ME 04553; (207) 563-5685; (800) 832-8669 (except Maine).

The Bradley Inn at Pemaquid Point

The Bradley Inn is located several hundred yards from the Pemaquid Point lighthouse, one of the icons of the American landscape. The rooms in the main building have been totally refurbished with wall-to-wall carpeting, new mahogany furniture, new bathrooms, cable television, and telephones. The best rooms in the inn are the three rooms on the third floor—301, 303, 305—each with cathedral ceilings and limited views of John's Bay. The top accommodation is the cottage suite, which has a queen-size bed, a fieldstone fireplace, a refrigerator and coffeemaker, and a screened porch. The renovated barn has three units, each with a full kitchen and living room.

Sixteen rooms and suites, all with private bath. June through October, $100–$195. Other times $100–$125. Continental breakfast included. Children welcome. No pets. Bicycles available. Two-night minimum in season. Route 130, H.C. 61, 361 Pemaquid Point, New Harbor, ME 04554; (207) 677-2105.

Monhegan Island

If you stay overnight on Monhegan Island, don't expect creature comforts. The island is beautiful but accommodations are rustic.

The Island Inn

This is the best hotel on the island. The better rooms, those with great sunset views over the water, are often booked far in advance by returning guests. The Island Inn serves three meals a day to guests and to the public. Lobster is always available, although if you want it baked or stuffed you need to order in advance.

Open mid-May through mid-October. Thirty-six rooms, seven with private bath, $98–$155. Full breakfast included. Lunch and dinner ($16/houseguests, $18/nonhouseguests) is available. Children welcome. Pets permitted. Box 128, Monhegan Island, ME 04852; (207) 596-0371.

Monhegan House

At this basic guesthouse the best rooms are on the second floor near the baths and showers. The first, third, and fourth floors have rooms only.

Open late May through mid-October. Thirty-two rooms, all share the baths on the second floor, $75. Meals are not included. Breakfast, lunch, and dinner available. Children welcome. No pets. Monhegan Island, ME 04852; (207) 594-7983.

Trailing Yew

Come with the expectation that a stay here is one step above camping. The buildings are not heated. The best rooms are the three in the Sea Gull building. Meals are basic and hearty, reminiscent of summer camp food.

Open mid-May through mid-October. Accommodations for sixty guests, $54 per person including breakfast, dinner, taxes, and gratuity. Children welcome. All rooms with shared bath down the hall. Monhegan Island, ME 04852; (207) 596-0440.

Shining Sails Real Estate, Inc. House Rentals

Bill Baker and Amy Melenbaker rent four housekeeping efficiency apartments and three rooms in their home. Rooms 1, 2, 3, and 6 all have ocean views. The agency owns or represents the owners of twenty-six cottages on Monhegan Island. Nigh Duck Cottage is our favorite since it is perched on a fifty-foot bluff overlooking a private cove. Baldwin has ocean frontage and a view of the harbor. Cottages generally have gas or kerosene lighting and gas appliances instead of electricity. All have hot and cold running water and equipped kitchens.

Open year-round. Four apartments and three rooms, available by the night or per week. Nightly rate $65–$100. Breakfast included. Cottages available for weekly rental, some available for nightly rentals, $500–$1,200 per week. Most permit children and some permit pets. P.O. Box 344, Monhegan Island, ME 04852; (207) 596-0041.

WHERE TO DINE

The Belmont, Camden

This is a favorite haunt of the Camden summer community, who quickly tire of eating lobster every night. This white Victorian with green shutters is located two blocks off Route 1 in a quiet residential section of town. The restaurant has a refined atmosphere, two dining areas, an enclosed porch, and a small bar.

The short menu changes frequently. The night we dined we started with a refreshing cold cucumber buttermilk soup and cod cakes served with red pepper mayonnaise and Southern cole slaw. A Caesar salad came with the meal. Roast duck came with a berry glaze and cherry rhubarb and onion chutney. The filet of veal was a thick loin covered with mushroom sauce.

Dinner served May through December, Tuesday through Sunday (daily during July and August), entrées $14–$22. 6 Belmont Avenue, Camden, ME; (207) 236-8053.

Frog Water Cafe, Camden

This storefront restaurant in the middle of town has quickly gained a wide local following. With large portions and very reasonable prices we can certainly understand why. Bread is served with a baked head of garlic to use as a spread, like butter. The hamburgers are two six-ounce patties. The double-dipped onion rings have a light, crunchy, tempura-like taste. Mushroom ravioli, pasta with eggplant and artichokes, chicken breast stuffed with goat cheese and bell peppers, curried mussels, crab cakes, braised lamb shanks, and grilled monkfish are other items on the menu.

Lunch and dinner, Tuesday through Sunday. Entrées $8–$14. Elm Street, Camden, ME; (207) 236-8998.

The Sail Loft, Rockport

When you make reservations, ask for a window table with a good view of the harbor. The preparations here are standard, but the portions are large and the prices fair. The baked local haddock with a crabmeat stuffing was moist and tender. The fisherman's platter includes fried clams, scallops, shrimp, haddock, and steamed mussels along with half a steamed lobster. One column of the menu describes the various lobster offerings, which include a shore dinner of clam chowder, steamed clams or mussels, and a lobster up to two pounds; a one-and-a-half- or two-pound baked stuffed lobster; a steamed live lobster; and lobster sauté or lobster Newburg served in a casserole with toast points. After dinner you can stroll around the intimate harbor for a look at the wooden boats and the statue of Andre the seal.

Open daily for lunch, dinner, and Sunday brunch. Dinner entrées $10–$37. Town Landing, Rockport, ME; (207) 236-2330.

The Bradley Inn, Pemaquid Point

Public dining areas at this country inn include a long granite-and-mahogany bar with ship models at each end and a lounge with a wood stove decorated with nautical oil paintings and prints. For starters, try the gravlax. A creative lobster dish such as lobster chardonnay with cracked mussels and pasta is always on the menu. Grilled swordfish, poached salmon with mussels, and steak are typical menu items. Desserts include homemade ice cream and sorbets as well as pecan pie, white chocolate cheesecake, and rhubarb and blueberry pie.

Dinner, daily, June through October. Weekends at other times. Entrées $15–$25. Route 130, 361 Pemaquid Point, New Harbor, ME; (207) 677-2105.

Cappy's, Camden

If there wasn't already a Cappy's in Camden, some entrepreneur would invent it. This restaurant and sailors' bar is in the center of town at the busiest inter-section. The favorite saying at this local haunt is true indeed: "Eventually everyone shows up to share a good time at Cappy's."

The booths are old and wooden; nautical parephernalia hangs from the rafters. This is a fun place and a good choice for standard, basic fare and a draft of beer. We were pleased with our Roseway burger served on rye with cheese, peppers, onions, and mushrooms, and the Mexican salad served in a large tortilla shell. The wide-ranging menu includes frittatas, seafood pie, Sze-chuan noodles, and steamed mussels.

Open daily. Breakfast, lunch and dinner, $5–$13. Main Street, Camden, ME; (207) 236-2254.

Sea Dog, Camden

This brew pub, located in the large nineteenth-century historic Knox Mill in the center of town, has a spectacular setting with a wall of glass overlooking the river. The corn chowder is excellent. Come for a pint and some "wicked good" nachos. The full menu has many options for a casual meal. Daily brew-ery tours are conducted June through October at 11 A.M.

Lunch and dinner daily. 43 Mechanic Street, Camden, ME; (207) 236-6863.

Miss Plum's Ice Cream, Rockport

You can't miss this plum-colored building as you drive south from Camden. This is the best ice cream in the area—flavors are intense. Blueberry is a favorite. There is a take-out window, picnic tables, and an attractive café serv-ing a wide selection of imaginative ice-cream sundaes, soups, sandwiches, and lighter fare. If you arrive at the take-out window with your pet dog, cat, or even a horse, the staff will provide a free scoop of the animal's favorite flavor.

Open daily. Summer hours, 7 A.M. to 10 P.M.; winter hours, 7:30 A.M. to 5 P.M. Sandwiches and meals $3–$9. On Route 1 south of Route 90, Rockport, ME; (207) 596-6946.

Captain's Catch, New Harbor

"We pride ourselves in being small and serving real fresh homemade food," Cindy Brackett told us as she dipped the freshly shucked locally dug whole clams (not strips) in flour, egg, and fine cracker meal and lightly fried them. This small seasonal roadside restaurant has indoor and outdoor picnic tables and does a large take-out business. This is the kind of place we always look for—away from the major tourist areas, frequented by the locals and the reg-ular summer people, and supplied with lobsters, clams, and fish caught by local fishermen.

Open early May through October, lunch and dinner. Pemaquid Beach Road, New Harbor, ME; (207) 677-2396.

Coveside, Christmas Cove

Since Captain John Smith dropped anchor here on Christmas Day in 1614, this natural harbor has been a port of call for sailboats from around the world. At the Dory Bar every square inch of space on the walls and rafters is covered with pennants from sailing clubs and sailboats from around the world. On summer evenings the bar and deck are packed with sailors and landlubbers alike.

Open mid-June through mid-September for breakfast, lunch, dinner. Lunch $5–$11; dinner entrées $12–$25. Route 129, Christmas Cove, ME; (207) 644-8282.

Moody's Diner, Waldoboro

Everybody stops at Moody's at one time or another if they have driven up the coast of Maine. During the summer it's packed all day and into the night. The food is traditional New England fare: chowders, pies, blueberry muffins, pancakes, and New England boiled dinners, all at prices that won't break anyone's budget.

Open daily and nightly except 11:30 P.M. Friday to 5 A.M. on Saturday and 11:30 P.M. Saturday to 7 A.M. Sunday. Route 1, Waldoboro; ME; (207) 832-7468.

Lobster Pounds

No trip to this area of the coast of Maine is complete without a lobster dinner. Here's a selection of our favorite lobster pounds, where you can roll up your sleeves and attack your lobster with gusto.

There isn't a more idyllic spot than Miller's to enjoy lobster in the rough.

Miller's Lobster, Spruce Head

This quintessential Maine lobster-in-the-rough business is owned and operated by the Miller family and is located at the end of a dirt road in a quiet cove. There isn't a more idyllic spot in the area. We sat at a picnic table enjoying our lobster and steamed clams and watched the ospreys fishing in Penobscot Bay right in front of us. The menu is short and sweet: lobster, steamed soft clams, lobster rolls, crabmeat rolls, fresh homemade pies, and for nonseafood eaters, hot dogs and potato chips. Bring your own beer, as they sell only soft drinks.

Open in season, 10 A.M. to 7 P.M. Down a side road off Route 73 between South Thomaston and St. George, Spruce Head, ME; (207) 594-7406.

Shaw's, New Harbor

This rustic dining spot overlooks one of the most photographed and painted fishing harbors in Maine. It has gone upscale just a bit as the crowds of tourists continue to grow. The lobster and commercial fishing boats still unload their catch here and next door at the lobstermen's co-op. The Hardy boat leaves from this dock for trips to Monhegan Island and for trips to see the puffins at Eastern Egg Rock.

Open seasonally, lunch and dinner. On Shaw's Wharf off Route 32, New Harbor, ME; (207) 677-2200.

Young's Lobster Pound, East Belfast

Nothing fancy here: the large first floor is filled with the sound of salt water circulating through dozens of lobster tanks holding thousands of lobsters that are shipped throughout the United States and worldwide. Order your lobster or shore dinner from the counter and take it upstairs to the picnic tables or outside on the back deck, which has an excellent view of downtown Belfast across the Passagassawakeag River.

Open seasonally, 7 A.M. to 6:30 P.M. Mitchell Avenue, just across the bridge from Belfast; (207) 338-1160.

Lincolnville Lobster Pound, Lincolnville

This is the largest and the most accessible of all the lobster pounds. It's on Route 1 a few miles north of Camden. You can eat inside at the family-style restaurant that seats over 200 and serves a full menu of lobster, seafood, ham, chicken, and steaks, or outside on picnic tables by the beach.

Open seasonally, May through mid-October, lunch and dinner. Route 1, Lincolnville Beach, ME; (207) 789-5550.

ITINERARY

DAY ONE. Start by getting oriented in Camden. Take a walk along the harbor, then take a drive to the top of Mount Battie in the **Camden Hills State Park** to see the view. Follow the **driving tour** from Camden to Rockport. If you want to bicycle, try the loop from Camden to Rockport and back. Have lunch overlooking the harbor at the **Sail Loft**. Continue to Rockland and visit the **Farnsworth Museum, Owl's Head Transportation Museum,** and **Owl's Head lighthouse**. Drive to Port Clyde. For dinner, stop at **Miller's** for lobster in the rough.

DAY TWO. Follow the **driving tour** from Waldoboro along Route 32 to New Harbor. Back Cove is worth the excursion, as the view is idyllic. Continue on to Pemaquid Point to visit the lighthouse, walk on the rocks, and follow the path to Kresge Point. Get some fried clams at **Captain's Catch**. Other places to visit include Pemaquid Beach and **Fort William Henry**. Drive to South Bristol, then continue to Christmas Cove to see the view and to have a drink on the outside deck at **Coveside**. Return on Route 129 to Damariscotta. Have dinner at The **Newcastle Inn,** or return to Camden for a casual dinner at **Cappy's, Sea Dog,** or **Frog Water Cafe** or a more formal one at the **Belmont**.

DAY THREE. Take a two-hour sail on the *Surprise* or a **harbor kayak** tour. Follow the driving tour north to Lincolnville for lobster here or at **Young's** in Belfast. Spend the afternoon visiting the antique shops in Searsport and the **Penobscot Marine Museum**.

DAY FOUR. Spend the day on **Monhegan Island**. You can also stay overnight or just spend a few hours walking the trails and visiting the artists' studios. For dinner on Monhegan Island we suggest the **Island Inn** or, if you return to the mainland, have another lobster dinner at **Miller's** or return to Camden to the **Frog Water Cafe**.

BUDGETING YOUR TRIP

To help you get the most for the time and money you have to spend, here are some travel suggestions at three budget levels (cost per day with two people sharing a room), including lodging and meal tax, gratuity on meals, and service charge when it is added to your bill. Prices on lodgings are based on peak rates. Prices are approximate and are intended for planning purposes only. Note: lodgings are categorized by price and depending on the room selected may appear in more than one category. Meal prices at lunch include an average entrée and beverage. Dinner prices include an appetizer, entrée, dessert, and beverage. Wine or alcoholic beverages are not included.

Staying and dining at expensive lodgings and restaurants: From $320 to $590 per day for two.

Lodging: Norumbega, Samoset Resort, Newcastle Inn.

Dining: Breakfast: included except at Samoset Resort. Lunch: Sail Loft, Miller's, Shaw's. Dinner: The Belmont, Newcastle Inn, Sail Loft, Bradley Inn.

Staying and dining at moderately priced lodgings and restaurants: From $210 to $300 per day for two.

Lodging: A Little Dream, Maine Stay Inn, Blue Harbor House, Newcastle Inn, Bradley Inn, Island Inn.

Dining: Breakfast: included. Lunch: Miss Plum's, Sail Loft, Coveside, Cappy's, Shaw's, Captain's Catch, Lincolnville Lobster, Miller's Lobster, Young's Lobster. Dinner: Sail Loft, Frog Water Cafe.

Staying and dining at less expensive lodgings and restaurants: From $125 to $160 per day for two.

Lodging: Blue Harbor House, Maine Stay Inn, Newcastle Inn, Island Inn, the Trailing Yew, Monhegan House, Shining Sails.

Dining: Breakfast: included except at Monhegan House. Lunch: Miss Plum's, Moody's Diner, or less expensive sandwich or fried food at Shaw's, Captain's Catch, Miller's Lobster. Dinner: Cappy's, Sea Dog, Miller's Lobster, Miss Plum's, Captain's Catch, Moody's Diner, Young's Lobster, Shaw's.

8

East Penobscot Bay, Maine

Centuries ago, the Penobscot Indians summered here, fishing and harvesting shellfish. The first Europeans to visit the region were the explorers Samuel Champlain (1604) and John Smith (1614). Eventually, a trading post was established by Baron Castine, who arrived from France with a band of colonists in 1667. The trading post and the town became a strategic pawn in the struggles for control of the continent, and the region changed hands many times during the French and Indian War, the American Revolution, and the War of 1812. By the mid-nineteenth century, the residents had settled down to a life of logging, shipping, coastal trading, and fishing. Many a Maine skipper sailed his Down East clipper ship "round the horn" during the California Gold Rush.

As early as the 1880s, however, the Maine coast was becoming known as an attractive summer resort area. The town of Castine in particular, with its excellent harbor, offered the wealthy an escape from the Northeast's humid summertime climate. The 1930s saw the first wave of craftspeople arrive, principally in the Blue Hill area. Thirty years later, as the children of the sixties searched for alternative lifestyles, a second wave hit. Today, craftspeople throughout the area—potters, weavers, woodworkers, and artisans in every imaginable medium—complement one of our nation's most famous craft schools, the Haystack Mountain School of Crafts in Deer Isle.

WHERE TO GO, WHAT TO DO

Driving Tours

If you are coming from Mount Desert Island, we've found a route that avoids all of the commercialization and traffic of Ellsworth. When you cross the bridge leaving Mount Desert Island at Trenton, turn left almost immediately on Route 230. Turn right on Goose Cove Road and right again on Route 230 (this is a shortcut across the peninsula). At Route 1 turn left, cross the bridge, and take the first left onto Route 172 heading toward Surry and Blue Hill.

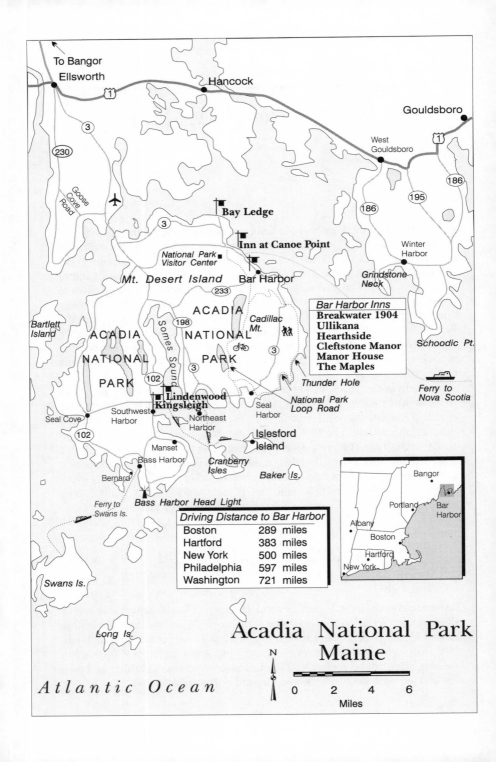

To Bangor
Ellsworth

Hancock

Gouldsboro

West Gouldsboro

Winter Harbor

Grindstone Neck

Bay Ledge

Inn at Canoe Point

National Park Visitor Center

Mt. Desert Island

Bar Harbor

ACADIA

NATIONAL

Cadillac Mt.

Bartlett Island

Somes Sound

ACADIA

NATIONAL

PARK

PARK

Schoodic Pt.

Bar Harbor Inns
Breakwater 1904
Ullikana
Hearthside
Cleftstone Manor
Manor House
The Maples

Thunder Hole

National Park Loop Road

Ferry to Nova Scotia

Seal Cove

Lindenwood
Kingsleigh

Southwest Harbor

Northeast Harbor

Seal Harbor

Islesford Island

Manset

Bass Harbor

Bernard

Cranberry Isles

Baker Is.

Ferry to Swans Is.

Bass Harbor Head Light

Driving Distance to Bar Harbor	
Boston	289 miles
Hartford	383 miles
New York	500 miles
Philadelphia	597 miles
Washington	721 miles

Bangor

Portland

Bar Harbor

Albany

Boston

Hartford

New York

Swans Is.

Long Is.

Acadia National Park
Maine

N

Atlantic Ocean

0   2   4   6
Miles

Blue Hill–Deer Isle–Stonington

Blue Hill is a year-round community with a number of fine galleries, potters, and restaurants, including three for fine dining. **Rackcliffe Pottery** is on Route 172 north of town and **Rowantrees Pottery** is on Route 177 also north of town. **Leighton Gallery** on Parker Point Road, off the main street, is one of the top galleries in the state, featuring fine contemporary paintings and a large sculpture garden. **Jud Hartman's Gallery** on Main Street (207) 359-2544) features a unique series of museum-quality bronze sculptures entitled *The Woodland Tribes of the Northeast.* **North Country Textiles,** which sells handwoven shawls, tablecloths, and blankets, is also on Main Street. **Handworks Gallery,** stocking locally produced clothing, jewelry, and contemporary crafts, with many local artists represented, has a second-floor location with an entrance on a side street off the main street. For lunch in town during the summer we suggest **Jean-Paul's Bistro**, where you can sit on white Adirondack chairs outside in a garden setting overlooking the bay. For a quick bite, eat in or take out at Red Bag Deli. For dinner in town choose from the **Blue Hill Inn, Firepond,** or **Jonathan's**. Chamber music is played at **Kneisel Hall** Sunday at 4 P.M. and Wednesday at 8:15 P.M. from early July through mid-August; (207) 374-2811.

Heading south of town on Route 15, stop at **Caterpillar Hill Overlook**, which has the best view on this peninsula of blueberry fields, Penobscot Bay, the islands, and the Camden Hills. Cross the high suspension bridge to Little Deer Isle. **Eaton's Lobster Pool** (*see* Where to Dine) is to your right down a side road. **Harbor Farm**, a store just before the causeway, is filled with top-quality gift items from around the world, and is a great place to browse year-round. After you cross the causeway to Deer Isle, bear left on Old Ferry Road to get to **Ronald Pearson Jewelry Design Studio,** a goldsmith (207-348-2535) or to **Kathy Woell,** a weaver whose chenille sweaters we saw at Handworks in Blue Hill (207-348-6141). Take a left on Reach Road and go 3.2 miles to get to **Bill Mor's** studio and showroom of stoneware and tribal Oriental rugs (207-348-2822).

Continue on Route 15 to Deer Isle Village. **The Maine Crafts Association,** a right turn on Dow Road just before you get to Deer Isle Village, is the place to go to research Maine crafts.

In Deer Isle Village stop to see **Terrell Lester's** (207-348-2676) wonderful large color photographs (he also has a gallery in Stonington). Walk across the street to the **Turtle Gallery**. Just after Route 15 turns left at Deer Isle Village look for the **Blue Heron Gallery** on your left. This is a top gallery with glass, pottery, jewelry, and other pieces, many of which are done by artists who teach at Haystack.

Continue on Route 15. Make a left turn at signs pointing the way to **Sunshine** and **Haystack**. This is a particularly lovely unspoiled road with wonderful water views. Go two miles to FR523, a dirt road that leads to the **Edgar**

M. Tennis Preserve. Return to the main road and continue toward Haystack with a stop at **Nervous Nellies Jams**. You can sample the jams and have tea and scones during the summer. For lunch we like the informality of **Eaton's Pier**, where you can eat lobster and clams outside at picnic tables next to the water. **Haystack School of Crafts**, one of the country's top craft schools, is at the end of the road. This school has given people of all ages and skill levels a solid grounding in the crafts since its founding in 1950. Visitors are permitted once a week on Wednesday at 1 P.M. for a tour of the school. You are welcome to walk down to the magnificent point at the end of the steps that are built over the giant boulders for a panoramic vista of the Atlantic Ocean; (207) 348-2306.

Return to Route 15, make a left and a right on the first road (Joyce's Cross Road) to **Wheeler Gallery** (207-348-5267), where we purchased a pair of Fred Woell's earrings. **Finest Kind Dining**, a little farther down this road, has good lobster rolls on grilled hot dog buns. Return to Route 15 and continue to Stonington. During the summer about eight galleries are open along Main Street. A favorite is the **Hoy Gallery. Eastern Bay Gallery** carries the work of local artists. For lunch or a snack stop at **Penobscot Provisions** (*see* Where to Dine) for a take-out sandwich on homemade bread and superb brownies made with Callebaut chocolate. The mail boat to Isle au Haut leaves from the dock behind Atlantic Hardware. Around the corner on Main Street notice the sculpture of the stonecutter, a monument to the thousands who worked the granite quarries that provided much of the employment in the town for more than 100 years. Follow the shore road to **Ames Pond**, a lily pond that's a mass of flowers during the summer. To return to Deer Isle Village take Route 15 or for a different route follow signs to West Stonington and Sunset. Walkers will want to see **Barred Island**, an island owned by the Nature Conservancy and accessible at low tide, next to Goose Cove Lodge (see Where to Stay).

Blue Hill–Castine

From Blue Hill take Route 177 to South Penobscot. Visit **North Country Textiles**, where designer shops and boutiques throughout America come to obtain handwoven garments. We saw lightweight open-weave jackets, capes, scarves, and table linens—all in a variety of pastel and muted colors, (207) 326-4131. Upstairs, **David Larson** has been painting and showing his haunting scenes for more than twenty-five years.

Take Route 175 to Route 199 south to Route 166 to **Castine**. A French trading post was erected here in 1613, nine years before the pilgrims landed at Plymouth. This waterfront community has an impressive number of restored eighteenth- and nineteenth-century homes. The state of Maine training ship of the Maine Maritime Academy (campus located in town) is docked at the foot of Main Street. Start a walking tour at the top of Main Street at **Chris Murray's Studio**—Murray is a world champion bird carver; stop at **Leila Day Antiques**; walk through the gardens at **the Castine Inn**, admire the **Penta-**

göet Inn and visit **Water Witch**, a store whose shelves are filled with batiks from Indonesia, Africa, and the Netherlands, made into shirts, vests, skirts, purses, and quilted mats—all designed by owner Jean de Raat; (207) 326-4884. Notice the well-cared-for magnificent American elm trees that line Main Street.

Dennett's Wharf along the water is a good lunch spot. Scattered throughout town are about a hundred markers that point out historic buildings and sites. Head down Perkins Street, which is lined with historic homes. Stop by the **Wilson Museum** (2 to 5 P.M., Tuesday through Sunday, June to October), especially to see the collection of photos of turn-of-the-century Castine. Next door, visit the blacksmith shop and antique hearse house (2 to 5 P.M., Sunday and Wednesday during July and August), or take the path to **Fort Madison**, where you can picnic overlooking the harbor. At the end of the road, bear left to **Dyce's Head Light** and follow the forty-seven steps down to the rocky shore below. Return to town via Battle Avenue, the next street north of Perkins Street.

After visiting Castine, return to South Penobscot. You have a choice of returning directly to Blue Hill on Route 177 or continuing on a circular loop around the peninsula. To do the loop, go south on Route 175. Turn right on Route 176. Stop at **Bagaduce Lunch**, a roadside lunch stand next to one of the reversing falls that change directions with the tide. Take Route 176 south. Hikers or birders can follow signs to **Holbrook Island Sanctuary**, a state park on Cape Rosier. Continue to South Brooksville. Stop at the **Buck's Harbor Market** and go to the back of the store to the **Pain de Famille bakery**, where European-style bread is baked in a wood-fired brick oven. Get a loaf of bread, a focaccia, or some wrapped slices of whole grain fruit and nut bread. **Buck's Harbor Yacht Club**, **Fiddlehead Gallery**, and **Landing Market and Restaurant** are across the street. For sailing on Penobscot Bay, we went with **Gil Perkins**, who takes only six passengers and sails out of Buck's Harbor marina; entrance is a half mile down the road. Stop at **Sow's Ear Winery** in Brooksville to try the English-style ciders or the rhubarb wine. To return to Blue Hill go north on Route 15.

To get to the east side of the peninsula and to the **Wooden Boat School** in Brooklin take Route 175 south to Sedgwick and then on to Brooklin. If you are fascinated by wooden boats, or have ever wondered where *WoodenBoat* magazine is published, this is the place! The school welcomes visitors, and has courses on building everything from canoes to twenty-seven-foot sailboats, and on photographing boats; (207) 359-4651.

Continue on Route 175, with stops at **Haight Farm** for hydroponically grown produce and at the Phoenix Center if you are interested in kayaking. Stop at the **Blue Hill Falls**, another reversing falls, and continue to Route 15 and Blue Hill. As you drive around the peninsula tune your radio to **WERU 89.9**, a local station broadcasting from Blue Hill. For evening entertainment, find out who's at the **Left Bank Cafe**; top folk, blues, and jazz artists are featured most weekends.

Craft Galleries

Leighton Gallery. This is one of the top galleries in the state, and we never miss an opportunity to visit. Serious collectors also have discovered this gallery, which exhibits the work of Maine artists as well as others. You won't find typical Maine coast scenes of water, rocks, and lighthouses; the contemporary works on display would be at home in sophisticated New York galleries. Be sure to visit the sculpture gardens. Open daily, Memorial Day to mid-October. Parker Point Road, Blue Hill, ME 04614; (207) 374-5001.

Rowantrees Pottery. Striking turquoise, evergreen, yellow, white, and blue glazes made from local ores decorate the dishes, pitchers, cups, bowls, and other attractive items made and sold here. The entire operation is open to the public, so you can see the potters at work. Open daily in summer; Monday through Friday the rest of the year. On Union Street in Blue Hill; (207) 374-5535.

Rackliffe Pottery. Phil Rackliffe was trained at Rowantrees, spent twenty years of his career there, then moved across town, where he now makes similar items alongside his children and grandchildren. The selection is not as grand, but neither are the prices. Open daily in summer; closed Sundays at other times. On Route 172 as you head north out of town. Blue Hill; (207) 374-2297.

Blue Heron Gallery. Here you will see works from some of the finest craftspeople working in America today, many of whom teach at Haystack. Owner Mary Nyberg features the work of Haystack faculty members as well as other American artists. Open May through September, Monday through Saturday. Located on Route 15. Deer Isle Village; (207) 348-6051.

The Maine Crafts Association. More than 100 craftspeople produce superb handmade items in this area. The Maine Crafts Association has crafts for sale as well as an extensive archive of photographs and slides of its members. While you're here, pick up a booklet describing the artists who belong to the association, the hours their shops are open, and how you can contact them. For a brochure of Maine Crafts write to Maine Crafts Association, 6 Dow Road, Box 228, Deer Isle, ME 04627; (207) 348-9943.

Eastern Bay Galleries. Works of local artists and crafts are exhibited. Make sure to check out the old granite cistern room located in the back of the gallery, where changing exhibits are held throughout the season. Open daily mid-May through mid-October, weekends through Christmas. On Main Street in Stonington; (207) 367-5006.

Hiking and Walking

Isle au Haut. This little-known appendage of Acadia National Park offers more than 32 miles of hiking trails. The 3.8-mile Duck Harbor Trail winds through a moss-carpeted forest that looks like a naturalistic bonsai garden. In summer the 10 A.M. boat leaves from the Stonington docks and sails to Duck Harbor, where it is met by park rangers who will answer questions, hand out trail maps, and lead hikes. The park accepts only fifty day-trippers at a time during the summer.

Mail boat to Isle au Haut, Stonington. Boats run daily except Sunday and postal holidays. Operated by Isle au Haut Company, Isle au Haut, ME 04645; (207) 367-5193. Call ahead, as the schedule can be confusing and varies with the season.

Holbrook Island Sanctuary. The network of old roads, paths, and animal trails that laces the forests of this 1,200-acre preserve, located off Cape Rosier Road, leads you to beaches, mudflats, rocky coasts, and ponds. When this land was given to the state of Maine, provisions stipulated that the sanctuary not be altered by modern park facilities or management techniques. Pick up a trail map at a local inn or contact the sanctuary at Box 280, Brooksville, ME 04617; (207) 326-4012.

Barred Island Nature Preserve, Sunset. Surrounding Goose Cove Lodge (*see* Where to Stay) are seventy acres owned by the Nature Conservancy with miles of nature trails open to the public. Take the road to Goose Cove Lodge and park in the lot that says "Parking for Barred Island." The Cliff Trail goes to Barred Island, which can been reached by a sand bar for three hours on each side of low tide.

Blue Hill Mountain. Take the road opposite the Blue Hill Fair Grounds on Route 172 eight-tenths of a mile to the parking lot. Hike the one-mile trail to the top of this mountain that overlooks the town of Blue Hill, Penobscot Bay, and Acadia National Park.

The Edgar M. Tennis Preserve. Take the road to Haystack and Sunshine. Go two miles; turn right at FR (fire road) 523. Take this dirt road to a trail sign and wooden box with trail maps. A number of trails lead through the woods, along the water, and to the tiny cemetery with a headstone for William Toothaker, a soldier who died near Richmond, which Ken Burns showed in the popular *Civil War* television series on PBS.

Getting out on the Water

Sailing. Captain Gil Perkins takes six people on half-day or full-day sails on *2nd Fiddle,* his Catalina 30, sailing on Penobscot Bay out of Buck's Harbor Marina. Gil was born in the area, knows the waters, and answered every question we asked. His wife makes great chocolate chip cookies (box lunches are provided for full-day sails), which are served along with cold drinks. His trips are very popular, so call early or have your innkeeper book in advance; (207) 326-4167.

Kayaking. For kayaking in East Penobscot Bay in the Blue Hill area contact the Phoenix Center. In addition to day trips the center offers a romantic

The Blue Hill Inn is a classic 1830s brick-and-white-clapboard New England building in the center of Blue Hill.

package called Fantasy Isle Escape. You kayak to a private beach, where a guide will set up the tent for you, prepare a campfire and dinner, and return the next morning to make breakfast. Route 175, Blue Hill Falls; (207) 374-2113. Registered Maine Guides accompany each group.

WHERE TO STAY

East Penobscot Bay lodgings arranged geographically from Blue Hill south to Deer Isle to Castine.

The Blue Hill Inn, Blue Hill
Opening the front door of this traditional brick-and-white-clapboard 1830s New England village inn on a chilly fall afternoon, seeing the fireplace and the couches invitingly set on either side, and being warmly greeted by innkeepers Mary and Don Hartley, we felt right at home. The tastefully coordinated rooms vary in size from enormous to comfortable. Many have yellow-pine floors original to the house and nineteenth-century antiques.

If reading in bed and watching the fire after a delicious dinner fit your image of a romantic New England inn, choose room 5, a second-floor corner room with a queen-size four-poster cannonball bed; room 10, a first-floor corner room with a fireplace and a queen-size bed; or room 4, with a king-size bed, a fireplace, and an old-fashioned claw-foot tub. Room 3 has a queen-size bed, a large sitting area, and a bath with a claw-foot tub. Room 9, a third-floor room, is the only one that can accommodate three people.

Breakfast includes a choice of five entrées such as amaretto French toast, waffles with strawberries, olive and chive omelettes, or blueberry pancakes.

Open mid-May through November. Eleven rooms, all with private bath, $140–$190; includes breakfast and dinner for two. B&B rates available. 15% service. Not recommended for children under 13. No pets. No smoking. Two-night weekend minimum. Union Street, Box 403, Blue Hill, ME 04614; (207) 374-2844; (800) 826-7415.

John Peters Inn, Blue Hill

This Southern plantation-style mansion owned by Barbara and Rick Seeger is situated on twenty-seven acres. The inn overlooks the inner harbor of Blue Hill Bay. The main inn has eight rooms. The Blue Hill Room, the most expensive and our favorite, has a king-size bed facing a wood-burning fireplace, a wet bar, a coffeemaker, a large private deck with a fabulous view, and a large bath with a claw-foot tub and a separate shower. The rooms throughout are decorated with Barbara's exquisite collection of Oriental rugs.

The Carriage House has six rooms with queen-size beds. Four have fully equipped kitchens, a wood-burning fireplace, and an outdoor deck. Our favorites are the two second-floor units: Searsport, with a view of the water, and Northport, with a view of Blue Hill Mountain.

An outstanding breakfast is served from 8 to 10 A.M. Guests sit at individual tables and select from a large menu that includes freshly squeezed orange juice, fruit with sorbet, grilled muffins, and a choice of ten entrées such as a lobster omelette, cheese eggs, poached eggs with asparagus, eggs Benedict, waffles with different toppings, or crabmeat Monterey Jack omelette.

They have a pool as well as a sixteen-foot sailboat, a rowboat, and a canoe for the guests to use.

Open May through October. Fourteen rooms, all with private bath, nine with fireplace, $95–$150. Full breakfast included. Children over 12 welcome. No pets. No smoking. Located a mile north of Blue Hill center just off Route 176. Route 176, Peters Point, Box 916, Blue Hill, ME 04614; (207) 374-2116.

Eggemoggin Reach B&B, Brooksville

The inn, located on a secluded rugged granite cove with a spectacular view of Eggemoggin Reach, Pumpkin Island Lighthouse, Penobscot Bay, and the outline of the Camden Hills in the distance, is a perfect hideaway for those who crave the seclusion of picture-book Maine coast. Don't attempt to find this inn without directions, as it is down a long entrance drive off a back road. Innkeepers Susie and Mike Canon turned their former summer house into a bed-and-breakfast in 1993. A wooden staircase leads from the house down to the dock and the rocky shoreline, where the Canons have a rowboat and canoe for guests' use. The first floor has an open plan with no doors separating the dining, living, and kitchen areas. The porch faces west for dramatic sunset views over the water; breakfast is served here in warm weather.

The three rooms in the main house and two studio cottages with screened porches all have water views. For privacy the two attached cottages are our top choice. Each pickled pine, cathedral-ceiling studio has a king-size bed, a fireplace stove, a couch, a fully-equipped kitchen, a screened porch, and a bath with a shower only.

The Wheelhouse Suite, the entire third floor of the main house, has a bedroom with a king-size bed, a full bath, and a very large living room with a desk, a couch, and two twin beds.

A breakfast buffet includes fresh-squeezed orange juice, cereals, yogurt, fruit, muffins, and a hot dish such as waffles, apple-cinnamon French toast, or sausage-and-egg casserole.

Open May through mid-October. Five rooms, all with private bath. Mid-June through Labor Day, $135–$165. 15% less at other times. Breakfast included. Children over 12 welcome. No pets. No smoking. Two-night weekend minimum. RR1, Box 33A, Herrick Road, Brooksville, ME 04617; (207) 359-5073.

Pilgrim's Inn, Deer Isle

Innkeepers Jean and Dud Hendrick have owned this fine large maroon 1793 Colonial country inn in tiny Deer Isle Village since 1982.

On the first floor there's a library filled with books relating to the area. On the ground level, a taproom and the wood-paneled lounge, each with a large eight-foot wood-burning fireplace, open onto the lawn that leads to the mill pond. A few Adirondack chairs are set out by the water, a relaxing spot to sit with a good book.

The guest rooms have pine floors and are furnished with country antiques. Favorites include room 4, a corner room with two double beds; room 5, with a queen cherry bed (made by Dud), a tub with a handheld shower, and the best view; and room 6, a spacious front corner room with a queen-size bed and a bath with a small shower. Rooms 11 and 14 are large third-floor rooms that have private baths with Deer Isle granite vanity tops.

Before dinner, guests gather for hors d'oeuvres followed by dinner at 7 P.M., certainly a highlight of your stay. For early risers, fresh-brewed coffee is left out in the hallways. Breakfast, served from 8 to 9 A.M., includes a buffet of juices, cereals, and breads plus a choice of entrée such as omelettes with bacon or sausage, blueberry pancakes, or waffles.

Open mid-May through mid-October. Thirteen rooms, eleven with private bath, and a one-bedroom cottage, $145–$200. Breakfast and dinner included. Bed-and-breakfast rates available. 15% service charge. Children over 10 welcome. No pets. No smoking. Bicycles available. Deer Isle, ME 04627; (207) 348-6615.

Goose Cove Lodge, Deer Isle

The lodge and cabins, surrounded by Nature Conservancy property with miles of walking trails in a private waterfront setting, are on a secluded cove of Penobscot Bay. The innkeepers are Dom and Joanne Parisi. During the summer season the water-view accommodations are reserved for guests staying a week or longer; woodland-view rooms can be reserved for shorter stays.

The rooms and cottages are rustic and simply furnished. Of the seven secluded cottages, each with a fireplace, kitchen, and deck, the two most popular for their proximity to the water are Elm and Linnea, which have a minimum three-person rate in season. Lookout, the second floor of the main lodge, is the most expensive accommodation, with two bedrooms, a living room, a kitchen, and spectacular water views.

Other accommodations include attached cottages, and rooms and suites in the annex off the lodge, almost all with fireplaces or Franklin stoves.

During the day you can use the lodge's canoes or kayaks to explore the cove, hike on the trails, or spend the day enjoying the solitude with a good book. A twenty-four-foot Rainbow sloop is available to rent. Goose Cove welcomes families and has a supervised evening children's program that includes dinner and entertainment.

The extensive breakfast includes juices, fruit, granola with toppings, yogurt, breads and muffins, and a hot dish such as delicious pan-fried wild mushroom risotto topped with chopped fresh tomatoes or poached eggs.

Open mid-May through mid-October. Twenty-three rooms, suites, and cottages. Late June through Labor Day, $87–$130 per person (some cottages with three-person minimums), breakfast and dinner included. Off-season $73–$110 per person, breakfast and dinner included, or $94–$160, lodging and breakfast for two included. 15% service charge. Water-view units, one-week minimum in season; off-season, two-night minimum. Children welcome, rates vary with age. No pets. Deer Isle, Box 40, Sunset, ME 04683; (207) 348-2508.

The Keeper's House, Isle au Haut

The Keeper's House is a most unusual inn located on rugged Isle au Haut, a little-known appendage of Acadia National Park in East Penobscot Bay, eight miles from Stonington, Maine. There are no phones and no electricity at the inn. Bathrooms are shared, and one of the little cottages has an outhouse.

This is not a destination that will appeal to everyone, but for those who find contentment in the splendor of thick forests and a pristine shoreline, we cannot recommend the Keeper's House strongly enough.

The largest room of the four in the main house is the third-floor Garret Room, which has a double bed. One of the inn's two bathrooms is on the third floor. The other three rooms, all with double beds and one with a trundle bed,

The Keeper's House is a most unusual inn located on rugged Isle au Haut, a little-known appendage of Acadia National Park, eight miles from Stonington, Maine.

are on the second floor. The Keeper's Room, the original master bedroom, is popular for its view of the lighthouse and for its wood stove. The Sunrise Room also has a wood stove. The Horizon Room looks westward and has the best view of any room in the main house.

There are also two tiny guest cottages. The Oil House (we think of it as a dollhouse, as it is only about ten feet square) is furnished with a double bed and a potbellied stove. Two chairs sit on a tiny deck overlooking the water; a short path leads to an outhouse; and the outdoor sink and outdoor shower are surrounded by a wood fence. The Wood Shed Room is the second floor of a small barn which shares the bathroom on the first floor with the innkeepers, Jeff and Judi Burke.

All the guests sit together at two candlelit tables for dinner, which the day we visited included homemade bread, eggplant Parmesan soup, baked salmon, bulgur pilaf, vegetables, and a garden salad with lettuces grown on the island. Dessert was a choice of apple charlotte or lemon tea cake. On Sunday nights the innkeepers steam lobsters on the beach.

Open May through October. Four rooms and two cottages, all sharing baths or outhouses, $268 for two (includes three meals a day, lodging, and taxes). Two-night minimum in July and August. Children welcome. No pets. No smoking. Box 26, Isle au Haut, ME 04645; (207) 367-2261 (off-island information and reservations).

The Pentagöet Inn, Castine

The exterior of this prominent Victorian bed-and-breakfast with its wide wrap-around porch, overflowing flower boxes, rocking chairs, and three-story turret, is a favorite of photographers and artists. Common space includes a sitting room with a turret window seat and view of the harbor and a plush library with a Bosendorfer upright piano. The innkeepers are Virginia and Lindsey Miller.

Most of the rooms have king- or queen-size beds. Our favorites are the turret rooms, room 1 on the second floor, with seven windows, and room 7 on the third floor, which has a good view looking down Castine's tree-lined main street toward the harbor.

The six-room Perkins House located just behind the inn is older than the rest of the inn. The suite is a favorite, as it is the only room with a wood-burning fireplace. We also like room 5, which has a king-size bed and a bright, sunny morning room.

For early risers, fresh-brewed coffee is set out in the hallway. A lovely breakfast buffet includes a sumptuous display of fresh fruits including, in season, a large bowl of Maine wild blueberries; cereals; many varieties of baked goods; and bagels. Guests can also order a cooked breakfast that includes a daily choice of three entrées such as glazed French toast, blintzes, blueberry pancakes, or omelettes with bacon or sausage.

Open Memorial Day through October. Sixteen rooms, all with private bath, $95–$125, breakfast, afternoon refreshment, and wine and cheese included. Children over 12 welcome. No smoking. Pets permitted in selected rooms. Main Street, Box 4, Castine, ME 04421; (207) 326-8616; (800) 845-1701 (outside Maine).

The Castine Inn, Castine

This breezy Maine hotel is owned by Mark and Margaret Hodesh. As you walk in the front door there is a living room with a fireplace and seating area on your right and a comfortable bar on your left. A recent addition is the Victorian garden next to the inn, created by Margaret over a number of years, with benches, a trellised walkway, and a small arched bridge over a stream. The garden is open to the public and has quickly become a favorite for summer wedding photographs. The sixty-foot wraparound porch extends along the side of the inn overlooking the garden.

The second floor has twelve rooms and the third floor has eight rooms, three of which are suites. Rooms have a queen-size bed or two twin beds. The third-floor rooms that face the water are the best and the most expensive since they offer great views of the garden, the town, and the harbor beyond. The rooms are airy and bright and the furnishings are sturdy functional country pieces.

Breakfast, served from 8 to 9 A.M., includes such choices as corned beef hash served with poached eggs, a baked omelette with spinach and mushrooms, and French toast.

Open early May through third week of October. Seventeen rooms and three suites, all with private bath, $75–$135. Off-peak rates available. Breakfast included. Dinner available. Children over 5 welcome. No pets. Box 41, Main Street, Castine, ME 04421; (207) 326-4365.

WHERE TO DINE

Fine Dining

The Castine Inn, Castine

The highlight of the dining room is the murals of Castine. Start with a glass of wine in the adjoining cozy bar; in warm weather, sit on the porch overlooking the beautifully landscaped strolling garden.

Homemade biscuits are served on a tray as they have been every day since the inn opened twelve years ago. We started with the freshly shucked Spinney Creek oysters and a salad of perfectly ripe local sliced tomatoes and chopped egg. Lobster was shelled and served over fresh corn. The large pan-seared Stonington diver scallops were superb, a highlight of the dinner. Traditional chicken-and-leek pot pie and crabmeat cakes with mustard sauce are always on the menu.

Don't miss the one-crust blueberry pie made with tiny wild blueberries. Other choices include gingerbread served with applesauce, baked Indian pudding, and a chocolate soufflé cake.

Early May through the third week of October. Dinner, weekends till Memorial Day; then daily till closing. Entrées, $14–$19. Tuesday is buffet night. Main Street, Castine, ME; (207) 326–4365.

Jonathan's, Blue Hill

Chef-owner Jonathan Chase has been at this Main Street location since 1982. The preferred seating is the newer back room with a high peaked wood ceiling and a more open feel.

For starters we liked the salad of Ducktrap Farm smoked mussels warmed in vinaigrette and served on baby greens with bits of chèvre and toasted pine nuts. Other first courses are steamed mussels; spanakopita; and a salad of smoked Ducktrap seafood and olives.

All the entrées come with a cup of soup. We had grilled loin lamb chops with Gorgonzola and walnut butter, a rich dish. The paella included pieces of chorizo, chicken, a lobster claw, clams, and mussels served over rice. Lamb shanks are a house favorite, a hearty dish simmered in Bass ale, bourbon, and maple barbecue sauce. Daily fish specials include boiled lobster, grilled swordfish, poached salmon, and baked haddock. Desserts are generous and traditional. Blueberry crisp with vanilla ice cream and four-layer chocolate cake were options the night we dined. The wine list is one of the best in Maine.

June through November, dinner nightly. Closed Monday and Tuesday in winter. Entrées, $15–$20. Main Street, Blue Hill, ME; (207) 374-5226.

Firepond Restaurant, Blue Hill

This large restaurant on two levels has an open, contemporary look. The first floor has a large bar with tables as well as an outdoor front bar area. An attractive staircase with a hand-wrought iron rail leads to the lower level, a candlelit country setting with hand-hewn wood-paneled walls, Oriental rugs, and the pleasant sounds and sight of a rushing stream.

During the peak months of July and August, the restaurant is very crowded. The prime seats are on the screened porch overlooking the stream. These seats can be requested but not reserved.

We give the food high marks. We started with the salmon ravioli, a single large filled pasta topped with Gruyère baked in a ramekin; chilled sweet berry soup; farm-raised oysters from southern Maine; and sautéed wild mushrooms on shredded radicchio. An excellent salad of local baby greens with crumbled blue cheese in herb vinaigrette was included with the entrée. Entrées we selected included pepper-encrusted tuna and grilled salmon. From the regular menu we also had veal with sun-dried tomatoes and shiitake mushrooms and grilled marinated chicken with grilled vegetable salsa and chèvre.

Mid-May to New Year's. Dinner daily late May through September. Fewer days at other times. Entrées, $16–$21. Main Street, Blue Hill, ME; (207) 374-9970.

The Blue Hill Inn, Blue Hill

A leisurely five-course dinner with a choice of two entrées is served to a maximum of twenty-four guests, all at individual tables. The dining room has a candlelit chandelier. The inn features locally raised produce, fowl, and Maine seafood.

Dinner starts with an appetizer such as leeks in puff pastry with a chervil sauce; fettuccine with lobster, arugula, and fresh tomatoes; or mussels Provençal. This is followed by a palate-cleansing ice. A choice of two entrées might include Spinney Creek oysters in curry sauce, roasted herb-stuffed loin of lamb, filet of beef with Roquefort sauce and walnuts, scallops with endive and lime, guinea hen with champagne grapes and wild mushrooms, and lobster with caramelized ginger served on spinach. Every Monday night the featured entrée is baked stuffed lobster flamed with brandy. The salad follows the entrée. Coffee and dessert such as a flourless chocolate torte or poached pears in red wine and cassis complete the meal.

Dinner daily, June through October; weekends other times. Dinner is included in the room rate. Limited reservations available for guests not staying at the inn. $35 per person. Innkeepers' reception at 6 P.M., dinner at 7 P.M. Union Street, Blue Hill, ME; (207) 374-2844.

Pilgrim's Inn, Deer Isle

Guests gather before dinner in the intimate bar or the two common rooms, each with an eight-foot wood-burning fireplace, to savor five to six creative hors d'oeuvres such as miniature crab cakes, smoked salmon, sliced apples and smoked trout pâté, marinated herbed mussels, corn tortilla pizza, and a cheese fondue. The hors d'oeuvres are a signature of this inn.

At 7 P.M. a set dinner is served in the barn dining room, where paintings by local artists hang on the walls. The basic entrée is the same each day of the week, but the first course, salad, and dessert change nightly. Sunday features salmon and trout; Monday, tenderloin of beef with lobster risotto; Tuesday, a mixed grill of pork, farm-raised chicken, and shrimp; Wednesday, crabmeat, salmon, and lobster cakes; Thursday, Deer Isle chicken or duck; Friday, bouillabaisse; and Saturday, loin of lamb, quail, and Maine scallops.

Mid-May through mid-October. Dinner is included in the daily room rate. For nonguests, $30 per person; reserve far in advance, as only a few outside diners can be accommodated. Cocktails at 6 P.M., dinner at 7 P.M. Deer Isle, ME; (207) 348-6615.

Goose Cove Lodge, Sunset

This lodge is on a secluded cove on Deer Isle overlooking Penobscot Bay. The dining area, which is a couple of steps below the great room, has large windows overlooking the water.

A choice of three entrées includes a vegetarian and grilled steak or chicken option, served each evening along with an appetizer, salad, and dessert.

The night we stayed we had sweet-potato-and-spinach gnocchi followed by entrées of steamed bass wrapped in banana leaves and the vegetarian entrée of rice cake and spinach sandwich with a mushroom-and-leek sauce. A romaine and tomato salad was followed by blueberry cake with English custard. Friday nights feature a lobster bake with mussels and corn plus grilled steaks, chicken, burgers, and hot dogs. In summer months when weather cooperates it is held on the beach.

Mid-May through mid-October, dinner nightly. Cocktails 6 P.M., dinner 7 P.M. Dinner included with room rate, for outside diners (a limited number of reservations only) $30 per person. Goose Cove Road, Sunset, ME; (207) 348-2508.

Informal Dining

Jean Paul's Bistro, Blue Hill

On a beautiful summer day it's idyllic to sit on white Adirondack chairs in the garden overlooking peaceful Blue Hill Harbor. Jean-Paul's menu is strictly French bistro fare, with such choices such as salad Niçoise, Caesar salad with grilled chicken breast, and sandwiches such as a croque monsieur, roast beef and melted Brie, or a "pizza" baguette. Finish with cappuccino and a chocolate croissant.

July and August, lunch, $4–$7. Main Street, Blue Hill, ME; (207) 374-5852.

Pie in the Sky Pizza, Blue Hill

This pizza parlor offers refreshingly different toppings, including jalapeños, tofu, and tempeh as well as the usual favorites. The "as you like it" pie features a whole-wheat crust, tomato sauce, spinach, fresh mushrooms, and ricotta and mozzarella cheese. This is the local teen hangout, and the wait in summer months can be long.

Open daily year-round, lunch and dinner. Mill Street, Blue Hill, ME; (207) 347-5570.

Left Bank Cafe, Blue Hill

Professional folk and jazz groups perform here almost every weekend throughout the year. The food is fine, but the entertainment is great.

Daily from 7 A.M. Located on Route 172 a mile or so north of Blue Hill; (207) 374-2201.

Dennett's Wharf, Castine

This lively informal restaurant and bar is directly on the water. The menu includes chowders; a salad bar; a raw bar; baked, broiled, or fried seafood; and charcoal-grilled steaks, chicken, and the like. Sitting on the outside deck eating a lobster dinner is a perfect afternoon pastime. Notice the ship's knees, joists from old sailing ships that here are used to brace the rafters.

May though early October, daily, lunch and dinner. Live music Wednesday through Saturday evenings. Dinner entrées $10–$20. On the wharf. Castine, ME; (207) 326-9045.

Penobscot Bay Provisions, Stonington

If you're planning a picnic, choose from excellent homemade breads, rolls and focaccio, sandwiches, soup, salads, and brownies made with Callebaut chocolate.

Open May though December. July and August, Tuesday through Saturday, 8 A.M. to 5 P.M., Sunday 10 A.M. to 2 P.M.; other times Thursday through Saturday, 8 A.M. to 3 P.M. West Main Street, Stonington, ME; (207) 367-2920.

Bagaduce Lunch, Brooksville

This unpretentious roadside take-out stand overlooking the Bagaduce River and one of the area's reversing falls has traditional fried scallops, shrimp, chicken, lobster and crab rolls, burgers, fried clams, ice cream, and hot dogs. After placing your order at the outside window, take your tray to a picnic table overlooking the water or bring a blanket and sit on the grassy slope.

Early May through mid-September, daily, lunch and dinner. Located on Routes 175 and 176 just east of Brooksville.

Buck's Harbor Market

The Pain de Famille bakery in the back of this traditional general store and market has a European-style brick wood-fired oven. The breads are superb. For snacking, try a focaccio and individual wrapped slices of the fruit and nut breads. Baker Stephen Lanzalotta has plans to open a café. Buck's Harbor, Route 176, South Brooksville, ME; (207) 326-9160.

Lobster Pounds

No trip to this area of the coast of Maine is complete without a lobster dinner. Here's a selection of our favorite lobster pounds where you can roll up your sleeves and attack your lobster with gusto.

Eaton's Lobster Pool Restaurant, Deer Isle

This building, which from the parking lot looks like it's about to fall down, is on the water at the end of a narrow road overlooking Penobscot Bay and the distant Camden Hills. The interior is a large room with rough wood walls. Bring your own wine or beer. We ignore the iceberg salad, the bags of potato chips, and the rolls that come with the dinners, and instead get to the basics: steamed soft shell clams, boiled lobster, and blueberry pie with ice cream.

Mid-May to mid-October. Dinner daily mid-June to mid-September, weekends at other times. Head south on Route 15 and cross the high suspension bridge onto Little Deer Isle. Turn right just before the information booth and follow the signs to Blastow's Cove and Eaton's Lobster Pool. Little Deer Isle; (207) 348-2383.

Eaton's Pier, Deer Isle

This casual lobster pound/restaurant owned and operated by Jim and Marianne Eaton and their children is on the road to Sunshine and the Haystack Craft School. You eat inside or outside at picnic tables at the water's edge, break your lobster claws with large rocks, and help yourself to soft drinks from the refrigerator. No alcohol is sold or allowed on the property.

Mid-June to mid-September, Monday through Saturday, lunch and dinner. (Call ahead early and late in the season to make sure they're open.) 491 Sunshine Road, Sunshine; (207) 348-2489.

ITINERARY

DAY ONE. Take the **driving tour of Blue Hill, Deer Isle, and Stonington.** Visit **Rowantrees** and **Rackliffe** potteries and the stores and galleries in Blue Hill. A good lunch stop is at **Jean Paul's Bistro.** Drive to Deer Isle, making sure to stop at **Blue Heron Art Gallery.** Continue to **Stonington** for more galleries and to Ames Pond if the water lilies are in bloom. Walk to **Barred Island Nature Preserve** and dine at **Goose Cove Lodge,** or take a walk on the **Edgar Tennis Preserve** followed by dinner at **Eaton's Pier, Pilgrim's Inn,** or **Eaton's Lobster Pool.**

DAY TWO. Drive to **Castine** and walk through town. Have lunch at **Dennett's Wharf** or continue the driving tour to South Penobscot and visit **Bagaduce Lunch** for fried clams. Take a sail with **Gil Perkins,** who leaves from Buck's Harbor. Alternatively, spend the afternoon visiting the many craftspeople and galleries in Deer Isle. Stop at the **Maine Crafts Association** in Deer Isle Village for a booklet of member artists. Have dinner in Blue Hill at **Jonathan's, Firepond,** or the **Blue Hill Inn.**

DAY THREE. Pack a lunch and take the mail boat from Stonington out to **Isle au Haut** for a day of biking or hiking.

BUDGETING YOUR TRIP

To help you get the most for the time and money you have to spend, here are some travel suggestions at three budget levels (cost per day with two people sharing a room), including lodging and meal tax, gratuity on meals, and service charge when it is added to your bill. Prices are approximate and are intended for planning purposes only. Lodgings are categorized by price and depending on the room selected may appear in more than one category. Meal prices at lunch include an average entrée and beverage. Dinner prices include an appetizer, entrée, dessert, and beverage. Wine or alcoholic beverages are not included.

Staying and dining at expensive lodgings and restaurants: From $250 to $350 per day for two.

Lodging: John Peters, Blue Hill Inn, Goose Cove Lodge, Pilgrim's Inn, Keeper's House.

Dining: Breakfast: included. Lunch: Eaton's Pier, Jean Paul's Bistro, Dennett's Wharf. Dinner: Blue Hill Inn, Jonathan's, Firepond, Goose Cove Lodge, Pilgrim's Inn.

Staying and dining at moderately priced lodgings and restaurants: From $200 to $250 per day for two.

Lodging: Eggemoggin Reach, John Peters, Castine Inn, Pentagöet, Pilgrim's Inn, Blue Hill Inn.

Dining: Breakfast: included. Lunch: Jean Paul's Bistro, Dennett's Wharf, Eaton's Pier. Dinner: Castine Inn, Dennett's Wharf.

Staying and dining at less expensive lodgings and restaurants: From $130 to $190 per day for two.

Lodging: John Peters, Pentagöet, Castine Inn.

Dining: Breakfast: included. Lunch: Penobscot Provisions, Red Bag Deli, Pie in the Sky, Bagaduce Lunch. Dinner: Eaton's Pier, Eaton's Lobster Pool, Pie in the Sky.

9

Bar Harbor and
Acadia National Park, Maine

J ohn D. Rockefeller Jr., one of the "rusticators," as the early twentieth century summer residents in Bar Harbor were called, became upset when the
first noisy and smelly automobiles appeared on Mount Desert Island. The
noise and fumes so irritated him that, from 1913 through 1940, he personally
supervised the building of forty-five miles of carriage roads for the private use
of his family and friends. These carriage trails, along with sixteen stone
bridges, two gatehouses, and about 12,000 acres, were donated to the national
park system to become part of Acadia National Park.

Today, 4 million people a year visit Acadia National Park on Mount Desert
Island (most during July and August), making it the second most visited national park in the United States.

The majority of visitors spend only about half a day in the park, however,
which barely gives them enough of a feel to say, "I've been there." These are
the tourists who drive the Loop Road, stopping at Sand Beach to dip their toes
in the fifty- to sixty-degree water; point their cameras at Thunder Hole and try
to snap a photo of the water rushing into the crevice; drive up Cadillac Mountain; then attempt to park in Bar Harbor, which is wall to wall with tourists
and day visitors from the cruise ships who wander the main streets and purchase an ice-cream cone and a trinket from the less discerning shops before
leaving.

There's a far more enjoyable way to gain an appreciation for this natural
wonder.

For information on special events, contact the following:

Acadia National Park. P.O. Box 177, Bar Harbor, ME 04609. Information,
(207) 288-3338. Reservation number for ranger trips, (207) 288-5262.

Bar Harbor Chamber of Commerce. P.O. Box 158, 93 Cottage Street,
Bar Harbor, ME 04609. Recorded info (800) 288-3393. Free visitors guide (800)
288-5103 or (207) 288-5103.

Bluenose Ferry. Information on trips to Nova Scotia, (800) 341-7981.

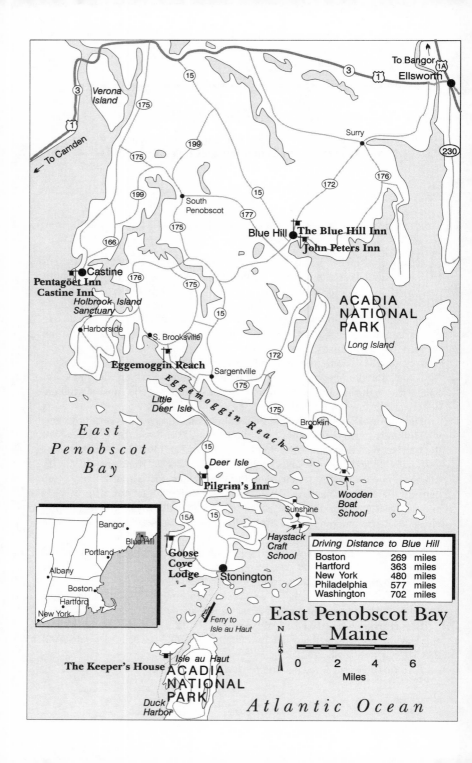

To Bangor

Ellsworth

1A

3

1

Verona
Island

3

1

175

230

← To Camden

175

199

Surry

175

15

172

176

199

South
Penobscot

175

15

177

Blue Hill

The Blue Hill Inn

John Peters Inn

166

Castine

Pentagöet Inn
Castine Inn

176

175

Holbrook Island
Sanctuary

Harborside

S. Brooksville

15

ACADIA
NATIONAL
PARK

Long Island

Eggemoggin Reach

Sargentville

172

175

Eggemoggin Reach

Little
Deer Isle

Brooklin

175

East
Penobscot
Bay

15

Deer Isle

Pilgrim's Inn

Wooden
Boat
School

Sunshine

Bangor

Blue Hill

Portland

15A

15

Haystack
Craft
School

Albany

Goose
Cove
Lodge

Stonington

Driving Distance to Blue Hill	
Boston	269 miles
Hartford	363 miles
New York	480 miles
Philadelphia	577 miles
Washington	702 miles

Boston

Hartford

New York

Ferry to
Isle au Haut

East Penobscot Bay
Maine

N

0   2   4   6

Miles

The Keeper's House

Isle au Haut

ACADIA
NATIONAL
PARK

Duck
Harbor

Atlantic Ocean

WHERE TO GO, WHAT TO DO

Acadia National Park

Stop at the Hulls Cove Visitor Center for a map of the park and a copy of the *Beaver Log*, a National Park publication with schedules of ranger-led interpretive talks, walks, and boat trips. There's also a video introduction to the park and a good selection of guidebooks here. We found booklets about the Loop Road (also available on audiotape), the booklet on the carriage roads for walking, and the detailed guide to hiking trails useful. Located on Route 3 just south of Hulls Cove. Open daily, 8 A.M. to 4:30 P.M. May 1 through October 31; (207) 288-3338. Other times of the year the park headquarters on Route 233 serves as the visitor center. Pick up a copy of *Acadia Weekly*, published eighteen times each summer mid-June to October. This is the best publication for a daily listing of events and activities in the area. We found it particularly useful for the listing and description of the ranger programs. Don't miss taking one or more of these hikes, walks, or boat trips; the ranger-led trips we took were excellent.

The Loop Road

The National Park Service charges admission to the twenty-seven-mile scenic Loop Road, which is one-way for most of the way and offers spectacular views. You can do the actual drive in just over an hour, but we strongly suggest stopping to enjoy the views and to take some of the walks and hikes.

Some highlights of the loop are the **Sieur de Monts Spring,** which features the **Wild Gardens of Acadia;** the **Abbe Museum,** with prehistoric pottery and bones and baskets, canoes, and a wigwam made from birch bark; and the **Park Nature Center. Schooner Head Overlook,** a turnoff just before the main entrance toll station, has a great view looking east over Frenchman Bay to Winter Harbor and Schoodic Peninsula. Take note of the monstrously large contemporary home to your left perched on the exposed bluff, both named Schooner Head.

Sand Beach is the only oceanfront beach in the park. Be aware that the water could be in the fifty-degree range, so swimming is for the hardy. Locals go to **Seal Harbor Beach** to avoid the toll and the crowds of Sand Beach. For warmer water, try **Echo Lake** close to Southwest Harbor.

There is always a crowd of tourist at **Thunder Hole** during the summer and fall. The "game" seems to be to get as close to the water as possible without being caught by a wave. The show everyone is waiting for is the vertical spray of water and accompanying boom caused by the ocean rushing into the mouth of the slot. As the rush of water compresses the air trapped at the back of the chasm it makes a booming sound. The best time to visit is at three-quarter rising tide when the seas are rough. **Otter Cliffs** are the highest headlands along the Atlantic coast north of Rio de Janeiro. On a clear day the views from here and Otter Point are spectacular.

At the Stanley Brook entrance, exit the Loop Road if you are headed to Northeast Harbor or if you want to take a carriage ride that leaves from the Wildwood Stables. Stop at the **Jordan Pond House** (*see* Where to Dine) for tea and popovers served outside on the lawn. This is a nice lunch stop before or after a hike on the carriage trails.

Bring a sweater when you drive to the top of **Cadillac Mountain.** At 1,530 feet, the highest point of land on the Atlantic coast north of Brazil, the views are spectacular and the air temperature at the summit is a mite chilly. On a clear morning consider getting up early to watch the sunrise at the top of Cadillac, or be there for sunset (visibility is best during fall and winter). Hikers can reward themselves with plenty of wild blueberries in mid-to late summer. In addition, stargazing programs are held on clear nights.

Mount Desert Island Driving Tour

This tour takes you to Northeast Harbor, Southwest Harbor, Bass Harbor, and Bernard, the less crowded areas of the island. Starting at Bar Harbor take Route 3 south. You will pass the **Burning Tree** restaurant (*see* Where to Dine) in Otter Creek. In Seal Harbor look for the **Bistro** (*see* Where to Dine), a tiny storefront restaurant high on our list of favorites. The entrance to the Rockefeller Gardens is off this road, but there are no signs; admission is by reservation only (see below). A little farther along Route 3 is the gate to the southern entrance of the **Carriage Roads,** across the road from a beach of large cobblestones. We walked along the carriage road to the **Cobblestone Bridge** during the height of the tourist season and met only two people.

Continue on almost to Northeast Harbor until you see the parking area on the left for **Thuya Lodge and Gardens**. Cross the road and walk up the steps and along the path to these exquisite azalea gardens. Across the street from the Asticou Hotel (a possible lunch stop) are the **Asticou Azalea Gardens** (entrance is on Route 198), which have the feel of a Japanese strolling garden. If you enjoy fine gardens we strongly suggest visiting both of these, and making reservations at the Rockefeller Gardens.

Northeast Harbor is a wealthy summer community with boutiques, expensive gift shops, and **Redfield's,** the top restaurant in this area (*see* Where to Dine). Rather than turning right on Route 198 in Northeast Harbor, go through the village and take **Sargent Drive,** which follows along Somes Sound with wonderful views. This road will eventually intersect with Route 3/Route 198. (At this point if time is short you can return to Bar Harbor on Route 233 and do the second part of this loop on another day.)

At the junction of Route 233 bear left on Route 198 to Route 102 to **Somesville.** We've enjoyed the plays we have seen over the years at the **Acadia Repertory Theater.** The **Port in the Storm Bookstore** on the left has readings and signings throughout the summer months by top authors (Julia Child had a large crowd for her signing the day we were there).

Southwest Harbor, a boatbuilding and fishing community, is quieter and not touristy like Bar Harbor. After exploring the main street and the shops at the beginning of **Clark Point Road,** continue down the road to the harbor. During the summer a ferry leaves from the Upper Town Dock in Southwest Harbor and goes to **Cranberry and Islesford Islands.** Islesford has a small maritime museum, and on Little Cranberry Island the Islesford Dock Restaurant serves lunch and dinner. For lunch or dinner in Southwest Harbor try Beal's Lobster at the end of Clark Point Road or Preble Grill (same owners as Fin Back in Bar Harbor) on Clark Point Road. Other places in town to visit are the **Wendell Gilley Museum** (corner of Main Street and Herrick Road, May through December, dates vary; (207) 244-7555), devoted to the work of this Southwest Harbor bird carver; and the **Oceanarium** (next to the Coast Guard station), a hands-on museum that will keep children and adults busy for a couple of hours with twenty tanks containing resident Maine sea life. We were fascinated by the touch tank, where we saw a "jet-propelled" sea scallop escape from a starfish. You can push a button to learn about fog or watch a diorama that explains how the tides work; (207) 244-7330, mid-May to late October.

Continue south of Southwest Harbor and turn left on Route 102A. Take a left in **Manset** to get to the waterfront. Hinckley Yachts, the top of the line, are made here. The boatyard is closed to visitors except for the **Ships Store,** which sells all kinds of sailing-related items (including bags, shirts, mugs, and belts with the Hinckley logo for your sailing friends). The *Rachel B. Jackson,* a sixty-seven-foot replica of an 1890s schooner, sails from Manset. Almost across the street is XYZ Restaurant, serving authentic Mexican food (dinner only). A great picnic spot is **Seawall Picnic Area** in the national park (no fee) with wonderful ocean views. The **Wonderland and Ship Harbor Nature Trails** are both easy walks. Years ago while taking these trails we discovered a massive stone throne made of local cobblestones set in a secluded cove overlooking the water, a magical spot we haven't been able to find on a map. Perhaps you'll find it. At **Bass Harbor Lighthouse** follow the steps and scramble over the rocks for a view of this much photographed lighthouse (now a private residence).

The ferry to **Swans Island** leaves from Bass Harbor. Have lunch or takeout at Maine-ly Delights opposite the ferry or at the Seafood Ketch Restaurant, also in Bass Harbor. A great day trip is to take the ferry to Swans Island, then rent bikes on the island. Another option is the Island Cruise that leaves from Bass Harbor and makes its way through the islands on the bay.

On your way to **Bernard** you pass **Keenan's** (*see* Where to Dine). The most photographed spot in Bernard is the colorful weathered wall of lobster buoys overlooking the water. The owners of the building restored the wall to commemorate the lobstermen who used to work here. Today the building is a shop and museum displaying and selling the largest collection of wooden typefaces in private hands. For lobster in the rough, look for the yellow awning of **Thurston's** (*see* Where to Dine) on the dock in Bernard. For the long route back continue on Route 102 to Somesville or take Seal Cove Road (a hard-packed dirt road) back to Southwest Harbor. From here go north on Route 102 to Somesville.

Hikes and Walks in Acadia

Bring a pair of broken-in hiking boots, as most of the trails are rocky and rutted with use. If you don't have hiking boots or want to take easier walks, stick to the forty-five miles of magnificent carriage roads. We suggest you go to the park information center located on Route 3 below Hulls Cove for a listing of hiking trails, their difficulty rating, the length of each trail, and the starting point. Rangers also lead hikes of various difficulties every day during the season, from pleasant walks along the ocean to strenuous hikes up the sides of mountains involving iron ladders and rungs imbedded in the rocks. Pick up a copy of *A Walk in the Park* by Tom St. Germain (Bar Harbor: Parkman Publications, 1995) for details and maps on many of the trails in the park. Here are a few of the trails we particularly like:

- **Bar Island.** This trail is fun—to get to the island you have to walk on a sandbar. Check the tide tables carefully, however, or you will end up stranded: the sandbar is accessible for only an hour and a half on either side of low tide. Start at the end of Bridge Street in Bar Harbor.
- **Compass Harbor.** The entrance to this flat trail is only one mile from Main and Mount Desert Streets in Bar Harbor. Continue south on Main Street with a keen eye for a parking area on the left with no identifying signs. (If you pass the Dairy Bar you've gone too far.) We walked a short distance on level ground, then scrambled down a few rocks to find a dramatic small rocky cove on Frenchman Bay. This harbor is secluded yet close to Bar Harbor—a great find.
- **Great Head.** Start at Sand Beach and climb 145 feet for wonderful views of Sand Beach, mountains, and the ocean. This short 1.3-mile hike gives you a lot of great views for small effort.
- **Penobscot and Sargent Mountains** is rated moderately difficult (6.5 miles), with parking at Jordan Pond. Bring a bathing suit and take a dip in the pond between Penobscot and Sargent Mountains. After your hike, treat yourself to popovers.
- **Acadia Mountain** is moderately difficult (2.5 miles). Park on Route 102 at signs for Acadia Mountain. The view of Somes Sound is spectacular.
- **Perpendicular Trail** just west of Southwest Harbor at the south

end of Long Pond is a masterpiece of trail building by the Civilian Conservation Corps in 1934. More than 700 granite steps, one small ladder, and three iron rungs make this a strenuous climb just shy of 900 feet to Mansell Mountain. You'll cross a gigantic rock slide, and the trail is very steep in sections. This is not a trail for those who fear heights or drop-offs.

The Carriage Roads. John D. Rockefeller Jr., one of the early summer residents on Mount Desert Island, personally supervised the building of forty-five miles of carriage roads from 1913 through 1940 for the private use of his family and friends. These carriage roads, along with sixteen stone bridges, built to preserve the line of hillsides, follow the contours of the land and take advantage of scenic views. The carriage roads were subsequently donated to Acadia National Park and are today one of its treasures. Pick up a copy of *A Guide to the Carriage Roads*, available at the visitor center, which has maps and descriptions of most of the roads. Jordan Pond House is a good place to begin walking or mountain biking the roads.

Carriage Rides. The carriage are large wagons with rows of seats holding ten or more people, pulled by beautiful matched pairs of draft horses that individual owners bring to the park each summer. Six one- to two-hour rides over some of the fifty miles of carriage roads in the park include a tour to Cobblestone Bridge with a park naturalist who relates the story of the carriage roads; a ride to Jordan Pond House for tea and popovers; and a sunset or a daytime carriage ride to Day Mountain. From Route 3 enter the park at the Stanley Brook entrance. Reservations suggested. Wildwood Stable, Seal Harbor; (207) 276-3622.

Camping. The National Park Service operates two campgrounds in Acadia—Seawall and Blackwoods—and one on Isle au Haut reached by mail boat from Stonington that has thirty primitive sites. Reservations are not accepted at Seawall, open May through September. Blackwoods is open year-round; reservations for June through September are taken no earlier than eight weeks before arrival; call Destinet, (800) 365-2267. Reservations for Isle au Haut at the Duck Harbor Campground must be postmarked after April 1. Write: Superintendent, Acadia National Park, Box 177, Bar Harbor, ME 04609; (207) 288-3338.

Aerial Flights. A scenic flight over Mount Desert Island was a highlight of our trip. The pilot pointed out many of the places we had visited. The rates were reasonable; a forty-five-minute flight around all of Mount Desert Island cost $27. Shorter and longer flights in the area are also available. Leaves from Bar Harbor Airport on Route 3 in Trenton; ((207) 667-5534.

Getting Out on the Water
Not surprisingly, many boating opportunities are available in this part of Maine. This is just a sampling of ones we like. A ferry goes from Bass Harbor

to **Swans Island** ((207) 244-3254), where you can rent bicyles to explore the island ((207) 288-9605). A ferry goes from Southwest Harbor to the **Cranberry Isles** ((207) 244-5882) and a mail-boat ferry goes from Northeast Harbor to the Cranberry Islands ((207) 244-3575). You can bring bikes, eat at the dockside restaurant, and visit the historical museum on Islesford.

For a **windjammer cruise** we suggest the *Rachel B. Jackson*, a sixty-seven-foot working replica of an 1890s coastal schooner that holds about thirty passengers and sails from Manset (207) 244-7813). For a more personal experience we like *Chamar*, a thirty-three-foot sloop captained by Bill and Maggie Johnston, teachers who have lived here for twenty years. They take up to six passengers and sail from Northeast Harbor; (207) 276-5352 or 276-3993.

The **M.V. Bluenose Ferry** to Yarmouth, Nova Scotia, departs daily at 8 A.M. from mid-June to mid-October, less frequently at other times, with no service in the winter months. Call (800) 341-7981 for up-to-date schedules and reservations. There are special rates for those who want to take the round-trip in one day.

Naturalist-Led Boat Trips. Because of our interest in the fishing, history, and birds of the area, we have always enjoyed the tours conducted by the National Park Service. Information about these trips is found in the *Beaver Log* and in *Acadia Weekly*.

- Islesford Historical Museum Cruise. Leaves from Northeast Harbor; (207) 276-5352.
- Baker Island Cruise. Leaves from Northeast Harbor; (207) 276-3717.
- Bass Harbor Cruise, (207) 244-5365.
- Frenchman Bay Cruise, (207) 288-3322.

Sea Kayaking. For kayaking in the Bar Harbor area we like National Park Sea Kayak Tours, 137 Cottage Street, Bar Harbor; (207) 288-0342. The groups are limited to six kayaks. Registered Maine Guides accompany each group.

Whale Watching. Half-day trips leave from Bar Harbor and all go to the same area. The major difference is the boat. *Friendship V*, leaving from the Bluenose Ferry Terminal, is a catamaran, so it gets to the feeding grounds faster than other boats. Check the weather conditions and recent sightings, as the seas can be rough. Mid-May to mid-Oct. 121 Eden St. (Route 3). Tickets available at 39 Cottage St; (800) WHALES-4 or (207) 288-2386.

Bar Harbor

Once you get to Bar Harbor, it's easiest to park your car and do your exploring on foot.

The craft stores featuring items made by Maine craftspeople are found on

Main, West, and Cottage Streets. **Island Artisans,** 99 Main Street, has excellent crafts by local artists including very affordable hand-painted tiles. **Eclipse Gallery,** 12 Mount Desert Street, has top contemporary American crafts. Next door is **Birdsnest Gallery,** with a large selection of oils, watercolors, and graphics. **Spruce Grove Gallery,** 43 Cottage Street, has prints of Anne Kilham, Jack Perkins's photographs, and custom-cut stones including Maine tourmaline. The **Lone Moose,** 78 West Street, has more items, all made in Maine, including furniture, pottery, Kulik prints, baskets, and cards.

The **Criterion Movie Theater** on Cottage Street is a real Art Deco gem and the movies are all first-run. Stop by the **Opera House** restaurant on Cottage Street for dessert and to listen to opera recordings in an eclectic Victorian atmosphere. **St. Saviour's Episcopal Church** on Mount Desert Street in the middle of town has a renowned stained glass window collection, including twelve made by Tiffany. Tours are given Monday through Sunday at 11 A.M. and 3 P.M. and Sunday at 3 P.M.; (207) 288-4215. Take the **Shore Path** that starts at the intersection of Main and West Streets at the Bar Harbor Motor Inn and goes for about a mile along the water.

Northeast Harbor Gardens

Asticou Azalea Garden. This relaxing Japanese-style strolling garden features wooden stepping-stones over a stream, Japanese stone lanterns, a replica of Kyoto's Ryoanji Rock Garden with freshly raked gravel, and paths lined with moss. Located across the street from Asticou Inn, Route 3. Entrance is on Route 198.

Asticou Terrace and Thuya Lodge and Gardens. A series of wooded switchbacks lead from Route 3 up the hillside to the gardens. Along the way, about a fifteen-minute walk, are shelters with wooden benches where we paused frequently to admire the views of Northeast Harbor. Thuya Lodge houses a botanical library; visitors are welcome to peruse the books or tour the building. If you come on the weekend, you're likely to see a wedding in the formal gardens. A donation is suggested for the tour of the lodge. Park along Route 3 and walk up or look for the sign to the parking lot.

The Abby Aldrich Rockefeller Garden. This garden, started by Abby Aldridge Rockefeller in 1928, is located in the midst of the Rockefeller summer homes in Seal Harbor. The English-influenced main garden is rectangular with a path surrounded by wide borders, mainly of perennials. The oriental influence is strong, with a Chinese Wall of coping tiles from the Forbidden City enclosing the garden, a Spirit Garden of sculptures, a Moon Gate, a Buddha, a pagoda, and reflecting ponds. The sculpture from Korea, Japan, and China dates from the tenth to the eighteenth centuries. The garden is open on Thursdays, 9 A.M. to 1 P.M., from the second week in July through Labor Day. Reservations (no charge) are accepted starting in mid-June; call on Tuesdays and Wednesdays from noon to 3:30 P.M.; (207) 276-3330.

The full fury of the Atlantic Ocean crashes on the rocks at Schoodic Point.

Schoodic Peninsula Driving Tour

The part of the park most often skipped by visitors is the rugged Schoodic Peninsula. Here the waves attack the shore with a fury unknown on Mount Desert Island. The waves are particularly impressive after a storm. Even at the height of the tourist season, we have never found this part of the park to be crowded. It's about forty-five miles from Bar Harbor over to the tip of the peninsula.

To get here take Route 1 from Ellsworth 19 miles to West Gouldsboro. Go south on Route 186 to **Winter Harbor.** Turn right, go through the village, and turn left on Beach Avenue. This will take you to **Grindstone Neck,** an area of large summer homes. There are no street signs. At the far tip of the peninsula is a small parking area and a rocky area open to the water. On the west side of Grindstone Neck we parked at a cul-de-sac circle with dramatic views of Mount Desert Island, Acadia Park, and Cadillac Mountain. A short shore path starts from this point with views across Frenchman Bay. To continue to Schoodic Point, go back through Winter Harbor (Route 186) and turn right at the signs. If you are not here during the summer the best place to eat is at **Chase's Restaurant** (Route 186 between Winter Harbor and Birch Harbor), a real local spot with lots of color. Allow enough time to sit on the rocks at Schoodic or at any of the turnoffs along the road. There are plenty of places for a picnic. When you leave the park road at Schoodic, stop for lunch or an early dinner at **Oceanwood Restaurant and Gallery** in Birch Harbor (*see*

Where to Dine). We had a relaxing lunch on the enclosed porch overlooking
the harbor. For a side excursion turn right in Prospect Harbor (Route 195) to
get to **Corea,** a quiet fishing village. Return to Prospect Harbor and go north
on Route 186 toward Gouldsboro. Stop at **Darthia Farm** (off Route 186), a
certified organic farm with fresh produce, jams, and wool yarn. From here it
is about a forty-five-minute drive back to Bar Harbor.

   A back road driving tip: If you are going from Mount Desert Island to
the Blue Hill area we've found a route that avoids the commercialization and
traffic of Ellsworth. When you cross the bridge leaving Mount Desert Island
at Trenton, turn left almost immediately on Route 230. Turn right on Goose
Cove Road and right again on Route 230 (this is a shortcut across the peninsula). At Route 1 turn left, cross the bridge, and take the first left onto Route
172 heading toward Surry and Blue Hill.

WHERE TO STAY

Mount Desert Island lodgings are arranged geographically from north of Bar
Harbor to Southwest Harbor.

The Inn at Bay Ledge, Bar Harbor

The inn, located off Route 3 a half mile down a quiet road about five miles
before Bar Harbor, is in a tranquil setting perched on a ledge eighty feet above
Frenchman Bay. From the inn you walk down a wooden staircase that hugs
the cliff to a rocky beach. Cavelike shelters called the Ovens and Cathedral
Rock, a massive rock formation with an opening you can walk through, are
natural features unique to this property owned by Jack and Jeani Ochtera.

   The inn has a lodgelike feel on the first floor with pine walls, two wood-
burning fireplaces with comfortable seating, and French doors opening onto
a wide deck overlooking the water. A few steps from this deck is a good-sized
heated outdoor pool with a view of the water. A large sauna and the steam
shower are on the first floor of the inn. You can see the water from all of the
rooms in the main building except for room 11. Room 7, the largest, and room
8, both with king-size beds, and room 9 with a queen-size canopy bed, have
full front views of the water, and a bath with a whirlpool tub. Room 10 has a
private deck with a water view. Our favorite cottage is number 1 since it has
a stone fireplace; however, none of the cottages has a water view.

   Breakfast, served from 8 to 9:30 A.M. on the terrace or by the fireplace,
features an egg dish, pancakes, or French toast.

   Open May through October. Seven rooms and three cottages. Mid-June
through October, $135–250; May to mid-June, $75–$150. Breakfast and after-
noon refreshment included. Not appropriate for children under 16. No pets.
No smoking. Two-night minimum in season. 1385 Sand Point Road, Bar
Harbor, ME 04609; (207) 288-4204.

Inn at Canoe Point, Bar Harbor

This 100-year-old Tudor-style home is tucked into a quiet cove on the rocky Maine coast. The inn's dominant feature is the living room with floor-to-ceiling windows looking out on Frenchman Bay. In summer, breakfast is served on the wide deck that wraps around the room. In colder weather a favorite spot is the curved sectional sofa in front of the granite fireplace.

The master suite has a chaise longue and two easy chairs set by a wood-burning fireplace, a queen-size bed with a view of the water, and a deck that is shared with the Anchor Room, which is smaller than the master suite but is the only one with a double whirlpool tub. In the secluded third-floor Garret Suite one room has a king-size bed and another has a sofa bed. The smallest room in the house, the Garden Room, has windows on three sides, letting you feel as though your toes are practically in the water.

Innkeepers Tom and Nancy Cervelli serve breakfast either outside on the deck or at tables that overlook the water. Freshly squeezed orange juice and a fruit course is followed by omelettes with a choice of filling, eggs Benedict, or fluffy apple or blueberry pancakes.

Five rooms, all with private bath. Late May through October, $135–$245; off season, $80–$150. Breakfast and afternoon refreshment included. Children over 12 welcome. No pets. No smoking. No required minimum stay. Located off Route 3 just beyond the entrance to Acadia National Park. Box 216, Bar Harbor, ME 04609; (207) 288-9511.

Cleftstone Manor, Bar Harbor

This thirty-three-room mansion has the feel of an English country house, with lots of common space for guests. The summery Piccadilly Room flows into the living room, which has a wood-burning fireplace, and the dining room, with its long table and heavy English chairs. From 7 to 8 P.M., innkeepers Pattie and Don Reynolds's favorite time of day, guests gather for wine and cheese.

The rooms are furnished with antiques, and some are quite impressive. Romeo and Juliet, formerly part of the ballroom, is an enormous room with a beamed ceiling, stately fireplace, and lacy canopy bed. Victoria and Albert has a great French armoire, one of the inn's treasures, as well as a private balcony. Glastonbury, the original master bedroom, has a queen-size bed with a burled six-foot-high headboard. Hampton Court is a two-room suite with a fireplace and an enclosed porch. Sherlock Holmes has a private balcony and a fireplace.

Breakfast is a buffet of bagels, scones, home-baked coffee cakes, yogurt, fresh fruit, cereals, juices, and hot casserole dishes.

Open May through October. Sixteen rooms, all with private bath, five with fireplaces, July to mid-October, $100–198. Other times $65–$170. Breakfast, afternoon tea, and evening refreshment included. Children over 8 welcome; third person $20. No pets. No smoking. Two-night minimum in season. Located on Route 3 just outside the town of Bar Harbor. Route 3, Eden Street, Bar Harbor, ME 04609; (207) 288-4951; (800) 962-9762.

The Inn at Canoe Point's dominant feature is the living room with floor-to-ceiling windows that overlook Frenchman Bay.

Manor House Inn, Bar Harbor

After an active day of hiking in Acadia National Park, we sat on the wide wicker-filled porch of this turn-of-the-century yellow twenty-two-room Victorian inn, munched on chocolate chip cookies, and talked with innkeeper Mac Noyes, who has lived here his entire life. The inn is on an acre of land on a quiet street conveniently located a couple of blocks from the center of Bar Harbor.

Two garden cottages each have a large pine-paneled room with a wood-lined cathedral ceiling, cable television, and gas fireplace.

The former chauffeur's cottage, located behind the inn, has three units. The best is the second-floor honeymoon suite: antique king-size bed, a sitting area with a gas fireplace, and a balcony. Both downstairs units have private entrances and a king-size bed. One has a gas fireplace and the other has a small sitting room with a refrigerator.

In the main house the favorite fireplace room is room 5, the former master bedroom, which has a queen-size bed with an impressive headboard. Room 6, another favorite, also has a massive headboard and windows on three sides.

The buffet breakfast includes a hot casserole dish as well as fruit, cereal, and sweet breads.

Open April to mid-November. Fourteen rooms and suites, all with private baths. Late June to mid-October $85–$175; other times $50–$145. Breakfast and afternoon tea included. Children over 10 welcome, third person $20 additional. No pets. No smoking. Two-night minimum in season. 106 West Street, Bar Harbor, ME 04609; (207) 288-3759; (800) 437-0088.

The Maples, Bar Harbor

This small bed-and-breakfast inn on a side street in the middle of Bar Harbor is owned by Susan Sinclair, a most energetic innkeeper whose attention to the thoughtful touches of innkeeping is remarkable. Common space includes the first-floor living room with a fireplace, the front porch, and a small library sitting area on the second floor.

All of the rooms have queen-size beds and are generally small but attractively furnished. The largest and our favorite is the White Birch Suite, which includes a bedroom and a sitting room with a wood-burning fireplace and convertible sofa. In summer, Red Oak is enchanting: the bed in this very small room is directly in front of a door leading to a large deck surrounded by trees, a wonderfully private hideaway.

For early risers who like coffee before breakfast, Susan puts a thermos outside your door. Breakfast, 8:15 to 9 A.M., is served at two tables and includes a fruit course such as blueberry crisp or peach schnapps soup, muffins, and a main course such as blueberry or raspberry stuffed French toast or orange omelette soufflé.

Five rooms and one suite, all with private bath. Mid-June to mid-October $90–$150; other times $60–$95. Breakfast and afternoon tea included. Children over 8 welcome, third person $15 additional. No pets. No smoking. No required minimum stay. 16 Roberts Avenue, Bar Harbor, ME 04609; (207) 288-3443.

Hearthside, Bar Harbor

Innkeepers Susan and Barry Schwartz have owned this solidly built 1907 bed-and-breakfast inn, located on a side street in the middle of Bar Harbor, since 1986.

All the rooms are named after literary figures and have appropriate reading matter to match. Rooms also have queen-size beds and air-conditioning, and three have fireplaces. Our favorite room is Winston Churchill, a first-floor room with high ceilings, a fireplace, a private porch, and a new bath with a whirlpool tub. The Emily Dickinson Room has a fireplace and a whirlpool bath. Romeo and Juliet is the most romantic room, with a white iron bed and fishnet canopy, and a bath with an old-fashioned claw-foot tub and shower.

For breakfast Susan serves a buffet of cereals, breads, fruit, juice, muffins or sticky buns, and a hot entrée such as baked apple French toast. Guests sit together at the dining-room table or on the small porch.

Nine rooms, all with private bath, three with fireplace. Mid-June to mid-October $85–$125; other times $60–$90. Breakfast, afternoon and evening refreshments included. Children over 10 welcome. No pets. No smoking.

Two-night minimum in season. 7 High Street, Bar Harbor, ME 04609; (207) 288-4533.

Ullikana, Bar Harbor

This large granite-and-stucco 1885 Tudor-style house is tucked in a secluded section of downtown Bar Harbor close to the waterfront and not more than 100 yards from the main street. The inn is filled with Roy Kasindorf and Hélène Harton's extensive collection of paintings, prints, art books, and books about Acadia.

The rooms are spacious; many are decorated with fabrics and wall coverings from France. Four of the rooms have fireplaces. Favorites are the two second-floor rooms with private decks. Room 6 has a queen-size wicker bed, and room 5, a particularly spacious room, has a king-size bed, a daybed, and a fireplace. Room 7, on the third floor, has a queen-size bed and an alcove with two twin beds, a deck surrounded by trees, and a large bath.

Hélène is known for her creative breakfasts, which are served on the terrace during the summer and include a fruit course such as baked apples with zabaglione or brochette of fruit with ricotta and a main course of individual puff pancakes filled with blueberries or chocolate crepes with ricotta filling and raspberry coulis.

Open May through October. Ten rooms, all with private bath, $115–$200. Lower rates May to early June. Breakfast and afternoon refreshment included. Children over 8 welcome; third person $20 additional. No smoking. No pets. No required minimum stay. 16 The Field, Bar Harbor, ME 04609; (207) 288-9552.

Breakwater 1904, Bar Harbor

This magnificent oceanfront thirty-nine-room English Tudor was totally restored by Bonnie and Tom Sawyer. Staying here is a way to experience what life must have been like for the ultrawealthy who summered in Bar Harbor at the turn of the century.

The mansion has eleven gas fireplaces. The spacious common rooms on the first floor include two living rooms each with fireplaces, a library with a magnificent replica of a period billiard table, and a dining room. The lawn sweeps down from the house to the rocky shore.

All of the rooms have gas fireplaces. Mrs. Kane's, the largest, and Mrs. Alsop's Chamber are the two second-floor rooms with the best views. Ambassador Jay's Room on the third floor also has a full front view of the ocean.

A breakfast buffet of breads and cereal is served with fruit and a hot entrée such as hot apple crisp or French toast with raspberry sauce.

Open mid-April to mid-November. Six rooms, all with private bath. Late June to mid-October $185–$325. Other times $145–$235. Full breakfast and afternoon refreshments included. Not appropriate for children; rooms are double occupancy only. No pets. No smoking. Two-night minimum in season. 45 Hancock Street, Bar Harbor, ME 04609; (207) 288-2313; (800) 238-6309.

The Kingsleigh Inn, Southwest Harbor

An abundance of overflowing window boxes, hanging plants on the wicker-filled wraparound porch, and a hand-painted sign beckoned us to this inn on the main street in the fishing and boatbuilding village of Southwest Harbor.

The entrance to the inn is through the kitchen, which has a high counter and a row of stools that invite conversation between guests and innkeepers Cyd and Ken Collins. The inn is furnished with antiques and fine art that have a nautical theme.

The prize accommodation is the three-room third-floor turret suite. Using the telescope, we observed lobster boats, the Hinckley boatyard, and distant coastal islands. A living room with a television and a separate bedroom with a gas fireplace make this a superb hideaway.

On the second floor we like the quieter back rooms, rooms 3 and 5, each with a harbor view and queen-size bed.

Breakfast includes a fruit course such as bananas Foster over vanilla ice cream or apple coffee cake followed by ricotta cheese blintzes, Belgian waffles, eggs Florentine, and omelettes with various fillings.

Eight rooms, all with private bath. Late May to mid-October $105–$175; other times $75–$105. Breakfast and afternoon refreshment included. Children over 12 welcome. No pets. No smoking. No required minimum stay. 373 Main Street, Box 1426, Southwest Harbor, ME 04679; (207) 244-5302.

Lindenwood Inn, Southwest Harbor

This Victorian inn, named for the massive linden trees that front the property, is located on a quiet side street by the harbor. Innkeeper Jim King has decorated with a contemporary flair using beige and white fabrics and rugs, vibrantly colored walls, and reproduction pre-Columbian and African sculptures and masks for accents.

In our favorite rooms you can lie in bed and see the harbor. In the main inn our choice is the Penthouse, a third-floor room with a cathedral ceiling, a queen-size bed and a gas fireplace, and a large deck with a hot tub. Room 6, on the second floor, is a larger room with a queen-size bed and a balcony. The bungalow has a small bedroom, a kitchen in the high-ceilinged living room, and a large deck.

Favorites in the Annex, a second building next to the inn, are rooms 15 and 16, each with a small gas fireplace and a harbor view; 16 also has a deck. If you want to do your own cooking, three one- or two-bedroom cottages can be rented by the week.

A dipping pool (twelve by twenty feet) and a hot tub are new additions, as is the Lindenwood Restaurant, a thirty-seat gourmet restaurant on the first floor of the inn, which features organic produce, fish, and free-range chicken and beef.

Twenty rooms and suites; three cottages with kitchens. July through Labor Day $85–$250; other times $75–$195. Breakfast included except for cottages. Not appropriate for children. No pets. No smoking. Three-night minimum stay in season. The restaurant is open Monday through Saturday, entrées $17–$22. 118 Clark Point Road, Box 1328, Southwest Harbor, ME 04679; (207) 244-5335; (800) 307-5335.

WHERE TO DINE

Redfield's, Northeast Harbor
A reservation at this forty-six-seat restaurant tucked among the boutiques and expensive gift shops on the main street of Northeast Harbor's wealthy summer community is difficult to get during the busy summer season. The magic that chef-owner Scott Redfield works in the kitchen has made this the top restaurant in the area. Maureen, his wife, tends to the enthusiastic diners.

A basket of superb focaccio slices came with the meal. Our table ordered appetizers of smoked sautéed mussels on buckwheat noodles, a torta of grilled eggplant and smoked mozzarella, and a thick piece of house-smoked salmon served on a thin buckwheat crepe. A house salad of baby greens in a flavorful white miso herb vinaigrette came with the dinner. A tart lemon sorbet was served as a palate cleanser.

Entrées included smoked mozzarella ravioli with black olive and sweet vermouth sauce, loin of lamb with rosemary Provençal sauce, muscovy duck breast served rare, fillet of salmon with saffron lemon yogurt sauce, and grilled fillet of beef with a maple mustard cabernet sauce. Unusual accompaniments included Thai red rice and bulgur wheat, rutabaga roasted in apple juice and cardamom, and sautéed sliced radish.

Desserts included intense sorbets, rich chocolate raspberry mousse terrine, and blueberry pie.

April to October, dinner daily except Sunday; October to mid-February, Friday and Saturday. Entrées $17–$24. Main Street, Northeast Harbor, ME; (207) 276-5283.

Porcupine Grill, Bar Harbor
This casually elegant, popular restaurant is in a turn-of-the-century storefront building decorated with period decor that includes polished antique oak tables, an oak L-shaped bar, and antique lighting. The bread, pasta, and desserts are all made here. In season the produce is local and the fish comes from Bar Harbor.

The Caesar salad is prepared with fried Maine shrimp. The quail appetizer is a boneless bird stuffed with currants served on mesclun.

The entrées range from hearty meats to fish. The black Angus fillet with portabella mushrooms is garnished with grilled wild-boar bacon. The veal tenderloin comes with steamed leeks, a tarragon cream sauce, and whipped potatoes. Grilled jumbo diver scallops are procured locally. Porcupine stew, a light fresh tomato broth with lobster, scallops, salmon, and mussels, is another specialty. For dessert good choices are the chocolate crème caramel, orange chocolate crème brûlée, and the homemade ice creams and sorbets.

June through October, dinner daily. Off-season, Friday and Saturday only. Entrées $16–$22. 123 Cottage Street, Bar Harbor, ME; (207) 288-3884.

George's, Bar Harbor

At this fine restaurant the menu includes a large number of appetizers and slightly larger portions called "grazers," which can also be ordered as a meal. We enjoyed the kasseri cheese broiled with garlic, tuna cooked rare with slices of pickled ginger and wasabi, and broiled extra-large shrimp in a spicy honey mustard sauce.

Lobster is steamed, or grilled if the lobster is larger than one and a half pounds. The incredibly rich lobster strudel is popular, and the large selection of meat entrées includes a changing selection of unusual cuts such as elk steak and buffalo. Lamb is prepared a different way each day. We had grilled lamb tenderloin with blackberry ketchup. Zucchini stuffed with vegetable couscous was a vegetarian option.

For dessert the macadamia nut and chocolate ice-cream profiterole was a standout. Lemon curd in a gingersnap crust tart shell was pleasantly tart. The large wine list has won a Wine Spectator Award of Excellence, and beer selections are extensive as well.

Mid-June through October, dinner nightly. Entrées $23, except lobster. Located behind the First National Bank on Main Street, 7 Stephens Lane, Bar Harbor, ME; (207) 288-4505.

The Burning Tree, Otter Creek

This chef-owned restaurant, a fifteen-minute drive from Bar Harbor, features local fish. The long blackboard menu that is brought to your table always includes eight to ten different seafood dishes. Other selections include two chicken dishes and three vegetarian entrées. Herbs and edible flowers from a large garden behind the parking area are used liberally in the dishes. The covered front porch has a lattice front and an old cast-iron stove. Inside, two intimate rooms, each with about six tables, are decorated with paintings by local artists.

A thick piece of smoked salmon was served with a horseradish sauce. Broiled halibut was topped with a spicy Pernod and green pepper sauce. Grilled tuna was served with Napa cabbage, fennel, baby green beans, and balsamic vinaigrette. Other selections included Cajun lobster and crab au gratin, grilled swordfish with mango and red pepper barbecue sauce, and smoked dark-meat chicken rolled with marjoram and spinach pesto.

June to Columbus Day, dinner Wednesday through Monday. Entrées $13–$20. Route 3, Otter Creek, ME; (207) 288-9331.

The Bistro at Seal Harbor, Seal Harbor

Donna Fulton is the chef in the tiny open kitchen and Terri Clements takes care of the loyal diners at this intimate six-table bistro. Everything is prepared here, from the outstanding crusty bread to the rich ice cream. Terri also makes the beautiful ceramic pitchers and wine buckets in the off season, and sells them to interested customers.

From the small menu we selected an appetizer of polenta with a sauce of tomatoes and melted Gorgonzola. The gumbo was mildly spicy with crabmeat, mussels, and tiny Maine shrimp. The moist swordfish came with a tapenade of capers, black olives, garlic, and olive oil. Spinach linguine was tossed with a basil garlic cream sauce topped with a piece of roasted salmon. Lamb chops, duck, and salmon with a porcini mushroom crust were other entrée selections. Jack Daniel's ice cream with roasted pecans and caramel sauce was a winner.

The restaurant is popular and small, so advance reservations are a must.

Mid-June thru mid-October, dinner Tuesday through Sunday. Entrées $16–$22. No smoking. Seal Harbor, ME; (207) 276-3299.

Keenan's, Bass Harbor

This weathered, ramshackle shingle building, a favorite casual restaurant on Mount Desert Island, has bright red trim, wooden lobster traps on the pitched roof, and large steaming pots of water out front, ready for lobsters. To start, try the lightly breaded fried clams and the seafood gumbo, a spicy soup made with lobster, shrimp, crab, and sausage.

For a main course we liked the Cajun shrimp étouffée and the blackened swordfish special, which was moist in the center. Locals pack this place (especially after the tourists leave for the season) and order the slab of ribs. The lobster dinner includes steamers, corn, mussels, and a crab.

Dinner nightly in season. Fewer days in the off-season. Sandwiches and entrées $4–$13, lobster dinner based on market price. Route 102A, Bass Harbor, ME; (207) 244-3403.

Fin Back, Bar Harbor

This small, narrow storefront Bar Harbor restaurant with an etched glass room divider has about a dozen tables for two. We started with grilled salmon sausage and wild mushroom ravioli. The main course, lobster pieces sautéed in a chèvre cream with grilled polenta triangles, was excellent, but a small portion for the price. For dessert we enthusiastically shared the frozen peanut butter and chocolate mousse pie with chocolate icing. The owner has also opened

Preble Grille in Southwest Harbor (14 Clark Point Road), which has a similar menu.

May through November. Dinner daily in summer, weekends at other times. Entrées $15–$22. 78 West Street, Bar Harbor, ME; (207) 288-4193.

Jordan Pond House, Acadia National Park

The nostalgia associated with this restaurant overlooking Jordan Pond has accrued from one generation to the next for 100 years. Although the original Jordan Pond House burned down in 1979 and was replaced with a large contemporary structure, the location still brings back fond memories.

As the only restaurant located in Acadia National Park, the Jordan Pond House is popular with tourists. In fact, the inside dining room is full throughout the day. Lunch choices include chicken salad, steak sandwiches, or lobster stew. After a hike or a leisurely stroll or bike ride on the carriage trails, we like to stop here for the extra-large, fresh-from-the-oven popovers served on the lawn overlooking Jordan Pond.

Mid-May to mid-October. Lunch, tea, and dinner daily. Lunch $6–$14; tea $6; dinner entrées $8–$16. Located on the Loop Road in Acadia National Park; (207) 276-3316.

Guests enjoy tea and popovers on the lawn at the Jordan Pond House overlooking Jordan Pond and the rounded mountains called the Bubbles.

Ocean Wood Restaurant, Birch Harbor

This restaurant, a few minutes' drive from Schoodic Point, overlooks Birch Harbor. The front room is a gallery stocked with crafts from natives of the Darien rain forest in Panama, including the Choco Indians. The dining room is an airy enclosed porch with a water view. For an added fee you can dine in the privacy of the gazebo about 100 feet from the restaurant overlooking Birch Harbor. We had a pleasant lunch that included a cup of rich lobster stew, a lobster salad plate, and a large tossed salad of organic greens. The dinner menu has the same salad and sandwich selections as well as entrées such as pork tenderloin, steak, vegetarian dishes, and fresh seafood.

Mid-June through Labor Day, daily, lunch and dinner. Lunch $7–$11. Dinner entrées $8–$18. East Schoodic Drive, Birch Harbor, ME; (207) 963-2653.

Lobster Pounds

No trip to this area of the coast of Maine is complete without a lobster dinner. Here's a selection of our favorite lobster pounds, where you can roll up your sleeves and attack your lobster with gusto.

Oak Point Lobster Pound, Trenton

Oak Point is situated on the water overlooking Western Bay, just far enough off the beaten path that you have to know about it to find it. Choose from full dinners, large lobsters, steamers, and homemade pies. Casual dining inside and outside at picnic tables along the water; the sunsets are breathtaking.

Mid-June through September, daily from 4:30 P.M. From Route 3 in Trenton take Route 230 about four miles to Oak Point Road. Follow the signs to the end of the dirt road; (207) 667-8548.

Thurston's Wharf, Bernard

You can't miss the long yellow awning that covers the two-level outdoor screened dining area on this wharf in Bernard, just across the water from Bass Harbor. Order your lobster by the pound and choose such extras as corn, salad, and steamed mussels or clams. Burgers, chicken, and hot dogs are available as well.

Memorial Day to mid-September, lunch and dinner daily. During the rest of the year live lobsters can be purchased to take home. Bernard; (207) 244-7600.

Beal's Lobster Pier, Southwest Harbor

Place your order and grab a seat at a wooden picnic table surrounded by the sounds of diesel engines, the smell of the docks, and salted-down sardines and herring used for lobster bait. Scallops, clams, shrimp, chowders, and the like can also be purchased at this wholesale lobster pound.

Memorial Day to mid-September, lunch and dinner daily. During the rest of the year live lobsters can be purchased to take home. Located on Clark Point Road next to the Coast Guard base; (207) 244-3202 or 244-7178.

Trenton Bridge Lobster Pound

Clouds of steam rise from the outdoor wood-fired stove at this roadside bare-bones, no-frills operation. Fifty cords of wood a season keep four large wash-tubs of salt water boiling for lobsters and clams all day long.

Late April through Columbus Day, lunch and dinner daily. Located on Route 3, just before the bridge to Mount Desert Island; (207) 667-2977.

ITINERARY

DAY ONE. Stop first at the **Acadia National Park Visitor's Information Center** for maps, lists of park programs, and guidebooks or the audio tape tour. Take the **Loop Road** and have lunch or tea at **Jordan Pond House,** where you can walk along the carriage road or the Jordan Pond Stream trail to the Cobblestone Bridge. Drive to the top of **Cadillac Mountain.** Dine in Bar Harbor at **George's, Porcupine Grill,** or **Fin Back.**

DAY TWO. Take the **driving tour around Mount Desert Island**. Stop to see the **Asticou Azalea Garden** and the **Thuya Lodge and Gardens.** Plan ahead if possible to see the **Rockefeller Gardens.** For lunch, go to the buffet at the **Asticou, Northwest Harbor Cafe,** or continue to Southwest Harbor to **Beal's.** Drive to Manset and take a walk on **Wonderland** or **Ship Harbor Trail.** Plan for an informal dinner at **Thurston's** overlooking the water in Bernard or at **Keenan's** in Bass Harbor.

DAY THREE. Follow the **driving tour to Schoodic Peninsula,** with lunch at **Oceanwood Restaurant** or **Chase's.** Have dinner at **Oak Point Lobster Pound.**

DAY FOUR. Plan to take a ranger-led hike or **boat trip,** go whale watching, **sea kayaking,** or biking on the carriage trails. You might also take bikes on the **ferry to the Cranberry Isles** from Southwest or Northeast Harbors or the ferry to Swans Island from Bass Harbor, where you can rent bikes to explore the island. For a sailing trip consider the *Chamar* from Northeast Harbor, or the *Rachel Jackson,* a schooner from Manset. Have dinner at **Redfield's,** the **Bistro at Seal Harbor,** or the **Burning Tree.**

BUDGETING YOUR TRIP

To help you get the most for the time and money you have to spend, here are some travel suggestions at three budget levels (cost per day with two people sharing a room), including lodging and meal tax, gratuity on meals, and service charge when it is added to your bill.

Prices on lodgings are based on peak rates. Prices are approximate and are intended for planning purposes only. Lodgings are categorized by price and depending on the room selected may appear in more than one category. Meal prices at lunch include an average entrée and beverage. Dinner prices include an appetizer, entrée, dessert, and beverage. Wine or alcoholic beverages are not included.

Staying and dining at expensive lodgings and restaurants: From $250 to $460 per day for two.

Lodging: Breakwater 1904, Inn at Canoe Point, Cleftstone Manor, Ullikana, Inn at Bay Ledge, Manor House, Lindenwood.

Dining: Breakfast: included except at Lindenwood cottages. Lunch: Jordan Pond House, Ocean Wood Restaurant. Dinner: Redfield's, George's, Bistro at Seal Harbor, Porcupine Grill, Fin Back.

Staying and dining at moderately priced lodgings and restaurants: From $210 to $250 per day for two.

Lodging: Inn at Canoe Point, Cleftstone Manor, Ullikana, the Maples, Hearthside.

Dining: Breakfast: included. Lunch: Trenton Bridge, Beal's, Thurston's Wharf. Dinner: Burning Tree.

Staying and dining at less expensive lodgings and restaurants: From $130 to $190 per day for two.

Lodging: Hearthside, Cleftstone Manor, Manor House, the Maples, Kingsleigh, Lindenwood.

Dining: Breakfast: included. Lunch: Take-out sandwiches. Dinner: Oak Point Lobster Pound, Thurston's Wharf, Trenton Bridge, Ocean Wood Restaurant.

10

Mystic and the Lower Connecticut River Valley

W here is all that squid going?" we asked the men who were unloading the boat at the Stonington Dock, home port of Connecticut's last commercial fishing fleet. "Japan—the squid will be on the plane tonight," we were told. The fishing boats here no longer roam the oceans of the world in search of whales, as they did in the nineteenth century. Nor do the fast clipper ships once built in this area make the journey around the Cape to the gold fields of California or to the Orient. Today, the docks along the lower Connecticut River and east along the Connecticut coastline to Rhode Island are home to thousands of pleasure craft. The commercial shops that outfitted the clipper ships and coastal traders have become art and antiques galleries, fashion shops, and trendy restaurants.

Long before Europeans arrived, this area was traveled by the Algonquin, Mohegan, and Pequot tribes. The early settlers came from Boston in the 1630s, not long after the Puritans stepped ashore. Many of the Native Americans were killed by European diseases in the early Colonial years. More were killed in battle as the English settlers expanded their holdings along the Connecticut shoreline and up the river valleys. Today, the remaining 300 Mashantucket Pequots have established one of the largest and most profitable gaming casinos in the world on their native land.

In the seventeenth century, tobacco, Indian corn, red onions, peas, and hay were traded first in Boston and then in the West Indies in exchange for rum and sugar. The necessities of trade soon gave rise to the area's second major industry, shipbuilding.

This maritime trade required ships. At one time more than fifty shipyards lined the banks of the river from Hartford to Saybrook and along the banks of Long Island Sound in Mystic, Noank, and Stonington. At the Mystic Seaport you can see and experience the grand nineteenth-century age of sail. The tradition of shipbuilding continued into the twentieth century as Groton became the world leader in nuclear-powered submarine construction.

As business prospered, so did the people. In the eighteenth century they

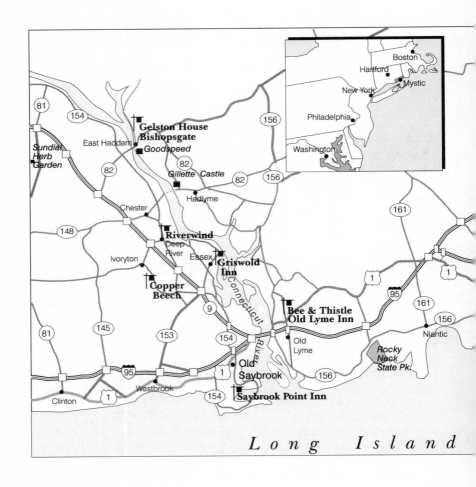

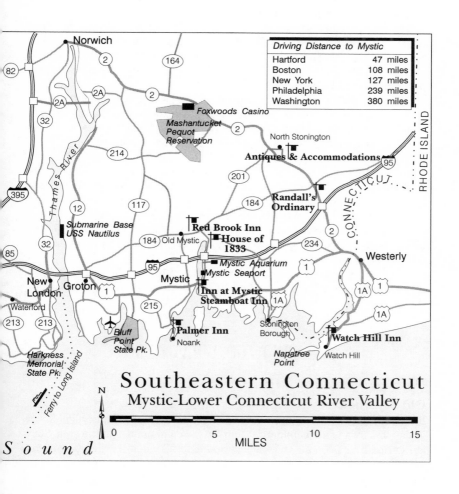

Driving Distance to Mystic	
Hartford	47 miles
Boston	108 miles
New York	127 miles
Philadelphia	239 miles
Washington	380 miles

Norwich

Foxwoods Casino

Mashantucket
Pequot
Reservation

North Stonington

Antiques & Accommodations

Randall's
Ordinary

Submarine Base
USS Nautilus

Red Brook Inn

Old Mystic

House of
1833

Westerly

Mystic Aquarium

Mystic Seaport

New
London

Groton

Mystic

Waterford

Inn at Mystic

Steamboat Inn

Harkness
Memorial
State Pk.

Bluff
Point
State Pk.

Palmer Inn

Noank

Stonington
Borough

Watch Hill Inn

Napatree
Point

Watch Hill

CONNECTICUT

RHODE ISLAND

Thames River

Ferry to Long Island

Southeastern Connecticut
Mystic-Lower Connecticut River Valley

N

0   5   10   15

MILES

Sound

began to furnish their homes in a higher style. Connecticut cabinetmakers crafted elegant cherry highboys and mahogany pie-crust tea tables. You can see examples in the Lyman Allyn Museum in New London. Joiners developed the high-style signature Connecticut River valley doorways. Be sure to look for them as you explore the area.

The Connecticut is the largest river in the Northeast without a major port city at its mouth. The beauty of the lower Connecticut River, especially its light and the changing colors of the water, marshes, and trees, attracted a summer colony of American Impressionists at the beginning of the twentieth century who came to Old Lyme to paint.

The Nature Conservancy has designated the lower Connecticut River one of the hemisphere's last great places, and has made monumental strides in protecting this magnificent resource. You can spot bald eagles in winter months along the river and ospreys in late spring and summer.

The interstate highways have made it easy to get to this area. The back roads will treat you to miles of stone walls, lovingly restored eighteenth-century homes around every bend, centuries-old unspoiled river towns, and irresistible antique shops.

For information on special events, contact the following:

Connecticut's Mystic and More. P.O. Box 89, New London, CT 06320; (860) 444-2206; (800) 863-6569. The Chamber of Commerce for the area from Old Lyme to Stonington.

Connecticut River Valley and Shoreline Visitor Council. 393 Main Street, Middletown, CT 06457; (860) 347-0028; (800) 486-3346. Covers East Haddam area to Old Saybrook.

WHERE TO GO, WHAT TO DO

Old Saybrook to Watch Hill

Old Saybrook

In 1632 English settlers put down roots at the mouth of the Connecticut River. Today the town is the commercial hub for the communities in the area. Start at the Amtrak station for an excellent driving, walking, or cycling tour of the town. Head south across busy Route 1 to the wide Main Street (Route 154), site of the most interesting shopping. North Cove Outfitters carries top names in fishing, hunting, camping, canoes, kayaks, and sportswear. At James Pharmacy, a 1790 building that has housed a pharmacy since 1877, you can enjoy an egg cream or an ice-cream soda at the 1896 soda fountain and then weigh yourself on the penny scale.

Continue on Route 154, detouring onto the side streets lined with large shade trees past attractive homes and well-kept yards. Continue to the end of Main Street. Turn left onto North Cove Road, which follows the shoreline and connects Old Saybrook and Saybrook Point. North Cove Road becomes Cromwell Place and returns to Route 154 just before Saybrook Point Inn. Fort Saybrook Monument Park has markers that explain the history of the town. The Connecticut River empties into Long Island Sound at this point. Saybrook Point Park includes a public miniature golf course during the summer, as well as picnic tables, a building housing Saybrook Artist's Colony exhibitions, and Dock and Dine, a large seafood restaurant on the water serving fried clams, fish, and lobster, across the road from Saybrook Point Inn.

Continue across the recently rebuilt causeway; make the first left to enter Fenwick, an enclave of large summer homes, which is particularly pleasant at sunset. The lighthouse pictured on the Connecticut license plate is at the end of Fenwick. Continue on Route 154 to the intersection of Route 1. Turn right to return to Old Saybrook.

Old Lyme

Florence Griswold Museum. From 1900 until the late 1920s, a summer colony of prominent American Impressionist painters rented rooms in Florence Griswold's 1817 late Georgian home. Childe Hassam, Willard Metcalf, William Chadwick, Henry Poore, and others came from New York City to live, work, and paint in the Old Lyme countryside.

Today the Griswold home is one of the more unusual small art museums in the country, housing one of the finest collections of American Impressionist paintings. Be sure to look at the hand-painted wall and door panels in the dining room, as well as the mantel painting of a mock fox chase that shows the former residents in characteristic poses.

After touring this intimate museum, you might want to visit some of the actual sites that these wonderful artists painted; you're sure to experience some of the special light that inspired them.

June through October, Tuesday through Saturday, 10 A.M. to 5 P.M. and Sunday, 1 to 5 P.M. Other times, Wednesday through Sunday, 1 to 5 P.M. Adults $4. 96 Lyme Street, Old Lyme; (860) 434-5542.

The center of Old Lyme is on the other side of I-95, under the highway bridge. Here you'll see the Congregational meetinghouse and church made famous by Childe Hassam's paintings. Walk the streets of Old Lyme, including Beckwith Lane, Academy Lane, and Lieutenant River Lane, all located off Lyme Street behind the town hall and library. Other places in town with paintings by the American Impressionists include the library (where the artists held their first shows) and the town hall (where paintings hang in the hallways).

The Cooley Gallery. If you have the interest and wherewithal to purchase a work by a painter of the Old Lyme School, you'll want to talk with gallery owner Jeffrey Cooley. More than 250 artists were associated with the Old Lyme art colony from 1900 to 1940, and the present-day value of their paintings varies tremendously. The gallery also represents the best of the painters currently working in the area. 25 Lyme Street, Old Lyme; (860) 434-8807.

New London–Groton

This large metropolitan area is the home of Electric Boat (a nuclear submarine plant), the Naval Submarine Base, the Coast Guard Academy, and Connecticut College.

USS Nautilus Memorial Submarine Force Library and Museum. Situated at the south end of the Naval Submarine Base, this site offers a self-guided audio tour of the *Nautilus,* the first atomic-powered submarine. The museum houses a collection of submarine memorabilia that includes working periscopes, an authentic submarine control room, and a model wall depicting the development of submarines. I-95 to exit 86; follow signs. Mid-April to mid-October, Wednesday through Monday, 9 A.M. to 5 P.M. Tuesday 1 to 5 P.M. Other times, Wednesday through Monday, 9 A.M. to 4 P.M. Free admission; (800) 343-0079 or (860) 449-3174 for recorded information on hours and exhibits.

Project Oceanology. Marine science instructors aboard an Enviro-lab research vessel offer a hands-on opportunity to learn about the marine environment. A trip includes pulling a trawl net, identifying the catch, collecting and examining plankton under a microscope, and collecting and testing samples of mud and sand from the ocean bottom with a gravity corer. Two-and-a-half-hour cruises twice daily, mid-June through Labor Day. Avery Point, Groton, CT 06340; (860) 445-9007; (800) 364-8472.

Buff Point State Park. This large, unimproved state park is great for walking or mountain biking. The main trail around the shore route has good views of Long Island Sound.

Noank

Quiet, unassuming Noank is several miles south of the active town of Mystic and is bordered by water on three sides. Most of the village (about 200 houses south of the railroad tracks) is on the National Register of Historic Places. The old homes are preserved, well-maintained, and quietly elegant. Marinas with 2,400 boat slips ring the town but are busy only on summer weekends.

Start your walking tour on Main Street at Carson's General Store, which is known for coffee, conversation, and ice cream. Across the street is the Pratt Gallery, which sells old oil paintings. The town dock, where the locals swim, is at one end of Main Street, and the little historical society is next door. Go down Pearl Street past Universal Food Store, where you can get a good grinder or white pizza with broccoli and chicken. Abbott's, the place for lobster and good views of the sound, is just a few blocks down the street. Continue past Abbott's, the marina (where the road ends), and the new homes to the completely restored Morgan Point Lighthouse, now a private home. Head back on Pearl Street toward Main Street. Take the first left and walk up the hill to High Street. You'll pass the Stone Ledge Gallery on the way.

Mystic

Mystic Marinelife Aquarium. This is a large, well-run, nonprofit aquarim. Highlights include a 35,000-gallon sixteen-window display tank with a collection of nurse and sand tiger sharks. Large windows allow visitors to watch the Beluga whale and Atlantic bottle-nosed dolphins as they wait to perform in shows held throughout the day in the 1,200-seat Marine Theater. You can watch African black-footed penguins from above or underwater in their outdoor rookery. The two-and-a-half-acre seal island has one of the largest collections of seals and sea lions in the world. Here you can watch seals and sea lions of different colors and regions. Check the schedule for morning and afternoon feeding times, as it's fun to watch the feeding antics.

Open daily except the last week of January. Adults $9.50. 55 Coogan Boulevard, Mystic, CT; (860) 536-9631.

Across from the aquarium is **Old Mystick Village,** a complex of stores in a nicely landscaped setting, and a shopping center of **factory outlets.**

Mystic Seaport. This late nineteenth-century recreated seaport village is the largest maritime museum in the United States. We like to walk around this seventeen-acre site along the Mystic River with its historic vessels, small craft collection, homes, shops, and places of work in the early morning or late afternoon. During the winter when the crowds thin out you can imagine what it might have been like here over 100 years ago. On the *Charles W. Morgan* (1841), the last surviving wooden whaling ship in America, we watched the sails being raised in midmorning, listened to the informative staff explain how the ship operated, and went below to see the the crew's quarters and the vast hold where the oak casks of whale oil were stored. Throughout the village, knowledgeable staff carry on the activities of a nineteenth-century New England village seaport. We saw open-hearth cooking, blacksmithing, sail setting and furling, chantey singing, a breeches buoy rescue drill, and anchoring and rope-making demonstrations. The site includes a planetarium, a preservation shipyard where skilled personnel work on the boats, a museum of scrimshaw and ship models, one of the finest galleries of paintings for sale by the most prominent marine artists, and the country's largest maritime bookstore. You can also take a cruise on the *Sabino,* the last coal-fired passenger steamer in operation in the United States. Reserve tickets early in the day for the popular sunset cruise.

Many visitors spend the better part of the day here or even make a return visit on the following day (no charge with a pass). The museum is a photographer's dream, and the large nineteenth-century sailing ships make a perfect backdrop. During the summer months, try to arrive as early as possible, before the rush of tourists. Lantern Light and Yule Tide tours in December are a fascinating way to experience a Mystic winter circa 1876. Actors portray the residents of the village, and visitors move in small groups from one scene to

The Charles W. Morgan *at Mystic Seaport Museum is the last surviving American wooden whaleship. It was built in 1841 and sailed for eighty years.*

the next. These wonderful tours sell out early. Open daily. Adults $16. (800) 522-1841. Route 27. Open daily, 9 A.M. to 6 P.M. (860) 572-0711.

Downtown Mystic. Beyond visiting the seaport and the aquarium we suggest you head to downtown Mystic, made famous in the 1988 movie *Mystic Pizza* (a pizza shop of the same name is at the end of the main street). A bascule bridge over the Mystic River has scheduled openings at a quarter past the hour during the summer. It is best to avoid this time, as traffic jams can be lengthy. Walk along the main street, which has a good bookstore, crafts shops, art galleries, and the usual tourist T-shirt and ice-cream shops. Sail on the river and into Long Island Sound on the *Argia,* docked in front of the Steamboat Inn next to the drawbridge. This eighty-one-foot vessel, a replica of a nineteenth-century gaff-rigged schooner, makes half-day, sunset, and full-day trips in summer and fall; (860) 536-0416.

Stonington–Mashantucket Reservation

In **Stonington Borough,** take a cooler to the Town Dock in the afternoon. You may be able to get a good buy on the catch of the day or some lobsters from the last commercial fishing fleet in Connecticut. The town is ideally situated for fishermen, as the narrow protected spit is inside Long Island Sound yet close to the open seas. The number of fishing boats is fast diminishing, but you'll see lots of expensive sailboats moored and docked at exclusive marinas such as the Dodson Boatyard. This historic community is an essential stop on a visit to the Connecticut shoreline. Pick up a copy of the walking tour of Stonington Borough at the **Old Lighthouse Museum** or in one of the shops along Water Street. This pamphlet describes many of the important village houses that were built in the eighteenth and nineteenth centuries.

Water Street is lined with antique stores, galleries, excellent restaurants, and a lighthouse museum. Start at the **Boatyard Cafe,** located in the Dodson Boatyard, just to your right after you cross the viaduct. Then poke your way down Water Street. The movie *Mystic Pizza* was filmed in Stonington at what is now Deja Vu Antiques. **Quimper** (prounced *kem-pear*) **Faience** (141 Water Street, (860) 535-1712) is the main retail store for a French pottery in operation since the seventeenth century. The business is now owned by an American group, and the store displays eighteen of the hand-painted patterns, including the famous Breton peasants. **Water Street Cafe** is an intimate restaurant that serves excellent food. Other restaurants to consider are **Noah's,** with moderately priced fare, and **Skipper's Dock**, with water views and Dixieland jazz on Sunday afternoon, March through October. At the **Anguilla Gallery** (72 Water Street, (860) 535-4399), go in the back room, place a dollar in the slot, and see a working model railroad of old Stonington come to life. **Orkney & Yost** (148 Water Street, (860) 535-4402) has high-quality antiques and rugs. At the south end of Water Street visit the old **Lighthouse Museum** (May through October, Tuesday through Sunday; (860) 535-1440) to see displays of nineteenth-century Stonington memorabilia such as stoneware, ship models, china trade and whaling gear, and climb to the octagonal lantern room. You can park at the **Point** just beyond the lighthouse. From here you can see Watch Hill to the southeast and Fisher's Island to the southwest. A public beach at the Point charges a modest admission fee. To continue the tour, walk north on Main Street to see more historic homes and explore the side streets.

Mashantucket Reservation–Foxwoods Casino

As you approach the casino on Route 2 (I-95, exit 92), a giant building seems to rise out of nowhere like Emerald City in the land of Oz. Foxwoods is the largest casino in the Western Hemisphere, with 190,000 square feet devoted to gaming. The 300 members of the Mashantucket Pequot Tribal Nation who own the complex are estimated to gross close to $1 billion a year. The casino has about 10,000 employees, nearly 3,900 slot machines, 230 table games, poker tables, a bingo hall, shops, restaurants, two hotels, and superstar entertainers like Frank Sinatra and Luciano Pavarotti. Other attractions include a Turbo Ride, a Cinedrome video theater, and an interactive virtual-reality theater. Open 24 hours. Hotel reservations; P.O. Box 410, Route 2, Ledyard, CT 06339; (800) FOXWOOD.

Watch Hill

From Stonington Borough take Route 1 to Westerly, Rhode Island, then take Route 1A to Avondale and follow the signs to Watch Hill. Street parking is limited and the police are vigilant about illegal parking, so it's best to pay the $5 parking fee. This is a quiet, moneyed beach community of grand old homes. Watch Hill is an ocean beach (as opposed to the Sound beaches along the Connecticut shoreline). To get to the **beach** (no charge), walk from the center of town up the hill to the left of the carousel past the road that goes to the **lighthouse.** Turn right down the pathway to a beautiful, unspoiled beach. Wander down the short paved drive to the lighthouse for excellent views of the water.

Napatree Point is a long spit of conservation land in Watch Hill that's privately owned but open to the public. It is located to the right of the carousel at the end of the parking lot beyond the cabanas of the yacht club. Go around the fence and follow the sand path over the dunes about a half mile to the end along the beach. Bring sneakers and binoculars, as the far end has boulders and pools of water that attract many birds.

The town has the breezy, lazy feel of a beach town. Stores along the Main Street sell high-quality gift items and clothing. For lunch or dinner, try the Olympia Tea Room (*see* Where to Dine). For homemade ice cream or a hot dog done the way we like—scored on the top, grilled and served in a buttered grilled roll—stop at **St. Clair's,** in business for 100 years. Enjoy your ice cream as you watch the children on the 1879 **Flying Horse Carousel**. Before leaving Watch Hill, take a drive along the roads next to the ocean to see some of the mansions.

Along the Connecticut River: Essex to Haddam

Essex

This riverfront town is one of America's little jewels. Stroll around town to see the many fine homes built by ship captains, and browse in the antique shops.

Have a look at the dining rooms in the Griswold Inn, even if you aren't eating here. Other restaurants include the Black Seal on Main Street and Olive Oyl, where we got great sandwiches to eat by the water at the Connecticut River Museum. She Sells Sandwiches has picnic tables overlooking the Connecticut River.

Connecticut River Museum. Between 1783 and 1900, several thousand commercial vessels were launched from more than fifty shipyards located between Saybrook and Springfield, Massachusetts. Situated on the river, this museum pays tribute to that long-ago maritime activity. In photograph and story, you'll learn of the journeys of ship captains who sailed the world and infrequently returned to the local river towns. Open Tuesday through Sunday, 10 A.M. to 5 P.M. Adults $4. 67 Main Street, Essex, CT; (860) 767-8269.

The Valley Railroad Company. Going for a ride on a train or riverboat was an adventure during the 1800s, and still holds an undeniable charm in this age of sophisticated travel. You certainly view the valley differently as you slowly steam through the countryside. The steam train ride lasts about an hour. You then can continue with a boat ride on the Connecticut River or return directly. The train runs daily May through October and weekends Thanksgiving to Christmas. Call for schedule. Box 452, Essex, CT 06426; (860) 767-0103.

Deep River

As you drive into town from the south you'll see the half dozen lighted horseshoe pits where the locals play on Thursday evenings. Concerts are held also on Thursday evenings in summer at the Green next to Riverwind or at the Town Landing along the Connecticut River. Deep River is the home of the largest fife-and-drum corps muster in the United States, held the third Saturday in July each year. The Great American Trading Company (39 Main Street) has a factory store that sells wooden games, surplus wooden boxes, and a great selection of marbles, puzzles, and rubber stamps. A number of antique stores line Main Street. A famous tattoo parlor is located along Main Street, as is Pasta Unlimited, an excellent source for picnic supplies.

Chester

Continue north on Route 154. A left on Route 148 brings you to Chester. Some twenty-five years ago, this was just another town that time and progress had forgotten, but now the houses and shops have been restored to the utmost degree. Restaurant du Village and Fiddler's are good choices for dinner; Wheat Market has picnic provisions, and the funky Mad Hatter Cafe is good for coffee and a pastry. Along the main street you can stop at Ceramica for fine hand-painted dinnerware from Italy, at Connecticut River Artisan Cooperative for local crafts, and at Spring Street Studio to talk with and see the paintings of local scenes done by Leif Nilsson. (One of his paintings hangs at Restaurant du Village).

Goodspeed-at-Chester. The Norma Terris Theatre, an old factory that once produced knitting needles, has been given new life as an intimate 200-seat testing stage for the development of new musical productions. For current productions contact the ticket office at the Goodspeed Opera House, East Haddam, CT 06423; (860) 873-8668.

Hadlyme

Take Route 148 to the eight-car Chester-Hadlyme ferry, which has been in continuous operation since 1769. The five-minute ride offers impressive views of Gillette Castle as well as pristine and isolated sections of the Connecticut River. The toll ferry runs from April to mid-December.

Gillette Castle. Perched 200 feet above the Connecticut River on 184 acres, the six-story granite castle was patterned after a medieval Rhenish fortress. This was the home of actor-playwright William Gillette (1853–1937), the incarnation of Sir Arthur Conan Doyle's Sherlock Holmes to audiences throughout the world in the early 1900s. Its twenty-four rooms range in size from the huge main living room—fifty feet long and thirty feet wide, with a lofty nineteen-foot ceiling—to Gillette's tiny bedroom, and each displays the skill of local craftsmen. Notice especially the glass lampshades along the walls made by Quezal, a designer from the Tiffany glass studios.

The myriad mechanical details that Gillette designed and built into his home during the eighteen years he lived here will be of interest to the tinkerer, especially the intricate hand-carved locking mechanisms for each of the castle's forty-seven doors and the locking liquor cabinet.

Open Memorial Day through Columbus Day, weekends only, through the last weekend before Christmas. On December weekends the castle is decorated for a Victorian Christmas. Adults $4. Hadlyme, CT; (860) 526-2336.

East Haddam

From Gillette Castle, follow the River Road north to Route 82 into East Haddam, home of the six-story Goodspeed Opera House, a landmark since 1876.

Goodspeed Opera House. Would you have guessed that in this picturesque, six-story Victorian opera house in the quaint and quiet town of East Haddam, *Man of La Mancha* (1966), *Shenandoah* (1974), and *Annie* (1977) got their starts? It's true, and to us, the Goodspeed is as emblematic of the lower Connecticut River valley as the Opera House is of Sydney, Australia.

The structure was built in 1876 by entrepreneur William H. Goodspeed to house his shipping business and, on the top two floors, a 400-seat theater. Steamboats came from Boston and New York and docked in front of the opera house. After several decades of decline Goodspeed was saved from the wrecking ball in the late 1950s. Today the bar is once again resplendent in English Victorian flocked wallpaper, while the elegantly decorated Green Room, the ladies' drinking parlor, and the carpeted grand staircase with its marbleized balustrade round out the exceptional restoration.

Be forewarned—70 percent of the seats are sold by subscription, so call ahead for tickets. During August a cabaret is held three nights a week at the Gelston House next to the theater.

The season runs from April through December, Wednesday through Sunday, Goodspeed Opera House, East Haddam, CT 06423; (860) 873-8668.

Cruises. If you prefer to see nature from the deck of a boat, consider a cruise on the Connecticut River. Camelot Cruises has daily two-hour cruises from Haddam, dinner cruises, Friday and Saturday night "Murder on the Connecticut River" dinner cruises, an all-day cruise to Sag Harbor, fall foliage lunch

Goodspeed Opera House, situated on the banks of the Connecticut River, was built in 1876.

cruises, and Sunday jazz brunch cruises. Call or write for a schedule. 1 Marine Park, Haddam CT; (860) 345-8591.

East Haddam airport can arrange twenty-minute sight-seeing flights. A tip for the flying enthusiast with a private plane: in East Haddam you won't have a problem getting around once you've landed. From the airport you can walk up the road to the Goodspeed Opera House and stay and dine at the Gelston House.

Higganum

The Sundial Gardens. The gift shop is located in the restored eighteenth-century barn located next to the meticulously maintained herb gardens of herbalist Ragna Tischler Goddard. Blended herbal teas from the gardens, as well as the highest-quality dried flowers from Holland and England, pepper mills, tea strainers, and the like are sold throughout the year.

Drop-in teas are held on Sunday and Friday afternoons, June through August. A pot of tea comes with scones served with clotted cream, fruit or jam, and lemon curd. Before or after tea you can wander through the garden. The gift shop is open weekends year-round, daily from November to Christmas. Exit 9 off Route 9; south on Route 81 (three miles); right on Brault Hill Road. At the end of the road, bear right and follow it for a quarter of a mile. Higganum, CT; (860) 345-4290.

Driving Tours

East Haddam to Mystic

Start on Route 82 at the Goodspeed Opera House or the Chester-Hadlyme
ferry and take Route 148 to Route 82. From East Haddam, take Route 82 east
for about fourteen miles to I-395 south. Get off at the next exit (79A) onto
Route 2A. Take the toll bridge over the Thames River, past the hospital, and
go right onto Route 117 (Ledyard Highway) for two and a half miles. Turn left
on Route 214 to the **Saw Mill Park**, which has a water-powered sawmill that
operates on Saturday, 1 to 4 P.M. Return to Route 117 and take the next left
onto Colonel Ledyard Highway (Route 117 goes straight). If you're here in the
fall, stop at **Allyn's Barn** (just after Ledyard High School) for apples, pies,
jellies, and pickles. Turn left on Route 184 past J. P. Daniel's. Turn right at
Lantern Hill Road, then jog immediately left onto Route 201 (North Stonington
Road). Stop at **Clyde's Cider Mill** (open the last weekend in September to
the day before Thanksgiving; (860) 536-3354) to watch this old steam-powered
cider mill at work; pressings at 1 and 3 P.M. on Saturday and Sunday.

   Detour 1. To get to the **Foxwoods Casino**, continue on Route 201 and to
left on Route 2. *Detour 2.* To get to **Randall's Ordinary** for a lunch or dinner
of open-hearth cooking, follow Route 201 but turn right onto Route 2.

   Turn right onto Route 184 and right again at the blinking light (Taugwonk
Road) to **Stonington Winery** (daily 11 A.M. to 5 P.M. (860) 535-1222). Taugwonk Road goes to the entrance to I-95 and continues to North Main Street,
which crosses Route 1 and continues to **Stonington Borough**, a town that is
tops on our list of places to visit. To get to Mystic, turn right on Route 1.

Lower Connecticut River Valley

This is the area once favored by the American Impressionist painters. Drive
north on Route 156 about three miles, then turn left onto Ely's Ferry Road.
Drive to the end; along the way you will pass rocky, glaciated terrain on one
side and salt marshes (most of which are now protected by the Nature Conservancy) on the other. Stone walls and pastureland are interspersed with well-
kept clapboard houses. At the end there is an excellent view of Essex and the
steamboat dock.

   Return on Ely's Ferry Road and take a left on Cove Road, which skirts
timeless Hamburg Cove, one of the finest harbors in the state. Bear left at the
beige arch bridge that crosses the cove. Continue on Joshuatown Road. At the
end of this road, turn left on Ferry Road (Route 148). Follow this road, with
its marshland views, to the small **Chester-Hadlyme ferry**. Before you take
the ferry, consider a tour of **Gillette Castle**, which is perched on the hillside
overlooking the river.

   Take Route 148 into **Chester**. A good lunch stop is **Fiddler's, Wheat-
market**, or **Mad Hatter Cafe** for sandwiches or tea and pastry. **Restaurant
du Village** is our favorite for dinner. Trace your way back toward the river

A moose head is the focal point of the first-floor front parlor at Riverwind.

and turn right on to Route 154 to **Deep River**. Turn left on Essex Street (just before you get to Riverwind), which becomes River Road. This is a scenic five-mile road along the river and through woods to Essex. For lunch, stop at **She Sells Sandwiches** or the **Griswold Inn** for more leisurely dining. Walk around the town and visit the **Connecticut River Museum**. Continue on River Road back to Route 154. Turn left. A number of antique stores are located along this stretch of Route 154. In **Old Saybrook**, have a soda at the **James Pharmacy** and follow Route 154 across the causeway to Fenwick. To return to Old Lyme, turn right on Route 1 and cross the river on I-95, getting off at exit 70 just over the bridge.

WHERE TO STAY

East Haddam to Old Lyme

Riverwind, Deep River

Riverwind, a jewel of Americana, is owned by Barbara Barlow, who also happens to be the local justice of the peace, and her husband, Bob Bucknall. Eight common living rooms (four with wood-burning fireplaces) provide a luxurious amount of space for guests' use. There's a front parlor with a piano and a fireplace, a porch, a game room with an antique checkerboard, a library, and a keeping room with a twelve-foot stone cooking fireplace. Scattered throughout is a collection of American folk art.

Champagne and Roses, the largest room, has a private porch, and a bath with a deep tub and separate shower.

Zelda's is a cozy dark-colored emerald green suite with a daybed and a double sleigh bed in the small bedroom. The Willow Room has a four-poster double bed and a private porch, the Quilt Room has two queen-size four-poster beds.

The country kitchen is picture perfect—dripping with hanging pots, Smithfield aged hams, old biscuit barrels, lard cans, tobacco tins, molds, and cooking contraptions of every shape and size. Amid the smells of baking biscuits and wood burning in the fireplace, we sat down to a breakfast of Smithfield ham, piglet-shaped biscuits, pastries, fruit, and hearty slices of artichoke quiche.

For total privacy, a two-bedroom house located about a mile away from the inn is generally available by the week. It has a kitchen, a living room with a wood-burning fireplace, two small bedrooms with double canopy beds, a sitting room with a television, and a bath.

Eight rooms, all with private bath, $90–$155. Full breakfast included. Cottage $200 for two nightly, continental breakfast supplied. Children over 12 welcome in the inn. No pets. Two-night weekend minimum. 209 Main Street, Deep River, CT 06417; (860) 526-2014.

Saybrook Point Inn, Old Saybrook

Location, location, location—with a site at the mouth of the Connecticut River, panoramic water views, and deluxe accommodations, this hotel has much to recommend it. Facilities include a 120-slip marina with deep-sea fishing charters, conference facilities, and a full-service spa with personal fitness training, Keiser exercise equipment, and indoor and outdoor pools.

Deluxe rooms have fireplaces and wet bars, and most have balconies. Our top choices are the third-floor rooms with balconies, panoramic views of the sound, and fireplaces. Six of the suites have double whirlpool tubs in addition to fireplaces.

The hotel will pick up guests at the train station and provides bicycles at no charge.

Fifty rooms and twelve suites. Memorial Day through October, rooms $188–$285, suites $319–$449. Other times, rooms $137–$200, suites $225–$425. All meals available. Children under 16 free. No pets. Inquire about available packages. Two-night weekend minimum in season only. 2 Bridge Street, Old Saybrook, CT 06475; (860) 395-2000; (800) 243-0212 (outside CT).

Copper Beech Inn, Ivoryton

The inn, originally constructed in the nineteenth century for one of the town's ivory merchants, was named for an enormous copper beech tree that spreads over the front lawn. The first floor of the main building houses an elegant gourmet restaurant. Innkeepers Eldon and Sally Senner added an attractive plant-filled Victorian conservatory onto the front of the main building. Upstairs are four bedrooms furnished with antiques, all have baths that are original to the house. Our favorite is room 1, an extremely spacious room with a blue canopy over the king-size bed, and a bath with a handheld shower.

The secluded rooms in the renovated carriage house, located behind the main building, offer more privacy. Each room has access to a deck overlooking a wooded area, wall-to-wall carpeting, a mahogany or pine queen-size bed, a television, easy chairs or a couch, and a bath with a single whirlpool tub. The exposed beams of the high cathedral ceiling give the rooms on the second floor a more spacious feel. Room 19 on the second floor and room 10 on the first floor are the two largest rooms in this building, each with a private deck. All the rooms have telephones.

Breakfast includes homemade turnovers and Danish baked fresh each morning.

Thirteen rooms, all with private bath, $105–$175. Continental breakfast included. Children over 8 welcome. No pets. Two-night weekend minimum. Main Street, Ivoryton, CT 06442; (860) 767-0330.

Griswold Inn, Essex

The Griswold Inn—or "the Gris," as it's affectionately called by loyal patrons— has continuously operated as an inn since it was built in 1776, and has the additional distinction of being the first three-story structure in Connecticut.

By staying overnight in season, you can enjoy the peace and quiet after the legions of day-trippers have left, and can rise early in the morning for an invigorating walk through the manicured streets of this historic riverfront town.

Suite 36, in a courtyard across the street, is our top choice. The bedroom has a king-size bed, a wood-burning fireplace, a small living room, a bath with both a claw-foot tub and a glass shower, and a private porch. Suite 37, the newest room, has a king-size bed and a sitting area with a daybed. The Garden Suite has a large living room with a wet bar and a wood-burning fireplace and a second floor with two bedrooms, each with a double bed. Suite 34 and 35 each have a large living room and a gas fireplace.

In the main inn, suites 4 and 5 have queen-size beds and sitting areas with gas stoves. Most of the standard rooms in the inn above the restaurant have exposed wooden beams and floors that slope slightly with age.

Twenty-eight rooms and suites, $90–$185, all with private bath. Children welcome. Continental breakfast included. No required minimum stay. 36 Main Street, Essex, CT 06426; (860) 767-1776.

Bee and Thistle Inn, Old Lyme

This well-known restaurant and inn owned by Bob and Penny Nelson is next door to the Florence Griswold Museum in the lovely town of Old Lyme. The first floor has a restaurant and a parlor, open to restaurant guests, with a wood-burning fireplace.

The guest rooms, located on the second and third floors, have canopied and brass beds covered with old quilts. The best are room 1, overlooking the garden, and room 2, recently redone, each with a queen-size bed with a canopy over the curved tester and two wing chairs. Room 11, slightly smaller, is the third room with a queen-size canopy bed. Room 3 is a corner room with twins that can connect to make a king-size bed. All rooms have paddle ceiling fans, central air-conditioning, and phones.

The first floor of a cottage behind the inn overlooking the Lieutenant River has a fully equipped kitchen, a library with a wood-burning fireplace, a family room with a brick floor, and glass doors that open onto a back deck that wraps around to the deck off the bedroom.

Eleven rooms, all with private bath, $85–$125; cottage $195. All meals available. Children over 12 welcome. No pets. No required minimum stay. 100 Lyme Street, Old Lyme, CT 06371; (860) 434-1667; (800) 622-4946.

Bishopsgate Inn, East Haddam

This 1818 center-chimney Colonial in the village of East Haddam down the street from the Goodspeed Opera House is owned by innkeepers Lisa and Colin Kagel and Colin's parents, Colin Sr. and Jane, who purchased the inn in December 1995.

The choice accommodation is the director's suite with its open-truss ceiling, queen-size bed, private sauna, large bath with double sinks, balcony, and an alcove with a sitting area. Four other rooms each have wood-burning fireplaces; three have double beds and one has a queen-size bed. All rooms have feather beds. A living room on the first floor has couches surrounding a wood-burning fireplace, and on the second floor there's a cozy sitting area stocked with magazines.

A full breakfast served in the country kitchen includes crustless spinach quiche, waffles, or an egg dish.

Six rooms $85–$120. Full breakfast included. Children welcome. No pets. No smoking. No required minimum stay. P.O. Box 290, Goodspeed Landing, East Haddam, CT 06423; (860) 873-1677.

Gelston House, East Haddam

This Victorian building overlooking the Connecticut River next to the Goodspeed Opera House is owned by Goodspeed. A restaurant fills the first and part of the second floor. The guest rooms on the second and third floors were all redone recently with new carpeting, matching draperies and spreads, and central air-conditioning (windows do not open).

Suite 302 has a perfect view of the river, the swing bridge, and the opera house. Suites 301 and 201 also have excellent views. Each has a bedroom with a queen-size bed and a large living room with a few antiques. Room 201, the best of the lower-priced rooms, also has a good view of the river and opera house. We do not recommend rooms 303 and 304, as they overlook either the parking lot, a tent used for outdoor dining, or the roof over the kitchen.

Six rooms and suites $100–$225. Continental breakfast included. Children welcome. No pets. No smoking. No required minimum stay. Goodspeed Landing, East Haddam, CT 06423; (860) 873-1411.

Old Lyme Inn, Old Lyme

This inn, across from the Griswold Museum, has been owned by Diana Field Atwood since 1976. The main part of the inn has a grill dining room, a formal dining room, and banquet rooms. Rooms 6 to 14 are larger, more upscale rooms located in a wing that was added to the inn about fifteen years ago. The best are rooms 7 and 11, both front corner rooms with canopy beds and Victorian furniture. Rooms 1 to 5 are in the old farmhouse section and have the nooks and crannies of an old New England inn. All rooms have antiques, queen-size beds, televisions, phones, and central air-conditioning.

Thirteen rooms, all with private bath, $99–$158. Closed first two weeks in January. Continental breakfast included. Children welcome. Pets welcome. No required minimum stay. 85 Lyme Street, Old Lyme CT 06371; (860) 434-2600; (800) 434-5352.

Mystic to Watch Hill

The Inn at Mystic, Mystic

This fifteen-acre complex consists of a series of buildings on a glacial hillside overlooking Mystic Harbor. You'll find a wide range of accommodations. Rooms at the Motor Inn range from upscale, nicely appointed motel-style to generous-sized rooms with wood-burning fireplaces and double whirlpool tubs. The Inn, a Colonial Revival mansion at the top of the hill, has five bedrooms, a large wood-paneled living room with a wood-burning fireplace, and an expansive veranda overlooking the harbor. Since a large tent attached to this building is used most weekends in warmer weather for wedding receptions, we suggest inquiring about this before deciding to stay in this building. The Gate House, formerly the guesthouse for the mansion, has four rooms, three of which are deluxe.

Facilities include a tennis court, an outdoor swimming pool, a small dock with a canoe and paddleboat, and beautifully manicured formal English and rock gardens for strolling and sitting. Guests also can use the indoor pool and exercise and weight facilities at a nearby community center. Try to arrive by 4 P.M. for tea, which is set out at the Flood Tide Restaurant and includes cakes, cookies, sandwiches, and cheese.

Sixty-seven rooms, all with private bath. July through October $140–$250. Other times $65–$250. Children welcome. Afternoon tea included. No pets.

Nonsmoking rooms available. Two-night weekend minimum in season. Junction of Routes 1 and 27, Mystic, CT 06355; (860) 536-9604; (800) 237-2415.

Steamboat Inn, Mystic

This deluxe inn located along the Mystic River just steps below the bascule drawbridge in the center of town has the feel of a little European hotel. The hallways have framed photographs of Mystic during the age of sail, and the rooms are decorated with maritime scenes. All the rooms on the second floor have wood-burning fireplaces and baths with single whirlpool tubs. All first-floor rooms except one have windows that look right onto the boardwalk along the river in front of the inn; for privacy, the blinds need to be kept drawn. These first-floor rooms are larger, have double whirlpool tubs, a separate shower, and a wet bar with a refrigerator. Two of these rooms have a microwave. All rooms have televisions, telephones, and individually controlled heat and air-conditioning.

Ten rooms, all with private bath. Late May to mid-September $150–$275. Other times $95–$250. Continental breakfast included. Children welcome on the first floor. No smoking. No pets. Two-night weekend minimum. 73 Steamboat Wharf, Mystic, CT 06355; (860) 536-8300.

House of 1833, Mystic

This early nineteenth-century Greek Revival home located on three acres was converted to a five-room bed-and-breakfast in 1994 by Matt and Carol Nolan. It is located in Old Mystic, a five-minute drive from the Mystic Seaport, and is across the road from Clyde's, one of the last steam-powered cider mills. The house is centrally air-conditioned and beautifully decorated, and the well-landscaped grounds include a pool as well as a tennis court. Six eighteen-speed bikes are also available to guests.

Common rooms include a double parlor with a Belgian marble fireplace, a pump organ, and a grand piano. Four of the guest rooms have fireplaces and one has a wood stove. The Peach Room, the former library with an eleven-foot ceiling on the first floor off the parlor, has a queen-size canopy bed and a bathroom with both a double whirlpool tub and a huge shower, and a private porch. The Veranda Room has a queen-size canopy bed and a Lady Slipper tub on a platform facing the fireplace. The third floor Cupola Room has a canopy draped from the high peaked ceiling, a wood-burning stove, a bath with a double whirlpool, and a cupola with two chairs and a little table.

Breakfast is at 9 A.M., with all guests sitting at one large table.

Five rooms, all with private bath, $95–$195. Breakfast and afternoon refreshment included. Children over 7 welcome. No smoking. No pets. Two-night weekend minimum. 72 North Stonington Road, Mystic, CT 06355; (860) 536-6325; (800) FOR-1833.

Antiques and Accommodations, North Stonington

Take two antiques dealers, give them an eighteenth- and nineteenth-century building, a barn full of antiques that are for sale, and a love of English perennial gardens, and you have a unique country inn. Anglophiles Ann and Tom Gray have made over thirty trips to England and have stories galore to tell of their antiquing adventures. The inn's living room is decorated with many fine antiques and a large collection of coffee-table books about England. A seating area in the midst of the garden is particularly inviting.

The bridal room has a double canopy bed, while the first-floor room has floor-length windows that overlook the front porch, a wood-burning fireplace, and a queen-size bed.

The top floor of the Garden Cottage has a common room with a wood-burning fireplace, a kitchen, and two bedrooms. The family suite has a living room, a porch, a master bedroom with a wood-burning fireplace, and two additional bedrooms.

Guests sit at one table in the beautifully appointed dining room. Our breakfast included chilled cantaloupe and mint soup, blueberry and lemon bread, and a choice of cornmeal pancakes with fried apples and sausage or a salmon omelette.

Five rooms and a three-bedroom suite, all with private bath, $119–$189. Full breakfast included. Children welcome. Smoking permitted in the cottage only. Two-night weekend minimum. 32 Main Street, North Stonington, CT 06359; (860) 535-1736; (800) 554-7829.

Red Brook Inn, Old Mystic

Red Brook Inn consists of two eighteenth-century buildings set on seven and a half acres furnished with innkeeper Ruth Keyes's vast collection of Colonial antiques. The main building is the Haley Tavern. Breakfast is served in the keeping room, which has a large open-hearth fireplace with all the cooking utensils in place for the Colonial dinners that Ruth prepares on winter weekends and for Thanksgiving and Christmas. This room is lit entirely by natural and candle lighting. The original tavern is now a game room with sofas, old books, scrapbooks about the inn, and a tavern ledger from 1809. The more formal front parlor has a long breakfront filled with Ruth's collection of Early American glass, a grandfather clock, and a beautiful Oriental carpet.

The large Ross Haley Chamber has an original 1790 high four-poster mahogany double canopy bed with fabric made in 1815. The Henry Haley Chamber and Mary Virginia Chamber each have a queen-size bed and wood-burning fireplace.

The Crary Homestead, down the hill, has four rooms each with a wood-burning fireplace and a country feel.

When we arrived for breakfast the fire was lit and candles were on the table for a meal of fresh fruit, juice, particularly delicious walnut waffles, and sausage.

Ten rooms, all with private bath, $95–$189. Full breakfast included. Children welcome. No pets. No smoking. Two-night weekend minimum. Saturday night hearth dinners November through March. Route 184 and Wells Road, P.O. Box 237, Old Mystic, CT 06372; (860) 572-0349.

The Palmer Inn, Noank

Noank is a quiet waterfront community next to Mystic that has the charm of a bygone era. Most of the village is on the National Register of Historic Places. Innkeeper Patti White has owned this 7,200-square-foot Southern-style 1907 house with massive two-story white columns since 1983.

This is not a designer-perfect inn. The charm is its casual, cordial homelike ambience. The main parlor has a wood-burning fireplace, easy chairs covered with throws, and games, books, and magazines.

The master bedroom, the largest and the only guest room with a wood-burning fireplace, has a carved walnut headboard on the queen-size bed. The Mahogany Room has twins that connect to make a king-size bed. The Oak Room has a double bed, a balcony, and a private hall bath. All rooms are air-conditioned.

Six rooms, all with private bath, $115–$215. Continental breakfast included. Children over 12 welcome; rooms are double occupancy only. No pets. No smoking. Two-night weekend minimum. 25 Church Street, Noank, CT 06340; (860) 572-9000.

Randall's Ordinary, North Stonington

This inn and restaurant is situated in a wooded setting off Route 2, a few miles from Mystic and from the Foxwoods Casino. The property is owned by the Mashantucket Indians. Rooms are furnished with reproduction Colonial antiques. Most guest rooms are in a large 200-year-old barn, and three are above the restaurant in the original 1685 center chimney Colonial house where meals are cooked on an open hearth.

The best accommodation is the duplex silo suite in the barn. A spiral staircase leads to the bedroom level, where there is an Adirondack twig-style queen-size bed, a large living room, a bath, and a kitchen. Continue up the spiral staircase to a double whirlpool tub in the middle of a room surrounded by windows with a high peaked ceiling. The rustic barn rooms have phones, televisions, and baths with single whirlpool tubs.

A continental breakfast is included, but for an additional charge you can have johnnycakes, codfish cakes, griddle cakes, or corned beef hash prepared over the open hearth.

Fourteen rooms and one suite, all with private bath. Weekends $115, midweek $75, suite $195. Continental breakfast included; full breakfast available. Children welcome. No pets. Route 2, P.O. Box 243, North Stonington, CT 06359; (860) 599-4540.

Watch Hill Inn, Watch Hill, RI

This old hotel located on the main street of a quiet Victorian seaside town is across the street from the water. What makes the inn appealing is its proximity to the beach (the ocean, not the sound) and the breezy, casual atmosphere of the town, particularly during the warmer weather, when the shops and restaurants are open. Restaurant tables are set on the outdoor terrace, which overlooks the harbor.

The regular rooms here are quite small. Rooms have phones, baths with showers or old-fashioned claw-foot tubs, and no air-conditioning.

Open April through December. Sixteen rooms, all with private bath. Late June through Labor Day, weekends $170–$190, midweek $100–$120. Other times, weekends $115–$135, midweek $75–$95. Continental breakfast daily April through August, weekends at other times. Children over 8 welcome. Two-night weekend minimum. *Note:* The phone is answered by an answering service at most times of the day and evening. 38 Bay Street, Watch Hill, RI 02891; (401) 348-8912; (800) 356-9314.

WHERE TO DINE

Chester to Saybrook

Restaurant du Village, Chester

Wrought-iron gates frame a courtyard entrance to this intimate bar and twelve-table dining room. Chefs Michel (who comes from Alsace) and Cynthia Keller have given their restaurant a French country feel with white lace curtains, white linen tablecloths, and white stucco walls. The feeling here is relaxed and friendly, and the food is exceptional.

The baguettes, made fresh every morning (you can purchase one to take home), are a signature item. For starters we recommend the rich flaky crusted wild mushroom tart or the ricotta cheese tart. Goat-cheese-filled ravioli, escargots in a puff pastry shell, and wood-smoked lobster are other outstanding appetizers.

Our swordfish was topped with a delicious tapenade of olives, anchovies, and sun-dried tomatoes. The duck, a speciality, is prepared with a cranberry-and-dried-cherry sauce, and Grandmother's roast baby chicken, a typical French Sunday dinner, comes with rissolé potatoes, caramelized pearl onions, and mushrooms.

An excellent lemon tart and a chocolate mousse cake along with strong dark French roast coffee and eau-de-vie from the Alsace region of France finished a memorable meal.

Dinner, Wednesday through Sunday (Tuesday in summer), entrées $22–$26. 59 Main Street, Chester; (860) 526-5301.

Fiddler's Seafood Restaurant, Chester

This unpretentious restaurant with two dining rooms decorated in white and blue with scallop stenciling has kept the same winning formula for years. The menu features locally caught fish with a choice of preparation—sautéed, poached, or mesquite grilled—and a choice of pasta, baked stuffed potato, or rice. More creative selections might include poached scallops with shiitake mushrooms served on spinach, or lobster meat and peaches cooked with shallots, mushrooms, and peach brandy. The toasted garlic bread with aioli dip is addictive.

Lunch, Tuesday through Saturday, entrées $5–$9. Dinner, Tuesday through Sunday, entrées $12–$19. 4 Water Street, Chester, CT; (860) 526-3210.

Copper Beech Inn, Ivoryton

The first floor of the main building is an elegant gourmet restaurant. The plant-filled Victorian conservatory is a great spot for drinks before or after dinner.

Copper Beech is a good choice for a special occasion. The menu is French, with classic picture-perfect presentation. We started with littleneck clams lightly steamed on the half shell with a mild curry sauce. Escargot and artichoke bottoms were rolled in puff pastry with a tomato sauce. The bouillabaisse had a light fennel-flavored broth. The lobster dish featured lobster pieces arranged over a sun-dried tomato sauce. Other selections included boneless breast of pheasant and sautéed medallions of veal sweetbreads, a specialty of the inn.

The desserts are works of art. Quenelles of white, orange, and dark chocolate mousses were served with a hazelnut-mocha custard sauce. The sorbet was intensely flavored and pots de crème was served with a warm chocolate sauce.

Dinner, Tuesday through Saturday; Sunday from 1 P.M. Entrées $23–$26. Main Street, Ivoryton, CT; (860) 767-0330.

Steve's Centerbrook Grill, Centerbrook

This restaurant fills the void for those times when you want a light meal, perhaps just a bowl of soup and an appetizer.

The fare is creative, with such appetizers as grilled Thai shrimp, lobster chowder, and mixed greens with goat cheese. Entrées include pork satay and sesame noodles, seared tuna, and cavatelli with greens and grilled chicken. Desserts are impressive creations, and Steve has an award-winning wine cellar.

Dinner, Tuesday through Sunday, entrées $10–$20. 18 Main Street, Centerbrook, CT; (860) 767-1277.

Griswold Inn, Essex

For over 200 years "the Gris" has been serving meals in this historic Connecticut River town. The building is a museum of collectibles, and even if you don't stay or eat here, be sure to take a look around. The main dining room was built from an old New Hampshire covered bridge and has a large wood-burning fireplace. The walls in the dining rooms are covered with firearms, Currier and Ives steamboat prints, and late nineteenth-century marine oil paintings. The library dining room is more intimate and also has a wood-burning fireplace.

Dinner here is hearty New England fare: bay scallops, broiled scrod, lobster, fried oysters, clams, prime rib with fresh horseradish, and New York strip steak. The Sunday hunt breakfast buffet fills a long table with chicken livers, creamed chipped beef, herring, lamb, fried chicken, grits, the inn's specially made 1776 sausage, and much more.

When you're tired of touring, visit the taproom in the evening (built from a 1738 one-room school) and enjoy nightly entertainment.

Three meals daily. Lunch entrées $7–$12, Sunday brunch $13, dinner entrées $15–$23. 48 Main Street, Essex, CT; (860) 767-1776.

Saybrook Point Inn, Old Saybrook

Be sure to ask for a window table at the Terra Mar Grill and arrive before the sun sets so you can enjoy the outstanding views of the marina and Long Island Sound. The restaurant has two dining rooms, both with tables overlooking the water, and a large bar area (active the night we dined with boaters from the marina) with a light menu.

For starters we had rich tortellini with sun-dried tomatoes, artichoke hearts, mushrooms, Gorgonzola cheese, and cream. In addition to such entrées as veal medallions with artichoke hearts and mushrooms, sirloin or filet mignon, the menu includes a number of spa choices such as farfel with shiitake mushrooms, artichoke hearts, roasted peppers and vegetables, and grilled salmon with tomatoes, basil, and olives.

Three meals daily. Lunch entrées $8–$14, Sunday brunch $22, dinner entrées $14–$24. 2 Bridge Street, Old Saybrook, CT 06475; (860) 388-0212.

Wine and Roses, Old Saybrook

This unpretentious chef-owned restaurant serves creative contemporary food. The second-floor dining room has a bar and a piano player on the weekends, while the first floor is more casual.

Lunch choices include bruschetta with Gorgonzola cheese, fish, tenderloin medallions, pastas, and chicken Caesar salad. At dinner, start with fried spicy crab wontons or ravioli filled with clams, garlic, pepper, and bacon served with a tomato vodka sauce. Entrée favorites include chicken Devon, a boneless breast filled with asparagus, pears, and cheddar cheese wrapped in puff pastry; curried shrimp Anna; and wild-mushroom-and-spinach ravioli with a Gorgonzola sauce.

Lunch, Tuesday through Saturday, entrées $5–$9. Dinner, Tuesday through Sunday, entrées $11–$17. 150 Main Street, Old Saybrook, CT; (860) 388-9646.

Stella D'Oro, Old Saybrook

This small family-owned fourteen-table Italian restaurant in the shopping plaza in the middle of Old Saybrook makes its own pasta, including creative flavors like salmon or smoked cheese ravioli and gnocchi. It's a bit more upscale than the usual Italian fare, with selections such as veal cubes with roast peppers, tomato, artichoke hearts, and a cream sauce, one of the most popular choices, as well as zuppa di pesce, calamari fra diavalo, capellini with seafood, and the Stella D'Oro combination of two pieces of veal, a piece of chicken, and two shrimp topped with an egg. For dessert try the homemade tiramisu.

Lunch, Monday through Friday, entrées $8–$12. Dinner daily, entrées $11–$19. 10 Main Street, Old Saybrook, CT; (860) 388-6590.

Aleia's, Westbrook

The best thing about Aleia's location is its ease of access if you are driving on I-95. The dining room is fairly standard, with a separate bar and an outdoor deck on the side of the building next to the parking lot, but the bistro-style menu is excellent. Our starters of whole grilled portabella mushroom cap topped with strips of roasted pepper and goat cheese and seared rare pepper-encrusted tuna slices were satisfying large portions. From a selection of six pastas we chose the rigatoni with a rich tomato sauce and roasted eggplant, sausage, and fresh mozzarella, as well as the flavorful tagliatelle with cubes of braised veal, mushrooms and a cream sauce, which at a half portion more than sufficed for a main dish.

Other entrées include veal chop, roasted cod, tuna medallion, tenderloin, strip steak, and salmon.

Lunch, Tuesday through Friday, entrées $7–$11. Dinner, Tuesday through Sunday, entrées $14–$24. 1353 Boston Post Road, Westbrook, CT; (860) 399-5050.

Light Bites and Takeout

She Sells Sandwiches, Essex. Order at the counter and sit at picnic tables on the deck overlooking the Brewer's Dauntless Shipyard and the Connecticut River. The blackboard menu has fried egg sandwiches, scones, bagels, or granola for breakfast, then switches to lunches of muffaletta, cheese steak, rolled tortillas, and prepared cold salads. Breakfast and lunch daily. Brewer's Shipyard, Essex; (860) 767-3288.

Mad Hatter Cafe, Chester. This tiny café and bakery specializing in hearth-baked breads has a few tables inside and on the street corner—fine for a snack, a light lunch, or tea. On Saturdays a set four-course dinner is served. Wednesday through Sunday. Main Street, Chester; (860) 526-2156.

Olive Oyl's. Tuesday through Sunday. This take-out shop has creative sandwiches, gourmet groceries, and prepared salads. 77 Main Street, Essex, CT; (860) 767-4909.

Pasta Unlimited. Take-out fresh-cut pastas, pasta salads, and creative sandwiches. Monday through Saturday. 159 Main Street (Route 154), Deep River, CT; (860) 526-4056.

Wheat Market. Monday through Saturday. Pick up gourmet groceries, creative sandwiches, and hot items for takeout, or to eat at a table in the store. Water Street, Chester, CT; (860) 526-9347.

Old Lyme to Watch Hill

Bee and Thistle Inn, Old Lyme

This eighteenth-century mustard-colored inn owned by Penny and Bob Nelson sits on five acres surrounded by large trees. The front parlor has a wood-burning fireplace. The glass-enclosed porch dining rooms have hanging baskets, while the larger main room has a wood-burning fireplace and a print by Roger Tory Peterson, author of the birder's "bible." Creative lunch selections include grilled Thai chicken tossed with angel-hair pasta, blini filled with sour cream and salmon, salmon lasagna, and crab cakes.

Starters at dinner include Gorgonzola tart, goat cheese terrine, and thick clam chowder. A selection of the more than a dozen entrées includes wild mushroom napoleon, grilled veal chop served with roasted red pepper and spinach fettuccine pie, panfried trout, sautéed rare duck breast with duck confit ravioli, and rack of lamb with garlic mashed potatoes and fried spinach.

Lunch and dinner, Wednesday through Monday. Lunch entrées $9–$12, brunch $12–$15, dinner entrées $19–$26. 100 Lyme Street, Old Lyme, CT; (860) 434-1667.

Old Lyme Inn, Old Lyme

This inn has many dining rooms. We like the Grill Room, which has an informal atmosphere and at night offers a lighter, lower-priced blackboard menu in addition to the regular menu. The Empire Room is more formal, with a high ceiling and widely spaced tables. The single-table Alcove Room is in demand for special occasions. A private dining room and banquet rooms are also available.

The menu is continental. Dinner entrées include sweetbreads served in a cream sauce, boned stuffed pheasant, fillet of venison served over johnny-cakes, lobster thermidor, seared tuna steak, and twin tournedos with baby artichokes. Lunch selections include spinach and tomato bow ties tossed with smoked salmon and cream, chicken fricassee, grilled salmon Reuben sandwich, and chicken and sweet pepper salad.

Lunch, Sunday brunch, and dinner daily. Lunch entrées $7–$10, brunch entrées $10–$15, dinner entrées $20–$30. Grill Room $10–$25. 85 Lyme Street, Old Lyme, CT; (860) 434-2600.

Abbott's, Noank

With its proximity to Mystic, lots of advertising, media coverage, and excellent waterfront location, it's no wonder that Abbott's is probably the most well known lobster-in-the-rough restaurant on the East Coast. Come here early or be prepared to wait as we did thirty minutes on a "quiet" weekday summer evening just to place and pay for your order. Your number is called when each item is ready. There are picnic tables with good views along the waterfront or inside the building where the food is prepared. (Bring a sweater, as it gets chilly on the water at night.) The menu includes steamed lobster from one and a quarter to four pounds (we split one of these), hot lobster rolls, steamed clams, clam chowder, oysters, shrimp, and hot dogs.

If you get tired of waiting in line at Abbott's, head down the street to Costello, two parking lots away in the Noank Shipyard. The restaurant is owned by Abbott's and the menu includes lobster dinners as well as fried clams, fritters, and fish-and-chips.

Daily, early May to Labor Day; weekends to Columbus Day, noon to 9 P.M. Lobsters $13–$35. BYOB. 117 Pearl Street, Noank; (860) 572-9128.

The Seahorse Restaurant and Tavern, Noank

This undistinguished weathered clapboard tavern and backroom restaurant is slightly off the usual tourist route next to Spicers Marina in Noank. Rave reviews go to the grilled chicken sandwich on focaccio topped with provolone cheese and roasted peppers. Sautéed calamari in spiced marinara sauce is served over pasta. The menu includes lobster, shrimp scampi, broiled flounder, fried fish, and steaks and prime rib.

Lunch and dinner daily. Entrées $6–$17. 65 Marsh Road, Noank, CT; (860) 536-1670.

Flood Tide Restaurant, Inn at Mystic, Mystic

This is our choice for an elegant, relaxed dinner in the Mystic area. We like the window tables overlooking the harbor and especially like the ambience of the smaller dining room (although it is also the smoking room), which has a wood-burning fireplace.

Since tableside preparations or carving are a specialty, consider the Caesar salad, classic beef Wellington, whole roast stuffed pheasant, rack of lamb, chateaubriand, or fettuccine Alfredo. If you and your dining partner don't want the same entrée, other good choices are baked two-tailed lobster with a shrimp stuffing, shrimp and artichoke hearts on linguine, roast duckling, and phyllo-wrapped lamb stuffed with spinach and feta cheese. For dessert go for the show with bananas foster or chocolate fondue.

The lunch buffet is beautifully presented with a bounteous selection of cold meats, salads, hot entrées, and desserts.

Three meals daily. Lunch entrées $6–$20, buffet $12; dinner entrées $14–$32. Junction of Routes 1 and 27, Mystic, CT; (860) 536-9604.

Bravo Bravo, Mystic

This is the hot spot in the center of Mystic for innovative Northern Italian and French fare. The tables are packed close together and the restaurant is noisy when it is full, which is every night in summer and fall.

Top choices we sampled included grilled shrimp wrapped in prosciutto with skewered artichokes and the seafood stew with a rich tomato broth. About half of the twenty-five entrées are made with pasta. Black pepper fettuccine was topped with grilled scallops and a rich Gorgonzola cream sauce. The chicken and walnut ravioli had a good flavor but was a small portion, while shrimp oregano and feta cheese over angel-hair pasta was a heaping portion.

Lunch, Tuesday through Saturday, entrées $6–$13. Dinner, Tuesday through Sunday, entrées $11–$22. 20 East Main Street, Mystic, CT; (860) 536-3228.

J. P. Daniel's, Old Mystic

This restaurant, located in an old barn a few miles from Mystic, has a strong local year-round following. The center of the barn is open to the rafters with tables on the first floor and the balcony. The rough-hewn barnboard walls are decorated with old photographs, hanging dried flowers, and a wood sleigh.

Almost all of the entrées, including seafood, beef, and veal dishes, can be ordered as half portions or appetizers—great for light eaters or as a way of increasing your choices. We started with linguine in a spicy Louisiana sauce with andouille sausage and baby shrimp. The bouillabaisse, our favorite, included a hearty portion of shellfish plus pieces of salmon and whitefish in a flavorful, rich broth. Desserts are traditional and come in hearty portions.

Lunch and dinner daily. Lunch buffet $10 and à la carte, Sunday brunch buffet $13, dinner entrées $7–$19. No smoking. From Mystic take Route 27N. Turn right on Route 184 for a half mile. Old Mystic, CT; (860) 572-9564.

Randall's Ordinary, North Stonington

The complex is owned by the Mashantucket Pequots. Watching and eating a meal prepared over the open hearth by cooks in Colonial dress was a memorable experience in this 300-year-old tavern.

Lunch is a bargain and includes hearth-grilled items such as sirloin steak, venison sausage, lamb chops, roast pork loin, and scallops, all served with homemade bread and vegetables.

Dinner guests stand around the hearth to watch the cooking preparations, munch popcorn, and have a drink. Throughout dinner you are entertained by a classical guitarist or a harpist. Our dinner included Shaker herb soup served with whole-wheat and corn bread, followed by a choice of three entrées. Spiced scallops, a specialty, are cooked in a black spider pan over the coals. The capon and loin of pork were both roasted in a reflector oven. Other cast-iron pots hung over the fire were used to cook the carrots, the mashed cauliflower and potato combination, and the beans. Dessert was baked apple with custard and whipped cream or bird's-nest pudding.

Three meals daily. Lunch entrées $5–$9; dinner at 7 P.M. (Saturday at 5 and 7:30 P.M.) prix fixe $30. Route 2, North Stonington, CT; (860) 599-4540.

Water Street Cafe, Stonington

This tiny eight-table café owned by chef Walter Houlihan and his wife, Stephanie, is a find. Curtains and chair covers are a brightly colored fish print and walls are sponge painted, both tributes to Stonington's fishing fleet and to the name of the street.

When possible, the fish comes from the docks in Stonington. Appetizers include a lobster hash made with roasted peppers, asparagus salad with sesame-orange dressing, goat cheese tartlet, and chilled grilled shrimp cocktail with tomato-olive salsa and avocado.

Fish entrées include the popular roasted salmon with a crust of mushrooms and arugula and seared scallops in a ginger-scallion vinaigrette. Medallions of pork, rib steak, and roasted duck are other choices. The chocolate flourless torte with whipped cream and fresh raspberry puree as well as a coconut chocolate and caramel wafer cake with vanilla ice cream were exceptional and well worth the calories.

Dinner, Wednesday through Monday, entrées $16–$20. BYOB. 142 Water Street, Stonington; (860) 535-2122.

Olympia Tea Room, Watch Hill

This delightfully old-fashioned restaurant on the main street is tucked among the upscale shops facing the water. Waitresses wear starched black uniforms with white aprons, lace collars, and cuffs. High-backed wood booths line the bright pink walls. Desserts like the Avondale Swan, a huge "head-turning" creation of puff pastry, ice cream, clouds of whipped cream, and hot fudge, remind us of a more innocent era. The children's menu also has a bit of whimsy that will make adults smile.

For lunch we had Italian sweet sausage and littleneck clams in marinara sauce with a split toasted grinder roll perfect for dunking. Other lunch items include clam chowder, fried calamari, lobster rolls, fish sandwich, or smoked bluefish pâté with bruschetta, olives, roasted peppers, and anchovies. In the evening steaks, pork chops, shrimp scampi, and pasta dishes are added to the menu.

Three meals daily, May through November. Lunch entrées $5–$11, dinner entrées $13–$18. Bay Street, Watch Hill, RI; (401) 348-8211.

ITINERARY

DAY ONE. Start at **Mystic Seaport** early in the day before the crowds arrive. Have lunch at **Bravo Bravo,** then return to see more of the seaport or go the the **Mystic Aquarium.** Take a sunset cruise on the *Sabino* or the *Argia* followed by dinner at **Flood Tide** or **J. P. Daniel's.**

DAY TWO. Visit the **Florence Griswold Museum** and the **Cooley Gallery** in Old Lyme. Lunch at **Bee and Thistle** or **Old Lyme Inn.** Follow the **driving tour** along Route 156 to Hamburg Cove and on to **Gillette Castle.** Take the Chester-Hadlyme ferry across the Connecticut River. This would be a good night to see a musical at **Goodspeed Opera** in East Haddam. Have an early dinner at **Fiddler's** or get sandwiches for a picnic at **Wheat Market** in Chester. For a leisurely, superb dinner, try the **Restaurant du Village** or **Copper Beech Inn.**

DAY THREE. Take a train ride on the **Valley Railroad** (outside of Essex), which connects to a boat ride on the Connecticut River. Walk through the town of Essex; have lunch at the **Griswold Inn** or at **She Sells Sandwiches.** Continue on Route 154, which is dotted with antique shops, to Old Saybrook. Follow the driving tour around the town. Have dinner at **Saybrook Point Inn, Wine and Roses, Stella D'Oro,** or nearby at **Steve's Centerbrook Grill.**

DAY FOUR. Take the **driving tour** starting in East Haddam and traveling the back roads toward Stonington. If interested, take a detour to **Foxwoods Casino.** The bargain lunch is at **Randall's Ordinary.** Choices in Stonington for lunch include **Noah's, Skipper's Dock,** and the gourmet takeout across the street from **Water Street Cafe.** In Stonington, allow plenty of time to see Water Street's many fine antique and gift stores, as well as the lighthouse museum and the commercial fishing dock. Have dinner at **Water Street Cafe** or at **Randall's Ordinary** for open-hearth cooking.

DAY FIVE. If it is a nice day, go to **Watch Hill** for swimming and surfing, walking along the shore to Napatree Point, and browsing through the upscale stores. Have lunch at **Olympia Tea Room.** Finish your trip to this area with a lobster dinner at **Abbott's** in Noank.

BUDGETING YOUR TRIP

To help you get the most for the time and money you have to spend, here are some travel suggestions at three budget levels (cost per day with two people sharing a room), including lodging and meal tax, gratuity on meals, and service charge when it is added to your bill. Prices on lodgings are based on peak rates. Prices are approximate and are intended for planning purposes only. Lodgings are categorized by price and depending on the room selected may appear in more than one category. Meal prices at lunch include an average entrée and beverage. Dinner prices include an appetizer, entrée, dessert, and beverage. Wine or alcoholic beverages are not included.

Staying and dining at expensive lodgings and restaurants: From $280 to $600 per day for two.

Lodging: Inn at Mystic, Saybrook Point Inn, Steamboat Inn, Gelston House (suites), Riverwind (cottage), Randall's Ordinary (suite), Antiques and Accommodations, Copper Beech Inn, Red Brook Inn, Palmer Inn, Watch Hill Inn, House of 1833.

Dining: Breakfast: included except at Inn at Mystic and Saybrook Point. Lunch: Flood Tide, Bee and Thistle, Saybrook Point Inn. Dinner: Copper Beech, Restaurant du Village, Old Lyme, Flood Tide, Bee and Thistle.

Staying and dining at moderately priced lodgings and restaurants: From $190 to $280 per day for two.

Lodging: Riverwind, Griswold Inn, Copper Beech Inn, Gelston House, Bee and Thistle, Old Lyme Inn, Palmer Inn, Inn at Mystic, Red Brook Inn, Randall's Ordinary, Bishopsgate Inn, House of 1833.

Dining: Breakfast: included except at Bee and Thistle, Inn at Mystic. Lunch: Old Lyme Inn, Griswold Inn, J. P. Daniel's, Bravo Bravo, Aleia's, Stella D'Oro. Dinner: Saybrook Point Inn, Aleia's, Randall's Ordinary, Bravo Bravo, Olympia Tea Room, Griswold Inn, Fiddler's.

Staying and dining at less expensive lodgings and restaurants: From $155 to $190 per day for two.

Lodging: Griswold Inn, Inn at Mystic, Bee and Thistle, Bishopsgate Inn.

Dining: Breakfast: included. Lunch: Randall's Ordinary, Wine and Roses, Seahorse Tavern, Abbott's, Olympia Tea Room. Dinner: Steve's Centerbrook Grill, Water Street Cafe, Boatyard Cafe, Wine and Roses, Stella D'Oro, J. P. Daniel's, Abbott's, Seahorse Tavern.

11

Newport, Rhode Island

W e don't know of another location in the Northeast quite like Newport.
As a seaside resort, it is renowned for its sailboats and sandy
beaches, deep foghorns and screeching seagulls, wind whistling through the
halyards, and waves crashing on the rocks. Chances are you've heard about
Newport's opulent and lavishly appointed summer estates called "cottages"
where, around the turn of the century, the outrageously wealthy outdid the
mere rich in a race to build the grandest mansions this country had ever seen.

The cottages tend to be the only thing tourists come here to see. But Newport is much more than just the town where American capitalists strutted their
turn-of-the-century *Lifestyles of the Rich and Famous.*

America's oldest library, tavern, and synagogue are all located in Newport.
Its streets are lined by more than 300 Colonial-era homes—many beautifully
restored and occupied. Newport also was home to a school of furniture makers
who turned their craft into an art form. Further back in history, this fashionable
resort was a major hub of the detestable triangle trade involving slaves, rum,
and molasses. Newporters fired on the British before the Revolutionary War
battles at Lexington and Concord. The town hosted the first national tennis
tournament, as well as America's first automobile race.

As we strolled along the brick sidewalks and gaslit streets of Newport's
Colonial section, we realized that this town offers the discerning traveler a
unique opportunity to view a city in transition. Newport is not content to live
in the past, with those extraordinary summer estates of a bygone era as its
sole claim to fame. Instead, it is hard at work trying to blend its rich heritage
with a burgeoning future.

A visit to the waterfront confirms this. Here, gentrification has rolled across
the wharves with the force of a raging nor'easter. The family businesses that
once lined the piers—fish processors, boatbuilders, marine repair shops, and
sail lofts—have all but given way to condos, gift shops, restaurants, and remarkable traffic jams.

Founded in 1639 by families fleeing the rigid Puritanism of the Massachusetts Bay Colony, Newport quickly became a haven for those seeking religious
freedom. Quakers came in 1657 from New Amsterdam; Jews came from Por-
tugal in 1658; and Baptists arrived soon thereafter.

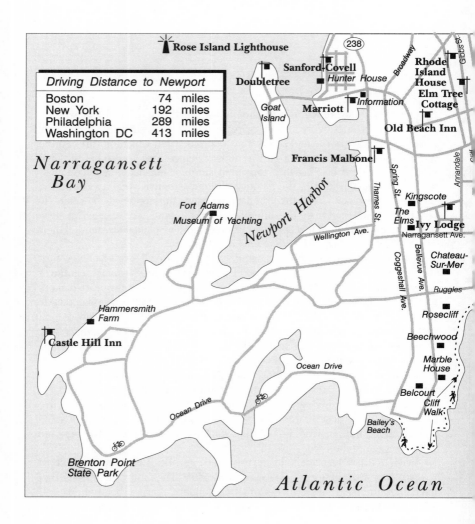

Rose Island Lighthouse

238

Sanford-Covell

Rhode Island House

Doubletree
Hunter House
Elm Tree Cottage

Driving Distance to Newport

Boston	74	miles
New York	192	miles
Philadelphia	289	miles
Washington DC	413	miles

Goat Island
Marriott
Information

Old Beach Inn

Narragansett Bay

Francis Malbone

Spring St.
Thames St.
Kingscote
The Elms
Ivy Lodge
Narragansett Ave.

Fort Adams
Museum of Yachting
Newport Harbor
Wellington Ave.

Chateau-Sur-Mer

Coggeshall Ave.
Bellevue Ave.
Ruggles

Rosecliff

Hammersmith Farm

Beechwood

Castle Hill Inn

Marble House

Ocean Drive

Belcourt

Ocean Drive
Bailey's Beach
Cliff Walk

Brenton Point State Park

Atlantic Ocean

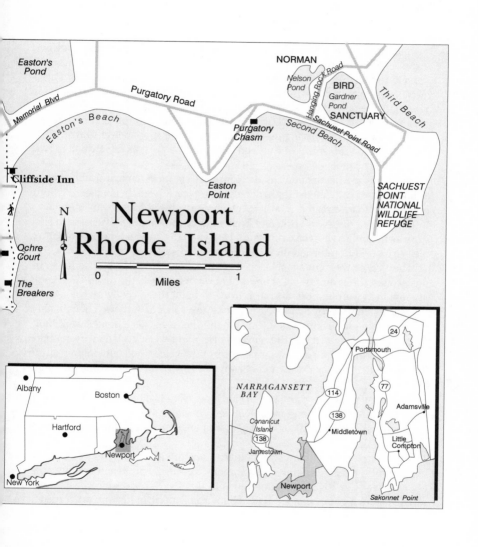

Easton's
Pond

NORMAN

Nelson
Pond

BIRD

Gardner
Pond

SANCTUARY

Third Beach

Purgatory Road

Memorial Blvd

Easton's Beach

Hanging Rock Road

Sachuest Point Road

Purgatory
Chasm

Second Beach

Cliffside Inn

Easton
Point

Newport
Rhode Island

SACHUEST
POINT
NATIONAL
WILDLIFE
REFUGE

N

Ochre
Court

0   Miles   1

The
Breakers

Albany

Boston

Hartford

Newport

New York

NARRAGANSETT
BAY

24

Portsmouth

114

77

138

Adamsville

Conanicut
Island

138

Middletown

Little
Compton

Jamestown

Newport

Sakonnet Point

The early residents were a melting pot of traders, merchants, shipbuilders, furniture makers, craftsmen, and intellectuals. By 1720 the population of the town had swelled to more than 38,000, and it ranked with Boston, New York, and Philadelphia as one of the foremost Colonial settlements. Even in its early days, Newport was a magnet for wealthy Southerners who flocked here seeking cool summer breezes.

But not all those who arrived on the town docks were so fortunate. Newport featured prominently in the notorious trade of slaves, rum, and molasses. A fiercely independent lot, Newporters were unhappy with the British Parliament's attempts to squelch their worldwide trading with heavier taxes. So in 1764, more than ten years before the start of Revolutionary hostilities, Newporters fired on British ships. Rhode Island also jumped the gun on the rest of the colonies by declaring its independence from England on May 4, 1776. As a result, the full wrath of England fell upon the port, as the British moved in and destroyed its commercial capacity.

The wars and occupations made Newport's status as a major trading center a thing of the past. Almost immediately, however, it became popular as a summer resort that attracted Southern plantation owners along with merchants from Philadelphia, New York, and Boston. Only the Civil War was able to slow its growth, and as soon as Grant and Lee signed the surrender at Appomattox, pleasure seekers returned on an unprecedented scale.

Then came the "cottages." Built between 1880 and 1910 by American industrialists, these huge estates brought new prosperity to the town. Thousands of craftsmen were imported from Europe to build these costly mansions, and thousands more were employed in backstairs roles as butlers, chefs, maids, valets, stableboys, nannies, and coachmen. And once these homes were built, the wealth that poured into them over a brief eight-week period every summer was staggering. The party went on, year after year, until the sinking of the *Titanic* in 1912 stripped Newport society of many of its most prominent members.

The First World War and the Great Depression brought the Gilded Age to its irrevocable end. The glorious cottages became the world's largest white elephants. By the late 1940s, Newport was once again a town in search of a new beginning.

Fortunately, certain farsighted citizens saw the incomparable wealth of architectural treasures scattered throughout Newport, and began serious preservation work in 1945 which continues to this day. This scenic coastal town gives visitors a glimpse of a unique chapter in American history, preserved in the wood, stone, bricks, and mortar.

For information on special events, contact the **Newport Gateway Visitors Center** (23 America's Cup Avenue, Newport, RI 02840; (401) 849-8048; (800) 326-6030).

WHERE TO GO, WHAT TO DO

Take time to stroll along Bellevue Avenue from Memorial Avenue to Bailey's Beach along the restored brick-and-gravel gaslit sidewalks canopied with ancient trees and grand mansions. You will pass many summer mansions along Bellevue Avenue in Newport; six of the most glamorous have been superbly restored by the Preservation Society of Newport County. These are open to the public, and each has its own unique charms.

Preservation Society Mansions

From November through March three of the six mansions are open weekends only, 10 A.M. to 4 P.M. From Thanksgiving through New Year's each of the three houses is decorated for the holidays. Starting in April, some of the mansions are open weekdays as well as weekends. May through October, all the houses and Green Animals, a topiary garden, 10 A.M. to 5 P.M.; in July and August, the Breakers stays open till 6 P.M. The Breakers Stable is open weekends only, Memorial Day through Labor Day.

Ticket prices at each mansion are $6.50 to $10 depending on the property. It is far less expensive to buy a combination ticket for two to eight buildings, available at any of the mansions.

If you plan to visit a number of mansions, you can save money as well as help a worthy cause by purchasing a membership in the Preservation Society. Benefits include free admission to all eight mansions and sites for a full year, a subscription to the society's newsletter, invitations to society activities, a handbook giving details of each property, and a 10 percent discount on purchases made at the society's gift shops. Memberships are $40 per person and $50 for a family, which includes children 17 and under.

To join, however, you must visit the society's office in Newport or contact the office by mail or phone, you cannot join at one of the properties. The office is open Monday through Friday, 9 A.M. to 5 P.M. 424 Bellevue Avenue, Newport, RI 02840; (401) 847-1000.

The Breakers

Most "executive" homes on the market today offer about 3,500 square feet of living space. Imagine living in a home that measures 37,000 square feet! We like as much elbow room as the next couple, but you literally can get lost in this place.

The Breakers was the summer home of Cornelius Vanderbilt II, grandson of the "Commodore," who, to his enormous good fortune, built the New York Central Railroad empire. It is by far the largest, most lavish, and most visited mansion.

The Breakers is by far the largest, most lavish, and most visited mansion in Newport.

Cornelius's "cottage" was modeled after a seventeenth-century Italianate palace and was built in only two years by 2,000 European artisans brought over for the purpose. (Remember, in the nineteenth century, construction work was done with picks, shovels, and horse-drawn carts.) Costly marble, alabaster, and stone imported from Italy, France, and Africa glint in the sunlight. In room after room, golden cherubs float in intricate friezes, rich tapestries hang from the walls, and gold-leaf ceilings remind visitors that no expense was spared for this summer residence. For something on a slightly smaller scale, take a walk through the Victorian children's playhouse: it's the size of a small home all by itself.

The Grand Salon was assembled in France, disassembled, crated, and then shipped, accompanied by the appropriate French artisans, across the Atlantic to be reassembled here . . . all for the Vanderbilts' eight-week stay each season. The irony of it all is that Cornelius—a shy, religious workaholic—had a stroke in 1896, just one year after the mansion was completed. His wife, known as Alice of the Breakers, continued to reign as the family matriarch and became an institution of the Newport social scene until her death in 1934.

The Breakers Stable. Make sure you drive down Coggeshall Street, which runs parallel to Bellevue. Here you'll see the stables and greenhouses that supported the mansions. Today many are leading a second life as private residences. The Breakers stable at the corner of Coggeshall and Bateman now houses the Preservation Society's horticultural department, and is also where the profuse quantities of flowers found in the mansions are grown. The carriage house includes a collection of Vanderbilt memorabilia and the Vanderbilt coach *Venture.*

Marble House

The second most visited cottage, this $11 million mansion was built by William Vanderbilt (brother of Cornelius II), the equivalent of a "jet-setter" in the Gilded Age, for his wife, Alva. The four white marble Corinthian columns along the front entrance were modeled after the Temple of the Sun at Heliopolis. The main floor comprises three major rooms, all thirty by fifty feet, surrounding an imposing marble foyer. The ballroom is the most ornate in Newport—a fantasy in gold leaf and ormolu modeled after the Hall of Mirrors at Versailles. The dining room of pink Numidian marble, modeled after the Salon of Hercules at Versailles, has bronze chairs so heavy (sixty pounds) that a footman was required for each one.

After the formal tour, we recommend taking the time to visit the restored Chinese teahouse at the rear of the property.

As you tour these mansions, notice that only the guest bedrooms enjoy ocean views. It was not the hosts' charity that yielded these prime vistas; damp sea breezes were considered less than healthful in those days.

The Elms

Even Horatio Alger never could have concocted a rags-to-riches story like this one. Born to German immigrants, Edward J. Berwind started out as a laborer in a piano factory. After decades of hard work, he ended up owning one of the largest coal mining and distribution companies in America, and then decided to build himself a comfortable nest to call his own—a $1.4 million mansion on Bellevue Avenue.

An eighteenth-century château was the model for this massive stone structure, which was completed in 1902. The exquisitely adorned interior in the French classical style has one of America's most significant collections of Venetian wall paintings and murals, all purchased from a single palace. The shimmering grand staircase is made of Italian Carrara marble (the stone Michelangelo preferred). Don't miss the Florentine table inlaid with cut stones in the second-floor hallway (like those found in the Pitti Palace). Take time to explore the twelve acres of landscaped grounds—because the property does not have ocean frontage, its specimen trees have been spared the deleterious effects of salt spray.

Rosecliff

Inspired by the Grand Trianon at Versailles, Rosecliff is today famous as the setting for the Hollywood versions of *The Great Gatsby* and *The Betsy.* The highlights at this H-shaped mansion are an ingeniously designed heart-shaped grand stairway and an eighty-by-forty-foot ballroom. A Stanford White design completed in 1902, this cottage has become a favorite site for lectures, dinners, balls, weddings, and receptions. Having already visited its larger sisters down the road, however, we felt the guided tour here was a bit too long, and found the upstairs bedrooms to hold no special charms.

Kingscote

With its turrets and gingerbread ornamentation, this Gothic cottage has a certain storybook visual appeal. One of Newport's first notable mansions, Kingscote was completed in 1842 as the summer home for a Southern plantation owner. An extensive remodeling included the addition of many Tiffany windows in the 1870s and 1880s. In spite of its many owners and renovations, this building got better as it got older. Our tour through this much more livable home allowed us to see how several eras of Newport society left their imprint on one structure.

Chateau-Sur-Mer

Originally built as a retirement villa, this 1852 Victorian was remodeled in 1877 into what was touted prior to the Gilded Age as the most "substantial and expensive" residence in Newport. We were particularly impressed by the walnut carvings depicting the pleasures of eating and drinking—immortalized in Renaissance style by Italian craftsmen. Notice the mural of the tree of life that wraps around the stairwell to the third floor, culminating in a blue sky populated with birds.

Other Mansions in Newport

The following are the best of the remaining mansions in Newport that you can visit. None is managed by the Preservation Society.

Belcourt Castle

The Tinney family, antique dealers and restoration experts, have turned this home, originally built by Oliver Hazard Perry Belmont in 1891 and modeled after a Louis XIII hunting lodge, into a vast depository for their extensive art and antique collections.

Artifacts on display here include the largest collection of thirteenth-century stained-glass windows in America, a Gothic ballroom complete with a large working pipe organ, a gold-encrusted coach, and the Tinneys' incredible collection of Chinese art. Belcourt Castle is not as well maintained as the homes owned by the Preservation Society.

Open daily mid-February through New Year's, 9 A.M. to 5 P.M.; 10 A.M. to 4 P.M. off-season. Adults $6.50. 657 Bellevue Avenue, Newport; (401) 846-0669.

Hammersmith Farm

This rambling twenty-eight-room shingle-style cottage set on fifty oceanfront acres is where four generations of the Auchincloss family spent their summers. Sentimental visitors dabbed their eyes when the guide took us into Jacqueline Bouvier Kennedy Onassis's childhood bedroom and the office that President John F. Kennedy used as his summer home away from Washington. The property, currently owned by a group of investors, was for sale when we visited.

Open weekends in March and daily April through mid-November, 10 A.M. to 5 P.M.; 10 A.M. to 4 P.M. off-season. Holiday tours in early December. Adults $7. Ocean Drive, Newport; (401) 846-0420 or 846-7346.

Ochre Court

Overlooking the ocean, and modeled after Edward VII's castle in Paris, Ochre Court, a fifty-room French château, was one of Newport's first palatial summer cottages when completed in 1892. It is now used as administrative offices by Salve Regina College. The two-story Great Hall is surrounded by an ornate balconied gallery. The exterior has carved gargoyles, griffins, high roofs, turrets, and tall chimneys—a photographer's delight. Best of all, our sight-seeing was unmarred by the crowds you often bump into (literally) at the other mansions. Salve Regina College has twenty historic properties along the waterfront that are part of its campus.

Open weekends April and October; daily May through September, 10 A.M. to 5 P.M. Adults $5.50. Ochre Point Avenue, Newport; (401) 847-6650.

The Astors' Beechwood

Here's your chance to say hello to the seventh serving man, chat with the first undercook, and banter with a visiting Bavarian baron. At this onetime home of Caroline Schermerhorn Astor, queen of Newport society during the Gilded Age, professional actors assume the roles of the masters, servants, and guests who once populated Beechwood.

It's fun to ask questions about those bygone days, and even to try to trick the actors. It's not your usual information tour, and we enjoyed the way the actors remained in character throughout our visit. Bring the kids—we guarantee they will not get bored. There's even a Victorian tearoom staffed by waitresses in period costume, so you can take the tour and then enjoy a spot of Earl Grey with your crumpets.

Open February to mid-May, Friday through Sunday; daily, mid-May through December, 10 A.M. to 5 P.M.; 10 A.M. to 4 P.M. off-season. Call for information on tea dances and murder mystery events. 580 Bellevue Avenue, Newport, (401) 846-3772.

Colonial Newport

It may come as a surprise that here in Newport you can walk through peaceful residential streets lined with one of the greatest concentrations of restored Colonial buildings in the United States. The Point section extends from about the Gateway Visitors Center approximately to the Newport-Jamestown bridge across America's Cup Avenue to the White Horse Tavern.

We found walking these historic avenues very restful, without the traffic noise you'll find in Colonial sections of Philadelphia or Boston, and none of the Williamsburg tourist crush. Much of the credit goes to the late philanthropist Doris Duke and the unique restoration organization she founded.

Newport Restoration Foundation. As you stroll the streets, you'll see small plaques reading "NRF" on many beautiful old buildings. This is the acronym for the Newport Restoration Foundation, which was funded by Doris Duke. The restoration of eighty-three eighteenth-century properties changed the face of Newport. Many of these restored homes feature distinctive gambrel roof, beaded clapboards, and lovely white doorways topped with pediments and fanlights. Most are leased to individuals, but the Whitehorne House and Prescott Farm complex are open as museums.

Rough Point. Doris Duke's Newport mansion at the end of Bellevue Avenue is expected to open for tours in the spring of 1997. Call the Newport Restoration Foundation for more information; (401) 849-7300.

The Samuel Whitehorne House Museum

This outstanding collection of furnishings by Newport craftsmen, including the Goddard and Townsend families (and some of their contemporaries), is the best-kept secret in town. Winterthur, one of the preeminent museums of American furniture and decorative arts, sends its guides here from Delaware for training. Sotheby's also slips its curators in and out.

What's surprising is that few visitors come to this venerable 1811 brick merchant's house on Thames Street. The earliest period is represented by the summer kitchen, a basement room furnished with authentic Pilgrim-period pieces. The house has three floors, including many pieces of furniture made by Townsend and Goddard. (The Newport style features innovative reverse-shell motifs and uniquely detailed ball-and-claw feet.) It also has a good collection of Chinese porcelains and silver by Newport silversmiths. Be sure to visit the cupola, which offers great views of the city and harbor. The tour is personal; if you show interest and knowledge, you may be permitted to inspect the pieces closely. The period garden on the premises has also been carefully crafted.

Open May through October, Friday through Monday, 10 A.M. to 4 P.M. Adults $5. 416 Thames Street, Newport; (401) 847-2448.

Hunter House

Located on the waterfront in the historic Point Section and built in 1748, this national historic landmark features a characteristic Georgian architectural trait: a balustrade circumventing a flat rooftop, commonly called a "widow's walk." Allegedly, this is where a sea captain's wife would pace while awaiting her husband's return from the treacherous, sometimes deadly seas.

Hunter House has been well restored and furnished with fine Newport pieces. Cabinetmakers Goddard and Townsend, who lived in this section of town, made many of the pieces you'll see here. The elaborate floor-to-ceiling wall paneling, thought to have been installed in the 1750s, makes the interior of the house rather unusual.

The carved pineapple over the front doorway represents hospitality. Since Colonial times, sea captains returning from a long voyage often placed a pineapple over their front door to let friends and neighbors know they were home and receiving guests.

Hunter House is owned by the Preservation Society. For hours and rates see the section on Preservation Society mansions.

The Historical Society

Too often we only see restorations after their completion. Here you'll find the fascinating "before" photos of many of Newport's restored Colonial homes. Exhibits on the Gilded Age—photos, newspaper clippings, accounts from diaries, and more—also are imaginatively displayed. A reproduction of a Newport merchant's parlor has fine examples of furniture made by Goddard and Townsend, but unfortunately you can only peer into the room.

Open Tuesday through Friday, 9:30 A.M. to 4:30 P.M. and Saturday mornings June 15 through September. One-and-a-half-hour walking tours of the Colonial district are held Friday and Saturday at 10 A.M. Admission is free. 82 Touro Street, Newport; (401) 846-0813.

Touro Synagogue

Notice that this synagogue is set on a distinct diagonal to the street: according to ancient tradition, worshipers were supposed to face east, toward Jerusalem. Built in 1759, this Georgian structure was the first synagogue constructed in the colonies. Inside, twelve Ionic columns, symbolic of the twelve tribes of Israel, support the gallery, where women traditionally sit during services. Five massive brass candelabra, dating to the 1760s, hang from the ceiling.

A little-known feature of the synagogue is a trapdoor leading from the bimah (an elevated platform where the Torah is read) to a tunnel, which presumably was part of the Underground Railroad.

Open July Fourth weekend to Labor Day, Sunday through Friday, 10 A.M. to 4 P.M. Labor Day through mid-October, Sunday 11 A.M. to 3 P.M., and

Monday through Friday 1 to 2 P.M. The rest of the year, Sunday through Friday 1 to 3 P.M. 85 Touro Street, Newport; (401) 847-4794.

Trinity Church

A town landmark since it was completed in 1726, this church has figured prominently in Newport's history. The exterior design was influenced by Sir Christopher Wren, who created much of London's architecture after the Great Fire of 1666. Interior features of note include the wineglass-shaped pulpit, a lovely organ, an impressive great clock, and a box pew where George Washington probably sat while attending services. Many of the gravestones in the church cemetery date back to the Colonial period. An interesting fact not readily apparent: while the church sits on its original foundation, the neighboring Colonial buildings were all moved here by the Newport Restoration Foundation.

Open Monday through Friday 10 A.M. to 1 P.M., until 4 P.M. on weekdays from May through mid-October and weekends as well during the summer. Queen Anne Street; (401) 846-0660.

Quaker Meeting House

Built in 1699, the oldest Friends Great Meeting House in the country has changing exhibits on Quaker life in Newport from the seventeenth century. Call for hours. Marlborough and Farewell Streets across the street from White Horse Tavern; (401) 846-0813.

Other Points of Interest

St. Mary's Church. Thrust into the limelight by the marriage of Jacqueline Bouvier to John Fitzgerald Kennedy (then a senator) on September 12, 1953, this is one of the finest examples of Gothic architecture in the East, as well as the oldest Roman Catholic parish in Rhode Island.

Open Monday through Friday, 7 to 11 A.M., except holidays. Spring Street at Memorial Boulevard, Newport; (401) 847-0475.

The Museum of Newport History. Through pictures, recordings, and videos, this museum offers an excellent overview of the history of Newport. A highlight was the 1890s omnibus that we boarded for a video tour of Bellevue Avenue. Guided walking tours leave from the museum, Thursday though Saturday, June through September. Museum open Monday through Saturday 10 A.M. to 5 P.M., Sunday 1 to 5 P.M. Closed Tuesday. Adults $5. On Thames Street, across from the Brick Market, Newport; (401) 841-8770.

The Museum of Yachting. We've always had special admiration for those hearty souls who single-handedly brave wind and wave to sail around the world. So we especially enjoyed the upstairs gallery here, which is devoted to their exploits. At the opposite extreme "The Mansions and the Yachts" exhibit depicts the turn-of-the-century luxury yachts owned by the Bellevue Avenue crowd. A good example was William Vanderbilt's 285-foot *Alva,* which carried a crew of fifty-plus, and had more hands manning the galley than many boats have on deck. The museum also has models, costumes, paintings, and photographs documenting the history of yachting. Alongside the museum's dock, you can see the 127-foot *Shamrock V,* the 1930 America's Cup challenger.

Daily, mid-May through October. Adults $3. Located in Fort Adams State Park (admission to which is separate), Ocean Drive, Newport; (401) 847-1018.

The Navy War College Museum. The navy is Newport's largest single employer. The navy museum, located on the grounds of the War College, features exhibits on the history of naval warfare and the navy in Narragansett Bay. Visitors are welcome to attend all graduations, pass-in-review, and color and awards ceremonies.

Open Monday through Friday, 10 A.M. to 4 P.M. daily June through September, noon to 4 P.M. Admission is free. Coasters Harbor Island (access through gate 1 of the Naval Education and Training Center), Newport; (401) 841-4052.

The Newport Casino–International Tennis Hall of Fame and Museum. These are the only competition grass courts in the country open to the public. The thirteen grass courts are open mid-May through early October, $35 per person for ninety minutes.

The multimillion-dollar Tennis Museum houses the world's largest collection of tennis memorabilia and depicts the history of the game with photos and exhibits from its inception. The gallery that simulates a tennis match with two large screens facing each other is particularly well done. After you tour the museum, walk back to the courts for lawn and court tennis, precursors of the game we play today. You can have a relaxing outdoor lunch overlooking the nineteenth-century Horseshoe Piazza at the La Forge Casino (*see* Where to Dine).

Open daily 10 A.M. to 5 P.M. Adults $6. 194 Bellevue Avenue, Newport; (401) 849-3990.

The Redwood Library and Athenaeum. The classic Roman Doric temple-like structure built in 1748 is made of wood, not stone. This is the oldest continuously used library in the United States. Stop in to see some of the hundreds of early American portraits, particularly the six by Gilbert Stuart, including one of George Washington. Visitors are welcome to use the library, but can't take out books. The reading room has a large collection of magazines and newspapers.

Open Monday through Saturday, 9:30 A.M. to 5 P.M. 50 Bellevue Avenue, Newport; (401) 847-0292.

Newport Art Museum. This large European chaletlike building built in 1862 is done in stick style with half-timbered beams on exterior walls, piazzas, gables, bay windows, and large interior spaces that hold changing exhibits. The adjacent Cushing Gallery, a modern building that looks like an ancient temple, also has exhibits. You don't have to pay museum admission to browse in the Griffon Shop, a consignment shop located in the back of the building, which had lots of glass and china items the day we were there.

Museum open Monday through Saturday, 10 A.M. to 5 P.M. Sunday, noon to 5 P.M. Adults $5. 76 Bellevue Avenue, Newport; (401) 848-8200.

Walks, Drives, Beaches, Parks

The Cliff Walk. This three-and-a-half-mile walk is one of the most famous in America, and justly so. On one side is a row of mansions like none other in existence, and on the other the mighty Atlantic pounds the rocky shoreline at your feet. The experience is unforgettable.

Having walked the entire length, from Memorial Boulevard to the free part of Bailey's Beach, we offer the following insights. If you park at the Cliff Walk Manor on Memorial Boulevard, you will be charged a parking fee; even more annoying, the dense shrubbery along the path from Memorial Boulevard to Narragansett Avenue precludes views of the "cottages."

Instead, park for free at the end of Narragansett Avenue and start your walk at the famous Forty Steps. The steps are built into the rocks and lead down to a small landing almost at the water's edge. Head south along the walk (to your right) for the best views of the ocean and grand mansions. Along the way you will pass Ochre Court, the Breakers, Rosecliff, the Astors' Beechwood, and Marble House. The path to Land's End is partly paved, partly dirt, and some sections are rocky. After a rain, some areas will be covered with water and may be slippery. There are also a few tunnels. The route from Land's End to Bailey's Beach is not marked. Just follow the rocky coastline, climbing along boulders. Return to your car on Narragansett Avenue by walking back along Bellevue Avenue.

The Ten-Mile Drive. You will see more mansions, grand estates, and dramatic ocean views than you can imagine along this route. If you have bikes the views are even better. Bring along a picnic lunch in good weather and stop at Brenton Point State Park.

Beaches

Bailey's Beach. Formally known as "the Spouting Rock Beach Association," this famous private beach club is situated on Ocean Drive. During the Gilded Age, membership in the club was restricted to the elite of high society. Today it is still private and exclusive, but there is a section of beach that has been opened to the public. The problem is that there is no parking nearby. There is a path at the far end of Bellevue Avenue near the intersection of Coggeshall Avenue that leads to the beach. Likewise, if you take the Cliff Walk to its very end, you will find yourself at Bailey's.

Easton's Beach. Also known as First Beach, it parallels Memorial Boulevard from the Cliff Walk's northern end to the Middletown town line. There is a rotunda with an arcade, a concession stand, a merry-go-round, and miniature golf . . . and often a lot of seaweed. You can walk to this beach from many of the inns in Newport. Parking $10–$15.

Sachuest Beach. Also called Second Beach, this three-mile stretch of sand is next to First Beach off Purgatory Road in Middletown. It is cleaner than First Beach, as it is more protected, and has the only sand dunes in the area. In addition, there is good surfing here. Because it borders Sachuest Point National Wildlife Refuge, it is also popular with hikers and anglers. Parking $10–$15.

Third Beach. Located in Middletown beyond Second Beach, it fronts on the Sakonnet River and has good views of the Sakonnet Hills. Popular with families with children and windsurfing enthusiasts looking for steady (but not overpowering) winds. Parking $10–$15.

Parks

Fort Adams State Park. Located off Ocean Drive, this small state park has a swimming area and a picnic area with grills. Sailboats and Windsurfers can also be rented. Admission $4.

Brenton Point State Park. Also located off Ocean Drive, Brenton Point affords panoramic views of Narragansett Bay and the Atlantic, and is a good spot for a picnic as well as a place to fly a kite.

Norman Bird Sanctuary. This 450-acre wildlife refuge with ten miles of trails and habitats ranging from marsh to forest has three large rock ridges that jut south from the office with great views of the two reservoirs that attract waterfowl. The unusual rock in the ridges is named "pudding stone" because of the presence of small cobblestones that reminded early travelers of the raisins and currants in plum pudding. Guided tours available. Open daily, 9 A.M. to 5 P.M. Adults $4. Third Beach Road, Middletown; (401) 846-2577.

Sachuest Point National Wildlife Refuge. This 242-acre peninsula, adjacent to Norman Bird Sanctuary, is best visited in the winter when you can see abundant bird life, including bufflehead and especially harlequin ducks. A two-and-a-half-mile nature trail encircles this point of land with observation platforms offering good views of the rocky coast. The refuge and the visitor center are open year-round, no admission. Before you head off for a hike through the grasses during spring and summer we suggest checking with the ranger as when we visited in May ticks were a problem. Located just beyond Second Beach; (401) 847-5511.

Purgatory Chasm. Look down into a narrow 150-foot cleft in the rocky cliff overlooking Second Beach. Just off Purgatory Road.

Shopping

At first glance Newport shops appear to be the usual tourist potpourri of gifts and T-shirts, but you'll find some gems if you look closely. We found a number of high-quality antique shops and several fine art galleries. **Rue de France** (78 Thames Street, (401) 846-3636) has French country-inspired furnishings, Pierre Deux gifts, and Palais Royal linens. **Army and Navy Surplus Store** (262 Thames Street, (401) 847-3073) is one of the few real ones still left from the bygone days.

You can't miss **Aardvark Antiques,** on lower Thames across from Pronto restaurant; it has a fenced-in yard filled with large statuary and iron fountains and a warehouse of antiques. **Flying Colors Ltd.** (468 Thames Street, (401) 846-0418) has flags of all types as well as wind socks and kites. The **Armchair Sailor,** (543 Thames Street, (401) 847-4252 or (800) 292-4278) carries every conceivable title on marine history, navigation, and cruising, along with technical publications, loran tables and charts, and a selection of books about Newport. At **Thames Glass** (588 Thames Street, (401) 846-0576) you can watch glass artist Matthew Buecher and his team create handblown vases, perfume bottles, ornaments, and bowls.

On Spring and Franklin Streets in the Historic Colonial Hill section, antique shops include the **Drawing Room** (152 Spring Street, (401) 841-5060) for furniture, porcelains, and lighting from the Gilded Age; **Newport China Trade Co.** (8 Franklin Street, (401) 841-5267), which has a nice selection of eighteenth- through twentieth-century export china; and **Liberty Tree** (128 Spring Street, (401) 847-5925) for high-quality primitive folk art.

Art galleries are located along Bellevue Avenue. **William Vareika Fine Arts** (212 Bellevue Avenue, (401) 849-6149) specializes in eighteenth-, nineteenth-, and early-twentieth-century American paintings, especially by artists with a Newport connection. **DeBlois Gallery** (138 Bellevue Avenue, (401) 847-9977) and **Spring Bull Studio** (55 Bellevue Avenue, (401) 849-9166) feature local artists. The **Newport Book Store** (116 Bellevue Avenue, (401) 847-3400) is a great source for fine military and art history books. **Waldenbooks,** in the Bellevue Shopping Plaza (401-846-5067), has a large selection of general books about Newport.

Aquidneck Lobster Company at Bowen's Wharf (401-846-0106) is one of the last waterfront links with the fishing industry. This large wholesale and retail operation has tanks of lobsters ranging in size from chix to over eight pounds. Come in just for a look, to have a box packed for home, or to order some for a picnic.

Tours

Newport on Foot. You can best understand a city (especially one that was built before the automobile) by walking. After you've seen a few of the mansions, explore Colonial Newport by taking a guided walking tour of the Point and the Historic Hill sections. Anita Rafael, who has led walking tours since 1990, makes you feel as though you are being shown around by a friend. Her tours are informative but informal. The one-and-a-quarter-hour tours cover a distance of about a mile. Most tours end at the White Horse Tavern for coffee or tea. Tours leave from the visitors center, April through November, Saturday through Monday. Adults $7. Call (401) 846-5391 for an updated recording of the next day's schedule.

Newport Harbor Cruises. For a view of Newport from the water we suggest a two-hour schooner trip on either the two-masted *Madeleine* or the *Adirondack.* The *Adirondack,* completed in 1994, is seventy-eight feet long, while the *Madeleine,* a slightly older boat, is seventy feet long. Both hold up to forty-nine passengers. The *Adirondack* leaves from the Newport Yachting Center on America's Cup Avenue at Commercial Wharf, (401) 846-1600. The *Madeleine* leaves from Bannisters Wharf, (401) 849-3033. Tours May through October at 10:30 A.M. and 1, 3:30, and 6 P.M. Adults $20.

Driving Tours

Newport to Sakonnet Winery and Little Compton. Take Route 114 north out of Newport. Be aware of the traffic and development as you leave Newport. Years ago the countryside around Newport was dotted with windmills. To see one, stop at **Prescott Farm.** This mill was built in 1812 and restored by the Newport Restoration Foundation. Grinding doesn't begin here until October, but you can climb the stairs to view the millstones and purchase corn, herbs, and honey grown on the farm. Open daily April through November, 10 A.M. to 4 P.M. Adults $1.50. 2009 West Main Street, Route 114, Middletown; (401) 847-6230.

Continue on Route 114 north (about nine miles from Newport). Turn left on Cory's Lane to get to **Green Animals.** Arranged in a charming garden setting overlooking Narragansett Bay are some eighty topiary pieces, including twenty-one varieties of animals and birds. Started around 1880, this garden features the oldest and most northerly examples of topiary in the United States. Open daily May through September, weekends and holidays in October, 10 A.M. to 5 P.M. Adults $6.50. 380 Cory's Lane (off Route 114), Portsmouth; (401) 683-1267.

Follow road signs to Tiverton across the Sakonnet River, then take Route 77 south to Tiverton Four Corners. For lunch stop at **Provender,** an upscale, enticingly displayed gourmet store with hot entrées, classic salads, fancy picnic baskets, sandwiches, smoked meats, cheeses, breads, and incredible desserts to go. Open daily except Tuesday, 9 A.M. to 6 P.M.; (401) 624-9991. **Gray's Country Store and Ice Cream,** across the road from Provender, has excellent homemade ice cream at a good price.

Turn left on Route 179 to Adamsville. **Gray's Store** (401-635-4566) claims to be the oldest continuously operating country store in the United States.

There's a marble-topped soda fountain, penny candy and stone-ground corn-meal, rye, and wheat flour from Gray's Mill next door, plus a little bit of just about everything else. **Gray's Grist Mill** has been in operation on this site since 1675. Using granite millstones and Rhode Island white flint corn, miller Tim McTague is helping to preserve the traditional methods of making corn-meal. The mill grinds corn, wheat, and rye flours, and produces a variety of bread and pancake mixes. Open weekends, but hours are irregular, so call ahead; (508) 636-6075.

Return to Route 77. Continue south to **Sakonnet Vineyards and Winery.** Visitors are welcome to wander the self-guided dirt path and enjoy the views. From May through November, guided tours are offered Wednesday, Saturday, and Sunday, on the hour, 11 A.M. to 5 P.M. You might want to stop at Provender for a picnic lunch, then purchase a bottle of wine here and enjoy them both at the picnic tables set out for visitors (162 West Main Road, Route 77, Little Compton; (401) 635-8486). Look for signs for the village of **Little Compton** as you drive south on Route 77. This is a perfect New England village with the Congregational church's soaring steeple, a cemetery with graves dating back to 1675, and a town green. **Olga's Cup and Saucer** (261 West Main Road, (401) 635-8650), a tiny place with no inside tables, has a widespread reputation for vegetable and fruit pies, cornmeal crust pizza topped with vegetables, and other home-baked items. Picnic outside and then go next door to **Cole Wal-ker's** roadside stand (401-635-4719), which supplies top-quality local produce to Olga's. Continue south on Route 77 to Sakonnet Point, a working harbor.

Jamestown (Conanicut Island). Take the Newport-Jamestown Bridge ($2 toll), then take the first exit and follow signs to Jamestown. This is a quiet village along the waterfront, a total contrast to Newport. The waterfront harbor, which was a much busier place until 1969, when the bridge opened, is a wonderful place to stroll. The waterfront hasn't been filled with shops and condos, so is open to view. The top restaurant in town is **Trattoria Simpatico** (*see* Where to Dine). **Jamestown Oyster Bar** (22 Narragansett Avenue, (401) 423-3380) is across the street, another favorite option for dining. The island has two state parks, both of which have no admission fee.

Beavertail State Park is at the tip of the island, with rocky cliffs over-looking the water. Beavertail Point is a spectacular place to view the Atlantic Ocean. An interesting **lighthouse museum** next to the still-active Beavertail Light tells the story of the region's lighthouses. Open mid-June through Labor Day. Rustic **Fort Wetherill State Park** (401-884-2010) has trails, a picnic area, restrooms, and excellent views of the harbor from rocky cliffs. Both are good places to get away from the crowds, bring a picnic, and enjoy the views. The day we visited we saw fishermen and scuba divers.

Hints for handling Newport on a summer weekend

- Do not park in fire lanes, loading zones, private lots, driveways, or along yellow curbs. A large fleet of tow trucks operates within the city limits.
- When you see the traffic building on Spring Street, don't be a sheep and stay in line. Bellevue Avenue and Annandale Street both run parallel to Spring and are usually much less congested.
- During the summer, the city operates a free shuttle bus to the major sites.
- If you are arriving late on a Friday night and are staying at any of the inns mentioned below (except Castle Hill Inn), take the time to park your car at your inn and then walk to town for dinner—or be prepared for steep parking fees. Parking is difficult on summer weekends.
- Don't panic if you see a line waiting to get into the Breakers, the most famous and most extravagant of the summer cottages. The line moves fast, but the best time to come is first thing in the morning or near the end of the day.
- Reserve well in advance if you want to dine in the better-known restaurants on weekends.
- If you plan to leave by the Newport-Jamestown Bridge at peak times during the summer, ask if your innkeeper will sell you a token to considerably shorten your wait at the toll booth.

WHERE TO STAY

Elm Tree Cottage

The amount of common space for the guests is extraordinary in this large gray shingle-style mansion built in 1882 on a street of large homes two blocks from the beach. The innkeepers are Tom and Priscilla Malone. The large living room has a wall of windows overlooking the back gardens, a pair of white couches, and two pianos. The adjoining morning room is more casual, with wicker furniture covered with pillows. Be sure to notice the two round stained-glass windows in the pub and the stained-glass pieces throughout the home, all of which were made by the Malones. The attention to detail and fine quality is evident throughout the inn.

The Windsor Suite, a 1,000-square-foot room overlooking the back of the inn with a carved Louis XV headboard, king-size bed, fireplace, television, CD player, and large bath, is truly sumptuous. Room 4, with a fireplace, sitting area, and king-size bed, is the second most requested room. Room 5 has a

The Eustis room is one example of the fine quality and attention to detail at Elm Tree Cottage.

king-size bed, a fireplace, and a bath with a double-size soaking tub. Room 2 has a more masculine, equestrian feel with a fireplace, a queen-size bed, and a bath with a shower and separate tub. Room 3, a smaller, feminine room, has a queen-size bed with a canopy crown. The Library, a first-floor room, has a fireplace and a smaller bath with a shower.

Priscilla is known for her beautifully prepared and presented breakfasts, served from 8:30 to 9:45 A.M. at individual tables in the formal dining room. They include a cold buffet plus a hot entrée such as eggs Benedict, eggs in a phyllo nest, orange waffles, or French toast soufflé.

The Malones have three daughters (Keely, Briana, and Erin) and run a stained-glass studio on the bottom floor of their home.

Five rooms and one suite. May through October $175–$325. November through April $115–$295. Breakfast included. Children over 14 welcome, rooms are double occupancy only. No smoking. No pets. Two- to three-night weekend minimum. 336 Gibbs Avenue, Newport, RI 02840; (401) 849-1610; (888) ELM-TREE (toll free).

Cliffside Inn

This turreted Victorian on a quiet residential street is close to the famed Cliff Walk. The mansion is filled with breathtakingly lavish rooms and suites all

Cliffside Inn is filled with lavish rooms and suites.

with phones, televisions, and VCRs. Eleven rooms have both fireplaces and double whirlpools. Throughout the house are more than 100 copies or originals of paintings by Beatrice Turner, a reclusive artist who painted over 3,000 works, including more than 1,000 self-portraits, and who lived here until her death in 1948.

The two-level Garden Suite is a spectacular space with an entrance off the front porch. The upper-floor bedroom has a fireplace and a narrow iron spiral staircase leading to the lower level with a floor of stunning pink Peruvian limestone, the largest double whirlpool in the inn facing a second fireplace, and a private patio. Other top choices are the Tower Suite, a two-floor suite with a twenty-five-foot turret tower; the Governor's Suite, with the largest bedroom, a double-sided fireplace that you can see from the bed and from the double whirlpool, and an antique birdcage shower that sprays water out of four circular bars; and Miss Beatrice's Room, with a bath as large as many rooms with a double whirlpool set in front of the bay window.

The Seaview Cottage, a ranch-style house next to the inn, contains two spectacular suites with a cathedral ceiling. The Cliff Suite, with a king-size bed, double-sided fireplace, large living room, and bath with a double whirlpool tub, is somewhat larger than the Atlantic Suite. Even the lower-priced smaller rooms without the whirlpools are lovely, with the same attention to detail.

Don't miss the Victorian tea, which includes superb pastries such as éclairs, tarts, scones, tea sandwiches, cookies, and cake all made by the inn's chef. This is one of the best teas we've ever had at an inn.

A tray of coffee or tea and juice is brought to your room before breakfast. A full breakfast is served from 8 to 10 A.M. in the parlor at two large tables. It includes a hot dish such as a croissant sandwich with scrambled eggs and sausage, banana-filled crepes, or almond French toast.

Fifteen rooms and suites, all with private bath, $175–$325. Breakfast and afternoon tea included. Children over 13 welcome. No smoking. No pets. Two- to three-night weekend minimum. 2 Seaview Avenue, Newport, RI 02840; (401) 847-1811; (800) 845-1811.

The Francis Malbone House

This 1760 Colonial mansion located in the heart of busy Thames Street, the central tourist artery of Newport, is a good choice if you want to be in the middle of the action close to the waterfront. In the 1970s the house was meticulously restored and in 1990 it opened as an inn. The owners have just added the two-story Carriage House, with nine additional rooms on two floors designed to blend into the existing structure. There is a central courtyard with a fountain and a brick-paved enclosed colonnade connecting the old and new buildings.

The original building has three common sitting rooms, each with a wood-burning fireplace. The best accommodation is the Counting House, a thirty-three-foot-long room with a king-size four-poster bed and a bath with a double whirlpool tub. Second- and third-floor harbor-front rooms have partial views of the waterfront, queen-size beds, and fireplaces. All of the rooms in the Carriage House have king-size beds, fireplaces, and televisions; seven of the nine rooms have double whirlpool tubs. First-floor rooms 1 and 2 as well as rooms 3 and 4 each share a common courtyard, making these good choices for two couples traveling together. The Courtyard Suite is a larger room with a wet bar.

The breakfast room has four tables seating ten guests each. The main course changes daily: eggs Benedict, stuffed French toast, eggs in puff pastry, or peach crepes.

Eighteen rooms and suites, $165–$325. Breakfast included. Children over 12 welcome. No smoking. No pets. Two- to three-night weekend minimum. 392 Thames Street, Newport RI 02840; (401) 846-0392; (800) 846-0392.

Castle Hill Inn & Resort

This rambling 1874 shingled Victorian mansion, located five miles from the center of Newport on a forty-acre promontory overlooking the Atlantic Ocean, has one of the finest locations on the East Coast. In the morning you wake to the muffled crash of the surf against the rocks and a private view of the yachts sailing in and out of Newport harbor. A deep foghorn warns mariners from the working lighthouse on the property.

The first floor of the inn includes four dining rooms, a bar that commands an impressive view of the water, and a lobby sitting room.

Be aware of dramatic variations in the size and type of accommodations. We recommend one of the six large rooms that face the water, as well as the suite in the main inn and the first-floor suite in the chalet. Room 6 has a large bay window offering panoramic water views; room 7 is completely wood-paneled, including the ceiling; room 9 on the third floor has a full front water view; room 10 is a suite with a very large sitting room and a wood-paneled bedroom. We do not recommend the three small rooms that share a bath and a half, as they are above the kitchen.

The chalet (the former laboratory of the original owner, Dr. Agassiz) has a magnificent first-floor suite, often used for conferences, that recently was redecorated. Harbor House is a motel unit of six simply furnished rooms, all with porches with water views. Beach cottages with decks are available for guests who want to stay right on the water and do their own cooking, and who don't mind rustic accommodations.

Inn, chalet, and Harbor House: twenty-one rooms and suites, fifteen with private bath. June through October $115–$325. Other times $65–$180. Two-night weekend minimum. Beach Cottages: 18 units $750–$850 weekly, available nightly in the off-season. Breakfast included except in the cottages. Children over 12 welcome in the inn. No pets. Ocean Drive, Newport, RI 02840; (401) 849-3800.

Rhode Island House

This bed-and-breakfast is located along a street of large Victorian homes built between 1881 and 1884. Owners and innkeepers Michael Dupré and John Rich, who have owned the home since 1993, have left most of the first floor as common space for the guests' use. The drawing room with a multipaned bay window and wood-burning fireplace is particularly inviting. Michael, who is also a caterer, worked for five years as chef for Mrs. Auchincloss, Jacqueline Kennedy Onassis's mother, at Hammersmith Farm.

The five large rooms are all on the second floor. The Hunter Room has a private terrace overlooking the garden, a large bedroom with a fireplace, and a room with a double whirlpool tub. The Auchincloss Room, the largest room, has a fireplace, a room with a larger double whirlpool tub, and a bath with a separate shower. Both the Garden Room, a bright, cheerful room with a multipaned window behind the bed, and the Mary Kay Room have a fireplace.

An excellent breakfast, served at individual tables from 8:30 to 10 A.M., includes three courses: fresh fruit cup, a bread course such as blueberry bread pudding, and a main course such as an omelette, eggs Benedict, or waffles.

Five rooms, all with private bath. May through mid-October $175–$225; other times $155–$175. Breakfast included. Children over 12 welcome, rooms are double occupancy only. No smoking. No pets. Two- to three-night weekend minimum. 77 Rhode Island Avenue, Newport RI 02840; (401) 848-7787.

The Old Beach Inn

This large Victorian home and the carriage house, separated by a lovely garden, are owned and operated by Cynthia and Luke Murray. Luke, who has been the manager at the prestigious Black Pearl restaurant for many years, is well informed about the Newport restaurant scene. As both Cynthia and Luke have outside jobs and two young sons, the inn has less innkeeper presence than other inns. The first floor of the inn has two living rooms with fireplaces. The garden has a gazebo with wicker chairs that overlooks a nicely landscaped lily pond with a fountain.

Five of the rooms have fireplaces, two of which are gas fireplaces. The most popular is the Rose Room, with a queen-size canopy bed draped with lace and chintz. The Ivy Room has a double-size cottage bed and a fireplace stove. Forget-Me-Not, Morning Glory, and Wisteria, the latter two with gas fireplaces, all have queen-size beds. Two additional rooms are located in the Carriage House, which is across the garden from the main inn.

Breakfast includes fresh-squeezed orange juice, fruit, yogurt, granola, and bakery items. Guests can sit in the dining room or outside at the umbrella-topped tables in the large garden.

Nine rooms, all with private bath. April through October $135–$165. Other times $100–$135.

Continental breakfast included. Children over 12 welcome. No smoking. No pets. Two- to three-weekend minimum. 19 Old Beach Road, Newport RI 02840; (401) 849-3479; (888) 303-5033 (toll free).

Ivy Lodge

Each time we walk in the front door of Ivy Lodge we catch our breath and marvel at the soaring thirty-three-foot Gothic oak entry hall with wraparound hall and balconies on the second and third floors.

Maggie and Terry Moy are the owners and innkeepers of this 1886 Queen Anne Victorian located just one block off Bellevue Avenue in the mansion area, about a five-minute walk to the most spectacular section of the Cliff Walk, at Narragansett Avenue and the famous Forty Steps. The large living room, furnished with a pair of green-and-white couches and a grand piano, opens onto a wicker-filled porch overlooking the yard.

Our favorite guest room is the Library, a first-floor room with a gas fireplace and a bath with a double whirlpool tub. The largest room is the Turret Room, with a king-size bed, a nook with two chairs, and a large private hall bath. The second floor Ivy Room has a queen-size four-poster bed and a private bath.

The two-bedroom family suite offers the most privacy. One room has a queen-size sleigh bed and the second room has twin beds.

A buffet breakfast, served at 9 A.M. at one long table, includes fruit, juice, granola, pastries, and a hot dish such as oatmeal soufflé, blueberry pancakes, stuffed French toast, or various egg casseroles.

Eight rooms, seven with private bath. May through October $125–$165,

other times $85–$125. Children welcome. Breakfast and tea included. No
smoking. No pets. Two-night weekend minimum. 12 Clay Street, Newport, RI
02840; (401) 849-6865.

Sanford-Covell Villa Marina

This waterfront Victorian mansion located in the Point section of Newport, one
of America's great restored Colonial areas, has been in innkeeper Anne Ram-
sey Cuvelier's family for over 100 years. The favorite summer spot is the wraparound porch with wicker chairs that looks out onto Narragansett Bay, a view
that reminded us of breezy summer porch scenes painted at the end of the
nineteenth century. A heated saltwater pool with a whirlpool at one end overlooks the water just below the porch. The views of the water from the pool,
the porch, or from one of the waterfront rooms are what make this bed-and-
breakfast special.

The entryway soars a dramatic thirty-five feet with wood-paneled walls and
decorative arts on the walls and ceiling. The Covell Room is a corner water-
view room with a private bath. The Virginia Covell Room has a small kitchen
and shares the shower with the Sanford Room. All three of these rooms have
wood-burning fireplaces.

The Dolphin Room, a first-floor room (and a former porch), has a full front
fabulous water view, but only a tiny bath. The lower level of the home is a two-
bedroom apartment.

Travelers who want a large private bath should be sure to ask for one; even
some of the best rooms with wonderful water views have shared baths, very
small baths, or such arrangements as a tub behind a screen in the bedroom
and a closet converted to hold a toilet and sink. If you have an interest in the
history of the house, check if Anne will be there during your visit; she generally spends the spring-to-fall season in Newport and the winter in San Francisco.

Nine rooms, four with private bath, and a two-bedroom apartment. Mid-
May through mid-October, rooms $125–$225, apartment $295. Other times,
rooms $75–$150, apartment $195. Continental breakfast included. Children
welcome. No smoking. Pets permitted in some rooms. Two-night weekend
minimum. 72 Washington Street, Newport RI 02840; (401) 847-0206.

Rose Island Lighthouse

Lighthouse buffs and the more adventuresome can spend the night in a lighthouse in the middle of Narragansett Bay just south of the Newport-Jamestown
Bridge. The lighthouse is operated by a nonprofit citizens group as an
environmental education center whose aim is to teach conservation, preservation, and personal responsibility. The lighthouse is open year-round and has
radiant in-floor heating. There is no electricity on the first floor and no showers. Guests do their own cooking and must bring all of their own food. Bedding
is provided. The two small rooms on the first floor have antique double beds

with down comforters and Oriental rugs. The second-floor keeper's apartment is rented by the week and includes daily chores.

Birders will want to come in early spring to mid-July to see great and snowy egrets, glossy ibis, little blue and black-crowned herons, and American oyster-catchers, as well as more common shore birds. During the nesting period guests are restricted to certain parts of the sixteen-acre island. You can go swimming from the shore, and a kayak is available. In the winter, harbor seals come to feed on the eel grass beds.

Two rooms. May through September, weekends $140, weekdays $125. Other times $20 less. Apartment, April through November $700; other times $400. Children welcome. Museum open mid-July through Labor Day or by appointment. The office is at 365 Thames Street, P.O. Box 1419, Newport, RI 02840; (401) 847-4242 (weekdays 9 A.M. to 1 P.M). Send self-addressed stamped envelope for brochure.

Doubletree Islander Hotel

This is the ideal choice for travelers who want to stay on the water, have the creature comforts of a hotel, be close to the center of Newport, but feel miles away from the crowds. This fine resort hotel and conference center is situated on Goat Island, about a ten-minute walk from the main harbor area. The large Doubletree chocolate chip cookies at check-in are a signature of this hotel group.

The hotel has three sections connected by covered corridors: the main eight-story section, the Captains Quarters (the newest, and generally the section with the best rooms), and the four-story Lighthouse Wing. For a room that is the closest to the ocean with a full front water view, ask for a third-floor king room in the Captains Quarters section.

Duplex suites are located in the Lighthouse Wing and in the Captains Quarters. The first floor has a full bath and a living room with a sleeper sofa and balcony. The second floor has a king-size bed and a second full bath. The six suites in the Captains Quarters are larger but have a spiral metal staircase.

Standard rooms have two double beds or a king-size bed. Some of the standard rooms have windows that only overlook the indoor pool, which would not be our choice.

Outdoors, you'll find a saltwater pool and two tennis courts. Inside, there's a large pool under a glass roof with a poolside bar, two racquetball courts, a health club with a beauty salon, and a small exercise room. A huge conference center was just added to the hotel. They have a shuttle bus to the wharf area.

Two hundred fifty-three rooms and suites, each with private bath. Mid-June through August, rooms $169–$284; suites (one- and two-bedroom) $375–$550. Rooms drop to a low of $89–$164, suites $200 during the winter and spring. All meals available. Children welcome. No pets. Fourteen-day advance purchase nonrefundable rate available for standard rooms. Call the hotel directly to inquire about packages and special rates (especially in the off-season). No required minimum stay. Goat Island, Newport, RI 02840; (401) 849-2600; (800) 222-TREE (central reservation).

Marriott

The rooms at this centrally located hotel, next to Long Wharf and the Gateway Information Center, wrap around a six-story central atrium. Rooms overlook the atrium, the city (or parking lot), or have partial harbor views. The top-priced rooms are the rooms on the concierge floor (city view only) and the deluxe rooms, which have partial harbor views or balconies that overlook the atrium. The rooms on the seventh (conciérge) floor all have city views; the lounge has the harbor view. Continental breakfast (7 to 10 A.M.), hors d'oeuvres (6 to 8 P.M.) and desserts (9 to 10 P.M.) are offered daily during the peak season only.

Standard rooms overlook the city or parking lot or have an interior view of the atrium only. There is a hallway outside these rooms, so the blinds need to be kept closed at all times for privacy. Suites all have double whirlpool tubs.

The hotel has an indoor pool and a health and fitness spa, which includes three racquetball courts, sauna and steam rooms, a free weights room, and Universal and other exercise machines. Massages are available. The hotel has a harborside restaurant and a nightclub.

Three hundred twelve rooms and seven suites, each with private bath. Late May through October, weekends $229–$269, weekdays $199–$239. Suites $400–$850. November through mid-May $84–$134. Two for Breakfast package available in the winter, $89. Children welcome. No pets. No required minimum stay. 25 America's Cup Avenue, Newport, RI 02840; (800) 228-9290; (401) 849-1000.

Taylor-Made Reservations

Karen Taylor, the owner, and her staff have seen all 128 properties they represent in Newport, Middletown, and Portsmouth. There is no charge for the service. The cancellation policy is that of the particular inn or hotel. Prices for inns and bed-and-breakfasts in Newport start at $125 and hotels/motels start at $99. Middletown and Portsmouth offer lower prices in season. All inns and hotels have two-night minimums on weekends in season; (800) 848-8848.

Newport Gateway Visitors Center

The center posts a list of the current day's available rooms. They can give names and phone numbers but will not give opinions. (401) 849-8048; (800) 326-6030.

WHERE TO DINE

The Place at Yesterday's

If you like creative new American cuisine and want to see what is on the cutting edge in Newport, make reservations for the Place, the fine-dining side of this restaurant. The front of the room is a large wraparound dining bar. The rest of the room is on two levels separated by a brass rail. The informal side of the restaurant is called Yesterday's, which serves more traditional pub fare. If you like beer, there are thirty-six on tap, and a sampler of four seven-ounce brews is served in an attractive wood rack.

One of chef Alex Dagliss's creations is lobster-and-shrimp chowder with sweet corn and pancetta. We also highly recommend the crab ravioli filled with crabmeat, ginger, and chèvre served on shredded cabbage.

The two most popular entrées are the pan-seared red snapper served with lobster and guava sauces over black and white angel-hair pasta, and the loin of lamb with a pecan crust topped with a mound of fried shredded sweet potato. Portions are particularly generous; we suggest sharing such desserts as chocolate crepes filled with cinnamon ice cream covered with chocolate ganache or peach bread pudding.

Dinner, Tuesday through Sunday, also on Monday July through September. Entrées $15–$24. Yesterday's open daily lunch and dinner. 28 Washington Square, Newport; (401) 847-0116.

Scales and Shells and UpScales

As we wandered down lower Thames Street, the delicious aroma of spicy garlic tomato sauce lured us to this storefront restaurant. Andy Ackerman artfully directs his staff in a culinary performance on eighteen burners in full view of his casually dressed patrons. The overhead racks of frying pans, the charcoal grill, the deep-fry area, and piles of fresh seafood along one wall of the restaurant likewise offered clear testimony to the no-nonsense dining found here.

You'll see no written menu, just a large blackboard that lists an enticing array of offerings—with nary a choice for the non–seafood lover. Lobster fra diavalo (thick, spicy tomato sauce peppered with clams, mussels, squid, and lobster) is served over linguine and comes to your table in a steaming hot pan. Littlenecks Roberto, Sicilian clams and mussels, scampi, calamari, scallops Marsala, mesquite-grilled swordfish, salmon, and monkfish were some of the other choices the day we visited. Marinated grilled toro tuna, the fatty underbelly of the fish and an expensive delicacy in sushi bars, is a specialty of this restaurant.

On a crowded night the noise level can be annoying, as the bar, kitchen, and dining areas are all in one room. The lines are long on summer weekends, so get here early or be prepared to wait.

The second floor houses UpScales, which is presided over by Deborah

Ackerman, the other half of the husband-and-wife team. Here the atmosphere is more serene, the tables are covered with linen, and reservations are accepted.

Dinner daily, entrées $9–$20. Reservations accepted at UpScales (open seasonally). No smoking. 527 Thames Street, Newport; (401) 846-FISH.

Puerini's

We have a soft spot for Northern Italian trattorias. Of course, the restaurant should be small and personal, with whitewashed walls, and serve good, strong espresso. We're not going to make it to Italy this year, but we're satisfied with the next best thing: a superb meal at Puerini's. That's the good news. The bad news is that we're not alone in our quest for authentic Italian cuisine and atmosphere. Don't be surprised to find a two-hour wait for a table here on a Friday, Saturday, or Sunday night in the summer. The first floor has a waiting room and one dining room, with two additional rooms upstairs.

The portions are generous. Split the antipasto salad or an order of sweet red roasted peppers in oil and garlic served with chunks of provolone.

All the pasta is homemade by the Puerini family. Dishes we like include lightly breaded chicken breast stuffed with fontina cheese, pignoli nuts, and marinated artichoke hearts; layers of spinach pasta with vegetables, cheeses, and the family's secret tomato sauce; littleneck clams sautéed with olive oil, garlic, and spinach served with penne; and thin swordfish with a seafood stuffing and choice of pesto or manicotti. The memory of all those wonderful tastes and smells, the reasonable prices, and the friendly attitude are good reasons for the success of this family-run restaurant over many years.

Dinner daily. Entrées $9–$15. No reservations. 24 Memorial Boulevard, Newport; (401) 847-5506.

The Black Pearl

This small, shingled "shack" on Bannister's Wharf has been accorded something akin to cult status, especially for the nighttime seatings in its intimate Commodore Room. Outside the restaurant are the intriguing sights and sounds of the harbor. Inside, waiters hover over well-dressed patrons, and candlelight flickers off the plaster walls. The stage is set for a memorable meal. You'll find nothing of the "new American cuisine" here, just the very best of traditional dining and a superb wine list, especially of properly aged Bordeaux and Burgundy. While the food is superb, the low ceiling and closely spaced keep the noise level high.

Start with the famous clam chowder, thick with clams, which also is available to take home (fresh or frozen). We asked for a thick piece of swordfish and received one that was two inches high and wonderfully tasty. The striped bass recommended by our waiter was a moist, large portion. Other top choices are the rack of lamb and the aged Black Angus New York sirloin.

The front of the building is an informal tavern. Black enamel walls decorated with nautical charts, floors worn from years of use, side windows, and a packed bar complete the scene. Tables on the dock are available seasonally.

The Commodore Room (jacket required) is open daily for dinner, entrées $18–$35. The Tavern is open daily for lunch, $5–$19 and dinner entrées $6–$23. Bannister's Wharf, Newport; (401) 846-5264.

White Horse Tavern

Come here and immerse yourself in the atmosphere of America's oldest tavern, built in 1687. Both the exterior, with its maroon clapboard walls and gambrel roof, and the interior, featuring giant exposed beams and immense fireplaces, have been impeccably restored by the Preservation Society of Newport. It is indeed a pleasure to walk the old, wide-plank floors and enjoy the large bouquets of fresh flowers as you are led to your table. With three fireplaces in the bar, the main dining room, and the second floor, the tavern burns a cord and a half of wood a week. The service is impeccable and the atmosphere makes it an ideal spot for winter dining.

The menu of traditional fare includes grilled breast of duck with maple-glazed potatoes, veal tenderloin layered with roasted garlic potatoes and braised spinach, individual beef Wellington, chateaubriand for two, New York sirloin, rack of lamb, bouillabaisse, sautéed lobster served over black pasta, sliced breast of chicken with black bean salsa and a tortilla salad, baked salmon, and poached sole with rock shrimp and spinach risotto. Men must wear a jacket and tie at night.

To enjoy the atmosphere without the high dinner prices, come for lunch. The menu includes a tavern burger, a club sandwich, a grilled chicken breast sandwich, and smaller portions of many entrées served in the evening.

Lunch, Wednesday through Monday, entrées $9–$17. Dinner nightly, entrées $23–$33. Marlborough and Farewell Streets, Newport; (401) 849-3600.

Pronto

This intimate corner storefront restaurant on busy Thames Street has a Victorian feel. The door and large windows are open in warm weather so you can watch the people out strolling. The decor includes the owners' collection of eight different glass chandeliers, as well as tin walls and ceiling and good-quality oil paintings. The kitchen is open to view.

For a first course we shared sliced wild mushrooms sautéed in a light flavorful veal broth topped with a Brie-filled puff pastry triangle. Other options for starters are steamed mussels, a grilled portabella mushroom with Gorgonzola and polenta, and a classic antipasto.

The menu includes about six pasta dishes, which offer a lower-priced alternative to the high-priced entrées. Grilled tuna with coconut-flavored jasmine rice; bow-tie pasta with shiitake mushrooms, sun-dried tomatoes, pine nuts, spinach, and chèvre; pan-seared salmon with spinach and ginger risotto; rack of lamb; and blue-corn-encrusted soft-shell crabs are selected entrées.

An upstairs dining room is used on the weekends and for jazz on Thursday nights.

Daily, lunch, $6–$14; dinner, entrées $11–$25. 464 Thames Street, Newport; (401) 847-5251.

Cooke House (formerly Clarke Cooke House)

Bannister's Wharf, jam-packed with tourists during the summer, has two very popular restaurants adjacent to each other: the Black Pearl and Cooke House. For fine dining at Cooke House in the summer, try for the second-floor porch, which has a fine view of the harbor; there's also a second-floor candlelit dining room. Specialties include lobster and wild mushroom ravioli and entrées of grilled Block Island swordfish and roast rack of lamb with caramelized onions.

The downstairs of this 1790s building is more informal. It includes the Candy Store and Grill Room, which has a working fireplace. The wood-grilled pizzas are popular, and a full menu is available.

Daily, lunch, $12–$18. Dinner, downstairs, entrées $12–$18; upstairs entrées $18–$25. Bannister's Wharf, Newport; (401) 849-2900.

Castle Hill Inn

This has to be one of the finest oceanfront locations in New England. The inn is on forty acres overlooking the Atlantic Ocean and the entrance to Newport Harbor. When the fog rolls in you can hear the drone of the bell from the lighthouse on the rocky promontory several hundred yards from the inn. The first floor of the inn has been completely refurbished. The rich butternut and pine woodwork was cleaned and lightened, new carpets and furniture added, and the four fireplaces on the first floor are now in working order. Of the four dining rooms, our preference is the Sunset Room, a curved bright room with large windows on three sides, as well as the outdoor terrace with water views.

Lunch selections include lobster salad or pan-seared salmon served in a croissant, sole cooked in parchment, steamed mussels, and lemon farfel with grilled chicken.

Entrées from the dinner menu include steamed lobster with vanilla butter; grilled lobster tail with a profiterole of leek, lobster, and mushrooms; barbecued veal sweetbreads with smoked bacon spoon bread; and Black Angus sirloin with horseradish mashed potatoes.

The dining room closes at the end of October, but the wood-paneled bar is open Friday through Sunday. We can imagine this would be a great place in a storm, with the fireplace burning, the wind howling, and the seas pounding.

Lunch, mid-May through October, Tuesday through Saturday, $7–$16. Sunday brunch, entrées $15. Dinner, Monday through Saturday, mid-April through October, entrées $19–$30. Ocean Drive, Newport; (401) 849-3800.

The West Deck

The restaurant is on the water at the end of Waites Wharf off lower Thames. There's a parking lot on the wharf. The blue-and-white tent next to the water covers a large deck with a bar, a party scene throughout the warm weather with loud music and crowds.

Inside there are two dining rooms. One, a new addition made from a porch, is the more formal, and is often used for groups. The main dining room, our preference, includes a large horseshoe-shaped eating bar that wraps around the open kitchen. At your ringside seats you can kibitz with the chefs, and watch as they work as a team. Yellowfin tuna with lemon basil oil and swordfish with Jamaican jerk sauce, our choices, were garnished with a sampling of eight vegetables. Potato crusted salmon with mushroom duxelle, grilled filet mignon with Stilton, rack of lamb, and a mixed grill were other entrées available the night we dined.

Dinner, Wednesday through Sunday, entrées $14–$27. Outside deck open in season daily from noon. 1 Waites Wharf, Newport; (401) 847-3610.

Asterix & Obelix

This hip restaurant is located in a former garage in the quiet section of lower Thames Street. Its trendy decor features large abstract paintings on mustard-colored cinder-block walls and well-worn Oriental carpets on the orange cement floor. Two large overhead garage doors, kept open on warm days (there is no air-conditioning), are reminders of the restaurant's past. Outside there are umbrella-topped tables.

The brunch/lunch menu includes eggs Copenhagen (poached eggs with smoked salmon and hollandaise sauce); raisin bread French toast; pizzas with toppings of pesto and grilled shrimp, or bianco with garlic and cheese; and penne with shrimp, pesto, and sun-dried tomatoes.

The dinner menu is more inventive. Appetizers include seared tuna with oriental vegetables, shrimp spring rolls with peanut sauce, mussels marinière, and arugula and celery root salad with portabella mushroom. Entrées include grilled tuna au poivre, grilled shrimp with salmon brandade, sirloin Stroganoff, medallions of lamb with mushroom mashed potatoes, and linguine with little-necks, tomatoes, and roasted peppers.

Open daily, lunch, $6–$15, and dinner, entrées $15–$28. 599 Thames Street, Newport; (401) 841-8833.

La Forge Casino

You can sit on the porch or outside under umbrella-topped tables alongside a perfectly manicured grass court and feel transported to 1890, when this was a private club for Newport society. Within this complex are a number of grass courts, the only ones in the country open to the public.

While the restaurant has a number of rooms, we recommend a table on the porch or outside where you can see the court and possibly watch an expert tennis player. The menu features traditional salads and sandwiches such as grilled chicken Caesar salad, cobb salad, lobster salad, milkshakes, and hot fudge sundaes.

Millions of dollars have gone into the recent sprucing up of the Tennis Hall of Fame located within this complex across from the restaurant.

Daily, lunch and dinner, $7–$15. 186 Bellevue Avenue, Newport; (401) 847-0418.

Canfield House

At the end of the nineteenth century this lavish interior of dark paneled walls, stained glass, and vaulted twenty-foot ceilings was a casino for the wealthy Newport summer crowd. Today, under new management, this large dining room is fast becoming one of the best in Newport. The Caesar salad is served in an edible Parmesan basket; the oysters are coated with blue corn meal and grilled; caramelized eggplant is filled with ricotta, smoked Gouda, and andouille sausage and grilled over wood.

Entrées include pan-seared lobster served over a baked portabella mushroom with Parmesan scallion fettuccine. A mixed grill of shrimp, scallops, and swordfish comes with a tomato salsa, basil oil, and chive cream. For dessert don't miss the chef's special, a superb flourless chocolate cake.

Dinner daily, entrées $14–$23. Memorial Boulevard, Newport; (401) 847-0416.

Flo's Clam Shack, Middletown

Located across the road from Easton's Beach (First Beach), Flo's has been a Newport institution since 1936. Line up at the counter and order fried whole clams, calamari, scallops, shrimp, onion rings, lobster and clam rolls, hot dogs, hamburgers, and clamcakes (golfball-size fried dough made with bits of clams). Sit on the first floor or on the outside deck on the second floor. Come to the second-floor raw bar in the late afternoon for raw clams and oysters and beer and look at the pictures on the walls of proud fishermen with their catch of large striped bass.

Daily, lunch through dinner. Thursday through Sunday in the spring and fall. Aquidnick Avenue, Middletown (parking lot is off Wave Avenue); (401) 847-8141.

Trattoria Simpatico, Jamestown

If you are tired of the hectic summer pace of Newport, cross the bridge to Jamestown and enter a quiet summer community. This restaurant, located just up the street from the water, is well worth the round-trip bridge toll. There's an outdoor bar and small tables set up on the grass, where you can order grilled items and some of the appetizers from the regular menu. For the most creative menu, eat inside. In nice weather we liked the garden room, with screened windows that overlook the outdoor dining area. The front of the restaurant has two rooms.

Portions are oversize. Fried calamari is tossed in a spicy vinaigrette. A meaty grilled portabella mushroom cap is topped with roasted pepper and served over spinach.

Tuna, a special of the day, was a very generous portion served on a bed of spinach and topped with a nectarine salsa. Bucatini, a pasta, mixed with scallops, spinach, peppers, and shredded cheese was excellent and more than we could handle. The restaurant has live jazz most of the year on Thursday evenings and on Sunday afternoons.

Lunch, Wednesday through Sunday, $7–$11. Dinner, nightly, entrées $16–$23. 13 Narragansett Avenue, Jamestown; (401) 423-3731.

The Newport Local Scene

Ocean Coffee Roasters and Wave Cafe. This is a favorite hangout of the locals, city politicians, and the Generation X crowd. The coffee is strong and is by far the best we've found in Newport. It is also sold by the pound, so you might want to stock up before you head home. The scones, bagels, and pastries make a good accompaniment for a light breakfast or a midafternoon snack. When we stay at one of the hotels where breakfast is not included we like to take an early morning walk around town followed by breakfast here. A low-priced full menu is available throughout the day.

Open daily, 7 A.M. to 10 P.M. Washington Square, Newport; (401) 846-6060.

The Market on the Boulevard. Need a picnic lunch to take to the beach? Stop at this large gourmet grocery store for a wonderful sandwich or salad.

Daily, 8 A.M. to 8 P.M. Sandwiches $5–$6. 43 Memorial Boulevard, Newport; (401) 848-2600.

The Salvation Cafe. Broadway is the center of Newport for the year-round residents. City hall and elementary schools are here, and so is the Salvation Army thrift store, where owner Sue Lamond got some of the decor for her funky '60s-style restaurant that appeals to a young local crowd. Sit at Formica-topped tables and order from a blackboard menu. The portions are huge and low-priced. Choices generally include some Asian noodle dishes and jerk chicken or pork.

Daily dinner, entrées $8–$13. Sunday brunch. Bring your own wine. 140 Broadway, Newport; (401) 847-2620.

Tuckers. This restaurant has a 1920s Paris bistro ambience with glazed red walls, antique lamps on the tables, and grapevine wreaths with tiny lights on the ceiling. Walls are covered with mirrors and lots of pictures. Try the calamari with a spicy jalapeño and butter sauce or the grilled portabella mushroom served over sautéed spinach covered with caramelized balsamic vinegar.

The pasta specials are usually very good. Shrimp soaked in rum is grilled and served with a mango relish or dipped in beer batter, rolled in coconut, deep-fried and served with a horseradish marmalade sauce.

Dinner, daily, entrées $11–$17. Bring your own wine. A local liquor store will deliver to your table. 150 Broadway, Newport; (401) 846-3449.

ITINERARY

DAY ONE. Head to the **Breakers** for a tour before it gets crowded, then take the Ten-Mile **Ocean Drive.** Have lunch at **Castle Hill Inn,** followed by a tour of **Hammersmith Farm**. Dine at **Scales and Shells** on lower Thames Street or at the **Black Pearl** on Bannister's Wharf.

DAY TWO. Head to **Marble House** for a tour, then to one of the other mansions on Bellevue Avenue. Lunch at **La Forge Restaurant** at the Casino, where you might see a tennis match. In the afternoon, take a tour of the **Samuel Whitehorne House Museum** on Thames Street. Browse through the stores on Thames Street. For dinner, go to the **Place at Yesterday's.**

DAY THREE. Park your car at the end of Narragansett Avenue and walk south on the **Cliff Walk.** Try to get as far as Marble House, as the view of the teahouse from here is spectacular. Have lunch at **White Horse Tavern** either before or after a walking tour with **Newport on Foot,** which explores the Colonial Point section. Stop in at **Touro Synagogue, Quaker Meeting House** and **Trinity Church.** For dinner we suggest **Puerini**'s or **Pronto.**

DAY FOUR. Head out to the country. Stop at **Prescott Farm** if the mill is working, then head to **Green Animals.** Pick up a lunch at **Provender** and picnic at **Sakonnet Vineyards** or have lunch at **Olga's Cup and Saucer** in **Little Compton.** Stop in at **Gray's Store** and **Gray's Gristmill** next door to buy some ground cornmeal or the excellent pancake mix. Walk around **Little Compton** and drive out to **Sakonnet Point.** Have dinner at the **West Deck** on Waites Wharf.

DAY FIVE. Tour another of the mansions or **Hunter House.** Then visit the **Astors' Beechwood.** Have lunch at the **Wave Cafe** and then take a sail on one of the schooners—the **Adirondack** or the **Madeleine.** For a quiet dinner, drive to Jamestown to the **Trattoria Simpatico.**

BUDGETING YOUR TRIP

To help you get the most for the time and money you have to spend, here are some travel suggestions at three budget levels (cost per day with two people sharing a room), including lodging and meal tax, gratuity on meals, and service charge when it is added to your bill. Prices on lodgings are based on peak rates. Prices are approximate and are intended for planning purposes only.

Lodgings are categorized by price and depending on the room selected may appear in more than one category. Meal prices at lunch include an average entrée and beverage. Dinner prices include an appetizer, entrée, dessert, and beverage. Wine or alcoholic beverages are not included.

Staying and dining at expensive lodgings and restaurants: From $330 to $600 per day for two.

Lodging: Elm Tree Cottage, Francis Malbone, Cliffside, Castle Hill, Sanford-Covell, Rhode Island House, Marriott, Doubletree.

Dining: Breakfast: included except at Marriott, Doubletree. Lunch: White Horse Tavern, Black Pearl, Cooke House, Castle Hill. Dinner: White Horse Tavern, Black Pearl (Commodore), Cooke House (upstairs), Castle Hill, Asterix & Obelix.

Staying and dining at moderately priced lodgings and restaurants: From $240 to $340 for two.

Lodging: Old Beach Inn, Sanford-Covell, Ivy Lodge, Rhode Island House, Castle Hill, Francis Malbone, Cliffside, Elm Tree Cottage.

Dining: Breakfast: included. Lunch: Pronto, Asterix & Obelix, La Forge Casino, Trattoria Simpatico. Dinner: Trattoria Simpatico, Pronto, the Place, Canfield's.

Staying and dining at less expensive lodgings and restaurants: From $170 to $240 per day for two.

Lodging: Castle Hill, Rose Island Lighthouse.

Dining: Breakfast included; bring your own food to Rose Island. Lunch: Wave Cafe, Flo's Clam Shack, the Market. Dinner: the West Deck, Scales and Shells, Black Pearl Tavern, Tuckers, Salvation Cafe, Flo's Clam Shack, Wave Cafe.

12

Cape Cod, Massachusetts

When you come over the last hill on the road to Provincetown, the sky suddenly seems to open. On your right, with the Atlantic Ocean in the distance, the muted colors of the moors are reflected in Pilgrim Lake. On your left, the symmetrical rows of nearly identical cottages facing Cape Cod Bay look like wooden soldiers standing at attention. Alongside the road, sand from great shifting dunes drifts onto the pavement, a visible reminder of the ever-changing contours of the land. Silhouetted against the horizon, a monument that looks like a large Italian bell tower comes into view as the outline of Provincetown's eighteenth- and nineteenth-century architecture becomes visible. It is a scene that never ceases to electrify the person fortunate enough to see it. Today these moors, marshes, dunes, beaches, and woodlands—collectively known as the Province Lands—are protected as part of the Cape Cod National Seashore.

In 1620 the Pilgrims landed at Provincetown and drew up the Mayflower Compact, that venerable precursor to the Constitution, before continuing on to Plymouth. In the early years the Wampanoag, a North American Indian tribe, occupied this area and showed these early seventeenth-century colonists how to collect local berries and plants, harvest shellfish, and grow beans, squash, and corn.

The outer Cape was settled by hardy fishermen and their families, many of Portuguese descent. The cod and mackerel they caught was dried and salted to preserve it. Saltworks that used windmills to pump sea water into large evaporation vats lined the harbors of the Cape's fishing villages. The *baccala,* or salt cod, was then shipped to cities along the eastern seaboard, as well as to Europe, where it has been a staple of the Italian, Spanish, and Portuguese diets for hundreds of years. Today fishing fleets still return to Provincetown and Chatham, where their catch is loaded onto trailer trucks for the journey to Boston, New York, or, increasingly, Tokyo.

During the first decades of the nineteenth century, whaling provided the wealth that allowed sea captains and merchants to build the splendid homes that add so much to the charm and character of Provincetown, Chatham, Wellfleet, Brewster, and other Cape towns. Although the days of the Yankee whalers are long gone, the whales are not. Today a new breed of entrepreneurs is

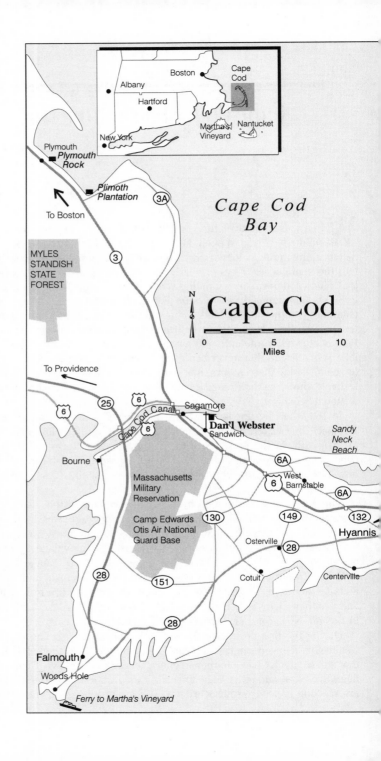

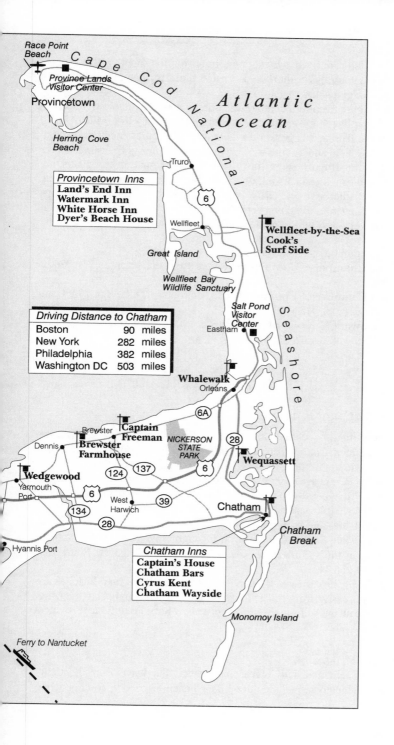

Race Point
Beach

Cape Cod

Province Lands
Visitor Center

Provincetown

Atlantic
Ocean

National

Herring Cove
Beach

Truro

Provincetown Inns
Land's End Inn
Watermark Inn
White Horse Inn
Dyer's Beach House

6

Wellfleet

Wellfleet-by-the-Sea
Cook's
Surf Side

Great Island

Wellfleet Bay
Wildlife Sanctuary

Seashore

Salt Pond
Visitor
Center

Eastham

Driving Distance to Chatham		
Boston	90	miles
New York	282	miles
Philadelphia	382	miles
Washington DC	503	miles

Whalewalk
Orleans

6A

Brewster **Captain**
Freeman NICKERSON
STATE
PARK

28

Dennis **Brewster**
Farmhouse

6

Wequassett

124 137

Wedgewood

Yarmouth
Port

6

West
Harwich

39

134

28

Chatham

Chatham
Break

Hyannis Port

Chatham Inns
Captain's House
Chatham Bars
Cyrus Kent
Chatham Wayside

Monomoy Island

Ferry to Nantucket

reaping a harvest from the sea by taking tourists out to "shoot" with a camera instead of a harpoon. Still others have turned these former captain's homes into gracious lodgings and restaurants.

For much of the twentieth century, the outer Cape, Provincetown in particular, has been a haven for artists and writers attracted by the brilliant light, the picturesque fishing villages, and a liberal tradition that encourages creativity. Eugene O'Neill and Tennessee Williams wrote some of their finest plays here, and Edward Hopper spent thirty summers in Truro. In the 1950s, abstract expressionists like Jackson Pollock and Franz Kline came to the Cape. Today the area is home to one of the largest art colonies in the United States. The waiter serving you, the chef preparing your meal, or the chambermaid at your inn may very well be the next great American novelist or darling of the art world.

For information on special events, contact the following:

Cape Cod Chamber of Commerce. Routes 6 and 132, Hyannis, MA 02601, (508) 362-3225.

Chatham Chamber of Commerce. 533 Main Street, P.O. Box 793, Chatham, MA 02633; (508) 945-5199.

Provincetown Chamber of Commerce. 307 Commercial Street, Box 1017, Provincetown, MA 02657; (508) 487-3424.

WHERE TO GO, WHAT TO DO

Cape Cod National Seashore

The scenery at the tip of Cape Cod is different from anything else you will see in the United States. Come during any season of the year and watch as nature displays its power along the forty-mile-long Cape Cod National Seashore. The wind and water are ceaselessly at work. Giant sand dunes encroach on the highway near Provincetown. The sand cliffs continue to erode at the Marconi wireless station site. A massive break in the barrier beach at Chatham draws crowds of spectators and surfers.

Salt Pond Visitor Center. Open March through New Year's 9 A.M. to 4:30 P.M. till 8 P.M. in the summer; weekends January and February. Route 6 in Eastham; (508) 255-3421.

Province Lands Visitor Center. The vistas of moors, dunes, and beaches are particularly impressive from this spot. Open mid-April through Thanksgiving, 9 A.M. to 5 P.M.; till 6 P.M. June through September. Race Point Road, Provincetown; (508) 487-1256.

Interpretive Programs

Ranger-guided activities and interpretive walks that leave from Eastham, Truro, and Provincetown include dune hikes; beach discovery; cranberry bog and early morning birding walks; a talk about the Cape's infamous storms and shipwrecks; and canoe trips. Check the listings of events in the visitor centers.

Self-Guided Nature Trails

If you like to do your walking in relative privacy, we recommend the trails in the Wellfleet, Truro, and Provincetown areas. Ask for the free leaflet "Self-Guiding Nature Trails" at the visitor centers. It also comes in braille and large-print versions. Beware of poison ivy; stay on the paths, as there's a lot of it on the Cape.

Atlantic White Cedar Swamp Trail, Wellfleet. The long boardwalk that winds its way through the moss-covered trunks of cedar trees is enchanting. Cedars were found in great abundance by the first white settlers on the Cape, and the decay-resistant lumber was widely used for joists, frames, floors, doors, rafters, water pipes, organ pipes, and whale-oil tanks. Sadly, over the last 300 years excessive logging has almost eliminated this tree from the Cape. Next to the Marconi wireless station site at Marconi Beach.

Great Island Trail, Wellfleet. Serious hikers will enjoy this eight-mile trail. The path is covered with soft sand for much of the way, making it more of a challenge than some of the other trails in the area. This tip of land, Jeremy Point, which is submerged at high tide, is a hangout for seals. Bring lunch, something to drink, and a hat if it's summer. Even if you don't feel up to this walk, the drive from the Wellfleet town pier along Chequesset Neck Road to the trailhead is spectacular and worth a special detour.

Cranberry Bog Trail, Truro. The paintings of Edward Hopper, who spent many summers in South Truro, capture the colors of these moors in all their subtle splendor. A short trail leads through an old cranberry bog and a stretch of the moors.

Beech Forest Trail, Provincetown. Birds flock to this colorful area. The one-mile trail, which winds around a lake and through a forest of pine, oak, and beech, has steep log steps, and the trail is mostly in soft sand. Notice how the dunes are moving and encroaching on the forest.

Fort Hill Trail, Eastham. The red maples on this one-and-one-half-mile trail bring out the crowds during the fall foliage season. Part of this trail is a boardwalk, and there are log steps on the slopes.

Swimming

The following beaches have lifeguards and bathhouses. Eastham: Coast Guard (where Henry Beston wrote *The Outermost House*) and Nauset Light. Wellfleet: Marconi Beach. Truro: Head of the Meadow beaches. Provincetown: Race Point and Herring Cove. *Note:* Sometimes you can see whales from Herring Cove Beach. Look for the whitish spouts of water in the distance. From mid-June to Labor Day there is a parking fee at the National Seashore beaches.

Fishing

Sixteen charter boats sail from Rock Harbor in Orleans for striped bass, blue-fish, mackerel, tautog, fluke, and sea bass from June to October, (508) 255-9757. Check with your innkeeper for a current list of charter boats on other parts of the Cape. If you're lucky enough to land a bluefin tuna, which can weigh up to 700 pounds, you can extend your vacation for another couple of months without worrying about how you're going to pay for it: the Japanese are paying about $16 a pound on the spot for unbruised tuna, which end up gracing the menus at Tokyo's sushi bars.

Bicycling

During the summer season, bicycles can be rented in most towns. At other times of the year it's best to check in advance or bring your own bike. Ask at the visitor centers for a leaflet describing the bicycle trails in the area.

Province Lands Trail, Provincetown. The almost eight-mile-long Province Lands Trail passes through forests and bogs and over spectacular sand dunes. Be warned, however, that in places the trail is steep. The Beech Forest parking area, Race Point Beach, or Herring Cove Beach offer easy access to the trail.

Head of the Meadow Trail, North Truro. This two-mile trail passes through sand dunes and then along the edge of Salt Meadow before it ends at Pilgrim Lake. Access at Head of the Meadow Beach parking area or High Head Road.

Nauset Trail, Eastham. This two-mile trail affords views of the old Nauset Coast Guard Station and Nauset Marsh. The trail begins at the Salt Pond Visitor Center.

Cape Cod Rail Trail. After train service to the Cape was discontinued and the tracks removed, the right-of-way was put to a new use: a thirty-mile stretch was tarred and is now used for bicycling and jogging. This is an easy trail over flat terrain. The trail starts at Route 134 in South Dennis and continues to South Wellfleet. There is parking at Nickerson State Park in Brewster, Route 124 in Harwich, and the Salt Pond Visitor Center. If you're out of shape, we suggest you tackle this trail and some of the shorter ones in the National Seashore before you attempt the Province Lands Trail over the dunes in Provincetown.

Wildlife Sanctuaries

Wellfleet Bay Wildlife Sanctuary. Wellfleet Bay Wildlife Sanctuary encompasses 700 acres of pine woods, moorland, and salt marsh. Take a self-guided nature walk along the five miles of trails or join one of the birding walks, canoe trips, or cruises run throughout the year. The environmentally correct visitor center has composting toilets and passive solar heat; sink water is recycled to provide water for the greenhouse. The building has a large room at one end with picture windows looking out onto many bird feeders.

The office is open 9 A.M. to 5 P.M. daily. The sanctuary is located on the west side of Route 6 a few hundred yards north of the Wellfleet-Eastham town line. Box 236, South Wellfleet, MA 02663; (508) 349-2615.

Monomoy National Wildlife Refuge. Both the Audubon Society and the Cape Cod Museum of Natural History lead trips to Monomoy Island, a 2,750-acre refuge which was cut in two by a winter storm in 1978. The two- and-a-half-mile-long North Island is about a fifteen-minute boat ride from Chatham, and offers tidal flats and a salt marsh where migrating shorebirds rest and feed. Most trips to the island last three to four hours.

The five-mile-long South Island is some forty-five minutes by boat from Chatham. In addition to supporting white-tailed deer, muskrats, reptiles, and a variety of migrating waterfowl among its pitch pines, sedge flats, and fresh-water ponds, it is also home to the piping plover and short-eared owl, both endangered species. Trips to South Island take seven to eight hours, and if you only have time for one island visit, this is the one we favor.

You can drive to **Morris Island,** the refuge headquarters, and hike along a three-quarter-mile nature trail that goes down a set of stairs and continues along the beach. On a recent November day we watched men digging for soft-shell clams in the mudflats and saw a large school of striped bass migrating south. To get here from Chatham, take the Shore Road past the lighthouse. At the fork, bear to the left to Morris Island Road. Follow this road across a narrow strip of land with water on both sides until you see signs for Monomoy parking on your left.

The Cape Cod Museum of Natural History. In addition to sponsoring trips to North and South Islands, the museum has excellent displays on the ecology of the Cape. Exhibits include a working beehive, a weather station, a bird room displaying stuffed specimens, and small aquariums filled with local marine life. You'll also find a natural history library, gift shop, and network of trails here, the best being the one-mile John Wing Trail that starts at Route 6A and crosses a long boardwalk over the salt marsh to Wing's Island and Cape Cod Bay. The causeway floods at high tide, so check at the front reception area before walking this trail.

Open mid-April to mid-October, Monday through Saturday, 9:30 A.M. to 4:30 P.M.; Sunday, 12:30 to 4:30 P.M. Adults $4. Call or write for information about the Monomoy Island overnight trips. Drawer R, Route 6A, Brewster, MA 02631; (508) 896-3867.

Whale Watching

If you're looking for a family activity that appeals to children, teenagers, and adults, whale-watching cruises are at the top of the list, those operated by the Dolphin Fleet are among the best. Researchers and guides from the Center for Coastal Studies are on board every cruise to answer questions and conduct whale research.

Sightings are likely to include some or all of the following: humpbacks, finbacks, minke whales, white-sided dolphins, and the occasional right whale. The two most common whale species in these waters, the finback and hump-back, are regularly sighted from April to October. Finbacks can be seventy to eighty-five feet long and weigh up to fifty tons. Humpbacks get their name from the way they arch their back before diving, and can reach fifty to fifty-six feet in length and weigh up to forty tons. As the most active, they are also the most fun to watch. Sometimes they will even come close to the boats and, when they breach, will seem to be "waving" their flippers.

The trips are exceedingly popular, especially on weekends and during the summer, so make reservations two or three weeks in advance. Cruises lasting three to four hours head out daily, weather permitting, to the Stellwagen Bank, about six to eight miles from Provincetown. (Pack some anti–motion sickness medication in case of rough conditions.)

Trips go from mid-April through October: summer rates, $17.50. Children under 7 free. MacMillan Pier, Provincetown; (508) 255-3857; (800) 826-9300 in Massachusetts.

Golf

Duffers love the Cape because they can indulge their habit almost year-round. A few suggestions: the captain's Golf Course, eighteen holes, Brewster; (508) 896-5100. Cranberry Valley Golf Course, eighteen holes, Harwich; (508) 430-7560. Chatham Seaside Links (next to Chatham Bars Inn), nine holes, Chatham; (508) 945-4774. Chequesset Yacht and Country Club, nine holes, Wellfleet; (508) 349-3704. Highland Golf Links, nine holes, North Truro; (508) 487-9201.

Route 6A, the Old King's Highway

Route 6A, the thirty-four-mile twisting stretch of road from Sandwich to Orleans that parallels the shore of Cape Cod Bay, is part of the Old King's Highway Regional Historic District. This road began as a Native American trail from Provincetown to Plymouth and became the main artery of Cape Cod in the seventeenth and eighteenth centuries. Today this stretch of road is home to numerous bed-and-breakfasts, restaurants, scores of antique shops, and antiquarian bookstores. A large number of craftspeople have studios and shops along the road. Hundreds of historic structures line the road, and specimen trees provide a graceful canopy. There are views of great salt marshes, harbors, and open lands. Development is tightly controlled along this road. Listed below, starting from Bourne, are selected galleries and shops that we have visited. There are many more.

Pairpoint Glass Works. At this nineteenth-century glassworks, you can watch the glassblowers at work creating pieces using the same techniques and in the same style as those displayed at the Sandwich Glass Museum (see below). Prices are as low as $7 for a classic commemorative cup holder and go up to hundreds of dollars. The shop is open daily year-round; glassmaking weekdays 9 A.M. to 4:30 P.M. 851 Route 6A, at the Sagamore Bridge, Sagamore; (508) 888-2344; (800) 899-0953.

Colonial Candle Factory Outlet. Located in the Cape Cod Factory Outlet Mall; has excellent prices on candles. At exit 1 off Route 6, Sagamore; (508) 888-6356.

Sandwich

Founded in 1637, Sandwich is the oldest town on the Cape. It was primarily a small agricultural settlement until the 1820s, when glassmaking came to the town. Several large glassworks prospered until the 1880s, when more efficient furnaces in the Midwest captured the business. In the past decade, the town has become a community for preservation-minded folks who discovered the treasure of historic houses just waiting for a little love. Many residents commute to Boston, just over an hour away. This is a town for browsing down narrow lanes past restored historic homes and shops.

Heritage Plantation of Sandwich. This fascinating seventy-six-acre site started as a horticultural center and has exquisitely maintained grounds. Highlights are the famous Dexter rhododendrons and azaleas, which bloom from mid-May through mid-June; a large collection of hollies, hostas, and heather gardens; and more than 900 different daylilies, which bloom from mid-July through early August.

The Lilly family purchased the property in 1969 and moved its large collection of Americana to the site. A replica of the Shaker round stone barn in Hancock Shaker Village (Pittsfield, Massachusetts) houses a superb collection of thirty-five mint automobiles on two levels, including a 1930 Duesenberg once owned by Gary Cooper. In the art museum building, take a ride on a 1912 working carousel in a glass-enclosed rotunda and view one of the finest collections of Currier and Ives prints and the large collection of Elmer Crowell decorative bird carvings and decoys. A military museum in a replica of a Revolutionary War structure houses 2,000 hand-painted military miniatures as well as antique firearms and more. An outdoor café serves breakfast, lunch, and snacks. Open daily, mid-May to late October, 10 A.M. to 5 P.M. Adults $8. Grove and Pine Street, Sandwich; (508) 888-3300.

Sandwich Glass Museum. Displays of the glass manufactured here in the nineteenth century include early pressed lacy glass and pattern glass in intense colors of canary, green, amethyst, and blue. Rare American glass of the same period and early glassmaking paraphernalia is well presented along with an historical overview of Sandwich. Open daily, April through October, 9:30 A.M. to 4:30 P.M.; shorter hours and days off-season. Adults $3. 129 Main Street; (508) 888-0251.

Stroll around the **Shawme Duck Pond,** see corn ground at the **Dexter Grist Mill** (open mid-June to early October), and stop in at the tiny **Thornton**

W. Burgess Museum (4 Water Street, (508) 888-6870; open year-round), dedicated to the man who brought Peter Cottontail alive for millions of children. The **Hoxie House** (Water Street, open mid-June to early October) is a seventeenth-century Cape house with a saltbox roofline and Colonial furniture from Boston's Museum of Fine Arts. After a storm destroyed the walkway the town raised funds to replace the 1,350-foot **boardwalk** that crosses marshland and low dunes to give expansive views at the far end. To get here, take Harbor Street off Factory Street.

At **Black's Weaving Shop** (seven-tenths of a mile west of Route 149 in West Barnstable, (508-362-3955), Bob and Gabrielle Black have been hand-weaving on eight looms for more than thirty-five years. Bob weaves original intricately patterned personalized jacquard coverlets, which can include your family tree and the outline of your home. As we discussed an order for custom place mats, Bob wove a few rows to show us how it would look.

At Route 149, turn right to get to two craftsmen located next to each other in West Barnstable. At **West Barnstable Tables** (2454 Meetinghouse Way, (508) 362-2676) you'll find high-quality trestle tables and furniture crafted from old pieces of wood such as 200-year-old planks, barnboards, and old window frames. At **Tern Studios** (508-362-6077) you can watch Albert Barbour make extraordinary bowls and other turned vessels from wood of every type and description.

Continue on Route 149 to the **West Parrish Meetinghouse** (1049 Meetinghouse Way, Barnstable; (508) 362-4445). Built in 1719, this meetinghouse has a five-foot gilded rooster weather vane and a bell cast in Paul Revere's shop in 1806. The fellowship that meets here traces its roots continuously to 1616 in England, where the Congregational Church was founded. This building was completely restored in the 1950s and is worth a visit.

Sandy Neck Conservation Area. As you drive along 6A in Barnstable and look across the Great Marsh, you'll see a line of sand dunes that stretches six and a half miles along Cape Cod Bay. If you want to hike the dunes, take Sandy Neck Road in East Sandwich to Sandy Neck Beach. This area can be very hot in the summer, the sand is tough walking, and there is no shade. Bring water, a hat, and sunscreen.

If you're thirsty for an old-fashioned ice-cream soda, stop at **Hallets,** (139 Main Street, Yarmouth Port, (508) 362-3362) and sit on a stool at the marble soda fountain.

Parnassus Book Service. Has a large collection of Cape Cod titles and much, much more. Outside under an eave of the building is a wall of books sold by the honor system. 220 Main Street, Yarmouth Port; (508) 362-6420.

Winslow Crocker House. Has a fine collection of American furniture—Jacobean through William and Mary and Queen Anne to Chippendale—in a large weathered-shingle late-eighteenth-century Cape house owned by the Society for the Preservation of New England Antiquities. Open June through

October 15, Tuesday, Thursday, Saturday and Sunday; tours noon to 4 P.M. Adults $4. 250 Main Street, Yarmouth Port; (508) 362-4385.

Pewter Crafters of Cape Cod. Has traditional satin-finish Colonial-style pewter candlesticks and bowls in shiny contemporary shapes. 927 Route 6A Yarmouth Port; (508) 362-3407.

Antiques Center of Cape Cod. One hundred thirty-five dealers are represented in this large two-story building, an antiquer's delight. 243 Main Street, Dennis; (508) 385-6400.

Scargo Tower. This 28-foot stone tower on the top of a 160-foot hill is located off Scargo Hill Road, a right turn off Route 6A. On a clear day the view from the top spans the Cape Cod Canal Bridges all the way to Provincetown.

Scargo Pottery. A large outdoor display highlights the bird-feeder castles for which this family of potters is so well known. Inside, you can learn how stoneware, porcelain, black sand porcelain, flameware, and raku are made. Follow the signs off Route 6A; it's just before the road to Scargo Tower. 30 Dr. Lord Road South, Dennis; (508) 385-3894.

The Spectrum. This gallery has an excellent selection of contemporary crafts gathered from around the country. 369 Main Street, Brewster; (508) 385-3322.

Kingsland Manor Antiques. This is one of the top shops. 440 Main Street, Route 6A, Brewster; (508) 385-9741.

Sydenstricker Galleries. Try to come during workshop hours, 10 A.M. to 2:30 P.M., Tuesday through Saturday. Glass plates and bowls are made with two sheets of glass and a decorative pattern of powdered glass between them. 490 Route 6A, Brewster; (508) 385-3272.

Lemon Tree Village. At this small shopping complex, our favorite was the Cook Shop, which stocks all kinds of cookware, and Cafe Alfresco (*see* Where to Dine), where you can get an informal lunch or coffee and pastry. 1061–1097 Main Street, Brewster.

Breton House. This shop has an eclectic collection of furniture and children's toys. 1222 Stoney Brook Road at junction with 6A, Brewster, (508) 896-3974.

Mark Lawrence Fine Period Antiques. Almost across the street from the Lemon Tree is one of the best shops for museum-quality eighteenth- and nineteenth-century French and English paintings, porcelains, and furniture. 1050 Main Street, Brewster; (508) 896-8381.

Heart Pottery. Watch Diane Heart working on her potter's wheel, turning out affordable pots, bowls, mugs, and other items in porcelain, stoneware, and raku. 1145 Main St., Brewster; (508) 896-6189.

The Brewster Store. This 1866 building is one of the most photographed buildings on Cape Cod. The general store has a nickelodeon, penny candy, cheap souvenirs (it's on the tour bus route), as well as lots of merchandise for the locals. A second floor has more merchandise. 1935 Main Street; (508) 896-3744.

Breakwater Fish & Lobster Company. Purchase fresh fish to take home. If you're here in November you can get succulent Cape Cod and Nantucket bay scallops. 235 Underpass Road, Brewster, (508) 896-7080.

Baxter Antiques. Visit these barns filled with high-quality items. Opposite the entrance to Nickerson State Park. 3459 Main Street; (508) 896-3998.

Bird Watcher's General Store. Everything and then some: more than 100 different bird feeders, books, recordings, carving kits, field guides, note cards, puzzles, bath heaters, fountains, and much more are available here for the birder in your life. 36 Route 6A, Orleans, (800) 562-1512.

Chatham

Band concerts, baseball, and white-steepled churches—all are found in this picture-perfect New England town. Situated at the "elbow" of Cape Cod, and bordered on three sides by water, Chatham was founded in 1656 by Pilgrims, and today is a prosperous community of just under 7,000 souls. Strict zoning and preservation laws have kept the town from becoming cluttered with ugly strip malls, and the views of Pleasant Bay and the harbor are breathtaking. Every Friday evening from June 30 to September 1, all roads on the Cape seem to lead to the traditional band concerts on the green here. Pop tunes, golden oldies, and sing-alongs—the colorfully uniformed forty-piece band plays them all for the thousands who have brought chairs, blankets, and picnic suppers.

Chatham Fishing Pier. Make your way to the observation deck at around 1 or 2 P.M., when the fishing boats return, and watch as they unload their catch of haddock, cod, scrod, flounder, pollack, and halibut.

Main Street. With Route 28 now rerouted away from the center of town, this has become an especially enjoyable place to shop and stroll. In addition to a fine assortment of clothing stores, there are several galleries worth a visit. The **Hearle Gallery** (488 Main Street, (508) 945-2406) and the **Falconer's** (492 Main Street, (508) 945-2867) are good for great prints and watercolors of the Friday-night band concerts. **Chatham Candy Manor** (484 Main Street, (800) 221-6497), a family-owned business, has produced fine chocolates since the 1940s.

Chatham Glass. The brilliantly colored bud vases made here have shapes like gourds or vegetable parts. You can watch the process and purchase the results. Glass from this shop is sold in fine craft galleries throughout the United States. 17 Balfour Lane off Route 28 in West Chatham; (508) 945-5547.

Cape Cod Baseball League. The Cape Cod Baseball League was organized in 1885, and today features ten teams stocked with top college players. From mid-June through mid-August they play a forty-four-game season using wooden bats paid for by the major leagues. The caliber of play is high: ninety-three current major leaguers played summer ball on the Cape. Veterans Field is the home park of the Chatham Athletics, and admission to the games is free—which makes it a great family entertainment bargain.

Chatham Breakthrough. Stop at the parking lot just below the Chatham lighthouse for a view of the massive break in the barrier beach. Come at high tide or after a storm, when the water is particularly turbulent, and you're bound to see windsurfers flying over the waves.

Boat Trips. Outermost Harbor Marine, Seagull Road, Chatham ((508) 945-2030) runs launches throughout the day to South Beach, one of the Outer Beaches. If you are a birder, they can take you to North Monomoy Island. Bring a picnic and stay for the day. They also run one-hour seal cruises.

Atwood House. The low door lintels of this 1752 Cape Cod cottage will remind you that people in Colonial times were quite a bit shorter than the average American today. Period furnishings and clothing, Sandwich glass, seashells, and an excellent collection of old Chatham photographs are on display. Open mid-June through September, Tuesday through Friday, 1 to 4 P.M. Adults $3. Stage Harbor Road.

Wellfleet

Native American tribes summered along Wellfleet Harbor and lived on the delicious oysters for thousands of years. By the middle of the nineteenth century, white settlers had turned Wellfleet into the oyster capital of New England. The oysters are still some of the best on the East Coast, though not as plentiful as they once were. Today the town is known for the number and quality of its summer art galleries.

Most of the galleries and shops are clustered along Main Street, Bank Street, Baker Avenue, and Commercial Street. Our favorite galleries include **Kendall Art Gallery** (East Main Street, (508) 349-2482); **Cherrystone Gallery** (East Commercial Street, (508) 349-3026); **Left Bank Gallery** (Commercial Street, (508) 349-9451); **Cove Gallery** (Commercial Street, (508) 349-2530); and the **Blue Heron** (Bank Street, (508) 349-6724).

More than 70 percent of Wellfleet is conservation land. After you've explored the village, drive by Mayo Beach to Chequesset Neck Road, where you'll find the start of the Great Island trail. Whether you decide to hike or not, the drive to the point takes you past some spectacular scenery. For a longer back-road tour, head north on Bound Brook Island Road and Old County Road, which eventually connects with Route 6 in Truro. If you are adventurous take some of the side roads and you'll see the sand hills overlooking the water and the vistas that Edward Hopper painted when he summered here from 1920 to 1967.

Provincetown

Only three miles long and about two streets wide, this liberal, closely knit community attracts a fascinating, cosmopolitan mix of people. During the summer, as many as 50,000 of them, locals and visitors alike, jam Commercial Street, creating traffic gridlock and a carnival atmosphere. The whale-watching fleet is the largest on the East Coast, and artists and writers have made this the most famous art colony in the country. Elsewhere, fishermen of Portuguese descent still leave early each morning in their colorful boats from the end of MacMillan Wharf and return in the afternoon to unload their catch of cod, mackerel, and flounder. The National Seashore's Province Lands wrap around the town from the tip of the Cape, with spectacular wild dunes and ocean surf.

Whether you've come to whale-watch, people-watch, or simply to experience the Cape light, you'll want to pick up copies of *A Provincetown Discovery* (free) and *The Historical Society's Walking Tour Guides* (75¢) at the Province Lands Visitor Center. The walking tours describe homes and buildings that were built by the prosperous ship captains and the merchants they supported in the first half of the nineteenth century. Another interesting and useful publication is the *Provincetown Gallery Guide,* which lists twenty of the best galleries in town. It's available in art galleries along Commercial Street and at the Chamber of Commerce.

Commercial Street is about three miles from one end to the other. We have listed a few of our favorite stops along the way, starting at the east end and heading west. June through mid-October, almost everything is open every day. If you are visiting off-season, shops and galleries have different hours.

Suzanne Sinaiko's Garden. Artists frequently come to paint in this manicured hillside garden with a gazebo in the middle. Next to 606 Commercial Street.

Long Point Gallery. Robert Motherwell, Judith Rothschild, Fritz Bultman, Paul Resika, and Tony Vevers are among the outstanding artists whose work is on display. 492 Commercial Street; (508) 487-1795.

Berta Walker Gallery. Of the fine Provincetown artists represented here many have been associated with the Fine Arts Work Center in Provincetown. 208 Bradford Street; (508) 487-6411.

Provincetown Art Association and Museum. This association was started in 1917 by members of the original Provincetown art colony. Today the association encourages local artists and holds shows of members' work. The gift shop has an excellent selection of books about Provincetown artists. 460 Commercial Street; (508) 487-1750.

Anne Packard Gallery. Stop in to see the highly regarded originals by Anne and her daughter. Anne does landscapes in oils; daughter Cynthia paints interiors and portraits of women. 418 Commercial Street; (508) 487-4690.

Giardelli Antonelli. Owner Jerry Giardelli visits Italy several times a year to purchase the fine yarns and fabrics from which he designs and makes classic high-style women's clothing. 417 Commercial Street; (508) 487-3016.

Fine Arts Work Center. Call for times and dates for readings, seminars, and exhibits held at this prestigious center for artists and writers pursuing independent work. 24 Pearl Street; (508) 487-9960.

Northern Lights Leather. This top-quality leather store sells full-length leather coats, bomber jackets, women's skirts, and pants. 361 Commercial Street; (508) 487-9376.

Heritage Museum. On display is a sixty-four-foot half-scale model of a 1907 fishing schooner, antique fire equipment, marine gear, and artifacts from Provincetown's early fishing days. Open mid-June to Columbus Day, 10 A.M. to 6 P.M. 356 Commercial Street; (508) 487-0666.

Ellen Harris Gallery. Stop in for a look at local sculptor Al Davis's work. (Look for his ceramic cats at Napi's; *see* Where to Dine.) You'll also find fine arts and crafts in all mediums, as well as Native American folk art. 355 Commercial Street; (508) 487-1414.

Town Hall. Besides the clean rest rooms on the second floor, this building has an impressive collection of works by Provincetown artists. 250 Commercial Street; (508) 487-3900.

Pilgrim Monument and Museum. The history of Provincetown is told through models and displays. Of particular interest is a diorama of the vanished whaling settlement at Long Point. The women who lived in this settlement rebelled against living near the stench of the whale oil rendering vats and the racks of drying fish, so the families floated their homes to the main settlement at Provincetown. Many of the houses that they floated across the water still stand today, identified by blue plaques depicting a house on a barge. A display of pirate treasure recently salvaged from the *Whydah* sunk off Wellfleet in 1717 is also on display.

The entry fee includes admission to the 252-foot-tall Pilgrim Monument, a replica of a Sienna bell tower with an interior ramp system modeled after that found in the campanile of San Marco, in Venice. The view is worth the hike: on a clear day you can see Boston's John Hancock and Prudential Towers. Open daily, April throuh November, 9 A.M. to 5 P.M.; until 7 P.M. in the summer. Times and days vary at other times. Adults $5. Off Bradford Street, north of Town Hall; (508) 487-1310.

Julie Heller Gallery. In this small building on the harbor, you can buy paintings by the founders of the Provincetown art colony—Charles Hawthorne, Milton Avery, Henry Hensche—and contemporary artists. 2 Gosnold Street; (508) 487-2169.

Provincetown Bookshop. You're sure to find almost any book that has been written about Cape Cod or Provincetown here. 246 Commercial Street; (508) 487-0964.

Universalist Meeting House. Be sure to stop in and take a close look at the outstanding trompe l'oeil interior of the sanctuary on the second floor. The ceiling is a copy of the marble dome of the Temple of Jupiter in Athens. Except on Sundays, the sanctuary is kept locked. Check the first-floor office for someone to let you in. 236 Commercial Street; (508) 487-9344.

Atlantic House. The locals call it the A-House. During the fifties and sixties, it was the summer hangout of the New York abstract expressionists. Jazz greats performed here frequently, and Tennessee Williams wrote *The Glass Menagerie* here. Today it is a popular gay bar. 6 Masonic Place; (508) 487-3821.

WHERE TO STAY

Cape Cod lodgings are arranged geographically from Sandwich to Provincetown.

Inns

The Dan'l Webster Inn, Sandwich

This modern full-service motor hotel/inn is discreetly hidden in the center of historic Sandwich, the oldest town (1637) on Cape Cod. The highly regarded restaurant features hybrid striped bass and fresh greens and edible flowers from the inn's state-of-the-art hydroponic aquafarm. Accommodations are in the main inn, in the newer Jarves or the Fessenden Wing, or in two historic houses, one next to the inn and the other a block from the inn that includes rooms with fireplaces. Facilities at the main inn include a large outdoor swimming pool and a large restaurant. All the rooms are air-conditioned and have phones and cable televisions.

The best accommodation is the Dan'l Webster Suite on the third floor. This incredibly large space includes a living room, a bedroom with a king-size bed, and a marble-tiled bath with a double whirlpool tub. Rooms 39 (king-size canopy bed) and 32 (queen-size canopy bed) are front corner rooms with a view of Main Street. For greater privacy we like the Quince Tree House, six houses away from the inn. The house (four suites and a deluxe room) is nicely furnished with the best antiques in the inn. All rooms have fireplaces.

Thirty-seven rooms and nine suites, all with private bath. Memorial Day through late October $129–$199, Dan'l Webster Suite $325. Other times $89–$169, Dan'l Webster Suite $250–$275. Children welcome. Meals available but not included. No pets. Two-night weekend minimum. 149 Main Street, P.O. Box 1849, Sandwich, MA 02563; (508) 888-3622; (800) 444-3566.

The Wedgewood Inn, Yarmouth Port

This large, imposing 1812 white clapboard home with dark green shutters is set on a knoll on a two-acre property with large specimen trees. Innkeepers Milt and Gerrie Graham have owned the inn since 1985. The entrance is a sitting room with a large bellows that serves as a coffee table. In this room and hung throughout the inn are eight large John Stobart marine prints.

Four of the rooms have wood-burning fireplaces. All rooms are air-conditioned and have queen-size beds. Our favorite rooms, the two largest, are the first-floor rooms with fireplaces and screened summer porches; one also has a sitting room with a bay window. Plans are under way to convert the barn into three deluxe suites with fireplaces.

Breakfast, served from 8 to 9:30 A.M. at individual tables, includes a choice of two entrées such as scrambled eggs and Belgian waffles with strawberries and whipped cream.

Four rooms and two suites, all with private bath, four with wood-burning fireplaces. Memorial Day through October $120–$165; other times $95–$135. Afternoon tea and breakfast included. Children over 10 welcome. No pets. 83 Main Street (Route 6A), Yarmouth Port, MA 02675; (508) 362-5157.

Brewster Farmhouse Inn, Brewster

Distinctive green-striped awnings over all the windows of this white 1850 two-family farmhouse give a welcome appearance as you drive along Route 6A. The two-story contemporary-feeling light-filled gathering room has a fireplace and couches at one end and a large dining table at the other end. Sliding glass doors open onto an extensive wooden deck that extends to and surrounds a forty-by-eighteen-foot pool that is kept at eighty-three degrees. A hot tub is adjacent to the pool. Three adorable miniature dachshunds are also in residence.

Carol and Gary Concors purchased the inn in June 1996 and plan to continue the previous owners' custom of fancy pastries at teas and outstanding breakfasts. Guests sit at one table for breakfast. Portuguese sweet-bread French toast with sautéed apples, cheese and blueberry blintzes, eggs Benedict, or herbed eggs in puff pastry with wild mushrooms are a sample of the main dishes.

Favorites are the Garden Room, with a king-size canopy bed and a sliding door that opens onto the deck near the pool, and the Shaker Room, with a queen-size bed facing a wood-burning fireplace.

Five rooms, three with private bath. Mid-June through mid-September $95–$150; other times $75–$110. Afternoon tea and breakfast included. Children over 10 welcome. No smoking. No pets. Two-night minimum in season. 716 Main Street (Route 6A), Brewster, MA 02631; (508) 896-3910; (800) 892-3910.

The Captain Freeman Inn, Brewster

This post-and-beam house built in 1866 by Captain William Freeman, located on two acres just off Route 6A next to the Brewster General Store (one of the most photographed buildings on Cape Cod), has a wraparound front porch with hanging baskets of flowers and rocking chairs. The first and second floors have twelve-foot ceilings and the third floor has ten-foot ceilings. From the inn it is a short walk down the street to Breakwater Beach.

The innkeepers are Carol and Tom Edmondson. The first floor has a living room with a fireplace, a breakfast room with a fireplace, and a screened porch that overlooks the large swimming pool. Our top choices are the three luxury rooms, each with a glassed-in porch off the bedroom with a four-person, eighty-gallon whirlpool tub, and a queen-size canopy bed that faces a fireplace.

Breakfast features a low fat/low cholesterol entrée.

Twelve rooms, nine with private bath. June through October $95–$225; other times $80–$170. Afternoon tea and breakfast included. Children over 10 welcome. No smoking. No pets. Two-night minimum in season. 15 Breakwater Road, Brewster, MA 02631; (508) 896-7481; (800) 843-4664.

The Captain's House Inn, Chatham

The inn, located a half mile from the center of Chatham, is easily recognizable by the long, perfectly manicured high clipped hedge and white gate out front. This Greek Revival home built by a whaling captain in 1839 was purchased by Jan and Dave McMaster in 1993. The McMasters run the inn with a well-trained staff of English hotel-school students who do their internships here.

Guests stay in one of the three buildings on this two-acre property—the main inn, the attached Carriage House, or the Captain's Cottage. Common space for guests includes a small living room with a fireplace and the adjacent glass-enclosed breakfast room.

Our favorite room, especially in cooler weather, is Hiram Harding, a very large room in the Captain's Cottage with 200-year-old walnut-paneled walls, a king-size bed with a striking headboard that almost reaches the ceiling, and a fireplace. The Stables, a newly constructed building, has three luxury suites. The first-floor rooms have queen-size canopy beds and gas fireplaces and a bath with a double whirlpool tub. The second is a suite with a king-size bed, gas fireplaces in both the bedroom and living room, and a bath with a whirlpool tub. For a summer stay we like Tradewind, which has a private patio, a king-size bed, and a gas fireplace.

Tea includes scones with whipped cream and jam, cake, and fancy cookies. Breakfast, served at individual tables, includes a buffet of cereals, fruit, and breads and a hot entrée such as Southwest breakfast pie served with salsa or lemon yogurt pancakes served with cranberry syrup.

Nineteen rooms and suites, all with private bath, ten with fireplaces. Mid-May through October $130–$300. Other times $112–$200. Breakfast and afternoon tea included. Children over 12 welcome (double occupancy only). No pets. No smoking. Two-night midweek and three-night weekend minimum in season. 369–371 Old Harbor Road (Route 28), Chatham, MA 02633; (508) 945-0127; (800) 315-0728.

Cyrus Kent House, Chatham

The Cyrus Kent House is well suited to guests who enjoy the atmosphere of an old home in a quiet area that's only a block from the center of Chatham. This solid white clapboard with a high-peaked roof was built in 1877 by yet

The Carriage House at the Cyrus Kent House has two rooms with wood-burning fireplaces.

another ship captain, was completely restored in 1983, and is now owned by Sharon Mitchell Swan, a longtime resident of Chatham.

The high-ceiling living room has a white plush carpet, a pair of white wing chairs and matching love seats, and a wood-burning marble fireplace.

Favorite rooms are the two in the Carriage House, each with wood-burning fireplaces and double beds. The first-floor room has a deck overlooking the parking area, and the one on the second floor has a cathedral ceiling and a large Palladian window.

Nine rooms, all with private bath. Late June to Labor Day $130–$175. Other times $85–$145. Continental breakfast included. Children over 8 welcome. No pets. No smoking. Two-night weekend minimum. 63 Cross Street, Chatham, MA 02633; (508) 945–9104; (800) 338-5368.

Chatham Wayside Inn, Chatham

This 1860 inn on Main Street in the center of Chatham has recently seen major changes. Rooms in the original inn were all refurbished. Additions include a new entrance and the Parkside Building behind the original inn.

Even-numbered rooms in the Parkside Building overlook Kate Gould Park, where Friday-evening band concerts are held in summer. The first-floor rooms on the park side open onto a long porch that is shared by other rooms, with groupings of wicker chairs outside each room. Rooms are large and fully carpeted; a television is hidden inside the armoire; and all have one king-size or two queen-size beds. There's also a heated outdoor pool, a restaurant, conference facilities, and an outstanding gift shop off the lobby.

Fifty rooms and six suites. July and August, rooms $145–$265, suites $285–$315; other times $80–$215. All meals available. Children welcome, third person over 13 years $20 additional. No pets. Packages available off-season. Two-night minimum in season and weekends. 512 Main Street, Chatham, MA 02633; (508) 945–5550; (800) 391–5734.

Chatham Bars Inn, Chatham

This resort, set on twenty-two acres close to the center of Chatham, has undergone and is continuing a multimillion-dollar complete refurbishing. Facilities and amenities include four tennis courts, a heated outdoor pool, a small fitness center, a private beach, and launch service to Outer Bar Beach. The town golf course is next to the inn. During the summer there is a complimentary children's activity program. The resort includes a large main building with two restaurants and lounges on the first floor and guest rooms on the second and third floors, twenty-six cottages ranging in size from one to eight bedrooms with some directly on the bluffs with water views, a beach house grill at the water's edge, and conference facilities.

The best accommodations are the sumptuous new one-bedroom suites and the two master suites in the main building (a one-bedroom and a two-bedroom suite). The one-bedroom suites have a seaside upscale country feel with custom hand-painted furniture, a bedroom with a queen-size canopy bed, a gas fireplace in the living room, which has a long window seat, and a private patio.

One hundred twenty-two rooms and twenty-eight suites, all with private bath. Mid-June through mid-September, rooms $170–$365, one-bedroom suites $385–$650, two-bedroom suites $760–$1000. Lower rates at other times. All meals available. Packages available. Children welcome, no extra charge. No pets. Shore Road, Chatham, MA 02633; (508) 945–0096; (800) 527–4884.

Wequassett Inn, Pleasant Bay

This resort is situated three miles north of Chatham on Pleasant Bay. The facilities include four tennis courts, a heated outdoor pool, a small fitness center, sailboats, a deepwater dock, and launch service to the Outer Beach. A golf course is under construction and expected to open by 1997 or early 1998. All the rooms have a sitting area, a minibar, phones, and televisions. The most expensive have decks with views of the water, while the less expensive ones have views of the tennis courts and the grounds.

The most requested rooms, and the ones we like the best, are the four located closest to the beach with a view of Pleasant Bay. All the other water-view rooms overlook Round Cove. Families like the H-frame cottages, the largest accommodations, with four rooms in each building, two with water views and two with views of the grounds.

Open May through October. One hundred four rooms and suites, all with private bath. July and August, rooms $230–$340; waterfront suites $480. Off-season, rooms $170–$320; waterfront suites $360–$400. All meals available. Packages which include meals are available. Children welcome, $20 additional. No pets. Pleasant Bay, Chatham, MA 02633; (508) 432–5400, (800) 225–7125.

The Whalewalk Inn, Eastham

From this 1830s whaling master's home located in a residential area of old, beautifully landscaped homes, Cape Cod Bay is a five-minute walk, the thirty-mile Cape Cod Rail Trail is a two-minute bike ride, and the Cape Cod National Seashore is a ten-minute drive. The three-acre property, owned by innkeepers Carolyn and Dick Smith, consists of the main inn and an attached barn as well as a guest cottage and a saltbox cottage. The inn has two living rooms, both with fireplaces, a breakfast sunporch, and a patio where breakfast is served in the summer.

All the suites are stocked with a coffeemaker, a coffee grinder, coffee beans, and assorted teas. The East and West Suites in the cottage, our favorites, have spacious living rooms with a wood-burning fireplace and a full kitchen. The saltbox cottage, set off by itself, is a single-room low-ceiling summery country cottage with a wood-burning fireplace, a Pullman kitchen, and an outdoor seating area with a view of the meadows. The second-floor suite in the barn and a first-floor room in the main inn each have gas fireplaces.

Dick, the breakfast chef, has a repertoire of entrées that include blueberry and cranberry corn pancakes, Grand Marnier French toast, crabmeat quiche, strawberry shortcake, and apple walnut crepes with ice cream.

Open April through November and winter holiday weekends. Twelve rooms and suites, all with private bath. Memorial Day through Columbus Day $120–$190; other times $105–$170. Breakfast and hors d'oeuvres included. Children over 12 welcome; third person $30. No smoking. No pets. Two-night minimum in season and on weekends. From the Orleans Rotary turn left on Rock Harbor Road and take the next right onto Bridge Road. 220 Bridge Road, Eastham, MA 02642, (508) 255–0617.

Watermark Inn, Provincetown

Watermark Inn, located in the quiet residential East End, is perfect if you want to stay directly on the water, watch the sun rise, or listen to the rhythmic pounding of the sea. At high tide the water comes to the edge of the decks outside the rooms, and at low tide the inn has a private sand beach.

The inn is owned by Kevin Shea and Judy Richland, who live and work in Cambridge during the week. A resident innkeeper is at the inn in season; during the off-season, office hours are greatly reduced.

The sleek, spacious, contemporary suites feature skylights and angled ceilings. The second-floor suites have triangular windows, and furnishings follow crisp, uncluttered Scandinavian style lines. Colorful contemporary designer quilts contrast with the white walls and furniture, which is upholstered in shades of gray and white. Six of the ten suites have sliding glass doors opening onto private decks with full front views of the water. Two have working fireplaces. One suite has a full kitchen; the others have kitchenettes with a sink, small refrigerator, coffeemaker, and toaster oven.

Ten suites, each with private bath. July through Labor Day $135–$290. Other times $65–$235. Children welcome, $20–$40 per person additional depending on the season. Mid-June to mid-September one-week minimum stay, two- to three-night minimum at other times. Meals not included. No pets. 603 Commercial Street, Provincetown, MA 02657; (800) 734-0165 (Massachusetts only) or (508) 487-0165.

White Horse Inn, Provincetown

This 200-year-old captain's house is the kind of inn favored by young Europeans, artists, and Harvard professor types—people looking for reasonable rates and places to stay that emphasize character over lavish amenities. Innkeeper Frank Schaeffer has owned the White Horse Inn for over thirty years.

We like the studio apartments more than the rooms. The studios often are rented for longer stays. What makes the rooms different from the run-of-the-mill is the quantity and quality of the original art hanging on the walls and the antique bureaus and dressers. All rooms have a double bed or two twin beds. To make calls, guests use the pay phone down the street.

Open year-round. Twelve rooms: two with private bath, ten that share three baths; six apartments. Mid-June through mid-September, rooms $70–$75; apartments $125. (Three-night minimum stay for the apartments.) Other times, rooms $50; apartments $75–$90. Meals not included. Children welcome; third person $15 additional. No pets. No telephones. 500 Commercial Street, Provincetown, MA 02657; (508) 487–1790.

Dyer's Beach House, Provincetown

We watched loons feeding in the grasses from the third-floor balcony of this quiet little motel located behind Dyer's Hardware Store on Commercial Street. The rooms are standard, those of an older motel, but appeal to us for the sliding doors opening onto a shared deck overlooking the water, and for the proximity to the center of Provincetown. There's also a two-bedroom apartment set farther back from the water, as well as two three-bedroom apartments a few blocks away.

Open March through November. Five rooms and three apartments (two are weekly rentals). July and August $135–$150. Other times $90–$150. Two-bedroom apartment $1,200, three-bedroom apartments $1,800/week. Children welcome in the in-town apartments. 173 Commercial Street, Provincetown, MA 02657; (508) 487–2061.

Land's End Inn, Provincetown

Sitting on a hilltop at the far west end of Provincetown, with panoramic views of the harbor, the bay, and the dunes, this is a one-of-a-kind seaside turreted Victorian bungalow. The common areas are decorated and overflowing with the extensive glass collection of the late innkeeper, David Schoolman, who spent twenty years building and decorating this ornate structure. The current innkeeper is Anthony Arakelian. Common areas include the solarium with a curved picture window overlooking the bay and the atmospherically lit living room with a stone fireplace, overstuffed easy chairs, Tiffany-style lamps, stained glass window, and exotic wood carvings. The walls throughout the inn are covered with paintings.

Our favorite rooms with the best views are those on the upper levels. The loft duplex suite has a large living room with picture windows and a kitchen, a huge bathroom with both a whirlpool tub on a raised platform and a stall shower, and a spiral staircase leading to the upper-level sleeping loft. In the New Tower Room, the bed is situated under a cupola lined with rare African wood and blue glass. A wraparound deck off this room affords a fabulous view. Other top choices are the Library, with a great view and balcony, and the Old Tower Room, with an almost round bed, a Turkish brazier, and peaked dark wood-paneled ceiling. All the rooms are highly decorated with a great deal of visual appeal and are wonderfully eccentric. Rooms have fans but no air-conditioning.

The views of Provincetown and the water are spectacular from the upper-level suites at Land's End.

Sixteen rooms and a loft suite, all with private bath, including two efficiency apartments. Memorial Day through Labor Day $103–$165, loft suite $250; off-season $82–$165, loft suite $185. Continental breakfast included. Infants and children over 9 welcome, $15 additional. No pets. No smoking. Five- to seven-night minimum stay during the season; two-night weekend minimum (except holidays) at other times. 22 Commercial Street, Provincetown, MA 02657; (508) 487–0706.

Cottages

Instead of staying at an inn in Chatham or Provincetown, you might consider renting a cottage or an entire house. Most Realtors will rent only for two-week periods (unless there's an open slot), and during July and August it is nearly impossible to rent a prime cottage, as families lucky enough to get them return year after year. It's worth trying, as there are always last-minute cancellations; however, your chances of securing a cottage will be much better during early June and after Labor Day. Fortunately, offshore ocean currents keep the weather far warmer here in the fall than one might expect.

While the Cape is dotted with cabins and cottages, the three establishments mentioned below offer spectacular ocean views—if not from every single cottage in the complex, then by simply walking a few feet from your front door. They are located in South Wellfleet among the dunes of the national seashore, and the cottages are well spaced to preserve your privacy. While many cottages have views of the bay, these are in great demand for their ocean frontage.

Guests from the previous summer are contacted in January about booking for the upcoming summer. Weeks that aren't booked are then given to new renters. If you're interested, write to the addresses below to register your interest, particular needs, and the weeks you can come.

• **Cook's Cottages**. Open Memorial Day through the third week in October. Fifteen cottages, all with kitchens. Cottages are also equipped with a toilet and sink, but showers are in a separate building. There are five cottages with fireplaces. Cottages sleep from two to seven people, $500–$700 per week. These cottages were built in the 1940s and are close to the water; some have water views. Laurie Sexton, Box 237, South Wellfleet, MA 02663; (508) 255-4783.

• **Wellfleet-by-the-Sea Cottages**. Open Memorial Day through October. Ten two- and three-bedroom 1950s cottages with knotty pine walls in the living room, a brick wood-burning fireplace, a full kitchen, and a deck or patio. They are staggered on a hillside close to the water so all have unobstructed water views. July through Labor Day $835–$915 per week, one-week minimum; lower rates at other times, three-night minimum. They are owned by the Crosen family. 275 Wolcott Hill Road, Wethersfield, CT 06109. Write for reservations or information.

• **Surf Side Cottages**. Open April through October. Eighteen cottages, all with kitchens, full baths, wood-burning fireplaces, phones, carpeting, knotty pine interiors, and screened porches. Half have dishwashers and some have rooftop decks. These cottages are set in a hollow (from 215 to 400 steps from the water), so none have ocean views. Cottages are located on both sides of Ocean View Drive. One- to three-bedroom cottages $700–$1,275 per week, one-week minimum. Can be rented by the night at half price on the shoulder season—generally before Memorial Day and after Labor Day. Jim and Marcia Sexton, Box 937, South Wellfleet, MA 02663; (508) 349-3959.

WHERE TO DINE

Cape Cod restaurants are arranged geographically from Sandwich to Provincetown.

The Dan'l Webster Inn, Sandwich

Our favorite dining room in this large restaurant situated in the middle of Sandwich is the glass-enclosed Conservatory. Executive chef Robert Catania grows his own hydroponic lettuces, herbs, and edible flowers, and raises tilapia in a large greenhouse a few miles away. Don't miss the delicately dressed tender aquafarm lettuce. We had the tilapia from the aquafarm, available as appetizer or entrée with a tamari honey glaze as well as the lobster chowder, which has become so popular it's sold in specialty shops throughout the region. We also had duck with a pear-and-ginger glaze and local scallops and monkfish in a sweet ginger and jalapeño pepper sauce.

The restaurant has a large, well-regarded wine list strong in bottle-aged red Burgundies, red Rhônes, first-growth Bordeaux, and California Cabernets. Prices are just above retail for many wines, and the older vintages are real bargains.

Lunch and dinner daily. Lunch $6–$11. Dinner entrées $15–$24. 149 Main Street, Sandwich, MA; (508) 888-3623.

Abbicci, Yarmouth Port

The interior of this bright mustard-colored clapboard roadside building is strikingly contemporary. The small dining rooms have black columns, white walls painted with outline maps of Italy, track lighting, black chairs, and white tablecloths.

A dish of roasted garlic cloves and a bottle of olive oil comes with the bread. We suggest the excellent lightly fried calamari with a spicy tomato sauce, a large portion plenty for two to share.

For a main course we had shrimp with olives, capers, and sun-dried tomatoes served on spaghetti and a fish stew with shellfish and salmon, a good flavored broth served with a garlic roll. Other choices included osso buco, braised rabbit with figs, breast of veal stuffed with sausage, gnocchi, and spaghetti with clams.

Lunch and dinner daily. Lunch $7–$11. Dinner entrées $14–$21. 43 Main Street (Route 6A), Yarmouth Port, MA; (508) 362-3501.

Inaho, Yarmouth Port

A Japanese restaurant with a genuine sushi bar and a Japanese garden in the back along 6A in Cape Cod might sound incongruous at first, but some of the most expensive tuna served in Tokyo restaurants comes from Cape Cod. You can't apply New York standards to this restaurant, but then again, the prices are far more reasonable. One person at our table of four had a bento box, a lacquered box divided into four sections with small portions of tempura, chicken teriyaki, and two other items. Guests can watch the fingers of the husband-and-wife chef/owners Alda and Yuji Watanabe fly as they slice the fish, make the hand rolls, and produce the plates of assorted sushi and sashimi.

Dinner, Tuesday through Sunday. Entrées $12–$22. 157 Route 6A, Yarmouth Port, MA; (508) 362-5522.

High Brewster, Brewster

A strong mood of tranquility and Old World charm pervades this 1738 house. Low ceilings with exposed beams, Blue Willow china, and oil lamps give a Colonial feel to the three small dining rooms. The Mural Room has walls painted by James Hansen. We dined in the Living Room with its open hearth filled with antique cooking utensils. The fireplace has been converted to gas, yet it gave the room a warm glow on a late fall night.

We started with sautéed sweet local bay scallops served with a mound of linguine tossed with arugula walnut pesto. Following a salad of baby greens we had the mixed grill, a tasty venison chop, and a fillet of trout. Other entrée selections from the fall menu included sirloin steak, pheasant breast, rabbit sausage pie, and tea-smoked salmon.

Open Easter through New Year's. Dinner nightly in season; Wednesday through Sunday off-season. Club dinners Wednesday through Friday off-season. Four-course prix fixe $32–$42. 964 Satucket Road, Brewster, MA; (508) 896-3636.

Cafe Alfresco, Brewster

Stop for a cappuccino and pastry, a creative sandwich such as New Orleans muffaletta, grilled vegetables with mozzarella on focaccia, turkey with stuffing and cranberry, and lobster and scallop rolls. Dinner is served in the summer.

Breakfast and lunch year-round, early dinner in season. At Lemon Tree Village, 1097 Main Street, Brewster; (508) 896-1741.

The Brewster Fish House, Brewster

Since this small ten-table restaurant serves some of the best fish around at moderate prices, it's no wonder that there's often a wait to get in. We came with locals who steered us to fried calamari with red pepper aioli. Grilled swordfish and sea scallops, our choices, were well prepared and served without sauces, so the flavor of the fish was not obscured. For more creative combinations, try baked pollack under a horseradish crust; grilled salmon with spinach, prosciutto and mustard sauce; and baked cod with stuffing.

Open April through December. Daily, Memorial Day through Columbus Day. Thursday through Sunday at other times. Lunch $5–$9. Dinner entrées $12–$20. No reservations. 2208 Main Street (Route 6A), Brewster, MA; (508) 896-7867.

Chillingsworth, Brewster

Chef/owners Nitzi Rabin and his wife, Pat, the hostess, are owners of this, the most elegant restaurant on the Cape. If you have a strong interest in fine food, dinner here is an event that you will long remember.

Of the seven dining rooms, our favorites are the intimate Library Room with a single table, the Fireplace Room in cool weather, and the elegant Empire Room.

Diners are served a seven-course meal with about a dozen appetizers and entrée choices, many of which change daily. Angel-hair pasta with morels, carpaccio of veal, or fresh sautéed foie gras are a sampling of appetizers. Main courses (which determine the price of your meal) have included seared salmon with orzo, grilled swordfish with garlic mashed potatoes, breast of duck with wild rice crepe, tenderloin of beef with Dauphine potato, loin of veal with truffle risotto, or rack of lamb. Desserts of passion fruit crème brûlée, warm chocolate cake with ice cream, lemon tart, or a poached peach with strawberry sauce are excellent. Separating these three courses are a soup, a mixed green salad, a sorbet, and coffee.

Luncheon and à la carte bistro dinner at Chillingsworth are served in the cathedral-ceiling greenhouse lounge. The gourmet shop sells desserts, cheeses, and other items prepared in Chillingsworth's kitchen, as well as a selection of gift items.

Open late May through Thanksgiving. Tuesday through Sunday, late June through early September; Wednesday through Sunday till Columbus Day, weekends till Thanksgiving. Lunch $9–$11. Dinner seatings 6 to 6:30 P.M. and 9 to 9:30 P.M. Other times of the year, except Saturday, a single seating 7 to 8 P.M. Seven-course dinners $40–$54. Bistro dinners, entrées $9–$23. Six special wine dinners offered throughout the season. Route 6A, Brewster, MA; (508) 896-3640.

L'Alouette Restaurant, Harwich Port

Chef Jean-Louis Bastres and his wife, Danielle, the hostess, have owned this exceptionally fine country French restaurant for many years. In our opinion this is one of the less well known finds on the Cape. For starters we really enjoyed the salty sweet Wellfleet oysters, one of our favorites of all oysters on the East Coast. They were opened to order and served on ice. Sea scallops were delicately grilled with a mound of sweet Maui onion rings. House salad with blue cheese was a welcome change from the norm, as it had a light dressing and chunks of cheese. Caesar salad is prepared tableside with plenty of garlic. Sweet local Pleasant Bay scallops were in season. Other options included rack of lamb, chateaubriand, braised lamb shanks, chicken breast stuffed with goat cheese, and scrod with basil pesto on linguine. For dessert, try the crème brûlée with a hard crunchy top.

Dinner daily. January through March closed Mondays. Entrées $15–$25. Sunday brunch in the off-season. 787 Main Street (Route 28), Harwich Port, MA; (508) 430-0405.

Christian's, Chatham

Upstairs is a local favorite spot—a relaxed, comfortable room with mahogany paneled walls hung with movie posters, tables tucked into niches, and an outdoor deck.

The dining rooms downstairs have a more formal feel. All the items on the menu are named after movies that reflect chef/owner Christian Schultz's passion. Appetizers include sautéed escargots with mushrooms, garlic, and tomatoes aptly named Casablanca; fried calamari, known here as 20,000 Leagues Under the Sea; and chicken fingers fried golden brown, served with "007 sauce" and called Goldfinger. The fun continues with Roman Holiday, a traditional Caesar salad; Sweet Bird of Youth, a boneless half duck; and A Fish Called Wanda, a salmon sautéed with mushrooms.

Open year-round for lunch and dinner. January through March closed Tuesday and Wednesday. Lunch, $5–$12. Dinner entrées $7–$18. 443 Main Street, Chatham, MA; (508) 945-3362.

The Impudent Oyster, Chatham

The quality of the food, creativity of the preparation, and value received are well above average at this popular upscale bistro. Closely spaced glass-topped tables line the edge of the room. The restaurant occupies two levels, with the nonsmoking dining room separated from the lower-level large bar area by only a few steps.

Should you not want a full meal, smaller portions of some of the entrées are available. The *pesca fra diablo,* fettuccine topped with shrimp, scallops, mussels, clams, and pieces of fish in a spicy sauce, was more than ample for the average appetite. Portuguese mussels in a spicy tomato broth with linguica sausage pieces was a winner.

Chatham scrod, scallops baked in a casserole with Monterey Jack cheese and bacon, chicken enchiladas, and steak Bernard with onions and mushrooms in a Marsala wine sauce are other dinner choices.

Open year-round. Lunch $6–$8. Dinner entrées $8–$19. 15 Chatham Bars Avenue, Chatham, MA; (508) 945-3545.

Chatham Bars Inn, Chatham

During the season there are three dining options. In the main inn, choose from the formal dining room or the North Beach Tavern and Grille for more informal fare. The Beach House Grill across the road from the inn by the beach also serves lunch and dinner in season. At lunch in the North Beach Tavern, a comfortable wood-paneled room decorated with historic photographs and furnished with widely spaced tables, we had the signature lobster club sandwich. Other choices included grilled swordfish or chicken breast sandwiches, and salads such as pan-seared sea scallops on greens or Caesar salad topped with grilled chicken or shrimp.

The formal main dining room has a view of the water and is a quiet, refined setting for a special meal. Appetizers include foie gras on an open ravioli with chanterelles, a selection of smoked and cured seafood, grilled lobster tail with soba noodles, Caesar salad, and lobster chowder. Entrées range from a two-pound boiled lobster with mussels and clams to a smoked veal chop to peppered tuna to mushroom polenta with greens and baby vegetables.

Lunch served daily in the North Beach Tavern and seasonally in the Beach House Grill, $6–$13. Dinner served daily in the main dining room mid-April to mid-November, entrées $19–$28 and daily in the North Beach Tavern, entrées $8–$19. 17% gratuity added. Midweek New England clambakes and barbecues are served seasonally in the Beach House Grill. Shore Road, Chatham, MA; (508) 945-0096.

Wequassett Inn, Pleasant Bay

The large formal dining room at this resort has a magnificent view of Pleasant Bay. Window tables are the prime seats. Seafood is the specialty. The menu changes yearly. A lobster preparation is always on the menu, along with such selections as baked shrimp stuffed with cheese and wrapped in puff pastry, lamb loin encrusted with macadamia nuts, veal porterhouse, and grilled swordfish with lobster sauce and shiitake mushrooms. During the summer the ideal breakfast or lunch spot is outside on the veranda at one of the umbrella-topped tables with a water view.

Open May through October. Breakfast, lunch, dinner. Lunch $8–$13. Dinner entrées $18–$32. 18% gratuity added. Jackets requested at dinner. No smoking in the main dining room. Route 28, Pleasant Bay, Chatham; (508) 432-5400.

Off-the-Bay Cafe, Orleans

This storefront restaurant has a long bar in the front room and a dining room with a tin ceiling, a waterfowl mural on one wall, and wooden booths. The lobster bisque is a house specialty, served with little containers of sherry and cream on the side. We had a dozen Wellfleet raw oysters, which you can also order grilled with champagne or as oysters Rockefeller. The house salad came with chilled salad forks, and the dressing had large chunks of blue cheese. The swordfish can be served blackened or topped with pineapple salsa or artichoke hearts. Halibut was covered with a beurre blanc sauce. Other hearty choices are twin tournedos with port and oyster sauce, grilled butterflied leg of lamb with Roquefort, and prime rib. Lobster is available boiled, broiled, or baked and stuffed. Lunch selections include fajitas, burgers, salads, and pastas.

Lunch and dinner daily. Lunch $5–$10. Dinner entrées $15–$24. 28 Main Street, Orleans, MA; (508) 255-5505.

Pucci's Harborside, Provincetown

At high tide you can practically feel the water as it slaps against the pilings. Although we prefer the window tables, any seat has a view of the water. This is a thoroughly casual restaurant specializing in solid, reasonably priced American food, and is popular with the residents at the East End of town. (It's far enough from the center of town that most day-trippers and whale watchers never find it.) For lunch or snacks try the nachos, chicken wings, hamburgers, or thick pan pizza.

Open April through October. Lunch and dinner daily. Lunch $6–$8; dinner entrées $7–$15. 539 Commercial Street, Provincetown, MA; (508) 487-1964.

Ciro and Sal's, Provincetown

This restaurant, down an alley in the quiet East End of Provincetown, is particularly inviting in the cooler months, when the warmth from a large wood-burning fireplace and the coziness imparted by the low ceiling are most welcome. Chianti bottles encased in straw baskets hang from exposed wooden beams; the walls are brick and plaster; and the room is illuminated by candlelight and dim orange lightbulbs hung inside metal cheese graters.

The veal Marsala was excellent, with a strong wine and garlic flavor; the veal was easily cut with a fork. The tender calamari was sautéed with whole anchovies, lemon, garlic, and cream. Fish and veal dishes are house specialties. Side orders of roasted peppers with prosciutto and anchovies and baked artichoke hearts were consumed with enthusiasm.

The dessert menu features all the traditional Italian specialties, from zuppa inglese and zabaglione to cannoli and cassata, as well as an Italian version of English trifle.

Dinner daily, June through September, Friday through Sunday October through May. Entrées $10–$22. 4 Kiley Court (430 Commercial Street), Provincetown, MA; (508) 487-0049.

Cafe Edwige, Provincetown

One of the joys of staying in Provincetown is taking a walk in the morning and going out for breakfast. Our first choice (if we can get in) is this small second-floor high-ceilinged A-frame. Start with a large slice of the homemade Danish pastry. The daily special might be pear and apple almond pancakes; a frittata with a healthy dose of creative ingredients; broiled flounder and stir-fried vegetables; or a casserole of tofu, cream cheese, veggies, and melted cheddar cheese.

Open April through October. Daily, Memorial Day through September for breakfast and dinner. Shorter hours and days at other times. Breakfast, 8 A.M. to 1 P.M., $5–$8; dinner entrées $11–$18. 333 Commercial Street, Provincetown, MA; (508) 487-2008.

Napi's, Provincetown

This visually stimulating restaurant serves creatively prepared, robustly seasoned food. The restaurant is filled with the works of local artists. Be sure to notice the three-dimensional sculptural brick wall next to the bar, as well as the carousel horses and African masks and sculptures.

Of all the different fish stews we've tried in Provincetown, our favorite variation is the Portuguese platter served here with half a lobster, littleneck clams, mussels, fresh fish, and linguica sausage smothered in a thick, spicy sauce. Other good choices are penne Athena, made with feta, calamata olives, and tomato; shrimp Santa Fe with chipotle lime butter; and stuffed fillet of beef with roasted garlic and Brie.

Open year-round. Off-season, lunch, and dinner; dinner only during the summer. Lunch $5–$10; dinner entrées $11–$22. Parking available. 7 Freeman Street, Provincetown, MA; (508) 487-1145; (800) 571-6274.

Dancing Lobster, Provincetown

To avoid a wait at this small restaurant located at the end of the main parking lot near the docks, a great spot for sunset viewing, get here when the restaurant opens at 6 P.M.

In the open kitchen chef/owner Nils Berg, who has worked with Harry Cipriani in Venice and New York, turns out imaginative light Italian fare. The tables are close together and covered with white paper torn from a roll.

We started with appetizers of bruschetta topped with chopped tomatoes and grilled squid and another dish of mussels steamed in a spicy sauce, both good choices. Carpaccio (which the menu says originated at the Cipriani) is prepared with three different accompaniments. For entrées we had Sicilian fish stew served over a large mound of couscous, and Provençal seafood stew, a lighter dish with a flavorful broth. We finished with an excellent piece of tiramisu, one of the desserts that are shipped frozen to the restaurant from Italy.

Open May through late November. Dinner nightly (closed Wednesday and

Thursday on the shoulder season). Entrées $10–$15. No credit cards. No smoking. No reservations. 9 Ryder Street Extension, Provincetown, MA; (508) 487-0900.

Front Street, Provincetown

Chef/owner Donna Aliperti's downstairs bistro includes high-backed wooden booths, glossy wood tabletops, and exposed brick walls decorated with the work of local artists.

Appetizers and soups from a fall menu include goat cheese tart with caramelized onions, Thai squid salad, veal carpaccio, smoked salmon nori rolls, and leek-and-lobster bisque. Entrée selections include angel-hair pasta with shrimp and artichokes, grilled quail with corn risotto, grilled tuna caponata, mixed game cassoulet, and shelled lobster au poivre with pasta. A full Italian menu offers large portions of lower-priced entrées.

Open the week before Easter through New Year's. Dinner, Wednesday through Sunday; daily during the summer. Entrées $8–$22. 230 Commercial Street, Provincetown, MA; (508) 487-9715.

Bubala's-by-the-Bay, Provincetown

You can't miss this bright yellow building overlooking the water in Provincetown's West End. The four booths along the front and the outdoor deck have the best water views. One wall is covered with an intriguing mural of people eating in a café, done in the style of Braque by noted artist James Hansen. (Even if you don't have time to eat here, stop in for a look.)

For lunch we had grilled tuna with wasabi and ginger, an excellent combination with a Japanese influence, and Cajun-style fried calamari served with lemon aioli. Cod is prepared with a spicy citrus marinade and served with mango chutney, black beans, and rice. Other selections include a fried fish sandwich, Caribbean fish cakes, and lobster roll. A variety of burgers and shrimp fajitas served with roasted red peppers, garlic, and cheddar cheese accompanied by black beans, salsa, and sour cream round out the menu.

Open April through November. Breakfast, lunch, and dinner daily. Lunch $6–$10; dinner entrées $9–$15. On-site parking. 183 Commercial Street, Provincetown, MA; (508) 487-0773.

The Moors, Provincetown

This is the place to try Portuguese specialties that reflect the cultural heritage of many local Portuguese fishermen whose ancestors came from the Azores. Buoys, nets, lanterns, ladders, and ropes hang from the ceiling; and walls and booths are built from driftwood planks.

Start with hearty Portuguese soup, made here with cabbage and spicy chorizo and linguica sausages. One of the most popular entrées is *porco em pau*— broiled pieces of marinated boneless pork. The *porco em vinho d'alhos,* two thick boneless pork chops marinated in a wonderful garlicky marinade is more meat than the average person will be able to eat. The *caldeirada* is a spicy variation of bouillabaisse with a thin broth. The sea-clam pie made with chopped clam meat, chopped linguica, onions, and spices in a pie crust is a local specialty.

Open early April to the end of October. Lunch and dinner daily in summer; closed Tuesday and Wednesday spring and fall. Lunch $5–$11; dinner entrées $12–$20. Bradford Street West, Provincetown, MA; (508) 487-0840.

ITINERARY

DAY ONE. Start at the **Salt Pond National Seashore Visitors Center**. Look at the video and obtain maps of nature trails. Drive to the Fort Hill area for a view of Nauset Beach, then go to the Marconi area to see the wireless station site. In **Wellfleet** explore the shops and galleries. In the summer you can have lunch at **Cap'n Higgins** or the **Bookstore**, which both have views of the harbor. Take a drive on Chequessett Neck Road and a walk as far as you want on **Great Island Trail**. Other options are a walk on trails at **Wellfleet Bay Wildlife Sanctuary** or one of the other **nature trails.**

DAY TWO. Head directly to **Provincetown**. Take a **whale-watching** trip. Have a late lunch at **Pucci's, Bubala's**; or **Napi's.** Follow the **walking tour** through Provincetown. Climb to the top of **Pilgrim Monument.** Go to **Province Lands Visitor Center.** Watch the sunset over the water at Race Point.

DAY THREE. Go to **Heritage Plantation** in Sandwich. Have lunch at the **Dan'l Webster Inn** or at the Heritage Plantation. **Drive along Route 6A** with stops at antique shops, galleries, and studios as interested.

DAY FOUR. Continue to explore Route 6A and/or take a bike ride on the **Rail Trail.**

DAY FIVE. Browse along Main Street in **Chatham.** Drive along the Shore Road to the **Monomoy National Wildlife Refuge** headquarters on Morris Island. Take the trail along the beach. Other options include **golf, fishing, tennis, horseback riding, scenic flights,** or one of the **boat trips** that leave from Chatham to go to Monomoy Island for birding, to the Outer Beach for swimming, or a cruise to see seals.

BUDGETING YOUR TRIP

To help you get the most for the time and money you have to spend, here are some travel suggestions at three budget levels (cost per day with two people sharing a room), including lodging and meal tax, gratuity on meals, and service charge when it is added to your bill. Prices on lodgings are based on peak rates. Prices are approximate and are intended for planning purposes only. Lodgings are categorized by price and depending on the room selected may appear in more than one category. Meal prices at lunch include an average entrée and beverage. Dinner prices include an appetizer, entrée, dessert, and beverage. Wine or alcoholic beverages are not included.

Staying and dining at expensive lodgings and restaurants: From $340 to $885 per day for two.

Lodging: Dan'l Webster (suite), Chatham Bars Inn (water view and suites), Wequassett Inn, Chatham Wayside, Captain's House (suites), Watermark Inn, Land's End (duplex).

Dining: Breakfast: included except at Dan'l Webster, Chatham Bars, Wequassett, Chatham Wayside, Watermark. Lunch: Chillingsworth, Wequassett, Chatham Bars. Dinner: Chillingsworth, High Brewster, Chatham Bars, Wequassett.

Staying and dining at moderately priced lodgings and restaurants: From $200 to $340 per day for two.

Lodging: Dan'l Webster, Wedgewood Inn, Brewster Farmhouse Inn, Captain Freeman, Chatham Bars Inn (non–water view), Captain's House, Cyrus Kent, Chatham Wayside, Whalewalk Inn, Watermark Inn, White Horse Inn, Land's End.

Dining: Breakfast: included except at Dan'l Webster, Chatham Wayside, Cafe Edwige, Bubala's. Lunch: Dan'l Webster, Abbicci, Christian's, Impudent Oyster, Bubala's, Pucci's, Napi's, Off-the-Bay Cafe, Moors, Brewster Fish House. Dinner: Abbici, Chillingsworth (bistro), Off-the-Bay Cafe, Front Street, Dan'l Webster, L'Alouette, Ciro and Sal's, Napi's, Front Street.

Staying and dining at less expensive lodgings and restaurants: From $180 to $215 per day for two.

Lodging: Wedgewood Inn, Brewster Farmhouse Inn, Captain Freeman, White Horse Inn.

Dining: Breakfast: included except at White Horse Inn. Lunch: Cafe Alfresco, Pucci's. Dinner: Inaho, Impudent Oyster, Christian's (upstairs), Moors, Dancing Lobster, Pucci's, Brewster Fish House, Chatham Bars Tavern.

Index

The Discerning Traveler®, the East Coast's premier travel newsletter is a tightly focused, thoroughly researched 16-20 page newsletter (more like a travel journal) to destinations from Quebec to Key West. The Glicksteins, authors of this guidebook, do all of the research themselves and spend weeks in the field staying at or extensively inspecting each inn, bed and breakfast, hotel or resort; eating at every restaurant; and visiting the sights that they review.

They always include their opinion of the best rooms at each property. Readers get an insiders' view of the area, including the locals' favorite restaurants, the best craft and art galleries, and directions for backroading with places to stop along the way. Special features for subscribers include:

- •toll-free number to ask questions about any of the areas covered
- •twice-yearly updates on all of the back issues
- •50% reduction on the purchase of all back issues

The annual Romantic Hideaways issue features 12 special places to stay throughout the East. The other five issues published throughout the year cover one destination each. Portions of some of these issues are included in *The Discerning Traveler's Guide to New England, The Discerning Traveler's Guide to the Middle Atlantic States and The Discerning Traveler's Guide to Romantic Hideaways of the East Coast*, all published by St Martin's Press.

Send in the postcard inside this book for a free sample issue of the newsletter or a reduced rate on a one-year subscription.

If the postcard is missing call **(800) 673-7834** in the U.S. or **(215) 247-5578** elsewhere for more information about this special offer. The Discerning Traveler, 504 West Mermaid Lane, Philadelphia, PA 19118